NATION-BUILDING IN AFRICA

AFRICA 1966

DATES INDICATE YEAR OF INDEPENDENCE
COUNTRIES NOT YET INDEPENDENT ARE SHADED

Source : The Times (London), October 11, 1966

Unakwenda wapi, mwanachi?
Where are you going, friend?

Nakwenda kujenga taifa.
I'm going to build the nation.

Swahili Political Dialogue,
Tanzania, 1965

NATION-BUILDING IN AFRICA

Problems and Prospects

by ARNOLD RIVKIN

Edited by John H. Morrow

RUTGERS UNIVERSITY PRESS

New Brunswick   *New Jersey*

Manufactured in the United States of America by Quinn & Boden Company, Inc.,
Rahway, New Jersey

CONTENTS

ACKNOWLEDGMENTS

I would like to take this opportunity to express my most sincere thanks to the following individuals who went out of their way to aid me in verifying and establishing footnote and bibliographical references: In the Rutgers University Library, Mr. Gilbert H. Kelley, head of the Reference Department and his assistant, Mr. Robert Joseph Mulligan; Mr. François-Xavier Grondin, head of the Government Publications Department and Mr. Leslie Ota, assistant; Mr. Francis A. Johns, University Bibliographer; and Miss Jane E. Wissel of the Periodical Department; in the Princeton University Library, Mrs. Katherine Cameron, Microfilm Librarian.

I wish also to thank Miss Kathleen Jones, secretary in the Department of Foreign Languages, Rutgers University College, for typing revisions and emendations to the manuscript, as well as typing the bibliography.

J. H. M.

FOREWORD

Arnold Rivkin was forty-nine at the time of his death on September 19, 1968. A member of the Development Advisory Service of the World Bank since 1962, he had become economic adviser to its African department. For five years prior to joining the World Bank, Mr. Rivkin served at the Center for International Studies of the Massachusetts Institute of Technology as director of its African economic and political development projects. Before this he had spent almost a decade and a half in the service of the United States Government, where he ultimately became Association General Counsel of the International Cooperation Administration (known today as AID). His law degree was from Harvard University.

It was during his tour of duty with the Government that Mr. Rivkin was assigned as Assistant General Counsel to the European Headquarters of the Marshall Plan. Thus he became involved with the administering of aid for Dependent Overseas Territories in what was then called the Economic Cooperation Administration. In this capacity he was sent on many missions to British and French African territories. He read widely on African affairs and seized every opportunity to talk with Africans—inhabitants of the territories, officials, functionaries, students—about their problems and aspirations. As Director of the African Project at MIT, he made frequent trips to Africa, especially sub-Saharan Africa.

In the period 1950–1958 there was probably no American who had more intimate economic, political, or cultural knowledge of Africa than did Arnold Rivkin. He wrote two books on Africa, several monographs and a large number of articles. His present volume illustrates his passionate conviction that the world should be made aware of opinions about developing African nations that differ from many of the prevailing ones.

It is painful that Arnold Rivkin did not live to see the publication of his book, but he did, at least, know that it was about to be published. He gave enthusiastic assent to certain suggested changes made by one of the readers of his manuscript. I happened to be the reader who made these suggestions and it was probably for this reason that his widow, Mrs. Jeannette Rivkin, requested me, through the Rutgers University Press, to prepare the manuscript for publication.

I have done nothing to alter the premises or the conclusions expressed by the author. I have attempted, however, to make necessary corrections and to update the material where possible. This course has been followed because of my firm conviction that this book, this legacy—debatable though it may be in some parts—should remain true to the intentions of its author.

John H. Morrow

Rutgers University
June, 1969

INTRODUCTION

INDEPENDENCE: POINT OF DEPARTURE FOR NATION-BUILDING

The central theme of this book is nation-building in Africa. We have taken the achievement of independence, in fact, in President de Gaulle's felicitous phrase about the French-speaking African states, of "international sovereignty," as our point of departure, for only with limited exceptions did the outgoing European colonial powers consciously set about building nations in their former African territories. Under the best of circumstances only, such as in Nigeria, where there was something of a scheduled progression toward independence, were any deliberate steps taken prior to independence to prepare the way for the growth of a cohesive national entity. For the most part, the tendency has been quite the contrary.

The French for a long time, in fact until the adoption of the Constitution of the Fourth Republic in the aftermath of World War II, had assimilation as their national aim in Africa. The Africans—*les indigènes*—were to become assimilated Frenchmen—"black Frenchmen" as the saying went—and the areas they inhabited were in some way to become part of a greater French Republic.[1] Except for French Somaliland * and the island of Réunion in the Indian Ocean, the French Empire and its post-World War II republican embodiments—the French Union and the Franco-African Community—have for practical purposes departed the African scene. The residue of the assimilation policy and its offshoots in the post-World War II era first precluded, and then inhibited, the development of the concept of the nation-state in French-speaking Africa, and the taking of positive steps toward its realization. When accession to international sovereignty became in 1960 the inevitable outcome of the evolving Franco-African situation, it was much too late to prepare the ground for nation-building, which has become the critical challenge for survival of the eighteen African states the French Empire has spawned.[2]

The British have not had a colonial concept comparable to the French

[1] Numbered notes appear at back of book.

* A referendum held on March 19, 1967, resulted in a vote favoring continued association with France. Serious rioting followed the referendum. However, in July 1967 the name, French Somaliland, was changed to the "French Territory of the AFARS and the ISSAS." France, under a new statute, kept control of defense, currency, internal order, communications, and foreign relations. J.H.M.

1

one of assimilation. Neither, however, have the British had a clear-cut concept of building distinctive national units in their African territories based on developing a sense of national identity in each territory. On the one hand, the British established in their African territories territorial-wide legislative councils, the famous "Legcos," which gave structural recognition and impetus to evolving a sense of national identity and nationhood in the territories. On the other hand, the British continued to utilize Lord Lugard's doctrine of "indirect rule" in varying degrees and ways throughout their African territories, buttressing and at times revivifying traditional, local, parochial and, in the context of subsequent national development, separatist tendencies.[3] In the "multiracial terri-tories," concentrating power in the hands of the European settler com-munity has also acted to forestall the development of national conscious-ness and identity, which lie at the heart of any nation-building effort. Thus, in twelve former British territories,[4] nation-building for the most part remains major unfinished business for the fledgling African states, and in the still "dependent" territories in Southern Africa has yet to begin. Egypt and the Union of South Africa, which were both under British rule, are excluded. They are considered *sui generis* cases for the reasons given in the ensuing discussion. The British Cameroons became inde-pendent as parts of Nigeria and the Federal Republic of Cameroon as the result of UN-supervised referenda. So too, earlier, British Togoland became independent as part of Ghana. And British Somaliland became independent as part of the Somali Republic. Rhodesia has been in a state of rebellion against the United Kingdom since November 1965.* Even in Nigeria, which had the advantage of some preparation on this score, it remains the central priority task confronting the new state. Generally speaking, however, as we shall see in our subsequent analysis, particularly in Part III, in the discussion relating to comparative prospects, the heritage of the former British territories appears more conducive to successful nation-building than that of any other group of former African territories.

The Belgians left Africa before developing a program for "preparing the Colonies for self-government," let alone independence. The crisis came in the Congo for Belgium in 1959–60, and Belgium quit the stage promptly. In fact, many would say "abandoned the stage." Rwanda and Burundi came to independence with even less sense of national identity, if that is possible, than their huge neighbor to the west. All three new states are desperately seized of the critical need to build nations if they are to survive as independent sovereign states.

Portugal and Spain remain as African colonial powers, and it is evident

* Rhodesia, under Premier Ian Smith, issued a Declaration of Independence in November 1965. J.H.M.

that neither has been doing very much, if anything, to develop a sense of nation in their African territories.[5] On the contrary, constitutional and legal doctrine, which in the case of Portugal makes the African colonies [6] provinces of mainland Portugal, precludes conscious efforts by the colonial powers, particularly by Portugal, to induce the growth of a separate sense of nationality in the African territories. Spain * has been content to use her bits and pieces of African territory around the rim of Morocco for political bargaining with Morocco, and to a lesser extent, with Mauritania. Portugal, on the other hand, has been actively involved in building the mystique of a nonracial Portuguese civilization with its overseas offshoots in Africa, which make the latter appendages of mainland Portugal. Independence would be tantamount to secession in this view, and nation-building would take on the overtones of subversion, looking toward secession.

The Sui Generis Cases

Thus, in our view, nation-building in Africa is a phenomenon associated with independence. Accordingly, we have excluded the remaining colonial territories—essentially the Spanish bits and pieces, the Portuguese "provinces," and the former British "High Commission Territory" of Swaziland and Rhodesia in southern Africa and the island of Mauritius † in the Indian Ocean—from our area of concern in this book.

We have also excluded two peripheral areas—the United Arab Republic (Egypt) in the northeastern corner of the continent, and the Republic of South Africa in the southern tip. For our purpose both are *sui generis* and have limited value with respect to contributing to our understanding of the process of nation-building in Africa.

The UAR in many ways belongs to the Near East or Middle East. From the vantage point of nation-building, Egypt would seem to have very much more in common with her Near Eastern Arab neighbors than either the North African Arab states or the Sub-Saharan "black African" states.[7] In any event, Egypt's nation-building experience first under the monarchy and then under President Nasser would seem to have only limited applicability to the rest of Africa. This is not to say that Egypt is unimportant on the African scene and does not play a discernible role. It is rather to establish that to the extent this study deals with Egypt, it is as a force impinging on the inner core of Africa rather than as a component of that core. For a long time President Nasser himself has

---

* Equatorial Guinea did achieve independence from Spain on October 12, 1968, as the result of a referendum supervised by the United Nations. J.H.M.

† Swaziland achieved self-government in April 1967 and independence on September 6, 1968. Mauritius became independent on March 12, 1968, after 158 years of British rule. J.H.M.

held this view, that Egypt's role in Africa is one of "manifest destiny," to bring civilization to the "interior of the Dark Continent." In his words:

> The people of Africa will continue to look at us, who guard their northern gate, and who constitute their link with the outside world. We will never in any circumstances be able to relinquish our responsibility to support, with all our might, the spread of enlightenment and civilization to the remotest depths of the jungle.[8]

The Republic of South Africa will be treated in the same way. Its total isolation from the rest of Africa—in fact, politically from the rest of the world by the many UN General Assembly votes of 100 or more to 1, 2 or 3—makes it abundantly clear that the South African experience holds little that is instructive, except from a negative point of view, for the nation-building efforts of the rest of Africa. The special position of the European governing class and the governmental structure it operates, and the application of the South African Government's concept of building Bantustans—separate self-governing "states" for the Bantu (i.e., the Africans) with separate development within the Republic—are subjects apart, with only limited applicability to nation-building for the rest of the continent, except insofar as these factors serve to forge an African unity against South Africa and its doctrine of apartheid. So too, we have omitted the mandated territory of South-West Africa which the Republic of South Africa administers under an old League of Nations mandate. It seems clear since the decision in July 1966 of the International Court of Justice denying the "right" of Liberia and Ethiopia to challenge South Africa's administration of that mandate, that South-West Africa is to be developed as a series of Bantustans, for which Transkei in South Africa proper, the first Bantustan to emerge, is likely to serve as the model.

PART I

CONCEPTS AND CONTEXT

The Addis Ababa charter [of the Organization of African Unity] *is indeed the consecration of an "Afrique des patries" with mutual respect and non-interference in the internal affairs of states. Starting from this, each country is master of its own destiny and will carry out its own revolution within the context of its own development. This revolution will be what its own people will want and not what another African country considers as the true revolution, rough and hasty. To end, we advise these brother countries to devote their energies, all their energies, to the more noble and more exalting task of building up their own countries rather than Africa. The realisation of African unity will not be the achievement of an African head of state or nation, but the task of 250 million Africans inhabiting our continent. Whatever happens, nothing will deflect the Congo from this path. We shall continue to seek friendship and cooperation with all our African brothers, without exclusion.*

CYRILLE ADOULA, *Ambassador to Belgium and Former Prime Minister, Democratic Republic of the Congo (Kinshasa), 1964*

CHAPTER 1

CONCEPTS

In free Africa . . . the dominant sentiment is different. Here the main desire is to create modern nations, modern states, founded on respect for the dignity of the human individual and the sanctity of his personality. . . . The new nations will aim to charge their citizens with a sense of mission in life, to foster the spirit of self-help, and promote creative activities among the masses, and to accord economic modernization the primacy it deserves. . . .

> DUNDUZU CHISIZA, *late Parliamentary Secretary to Ministry of Finance, Nyasaland, and Secretary-General of the Malawi Congress Party, 1962*

NATION-BUILDING IN AFRICA: OLD WINE IN NEW BOTTLES

The problems of nation-building are anything but new. Three thousand years ago the Israelites in Palestine were confronted with the same range of problems, the same dilemmas, and the same uncertain prospects as today's new states of Africa.

In 1000 B.C., King David in Canaan "reduced the nation's dependence on the tribal chieftains by establishing a standing army . . . and a civil service. . . . David deliberately set about replacing tribal consciousness with symbols of national authority. He set up his capital in Jerusalem. . . . He pledged to construct a Temple there, to which the entire population could repair. He dispersed . . . the lower clergy across the land as a further means of using the common faith to purge separatist tendencies. . . . He launched a series of brilliant expansionist campaigns. . . . He annexed states that resisted. . . ."[1]

It's all there; the formula for nation-building used three thousand years ago by David and again in broad outline more recently by the new state of Israel. The new states of Africa too have in one degree or another sought to apply the formula with more or less success.

The ancient formula gave rise to a critical sociopolitical dilemma:

Centralized authority was a boon to security and commerce, but had distressing moral after-effects, because no new standards had yet evolved to replace the tribal mores that had sustained the people since the Exodus from Egypt.[2]

Indeed, this is the same dilemma confronting developing African and Asian states today.[3]

And the uncertain prospects of the nation-state built in Canaan by David and his successor, King Solomon, after about one hundred years, culminated in the fall and decline of Israel at the hands of "tribal advocates of separatism who had chafed under centralization drives of David and Solomon, and were jealous of Judah's primacy in the southern region of the country." [4] Two separate kingdoms, which were subsequently themselves to disappear, resulted.

The fate of the new state of Israel in about 900 B.C. reads almost like an early dress rehearsal for the unfolding nation-building drama of an important part of Africa today. Every African state today faces the critical issues of nation-building: how much centralization and how much devolution of power, how much uniformity and how much pluralism? Even if matters in Africa do not go to the early Israelite extreme, it is apparent that the prospects at this juncture for successful nation-building in most of the new African states are no less uncertain than those of the early Israelite state in Canaan. If anything, the new factor present in today's Africa—the pressure of time—seems to make African prospects for successful nation-building even more hazardous and uncertain.

THE TIME FACTOR IN AFRICAN NATION-BUILDING

The time is truly "out of joint" for Africa and its nation-building. The leisurely pace of nation-building in Biblical times, in the European Middle Ages, in the American Revolutionary Period, and more recently in the era in which the older Commonwealth States of Canada, Australia, and New Zealand evolved, no longer seems possible, or at any rate, tenable, for Africa and the Africans. The new states are in a hurry and seek to compress into a single generation what has taken the older states many generations, and for some of whom there still remains important "unfinished business," such as the Quebec Province issue in Canada, and the recurrent Walloon-Fleming controversy in Belgium. This forced-draft pace, this compulsion to telescope a century of nation-building into a decade, has frequently become the justification for African leaders and political parties having recourse to authoritarian and coercive courses of political action. Everything has to be sacrificed—the rationale goes—to speed, any means to an end. And so for many African countries, independence has not necessarily meant freedom for the individual. It has frequently meant authoritarian one-party government as the preferred means of building a strong, integrated, cohesive nation-state, and as a concomitant, a dominant state sector and comprehensive government controls as the preferred means of building a modern economy, which is, in this view, indispensable for, an integral part of, and inseparable from, building a modern nation-state.

THE SPECIAL ROLE OF ECONOMIC DEVELOPMENT
IN AFRICAN NATION-BUILDING

The new African states are seeking too "to catch up" with the established states. And "catch up" in this sense means to achieve (in addition to political cohesion and modern political institutions) a comparable state of material development. Thus, for the African states, economic development has become inextricably and indistinguishably intertwined with nation-building. It is not only a question of using economic development as a technique, or regarding it as a factor, in nation-building. It is something more. It is viewing economic development as a goal inseparable from that of nation-building. In this view, a nation-state has not been built unless and until it has also produced a modern economy. Although largely inchoate, this is frequently what is meant by African leaders who talk of achieving "economic independence" for their countries to sustain their "political independence."

Thus, these African leaders are caught in still another dilemma. On the one hand, they want to produce instant national political symbols—national airlines, national armed forces, national television networks, national universities, integrated steel plants, capital cities to which all could repair as the pride of the nation—irrespective of their cost and at the expense of real economic development. On the other hand, they want to achieve economic development in a single generation, which implies a high savings level and a high investment level, primarily in the productive sectors. There is an obvious conflict here between prestige disbursements and productive investment, between spending and saving, between consuming and investing. This dilemma is only a cut less vital than the basic sociopolitical dilemma of centralization and uniformity on the one hand, contrasted with decentralization and pluralism on the other.

In fact, in the same way that the goal of economic development has become indistinguishable from that of nation-building, so too the dilemma of quick political types of economic activity contrasted with perhaps somewhat slower but more productive economic development investment has become inextricably interrelated with the dilemma of coercing development or inducing it. Frequently the pattern has been centralized, coercive political development accompanied by large-scale instant development and prestige expenditure in a strongly controlled-state economy. Far less often the pattern has been decentralized (plural) induced political development accompanied by a relatively open economy (with some but quantitatively and qualitatively less instant development and prestige expenditure).

APPROACH TO AFRICAN NATION-BUILDING:
PROBLEMS AND PRECONDITIONS

Much of the literature on nation-building treats with the process in a single country, and conceives of it as little more than the historical evolution of this or that country, recounting the story of the development of a country's government, economy, and society. At the other extreme, there is a growing literature of highly generalized studies which seeks to treat with the inner workings of the process of nation-building across the board in all the seventy-seven or more countries belonging to the underdeveloped world, almost without distinction for the special circumstances and conditions of countries in widely separated parts of the globe.[5]

Our treatment of nation-building in this book is somewhat different. We start with the view that nation-building is the central process in the life of all the new states of Africa (as we have now defined it), which can be *consciously* directed or at least influenced and which will determine what they are to become. If successful or to the degree that they are successful, they will have political stability and a capacity for peaceful change and economic growth. If unsuccessful or to the extent unsuccessful, they will lack political stability and will be bedeviled by disorder, *coups*, and even chaos, and will sacrifice or compromise their opportunity for economic development.

We also believe that the circumstances and conditions in Africa are sufficiently different from those in other areas of the underdeveloped world (which we examine in Part II) to give nation-building in Africa a different "mix" and lead to different interactions of the elements which go to make up the process and thus to quite different results. Africa is not Asia; nor is it Latin America. Nevertheless, there has been a strong tendency for specialists in these areas, drawing on their experience in and preconceptions of these areas, to view Africa through the same prism, making little or no allowance for Africa's many distinctive circumstances and conditions. Thus, for the most part the classic image of densely overpopulated, famine-prone, land-hungry countries ruled by a landed aristocracy in league with a military clique living in conditions of oriental splendor, deriving from wide-spread impressions of both traditional and contemporaneous life in the Near East, South Asia, the Far East, and Latin America, has little or no relevancy for Africa.

In our study we start at the beginning, and view the new states of Africa as they were at the moment of independence and, for the most part, remain today. We see them with ill-defined and conflicting boundaries, as contrived geographic creations seeking to delimit their borders and come to terms with their geopolitical heritage of size, shape and situs in the crazy-quilt pattern of Africa's three dozen-odd sovereign entities. We then proceed to the consideration of the problem of state structures with which the African states are grappling. Are they to be centralized or decentralized, unitary or federal, monolithic or pluralistic in conception?

Next we turn to the vital political question: what types of political systems are the new states to choose to operate their state structures? Which system will most effectively facilitate building cohesion, unity and a sense of national identity, a voluntaristic or coercive one? What blend of carrots and sticks is likely to produce the best results? What role does regional and cultural autonomy play in nation-building? What role is played by a free press, independent trade unions, the military, pressure groups, the Rule of Law, the one-party apparatus?

Then we proceed to an examination and analysis of the relation between economic growth and nation-building. In view of what we have already said about the special role of economic development in African nation-building, we shall consider economic development not only from the vantage point of a technique and instrumentality for nation-building, for forging national unity, by breaking down prescriptive norms and qualifications for social advancement and substituting ascriptive ones, of achievement and demonstrated merit, but also as a goal, which has become so coupled with nation-building as to be a Siamese twin—a precondition, a factor, and a consequence.

Our approach, therefore, to nation-building is to examine in detail the principal problems confronting the African states seeking to build nations within their existing borders. (We return to this question of borders later in this chapter and in Chapters 2 and 3.) We have sought to do this by analyzing African experience over the past decade, when the birth rate of African states accelerated dramatically. Our study has convinced us that an examination and analysis of the principal problems suggest or at least imply the preconditions necessary for successful nation-building. Once again, in the final chapters of the book, the analysis and assessment of the prospects of the several African countries for successful nation-building also suggest or imply the necessary preconditions.

PROSPECTS FOR SUCCESSFUL NATION-BUILDING IN AFRICA

The prospects or lack of them for effective nation-building are viewed in the book from several vantage points. They are treated incidentally in Part II in the discussion of problems and preconditions. Subsequently, they are specifically evaluated in Part III by the orientation of the departed metropolitan country. The heritage bequeathed by the various metropoles has materially affected the nation-building prospects of the former colonial territories. In addition, in our view, for the larger colonial empires at any rate, there is a range of prospects for the former component territories, say, of British Africa, varying with the colonial policy, resource base, presence or absence of European settlers, local leadership, etc., in the former individual territories.

Finally, in our concept, nation-building in Africa is both qualitatively and quantitatively different from the comparable process in other large areas of the underdeveloped world—from Asia, the Near East, and Latin America. The three dozen-odd independent African states are by far more numerous than any other concentration of new states elsewhere in the world. And the independence revolution in Africa has still to run its course. Before running out of steam, there are another half-dozen territories that are likely to push to decision their candidacy for independence.

There are striking differences between the new states of Africa and those of other underdeveloped regions of the world in population densities and composition, food availabilities and potential, cultural and religious backgrounds, social structure and mobility of population, the role of the military, historical development, recency of accession to independence, nature of the independence revolutions, etc. In short, we believe the nation-building process in Africa faces the same fundamental problems as it does elsewhere, but in such different admixtures and with such different proportions, as to lead to distinctly different results. African prospects must therefore be evaluated in light of African circumstances and conditions and not those of other major underdeveloped areas. For example, and we consider this in some detail in Part II, whereas the use of the military directly and in "civic action" programs as a technique or instrumentality for nation-building may hold some promise in Asia or Latin America, it is in our concept of nation-building in Africa not only of limited usefulness but also potentially a danger to successful nation-building.

The Nation-Building Arena: Africa of the Fatherlands

For our purposes, then, nation-building in Africa is the process of defining the geographic area in which a particular state is to be built and developing the constitutional structure to give the state form and shape, the political system to give it life and provide the means for the population to relate to the state, and the economy to sustain the state structure and political system—all with a view to welding the multiple, disparate, noncohesive and unrelated population groups to be found in all the new states of Africa into identifiable and integrated nations within their respective borders. All of which leads up to the basic question underlying all others—of overall geographic limits within which African states are to be built—continental, regional, subregional or individual country boundaries. Until this question has been settled in principle, nation-building cannot start in earnest. So long as some wider unit is conceived of as the one to which loyalty and allegiance is due, the focus and concentration on building a Nigerian, Congolese, Kenyan, or Zambian nation will be badly diffused. Until there is definition as to area, it is difficult, if not impossible, to cope effectively with the problems of nation-building.

Hence, before proceeding to full-time and dedicated nation-building, African states have had to make a crucial decision on the framework within which the process was to take place. Africa had to come to terms with itself on Pan-Africanism. In an earlier volume, we dealt with the broad lines of choice—Pan-Africanism, Eurafricanism and nation-building in individual countries.[6] The last two choices in our view are not mutually exclusive and can be reconciled, as they have been by various of the French-speaking African states.

In this book, where our focus is nation-building, we will confine our consideration to an analysis of the choice made and the implications of that choice for nation-building on the continent. In fact, the choice provides the context in which nation-building will take place. It therefore seems useful to consider the nature and meaning of the African choice —summed up so nicely in the phrase of the former Prime Minister of the Congo, M. Adoula, and the poet-president of Senegal, M. Léopold Sédar Senghor, "Africa of the Fatherlands"—as our point of departure for analyzing and assessing the nation-building process and prospects of the nascent African states.

CHAPTER 2

CONTEXT: AFRICAN POLYCENTRISM

The baby millipede to its mother: "With so many legs which one do I move first?"

The mother's response: "Just move, child, move!"

> A Parable on African Unity and Development by Julius K. Nyerere, President of the United Republic of Tanzania at the Cairo Conference of Heads of State of the Organization of African Unity, 1964

THE MEANING OF THE ADDIS ABABA CONFERENCE (1963)

There can be no lingering doubt that there are to be many centers of power, authority, doctrine, policy, intrigue, and attraction in Africa.[1] The multidimensional African presence can no longer be denied; African states, like states everywhere in the world, will develop their own national personalities, their own national interests, and their own national styles for expressing their personalities and interests.

Polycentrism, not Pan-Africanism, at least as conceived of by its foremost apostle, former President Nkrumah of Ghana, is to be the guiding force in African interstate relations. The historic conference of thirty-one heads of state and government held at Addis Ababa, in May 1963, spelled this out for all who would see in the charter of the newly constituted Organization of African Unity. And two of the leading statesmen at the Addis Ababa Conference, one from the French-speaking world and one from the English-speaking world, left no room for doubt about the meaning of Addis Ababa for all who would take heed, in major public pronouncements soon after the Conference.

In somewhat stylized but nevertheless precise Gallic formulation, the President of Senegal, Léopold Sédar Senghor, commenting on the Addis Ababa Conference stated:

> We overcome this opposition ["between reformers and revolutionaries"]. We have united that which unites us and left aside that which

14

divides us. It is one step toward African unity: the assembly of heads of state [of the Organization of African Unity founded at the Addis Ababa Conference] has in effect a decision-making power. There is in addition a secretariat, an African group at the UN, specialized commissions, etc.

At no time did we renounce collaboration with Europe or with Asia or with France. Also in Africa, we do not envisage the disappearance of the Union of African and Malagasy States which constitutes a regional group.[2]

I have the same idea of African unity as General de Gaulle has of European unity. It is necessary to build an Africa of the Fatherlands. We are in fact very different from one another, from the point of view of culture and language as well as race.[3]

In the understated English idiom of the late Prime Minister of the Federation of Nigeria, Alhaji Sir Abubakar Tafawa Balewa, reporting to the Nigerian nation on the Addis Ababa Conference:

Just as we in Nigeria have been laying down one stone after another in the process of nation-building, thus ensuring that a solid foundation is laid; just as we are determined to preserve our unity in diversity; so the Addis Ababa Conference concentrated in those fields where the links between our states can be reinforced and strengthened and where new links can be forged while recognizing the fact that unity should not be tantamount to uniformity.[4]

In short, the total leadership of independent Africa assembled in Addis Ababa officially discovered (what many of the leaders had long sensed), after listening to what each of the national delegations had to say, that there was an African consensus—approaching unanimity—on the guiding principles for the organization of their vast continent. In the words of the charter of the Organization of African Unity:

The Member States . . . solemnly affirm and declare their adherence to the following principles:
(1) the sovereign equality of all Member States;
(2) non-interference in the internal affairs of States;
(3) respect for the sovereignty and territorial integrity of each Member State and for its inalienable right to independent existence;
(4) peaceful settlement of disputes by negotiation, mediation, conciliation or arbitration;
(5) unreserved condemnation, in all its forms, of political assassination as well as of subversive activities on the part of neighboring States or any other States.[5]

This is, purely and simply, the inter-African code of behavior of the Monrovia bloc of African states, and, just as purely and simply, the repudiation of the inter-African code of behavior of the Casablanca bloc of

African states. The Monrovia bloc of Nigeria, Liberia, Ethiopia, Congo (Kinshasa) Sierra Leone, Togo, and the Brazzaville bloc of twelve French-speaking African states had its code of behavior ratified and adopted by the thirty-one states in attendance at Addis Ababa. The Casablanca bloc of Morocco, Algeria, the United Arab Republic, Ghana, Guinea, and Mali, already in serious internal disarray before the Addis Ababa Conference, completed the formalities for making its demise official by acceding to the Monrovia bloc code of nationalism in one land, or multiple roads to national, political, and economic development, and foregoing its doctrine of continent-wide "political union now," as the sole road for African nationalists to travel to the promised land of development.

There could be no misunderstanding about what happened at the Addis Ababa Conference. At the very time it was happening the then Nigerian Prime Minister, Sir Abubakar, clearly enunciated it in his forthright address to the Conference. He then said:

> As I have said, we have to start from the beginning. I have listened to speeches in this Conference, and there have been only a very few members who spoke on the desirability of having a political union. Almost all of the speeches indicate that a more practical approach is much preferred by the majority of the delegations. I am glad to say that the stand we have taken right from the beginning is the stand of nearly all the countries in the Conference.[6]

Although the implications of what amounted to the absorption of the Casablanca bloc by the Monrovia bloc at Addis—the recognition of African diversity, of African polycentrism, of multiple roads to national development and nation-building—are many and varied, the inescapable implication that, for the most part, the African states would now proceed with their nation-building, by and large, within the geographic borders within which they came to independence—except in special, and probably relatively rare cases, where altered by peaceful negotiation of *all* of the equally sovereign parties—is in the view of the author so central to the future pattern, scale, and prospects for African political and economic development, as to be singled out as one of the keys to what lies ahead for the whole continent.

THE MEANING OF THE DEMISE OF THE CASABLANCA BLOC

Obviously the demise of the Casablanca bloc has not meant the automatic or total disappearance of the Casablanca approach of first the "political kingdom" and then all else would follow, or at least, should follow. Dr. Nkrumah, the leading exponent of this approach, has, even in exile in

Guinea, continued to urge that "Africa must unite" now in political union,[7] and that the Organization of African Unity, founded at the Addis Conference, is only a half-way house, or not much more than a starting point. However, the possibility of organized collective bloc action for political union now by the Casablanca bloc as such or any other African bloc has receded into the backwaters of history, more than likely forever. This does not mean that many of the practices or activities frequently justified under the cloak of Pan-Africanism (any means to this noble end) will disappear. On the contrary, it means that the practices and activities will have to stand on their own, will be harder to justify, and will have to be seen for what they are and in large part have always been—practices and activities associated with or deriving from the conventional and traditional kinds of disputes between states relating to conflicting boundary claims, irredentism, arms races, competition for spheres of influence, intrusions of states in the internal affairs of other states, externally-organized subversion, ideological controversies, hostile action of exiles or defectors launched from the sanctuary of neighboring states, and even overt aggression.

And so within months of the Addis Ababa Conference, the African scene became deeply troubled and remains deeply troubled by a series of disputes of the conventional and traditional type between states, arising from just about every given classic cause. Many of the incidents were in fact the renewal, continuation, or collateral descendants of earlier pre-Addis incidents. The earlier practices had not changed. They just became more visible. Many of the incidents still continue. In the few instances where the incidents have drawn to a close, others have taken their place. Although the actors and venue may change from time to time, the issues and conflicts persist and recur with more or less regularity.

Typical of the more disturbing incidents in the immediate post-Addis period were the outbreak of armed hostilities between Morocco and Algeria in the disputed border area to which both countries lay claim; the resumption of armed Somali raids (and Ethiopian reprisals), which were temporarily interrupted for the Addis Conference, on a stepped-up scale in the adjacent Ethiopian areas of Ogaden and the Haud, and in the Northern Frontier District of (subsequently independent) Kenya; the sporadic armed exchanges and continuing verbal thrusts between Dahomey and Niger, which disturbed the quiet of the tiny and little-known Lette Island in the Niger River lying between the two countries; Somalia's agreement to take substantial shipments of arms from the Soviet Union to build up its army to a strength of twenty thousand, while Kenya looked increasingly to the United Kingdom for military assistance and concluded a mutual defense pact with Ethiopia; the Congo's (Kinshasa) ouster of the total personnel of the Soviet Embassy following the arrest of two Soviet diplomats, allegedly found with compromising documents revealing a conspiracy between the Soviet Embassy and Congolese (Kinshasa) political exiles based in Brazzaville; Guinea's and Ghana's attacks on the then Union of African and Malagasy States for not dissolving in "the spirit of Addis" and for maintaining their separate "bloc structure"; Ghana's continuing unabated attack on the remodeled new association of eighteen African states with the Common Market and on the late Sir Milton Margai for contemplating possible association of the first English-speaking African state, Sierra Leone, with the Common Market.[8] And so the list goes and so too with the passing of time the list grows. With the exception of the "armistice" in the Moroccan-Algerian conflict, and the "provisional" settlement in the Dahomey-Niger contretemps, just about every incident, with minor variations, in scenario and casting, present in the post-Addis summer of 1963 was present in the post-Cairo OAU Conference summer of 1964 and post-Accra OAU Conference autumn of 1965, and will probably be present for a good many more African summers and autumns to come.

All that has changed has been the growing unavailability of the rationale provided by the Pan-African umbrella; now the incidents stand out in bold relief for what they are—conventional and traditional initiatives and maneuvers growing out of disputes among sovereign states seeking to influence events beyond their borders in their own national interests, as perceived by them, in keeping with their evolving national personalities and their new national styles.

Once this multiplicity of national characteristics has been recognized and admitted, the task, formidable enough when being dealt with in terms of the existing hard realities, and all but impossible when dealt with in terms of misleading myths, could at last be started—the task of organizing interstate African relations on a realistic, durable, and peaceful basis. It also becomes possible, as the other side of the coin, for African states to start to concentrate their attention and their efforts on their pressing, priority problems of internal development—subsumed in this study in our concept of nation-building; and to do this, without constant nagging, distractions, and fears of losing out in the Pan-African competition for position, prize, and pride of place, and without constant pressures and fears of being blackmailed into more "militant" Pan-African positions or actions by accusations of being "stooges" of the colonialists or "neo-colonialists." The emphasis is on the word *constant*. Nothing, of course, is likely to remove totally the Pan-African distractions, pressures, and fears. One or another African state is likely at one time or another to find it useful to resurrect and beat one or another of the muffled Pan-African drums. The difference, however, is important; it is the difference between a rhythmic drum beat, which sets the pace and the mood, and the infrequent

crash of cymbals, which punctuates or disturbs the otherwise orderly unfolding of a drama. The countries concerned with building their own
nation-states or with Eurafrican ties no longer have to devote energy and
allocate resources to rationalizing their every policy and action in a welter
of words and ritualistic actions to prove that they are as strong and as
pure in their advocacy of African unity, anticolonialism, and independence, as the radical nationalist Pan-Africanist Casablanca bloc.[9] Now all
independent and sovereign African states were deemed to be equal in
their independence and sovereignty.

Only Ghana claimed for herself the status of being "more equal" than
her fellow African states in her independence and sovereignty. But even
Ghana found it temporarily prudent after Addis to gild the lily, and her
advocacy of Pan-Africanism, although basically unchanged, became for a
time somewhat more muted. And so Nigeria could reach a short-lived
rapprochement with Ghana late in 1963 for the first time since Nigerian
independence in 1960, and Togo too could negotiate a brief temporary
respite with Ghana for the first time since Togolese independence in 1960.

Notwithstanding Ghana's tactical modulation of its public Pan-African
image, after Addis it stood very much alone. There was no longer an
organized claque to cheer on Dr. Nkrumah's Pan-African legions and
impugn the motives of any who would resist his doctrine of continental
union now. In isolation, Dr. Nkrumah's tactical shift away from his
evangelical Pan-Africanism and hard-fisted covert activity to help along
"the historical inevitability" of the triumph of his doctrine proved short-
lived. By the next conference of heads of state of the OAU at Cairo
about a year after the founding Addis Conference, the pretense of unity
achieved implied by the choice of that preposition *of* (instead of *for*) in
the title of the Organization of African Unity would clearly yield to the
reality of polycentrism in African internal development and external policies and relationships.

The Cairo Summit Conference of Heads of State (1964)

What the Addis Conference suggested the Cairo Conference of heads
of states and government of July 1964 crystallized. The African presence
in world affairs is most clearly characterized by the "unity amidst diversity" being practiced within the very framework of the Organization of
African Unity, and by the rejection or exposure at the Cairo Conference
of the dream of organic continental unity "here and now" as a myth or
"cover" for the national interests of particular African states.

The clash at Cairo at the second Heads of State Conference of the OAU
between President Nyerere of Tanzania and President Nkrumah made this
unmistakable. Commenting on Dr. Nkrumah's renewed plea for an im-

mediate union of all independent African states at the Cairo Conference, Dr. Nyerere declared:

> This union government business has become a cover for doing some of the most unbrotherly things in Africa.[10]

Dr. Nyerere went on:

> What was needed was not more preaching about unity but the practicing of unity.[11]

Finally, summing it all up the Commonwealth Correspondent for *The Observer* (London) wrote:

> The clash between Nyerere and Nkrumah today was not just a clash of personalities or between two jealous rivals. It reflected deep seated difference of policies and attitudes between Africa's leaders.
> The minority view is Nkrumah's—indeed it is difficult to find any other leader committed to supporting his crusade to set up an African union here and now. Nyerere speaks for the great majority, but unlike the great majority, Nyerere showed himself ready today to say what his colleagues prefer to say in private.[12]

There could be little doubt about the majority position. In the words of the *New York Times* despatch from Cairo:

> Mr. Nyerere espoused the more popular step-by-step approach, on the ground that final union now was impossible. The Tanganyikan received an ovation at the close of his speech, which he said he had not wanted to make.[13]

AFTER CAIRO: HIGH ROADS AND LOW ROADS

Everything that has happened since Cairo has served to reinforce the "spirit of Addis"—multiple roads to national development and nation-building.

The accession to independence of Malawi and Zambia during the second half of 1964 buttressed the tendency of African states to develop their own approach to nation-building and foreign policy based on self-assessment of their respective national interests. These two landlocked countries are dependent on reasonable—if not friendly—relations with the European-dominated government of Rhodesia and/or the Portuguese-run colony of Mozambique for primary access to the sea and a significant share of their economic activity. In the vivid words of Dr. H. Kamuzu Banda, then Prime Minister, and now President, of Malawi, responding to criticism of his frankly accommodationist policy toward Rhodesia and Portugal:

> I have four million people to look after. To do what I think is best in their interest I will do anything. I will even have the devil as my ally.[14]

So too, in East Africa, the growing polycentrism of the continent has led to loosening ties of the three states—Tanzania, Kenya, and Uganda—composing the East African Common Market and Common Services Organization. The proposal so rapturously embraced by the leaders of the three East African states *before* achieving national independence to federate their three countries into one sovereign federal state has receded more and more into the realm of things not to be. And since this has become recognized, President Nyerere of Tanzania, the principal proponent of East African federation, concluded during the summer of 1965:

> For a time we were willing and able to accept the *status quo*, and all of its disadvantages to us, as a necessary price to pay for East African unity. But in the absence of any progress or any hope of an early federation, we had no alternative but to seek activity for an equalization of the advantages and disadvantages of the Common Market. Only when our efforts failed to bring practical agreement on an East African basis did we, reluctantly, take steps on our own.[15]

The steps taken by Tanzania were to put into practice the agreed principles of the nonratified "Kampala Agreement" of March 1964, permitting the imposition of quotas on "imports" from Kenya to protect or encourage Tanzanian local industry, the creation of a separate central bank for Tanzania to replace the East African Currency Board, and the issuance of a separate Tanzanian currency to replace the East African shilling used in the three East African countries. The Kampala Agreement itself, providing as it did for quotas and for the location of industry by category and type, was a major step back from the existing common market. Unilaterally imposed, it was a violation not only of the letter but also of the very concept of a common market. The decision to have separate central banks in the three states, and also separate currencies, no matter how it is presented or rationalized, can only be seen as a fragmentation of the strongest financial bonds, a real set-back for economic integration, to say nothing of political union—now or later.

The dissolution of monetary and banking unity, the imposition of trade barriers, the development and protection of "infant industry" within each of the member states, when reinforced by the growing political differences and conflicts among the three states, leave little basis for concluding anything other than that even in East Africa, the most advanced area on the continent for a *regional* approach to development, and conceivably for nation-building too, the choice in principle and practice which has been made is clearly that each state will follow its own separate and quite distinctive road.

President Nyerere, referring to the publicly displayed indignation of President Kenyatta of Kenya over two incidents involving the discovery of Communist Chinese arms caches in Western Kenya, originating in Tanzania and ostensibly consigned to Uganda, declared:

> It is now clear that the pressures of our separate domestic problems can bring us more easily than we would have thought possible a few years ago, to a position where we are prepared to believe slanders about each other. And this is the greatest danger of all; for if we take that road it is not only East African federation which is gone for all time. So too has economic co-operation, and so has our ambition for continent-wide unity.[16]

Not only in Central Africa, and in East Africa, but also in West Africa, polycentrism and multiple roads to internal development became increasingly manifest after the Cairo Conference. In February 1965 the francophone states revived in effect the Union of African and Malagasy States under the style of the Common Organization of African and Malagasy States (OCAM after its French initials) as a rebuff to the radical nationalist African states, particularly Ghana and its persistent campaign of interfering in the internal affairs of other African states. Stripped bare of their Pan-African overtones, the Ghanaian policies and programs for influencing African governments enraged the French-speaking African states. They denounced Ghana, formed the OCAM, and stayed away in large numbers from the third meeting of heads of state of the OAU in Accra in October 1965 as a protest against Ghana and Dr. Nkrumah, and their "unbrotherly" policies of "subversion, infiltration and interference."

THE ACCRA SUMMIT CONFERENCE OF HEADS OF STATE (1965)

The distinguishing feature of the Accra Summit Conference was the public stock-taking by the membership of the nature of their organization —"merely a loose association of egocentric states," [17] intent on pursuing their own policies in national development and nation-building, and on a wide range of foreign policy issues. The Conference refused to take formal action on the Ghanaian proposal for a "permanent political executive council" within the OAU to coordinate political policies of African states on major issues affecting national development, inter-African affairs, and world affairs. The Ghanaian proposal itself represented a step backward by Ghana from its "union now" posture in recognizing that for the foreseeable future political union in Africa was not a realistic goal. In fact, so far did the Conference go in its recognition of its own basic nature that "because of its close association with Ghana's blueprint for a single continental government, the delegates refused even to approve the creation of a special commission to study the [new Ghanaian] council plan." [18] The delegates appeared to bury for good the repeated appeal of Ghana's President, Kwame Nkrumah, for a continent-wide union government.[19] The attitude on African union government was summed up by President Tubman of Liberia in these words:

> I have no objection to it in principle. But with the kind of confusion we have seen among ourselves right here—can we have one government functioning for us all? [20]

As for the OAU itself, the report of Secretary General Telli Diallo revealed the deplorable state of the organization's finances—the failure of members to pay their dues and assessments (24 of 36 had not paid in full or in part) and mounting debt ($2.5 million); the deplorable attendance of governments at the multiplicity of commission and committee meetings of the organization, and the incredible volume of meetings (an average of one every other week over the last two years). In the words of M. Telli Diallo, "the secretariat is in danger of becoming merely a conference-servicing machine." [21]

And finally, the most vivid testimonial of all of the growing polycentrism of the new African states was the record of attendance at the Accra Conference. Eight countries did not participate at all—the Ivory Coast, Niger, Upper Volta, Dahomey, Togo, Gabon, Chad, and the Malagasy Republic. Almost 25 percent of the membership stayed away. Ten countries were represented by ministers rather than heads of state. Half of the African heads of state stayed away. And of those that came, some, such as President Tubman, left early.

The poor attendance reflected two central themes—both of which illustrate Africa's decision to pursue many different roads in national policies and nation-building. First, it represented disapproval of President Nkrumah and Ghana, and their Pan-African policies and actions. Second, it was a reflection of the growing feeling of irrelevancy and ineffectiveness of so much that the OAU undertook to do. In the words of a discerning "news analysis" of the conference:

> The Africa of 1965 is turning inward, concentrating on nagging economic and social problems at home. So far, the OAU has paid scant attention to this set of problems, although it is the biggest common denominator within the organization.[22]

In fact, as early as 1963 and the founding of the OAU at the Addis Ababa Conference, Africa had rejected supranational versions of Pan-Africanism, and had opted for national development within inherited colonial boundaries. Many states shaped their policies accordingly, and turned increasingly to nation-building and economic development; others, such as Ghana, persisted in their ways. The Cairo Conference confirmed and expanded the African commitment to national development without interference by sister states. And the Accra Conference reaffirmed the African commitment to multiple roads to development and foreign affairs.

POLYCENTRISM: FRAMEWORK FOR NATION-BUILDING

Thus, a study of internal development and nation-building in Africa must take into account, and would seem well advised to take for its frame of reference, the context in which such development must take place, African polycentrism. It is in this context in any event, that we shall explore and analyze the crucial internal African development problems of nation-building in Part II and assess the prospects for such nation-building efforts in Part III of this book.

PART II

NATION-BUILDING AFTER ADDIS: PROBLEMS AND PRECONDITIONS

Taking our ideal for a reality, we thought we had only to condemn territorialism and its natural product, micronationalism, to overcome them and assure the success of our chimerical undertaking [the short-lived union of Senegal and the Soudan in the Federation of Mali]. . . . *We are faced with micronationalisms that need to be tamed, micronations that will have to be organized. Thus it is necessary for us to start with these micronationalisms and micronations, which are the realities of this strange twentieth-century African universe. Then we can build modestly, gradually, the bases of a great African nationalism and the foundations of a great African nation.*

MAMADOU DIA, *economist, author, and former Prime Minister of Senegal, 1961*

CHAPTER 3

THE GEOPOLITICAL PROBLEM:
SIZE, SHAPE, AND SITUS

With regard to its shape and size we might follow the Prince of Denmark and liken it [Nyasaland] to a camel or a weasel or a whale and still be as puzzled as was Polonius.

FRANK DEBENHAM, *Nyasaland: The Land of the Lake, 1955*

THE CASE OF THE REPUBLIC OF MALI

The country feels beset, too, by African neighbors with a potential stranglehold on its trade routes. Four years of independence is not long enough to learn to live with nightmare geography; a shape that, until 1956, few people imagined would one day be put forward as a viable republic. Mali has four thousand miles of land frontiers, enfenced by seven independent countries. About 200,000 square miles of it is in full Sahara. This is a territory tenable by a roving cavalry, perhaps, but a difficult one in which to build a modern state, dependent for most of its government revenue on licensed imports and exports.[1]

Almost more than any other African state the Republic of Mali raises and at the same time illustrates the problem of nation-building in Africa. We shall therefore open our consideration of the geopolitical factor in nation-building with the case of Mali, and then move on to the cases of the Sudan and Senegambia, and incidentally and in considerably less detail, to other African cases. We shall defer until subsequent chapters the problem of political and economic structures and systems. We are here concerned with the problem of the geographic limits—size, shape and situs —within which a sovereign state is to be constructed and thus the physical framework for the constitutional, legal, and political limits within which nation-building is to take place.

What is the Malian nation to be? The future tense, strange though it may sound to use it some years after the achievement of independence, is the correct one, for as yet no such nation exists. It must be conceived, constituted, and constructed. Is the Malian nation to encompass the in-

27

habitants, as at present, of the former French territory, the Soudan, or the inhabitants of the far larger area, of the former Soudan and the former French territory of Senegal, as was the case in August 1960, just prior to the disruption of the ill-conceived Federation of Mali, or the still larger area of the originally conceived Federation of Mali, consisting of the Soudan, Senegal, Upper Volta and Dahomey, which was discarded in the face of the determined opposition of President Houphouët-Boigny of the Ivory Coast?

Apparently, at the present juncture in African affairs, the answer is that within the geographic limits of Mali as presently constituted, within the size and shape of this residual "nightmare geography" the Malian nation is now to be built. This very basic and very important decision has resulted, not from a considered study and assessment of the geopolitical factors involved, not from a chance accident of history or, as is more fashionable at present, from colonial design or callousness, but primarily from the failure of the ill-considered and ill-conceived project of two African states to launch the Federation of Mali, which burst asunder almost before its existence could be acknowledged by other states.

To be sure, the colonial past of the two areas involved, as well as the incompatibility and lack of complementarity of the political structures, systems, economies, personalities, and philosophies of the partners in the enterprise, was an important element in the rupture, but no more so than the geopolitical factor. The size, shape, and situs of the individual part-ners, and of the resultant federal union, were at best considered little more than the crucial element of timing in assembling the federation. Were either or both of the partners ready to subvert their sovereign status, share their wealth or poverty, sacrifice inherited or geographic advantages, and submerge the advantages and disadvantages of the respective territories arising from their respective size, shape and situs for the benefit of the larger federal union? In all its manifestations, and particularly from the point of view of geopolitical considerations, the consequences of the abortive and short-lived attempt to launch the Federation of Mali serve to point up the manifold problems of nation-building in even more acute form than they ordinarily arise within the inherited geographic limits of the new African state.

We shall now consider in detail the geopolitical problem as a factor in Mali's nation-building. We shall pay particular attention to the problems of external relations arising from Mali's size, shape and situs, whereas in other cases we shall pay particular attention to problems of internal affairs arising from a country's size, shape and situs.

PROBLEMS OF EXTERNAL RELATIONS:
HINTERLAND FOR SENEGAL

Taking the residual area of the Republic of Mali and considering its size, shape and situs, what problems are posed for the nation-building task by the country's landlocked interior location and four thousand miles of land frontiers with seven independent countries?

Mali's interior location in West Africa has made it a hinterland, and this fact perhaps more than any other accounts for Mali's policy of aloofness, bordering on isolation, from its neighbors, and its passion for nondependence on, or independence of, the former metropole. Both as an inland colony (the former Soudan) and as the interior region of the independent Federation of Mali, the present Republic of Mali has felt the effects of being treated as a hinterland for the more accessible and attractive coastal area, centering on Dakar. Mali was thought of as an outlet or market for the commercial and industrial enterprises which developed in Senegal, in and around Dakar, particularly in the aftermath of World War II, and as a source of primary products to be processed and handled commercially in Senegal and shipped through its ports. Mali was also thought of as a supplier of foodstuffs for Senegal.

Thus, prior to 1960 Mali purchased some 30 percent of the industrial output of Senegal, 50 percent of its refined sugar, 35 percent of its matches, 3 percent of its tobacco, 20 percent of its shoes, and 15 percent of its cement. The Senegalese port of Kaolak exported some 90 percent of Mali's groundnuts, which constituted 95 percent of the port's activity (see the discussion of Senegambia below), and the port of Dakar handled some 244,000 tons of Malian goods. In addition, the bulk of Mali's imports came through Senegal's ports, primarily through Dakar.

This hinterland dependency of the Soudan was undoubtedly resented by the Soudanese leadership, and certainly contributed to the multiple economic and political problems which combined to undermine the Federation. The breakup of the Federation only served to reinforce Mali's psychological resentment of being a hinterland by adding the very tangible impact of the disruption of the Dakar-Bamako Railway, which cut off Mali from its only outlet to the sea. Landlocked, dependent on other states for access and outlet, Mali turned inwards. The consequence has been something of a "siege neurosis" in Mali's relations vis-à-vis her neighbors.

Some three years after the disruption of the Federation of Mali, the Republic of Mali resumed relations with its erstwhile partner in the defunct Federation, the Republic of Senegal, and, as a concomitant, the Dakar-Bamako railroad resumed operations. More than a residue of suspicion and doubt, however, still lingers to color the relations between the two states. Mali is apparently determined not to become so dependent ever again on a single route to the sea through Senegal as it was before the collapse of the Federation. The costly alternative trucking routes via the Ivory Coast and Upper Volta, pioneered during the three-year economic and diplomatic breach with Senegal are apparently, if at all possible, to be kept operational.

PROBLEMS OF EXTERNAL RELATIONS: SHARED BORDERS

Mali has reached understandings with Mauritania and Algeria concerning their shared borders. However, the Malian concern persists about the Touareg tribesmen who inhabit the northern reaches of the country and freely wander the Sahara on both sides of the shared borders with Mauritania and Algeria. It is a built-in source of continuing suspicion and doubt between Mali and its neighbors. Thus, as recently as August 1964, President Modibo Keita in denouncing "imperialist forces" for attempting to promote a "military putsch" laid the blame on "traitors who were refugees in certain neighboring states and had covered their subversive activities thanks to certain Malians originating in Kayez, Doventza and Goudam, localities situated in the Sahara, in the proximity of the frontiers of Mauritania, Senegal, Algeria, Niger and Upper Volta." [2] In addition, smuggling and illegal currency transaction, discussed below, have acted to exacerbate the relations of Mali with her neighbors, particularly with Niger, Upper Volta, and the Ivory Coast.

Mali's relations with her three southern neighbors, the Ivory Coast, Upper Volta, and Niger, however, although largely correct, are far from intimate. This reserve in neighborliness, notwithstanding the new trade routes, derives in important part from Mali's special political orientation, discussed in the chapter on political systems. Mali has deliberately remained out of the Union of African and Malagasy States, and successor organizations, the Union of African and Malagasy States for Economic Cooperation and the Common Organization of African and Malagasy States. She has also developed a somewhat more attenuated set of relations with France than all of the other states of l'expression française, excepting Guinea. These differences have caused a certain strain between Mali and the other former French territories and have led to unpleasant recrimination as they have enabled Mali to stand off and accuse her neighbors of being colonialist pawns or victims, i.e., maintaining too intimate connections with the former metropole.

As for Guinea, the seventh neighbor, Mali's relations with her are perhaps the most cordial of those with any of her near neighbors. They are perhaps closest ideologically. Economic relations are limited, however, and there are few other major ties presently discernible. The attempt at nation-building in the enlarged area of the Ghana-Guinea-Mali union, the Union of African States, has proved every bit as abortive and as futile as the effort in the defunct Federation of Mali, and has by common consent been allowed to fade away. There has in fact never been an official dissolution of the Union, but the aftermath has been, if nothing else, a certain coolness and tension among the former partners—Ghana, Guinea and Mali.

IMPLICATIONS OF MALI'S ISOLATION FOR NATION-BUILDING

Nation-building in Mali may be facilitated by the lack of intimacy of Mali with its neighbors, or stated otherwise, by the isolation Mali has achieved or imposed upon itself through its "passionate desire to avoid foreign interference, and a willingness to develop at a slower rate than its neighbors, if it must, to avoid the cost they pay in commitment." [3] The "commitment" alluded to is that of the members of the Common Organization of African and Malagasy States to one another, and also and more significantly of these francophone states to the former metropole, France. Mali's "siege neurosis," like the convenient and now commonplace external threat technique so freely invoked by new states to divert attention from internal difficulties, may lend a helping hand to its cohesion, based on an induced fear of an alleged "foreign devil." On the other hand, isolation and a "siege neurosis," as is suggested in the foregoing quotation, not only may slow down development, but in the case of Mali, seems actually to have done so. The price for less or slower development appears to be less rather than more national cohesion. To the extent that economic development breaks down tribal, local, and regional barriers, rewards performance rather than status, overcomes traditional and customary barriers to economic growth and political change, and generally contributes to the modernization of a society, then to this extent the self-imposed politico-economic and financial isolation of Mali, and its negative effects on development, will act to retard nation-building, not to facilitate it.

Less dramatic perhaps than Mali's 1960 decision "to go it alone," when Mali opted out of the accords between the defunct Federation of Mali and France, decided against any link with the Franco-African Community, and required the withdrawal of French military bases and personnel from the country, but no less important, however, has been the near total financial isolation Mali achieved following its withdrawal from the franc zone and unilateral issuance of a new and unsupported currency in July 1962. Ever since the new Malian franc appeared, it has been largely inconvertible in world trade; there has been an unwillingness on the part of traders, merchants, and others in the neighboring states as well as in Mali itself to accept Malian francs. There has also been a related inability or unwillingness of the neighboring states to control smuggling, particularly of cattle from Mali to traders in the neighboring countries who could pay the Malians in "hard currency" and consumer goods, which because of Mali's foreign exchange shortage have been in short supply. Mali's loss in foreign exchange earnings and revenue resulting from this illegal trade and related currency transactions has served to aggravate the already seriously deteriorating financial situation. This has been but one more cost of Mali's policy of isolation and "economic independence." The adverse impact on development and hence on nation-building is all too clear.

To the consequences of the policy of isolation must also be added the economic cost of premature or ill-founded political unions, such as the Federation of Mali, which are, as has already been suggested for purposes of the present discussion, merely enlarged postindependence geographic areas in which nation-building has to take place. The abortive Federation of Mali has led to the diversion of "ten thousand million francs worth of ground-nuts and cotton" from transportation by the Dakar-Bamako railroad to transportation over a hastily improvised road by three hundred heavy trucks to a railhead in the Ivory Coast, and then to final evacuation by railroad through the port of Abidjan.[4] The extra costs can only be imagined—loading and reloading, high-cost imported gasoline, the cost of vehicles and their maintenance, wear and tear of trucking on improvised roads, the extra time involved, and, finally, the Ivory Coast railroad haul.

In any event, it seems obvious that Mali's relations with its neighbors, based as they are on its landlocked location and its vast area of shared frontiers, are important factors for the crucial task of nation-building. No less important, however, are the internal problems for nation-building thrown up by its sprawling geographic shape and size, and location astride the Sahara Desert. We now turn briefly to a consideration of these internal problems.

Problems of Internal Cohesion

The interior location and the attendant "siege neurosis" of Mali has served to solidify the one-party mentality already present in the *Union Soudanaise*, and has contributed to one of the tightest one-party states on the African continent. The implications for nation-building of the one-party approach are many, important and varied. We treat with them in the chapters on political and economic structures and systems. Our purpose at this point is merely to take account of the implications of Mali's location for nation-building. The confluence of geography and doctrine in Mali has, probably more so than in many other African states, led to the one-party, "mass-mobilization," authoritarian approach to building national cohesion and internal unity, and all the problems attendant on that approach, discussed in subsequent chapters.

Against the background of the country's locus, we now consider the implications of its size and shape for nation-building. Mali is a large country—1,200,000 square kilometers. It is a thinly populated country—an estimated 4.3 million people. The average population density is about 3.5 per square kilometer. The population is unevenly distributed throughout the country. The largest part of the population is to be found along the rivers in the southern third of the country, particularly alongside the major river in the area, the Niger. The largest urban concentration is in the capital, Bamako, with an estimated population of 50,000; the next largest urban centers are really little more than small towns of some 25,000 to 30,000 people, Kayes and Ségou.

When the peculiar elongated "J" shape of the country, with its vast desert wastelands in the north, is taken together with the thin and uneven population distribution, the enormity of the nation-building problem from just the physical point of view becomes strikingly apparent. How are common bonds, shared interests, and reciprocal loyalties to be created among peoples scattered over so large an area, with limited contact, and without motivation or incentives for coming together beyond what may be provided by the nation-builders?

In addition to the difficulties of its size and shape, Mali is confronted by the physical barriers of desert, scrub land and an arid climate. The universal characteristics of underdevelopment, poor or totally absent transportation and communication systems, must also be added to round out the picture. How are the widely separate areas and harsh environmental factors of Mali to be coped with to weld together the white Arab-descended or Arab-influenced nomadic and desert tribesmen of the north and the black Soudanese farmers and forest-dwellers of the south?

The Malian government in an attempt to answer these questions, in its first development efforts has emphasized, in fact gone overboard, on transportation. It has worked itself into something of a dead end on this score with heavy investment, maintenance costs, and debt service charges for the foreign aid utilized in the road-building effort. To this continuing drain on national resources must be added the diversion of internal effort, energy, and resources from other possible uses which may well have been more productive for the economy, and so for nation-building. The sociopolitical motivation for the program is clear and understandable. Whether it is correct, however, is quite another question.

Would not more have been contributed to nation-building by judicious allocation of resources to more productive uses, to bring more people

into the market economy and to stimulate more economic exchanges and
contacts among producers and consumers than by a road-building program, which to understate the matter, has certainly been well ahead of
any discernible economic needs?   Or will the very existence of the roads,
as the Malian Government hopes, *ipso facto* lead to both economic growth
and sociopolitical links indispensable to national cohesion?   The roads
alone in the geopolitical circumstances of Mali can, in the author's judgment, hardly serve to induce the desired results.   Whereas in the far
more densely populated and economically advanced Federal Republic of
Nigeria further down the West Coast, where supply and demand justify
it, the road-building formula might pay off (in fact has already tended
to do so), it seems less likely that such a result could be achieved in Mali.
This being so, the imprudent use of scarce resources on road building in
the forelorn hope of contributing to national cohesion has tended to have
the contrary effect.   Economic development prospects have been impaired and along with them the prospects for drawing together the
heterogenous and scattered Malian population into a socially and politically cohesive nation-state structure.

From all that has preceded it seems fair to conclude that Mali, in consideration of both the external and internal aspects of its nation-building
efforts, has been in the few years of its existence, and will long continue
to be, confronted by a series of major geopolitical problems.   These problems are highly intractable, and will not be readily resolved.   Mali has
chosen a political approach to these and other problems of nation-building
which will be systematically examined in future chapters.   Our focus has
been the special and fundamental nature of the problems thrown up for
nation-building by the geography of the new state of Mali, including the
added geographical ramifications of the abortive political union of Mali
and Senegal.

In concluding this consideration of the geography of Mali and its bearing on the future of the new state, it should be noted that in greater or
lesser degree Mali shares many of the geopolitical constraints on nation-
building already examined with most of the new African states and particularly with the broad band of sub-Saharan states lying along the
southern fringe of the desert and merging into the savannah and tropical
forest areas further south.   Thus, in Mauritania, Niger, Chad, and the
Sudan, we find the same special admixture as in Mali of elongated countries running essentially along a north-south axis, with divided Arab-type
populations in the north and black Negroid-type populations in the south.
All too, like Mali, have ancient cultural and historical connections with
North Africa deriving from trans-Sahara trade routes of one sort or another, none though as important as the one that had its terminus at the
legendary city of Timbuktu, which lies near the geographic center of

Mali on a north-south axis. It is no traveler's tale or neocolonialist design
to recognize that many of the sociopolitical tensions in these sub-Saharan
countries derive from their basically different ethnic and cultural population groups. Whereas in Mauritania and the Sudan, at either end of the
sub-Saharan band, the Arab-oriented and Arab-descended group prevails
and holds political power, the reverse is true in the interior countries of
Mali, Niger, and the Chad. The Chad particularly has been the source
of considerable tension and some strife, revolving around the divided
population problem.

THE CASE OF THE REPUBLIC OF SUDAN

It is hard not to sympathize with both sides in the Sudan's tragic internal conflicts as violence continues to mount. The Arab Northerners, who
control the Government, do not want to see the country divided—especially since the situation they have to deal with is largely the result of
post-colonial mistakes. The Nilotic Southerners seek a federal constitution to allow them greater local autonomy—a desire strengthened by the
Northerners' mistakes made in the 10 years since independence.[5]

The Sudan, which shares most of the geopolitical characteristics alluded
to in our discussion of Mali, is singled out for detailed consideration here
because it so effectively complements the Malian case. Whereas in the
case of Mali we dwelt on the external relationship aspects of the geopolitical factor in nation-building, the reverse will be true here. Our
focus in considering the Sudan will be the internal aspects of the geopolitical factor in nation-building.

PROBLEMS OF INTERNAL COHESION

Although geography and history have tied the black, pagan and Christian Southern Sudan to the Arabic, Islamic Northern Sudan, "the ruthless
and indiscriminate maltreatment of Southerners by the military government [of the Sudan] only crowns an already obvious failure of the Sudan
as an Afro-Arab State." [6] Everything that has occurred since Mr. Makuei,
a close observer of Sudanese affairs, wrote these words in early 1964 has
tended to confirm his conclusion. The military regime of General
Abboud was overthrown in November 1964 as the climax of a series of
riots in Khartoum protesting the continuing military repression of the
political agitation for regional autonomy and even independence in the
southern provinces.[7] The continuing strife and mounting tempo of the
guerrilla warfare of the Southerners and counter-actions of the Northern-
dominated successor governments following the ousting of the Abboud

regime have revealed the true dimensions of Southern disaffection, which
had been earlier concealed by the policy of the Abboud Government of
sealing off the Southern provinces from outside contact.[8,] *

Mr. Makuei's point of departure in his analysis of the Sudanese situation
is the country's "geographic vastness." He then takes note of the location
of the country: "The Sudan has a more honoured role to play simply
because of its unique position as the only [?] State in Africa comprising
both African and Arab nationalisms." [9] From this base he moves to the
geopolitical heart of his assessment:

> The Sudan . . . brings with her an acute splintering problem in Afro-
> Arab relations. The position of the four million Negroid Africans of the
> Southern Sudan who are today subjected to the Arab North domination,
> and whose development is conditioned on their readiness to assimilate Arab
> culture and embrace Islam, cannot certainly be overlooked by their fellow
> Africans with whom they have common ideology, cultural, linguistic ties
> and political aspirations. The recent anti-Arab revolution in Zanzibar and
> similar tendencies in East Africa are a clear indication. . . .
>
> It is obvious that, geographically speaking, the Northern Sudan does
> belong to the Middle East. Economically, the two regions [Northern and
> Southern Sudan] could be interdependent, but in no way a firmer inter-
> dependence than between Nyasaland and the two Rhodesias. Economics
> alone, which Northerners are ignominiously using to make the South per-
> petually dependent on the North, could not be adduced to overstep glaring
> cultural, linguistic, religious and deeply rooted historical differences.[10]

From here the author throws out the possibility of the Southern Sudan
seceding from the Republic and possibly affiliating with a new East
African Federation. He then sums up in these critical words:

> The core of the Southern problem lies in the Northern rejection [sic]
> to the Sudan becoming a multi-racial state. This is shown by the Northern
> determination to obliterate African identity by the imposition of the Arabic
> language, of Islam, and by the subjugation of the African group econom-
> ically, politically and socially. Judging from the trend of development
> and of events, one can perceive that British and Egyptian colonialism has
> only been replaced by Northern colonialism.[11]

Perhaps the best testimonial to the validity of many of the points made
by Mr. Makuei is the admission contained in a letter by the Sudanese

---

* On May 25, 1969, a military *coup d'état* involving "middle-ranking" officers, led
by Maj. Gen. Jaafar Muhammed al-Nimeiry, overthrew the weak coalition government of the Republic of the Sudan, and declared as Premier and Foreign Minister
former Chief Justice Abubakr Awadallah. J.H.M.

press attaché in the London Embassy, written explicitly to rebut Mr. Makuei's allegations. The letter reads in part:

> Regarding the recent disturbances in the south, Mr. Makuei states that the "military government has ordered measures amounting to genocide in the South; and quotes certain figures to back his allegation. He does not mention the fact that the guerrilla campaign waged by a minority of Southern Sudanese has been financed and encouraged by a group from outside the Sudan, and that their activities have included the terrorising of villagers—their own people—who have shown their preference for a law-abiding life under the Government. The figure of 'more than 600' Southerners killed is greatly exaggerated; even if it were correct, 600 out of a total population (in the South) of over 4,000,000 could hardly be rated as genocide." [12]

The quotations from Mr. Makuei's article and the letter of refutation convey more vividly than any interpretative comments the flavor and intensity of the attitudes and views held among Sudanese, which have to be accommodated and reconciled in the country as part of the nation-building effort. The intractable nature of the problem of the regional, racial, religious, cultural, social, political, and economic disparaties between the North and South has been dramatically underscored by the events since the overthrow of the Abboud government, i.e., by "the terror and massacres in the Southern Sudan." [13]

Thus, in the Sudan the multidimensional problems of two radically different and mutually hostile ethnic, religious, and cultural population groups, associated with distinctly separate and different geographical regions, have converged to create a "nightmare" nation-building task to match the difficult geographic composition of the Sudan.

PROBLEMS OF EXTERNAL RELATIONS

Externally, the geopolitical factor has also had its impact on Sudanese nation-building. We now turn to this aspect, but only briefly. The obvious starting point is the size, shape, and situs of the Sudan, which gives it contiguity with nine other states, including for practical purposes Saudi Arabia across the narrow reach of the Red Sea. The country is a meeting place, crossroads, and locus of confrontation for the increasingly self-conscious Arab world and the vehemently nationalistic African world. The internal conflict in the Sudan itself between north and south reflects in microcosm this larger clash of nationalism. What may be synthesized, or alternatively rejected, here could have implications for the band of sub-Saharan states already discussed, and far beyond, given the sanctuary

Southern Sudanese have been finding increasingly in neighboring tropical African countries.

The privileged sanctuary which has been increasingly accorded southern Sudanese in the adjacent African countries, particularly in Uganda, Congo (Kinshasa), and the Central African Republic has evolved slowly but inevitably into a series of bases for guerrilla activity of the Sudanese underground, the Azania Liberation Front. The neighboring African states have been relatively slow to provide facilities or encouragement to the Sudanese exiles in their guerrilla warfare, in contradistinction to the willingness and readiness of the Sudan itself to provide such facilities and encouragement to Congolese rebel forces during late 1964 and early 1965 (after the overthrow of the Abboud regime).

The Sudan also has a long exposed border with the Chad, which has a less intense but troublesome ethnic problem. Only in the Chad, the power distribution, as we have already noted, is reversed, with the black African component of the population in the ascendancy. This contrasting power pattern contains the ingredients of possible Sudanese-Chadian difficulties. There have been intermittent incidents.[14] In the most recent ones, in mid-1965 and mid-1966, M. François Tombalbaye, President of the Chad, issued an "ultimatum" to the Sudanese Government concerning the presence of Chad political exiles in the Sudan. If the Sudan did not cease providing sanctuary to the "Islamic Republic of Chad in exile," Arabic emigrés disaffected from the Chad, then President Tombalbaye would not "return to the Sudan all black Sudanese and Christians who had sought refuge in Chad," as he did when General Abboud was in power.[15]

The Sudan's relations with Ethiopia have also been troubled by the Sudanese propensity since the 1964 *coup* to accord facilities to rebel forces. In this instance disaffected Eritreans incorporated into the Empire of Ethiopia found a sympathetic reception in the Sudan. Only after an arms shipment through the Sudan toward Eritrea got stuck in the pipeline in circumstances which suggested a threat to subvert the government of Sudan itself, and after the Ethiopian government made known its intentions to retaliate by granting sanctuary (with all the privileges that status now carries in most of Africa) to the Azania guerrilla forces, did relations between the two large neighbors improve. Previously relations were correct if not close. The Islamic Sudan had little in common with Coptic Christian Ethiopia.

A wholly different dimension is to be found in the relation of the Sudan to its powerful northern neighbor, the United Arab Republic. Although the relationship has improved in the last several years, the heritage of Egyptian intrusion in Sudanese affairs, including the still remembered and hated Arab slave trade in the Southern Sudan, throughout the Anglo-Egyptian condominium over the Sudan, and up to Sudanese independence in 1955, is still in evidence. The Sudanese have continued to experience Egyptian intrigue in the postindependence era with various Sudanese factions and political parties seeking Sudanese affiliation or association with Egypt. Various Egyptian territorial claims too, which have been settled or at least put temporarily in suspended animation, have been recent enough to still be a factor in Sudanese policy making.

On one important recent issue the Sudanese have ruffled Egyptian feelings; during the marathon Congo crisis, at various times, the Sudanese government first refused, then agreed, and once again refused the Egyptians transit rights for shipping arms and munitions into the northeastern part of the Congo (Kinshasa), to the rebel movements and bands operating throughout the area. On another recent issue the Sudanese government, at some cost to itself, pleased Egyptian sensibilities. The UAR broke relations with the Federal Republic of Germany, after a long period of deteriorating relations, early in 1965, on the specific issue of the establishment of diplomatic relations between West Germany and Israel. The Sudan, in a show of Arab solidarity, followed suit, and as a result, had to forego important amounts of economic and technical aid from West Germany, one of its principal sources of external assistance. Thus, the Sudanese government has maintained a somewhat ambivalent position *vis-à-vis* the United Arab Republic.

The impact of the Sudanese-Egyptian relationship on nation-building has been from time to time to divert attention, energy, and resources from the complicated and difficult internal situation. For example, the Egyptian meddling in the demoralizing interparty political strife contributed significantly to creating the conditions which led to the military *coup d'état* in 1958. The implications of the military regime for the Southern Sudanese and the country at large we have already discussed.

The rather aloof position adopted by the Sudan (except for a brief interval following the collapse of the Abboud government) from its near neighbors, primarily arising from its fear of external intrusion or support for the southern provinces, has acted to reinforce the divisive tensions in the country. The xenophobia has led to the ouster of all foreign Christian missionaries, and the almost total sealing-off of the Southern provinces to outside contacts. The self-imposed isolation, as in the case of Mali, has accentuated and interacted with the internal tensions. The short-lived tendency of the post-Abboud government to intrude in the internal affairs of her neighbors has led to a response in kind from the Congo, and to a lessening of the inhibitions of other neighboring states to providing sanctuary and arms to Sudanese rebel forces. The net result has been an intensification of the already intractable north-south problem. For the Southerners "the rebellion has become a way of life." For the

Northerners, it has become an "intractable" problem, "they will not concede the southern demand for federal status." [16]   The implications for successful nation-building are formidable.

THE CASE OF SENEGAMBIA

> By this settlement [with France drawing the Senegal-Gambia border] Great Britain was restricted to the areas over which it was exercising de facto influence and surrendered to the French a vaste hinterland extending on both sides of the river to the headwater of the Gambia, a hinterland to which we at one time had a better claim than the French and without which the Gambia . . . became a geographic and economic absurdity. The boundaries agreed upon with the French are frankly ridiculous; they take hold neither of the physical features nor of tribal divisions, and leave the Gambia a narrow enclave in French territory, some 200 miles in length.[17]

The double-pronged case of Senegal and Gambia illustrates still another aspect of Africa's nightmare geography, and the geopolitical problems for nation-building in yet another context.   Gambia is a tiny elongated English-speaking enclave or splinter of land lying on both sides of the mouth of the Gambia River, surrounded by the French-speaking Republic of Senegal, which is almost twenty times its size.   Gambia achieved internal self-government in 1963, and thereafter took rapid strides toward independence.   It was Gambia's actual accession to independence in February 1965 which thrust to the fore the question of the status of this small fragment of land, with only 300,000 people (compared to the three million in neighboring Senegal), and with hardly any known economic resources.

What is to become of this nonviable splinter of land?   Could a nation be built within its present geographical confines?   How much of an effort and how much of the world's resources should be devoted to develop a Gambian nation of 300,000, a population equal to that of a small American city, with all of the panoply of a sovereign state, including a vote in the United Nations?   Even its closest alphabetical neighbor in the United Nations, the small African state of Gabon, has a population estimated to be twice as large, and a rich resource base of okumé and other tropical hardwoods, oil, manganese, iron ore, etc.

Where is the point of diminishing returns?   Presumably there is some point in the crazy-quilt political geography of the African continent beyond which even the African thrust for independence would not venture in founding new states, and by doing so, require the building of new nations.   If such a point does in fact exist, however, it has yet to be revealed.   Quite the contrary.   Thus, with respect to the Gambia, in connection with British pressure on the colony to unite or federate with

Senegal, the African correspondent of *The Times* (of London) writing from Bathurst, the capital, chief city, principal port, and business center of the Gambia, a year before independence, reported that "opposition to any truly political association [with Senegal] or to any derogation from Gambia sovereignty is strong in Bathurst, a stronghold of the United Party (opposition)." [18]   And the Prime Minister, Sir Dauda Jawara, at the same time, a year before independence, spoke of Gambian "sovereignty": "We shall have to give up some of our sovereignty and the Senegalese will have to do the same. What we give up in local sovereignty, we share at a higher level." [19]   In the event, Gambia became independent on February 18, 1965, with no concession of and very few restraints on its sovereignty. It entered into limited agreements with Senegal for cooperation in defense and foreign affairs, and for joint development of the Gambia River Basin.

The Gambia River is the natural highway for the large hinterland lying in Gambia and Senegal, which has been severely restricted in its development and growth by the peculiar and artificial political geography of nineteenth-century colonialism. Nevertheless, the colonial legacy is real and significant. There is no stampede on either the Senegalese or Gambian side to federate and merge the two sovereign entities.

The scars of the abortive Federation of Mali are still visible, and the price Senegal has paid for the failure in political stability and economic loss still has some installments due, which continue to overhang the government's attempt to build in President Senghor's term "a fatherland" in an "Africa of the fatherland." Thus, it is with caution and studied care that Senegal has approached the possibility of another, and perhaps more logical, political merger with Gambia. Senegambia exists for the present as a political concept, and not as an aspiration or dream.

In addition to the political restraint being experienced by the Senegalese government, the marginal Senegalese ports of Ziguinchor and Kaolack are not overjoyed at the prospect of a program to develop their natural rival in the inherited postindependence context, Bathurst, the Gambian *sine qua non,* for any significant politicoeconomic association with Senegal. Thus, there is not only Gambia's shyness with respect to exposing its virgin sovereignty to Senegalese political embrace, there are also vested or vesting Senegalese economic interests which are fighting shy of the cost of any such embrace. The local ports are but a manifestation of these interests. Senegalese importers, exporters, processors, etc., locked into the French trading and monetary area are not exhilarated by the prospect of competition from the British trading and monetary area drifting in through the back door of the free port of Bathurst.

If both sides should overcome their initial shyness and reconcile their economic interests, the residue of nation-building problems for a Senegambia nationality would be formidable. There would be not only the Gambian "sovereignty" sentiment to accommodate, and the small but nonetheless in the given context important economic crosscurrents to consider, but also the curious cultural aftermath of colonialism to sort out. And the Senegambia case is a remarkably vivid example of this latter problem, which has one partial precedent, the Federal Republic of Cameroon, which combines the former French Cameroun and the former British Southern Cameroons. The report of the African correspondent of *The Times*, already alluded to, dramatizes the importance of the cultural issue in one long and suitably involved sentence:

> By all accounts the United Nations report [on the possibilities of Senegambia] accepts the fact that any close political association of the two neighbours is out of the question, at least for the time being, Gambia, a British colony, soaked in the British tradition, is fascinated by the wooing of Senegal, as French as Gambia is British; the flirtation will, however, go so far and no farther.[20]

Even more dramatically, the problems for nation-building posed by Senegambia are set out in the following excerpt from *New Africa:*

> What are the political implications of this geography? From a superficial glance at the map it may seem logical that in the long run Gambia should simply merge with Senegal. . . . [But] Gambia's three centuries of British rule cannot be wiped out in a single day. For many years the British have expounded with pride, the advantages, particularly in the field of justice, which have been derived from British rule. . . . To a passing visitor to Bathurst, one thing is certain, the difference in ways of thought and culture and in the very air itself between Gambia and Senegal is astonishing. The short motor journey from Kaolack—with its atmosphere of a small French town—across a barely noticeable frontier and finally over the river to Bathurst is like transference from one world to another.[21]

Even the partial precedent (for merging an English and a French African area) of the Federal Republic of Cameroon can be distinguished from the Senegambia case in one important respect. There is no throwback, no known historical past in which Senegambia existed as a unit,[22] with the emotional and evocative connotations now being found so useful in some quarters of Africa in nation-building. There is no dim but obviously glorious past which can be invoked as a goal to recapture, as a birthright, the enjoyment of which was interrupted by the colonialist, and now ripe for restoration, or as a colonialist act of "balkanization" which must be politically corrected as part of the emergence of the African personality. Ancient or medieval African kingdoms or empires are much preferred for this role of historical imperative—Ghana, Mali, Songhai, Bakongo, and Zimbabwe, but even former earlier colonial enterprises find some favor for this purpose. Thus, the reconstitution of the pre-World War I German colony of Kamerun has in the 1960 African independence era exercised a certain attraction and has been one of the factors in the founding of the Federal Republic of Cameroon, and in the Republic's irredentist claim on neighboring Nigeria with respect to the former British Northern Cameroons which voted in a 1960 UN plebescite for integration into Nigeria in preference to federation with Cameroun.[23]

How the European cultural legacy, and the lesser linguistic aspect of it, will affect the nation-building task is too early to say. It is not too early, however, on the basis of the evidence already in hand on the stresses and strains in the relations between English and French-speaking African countries, to hypothesize that the cultural factor will indeed play a major role and will add still one more difficult dimension to the already formidable nation-building task. Thus, associated with the geopolitical factor of size, shape, and locus—all present in Senegambia—is the cultural overlay, not only of African societies, but also of the European colonial penetration. This latter point was not developed in our consideration of the cases of Mali and the Sudan, although present in varying degrees in both cases, because in the instant case of Senegambia the clash of divergent European cultural heritages stands out so much more vividly. In Mali there have been differing impacts of the same European culture on different population groups—the nomadic Arabs and the settled black agriculturalists—in different geographic areas; in the Sudan, the situation has been much the same, complicated to a degree by the overlapping role of Egypt in the same area. In Senegambia, however, the distinctive and separate French and British impacts emerge more sharply and the possible confrontation in a single political union emphasizes the quality and extent of the problem of integrating into a cohesive unit culturally and linguistically diverse population groups, particularly where the population relationship is as disproportionate as in the Senegambia case.

OTHER CASES

The three principal cases of the geopolitical factor in nation-building, discussed in this chapter along with the incidental and comparative allusion to other relevant situations, have been drawn from French, British, and mixed French-British contexts. They have been drawn from Western and Eastern Africa; they have been drawn to emphasize external and internal aspects of geopolitical factors and their interaction with nation-building; they have been drawn to take account of varying situations with respect to size, shape and location; and they also relate to what has gone before in Chapters 1 and 2, and supply a natural bridge to what is to follow in subsequent chapters, where the geopolitical factor will be present but not the center of the discussion, as for example, in the discussion of the Congo (Kinshasa) in connection with its nation-building prospects. A discussion of the Congo in this chapter would, of course, be apposite and illuminating, but would also lead to a certain duplication of material as the same range of material will necessarily be considered in connection with other points in subsequent chapters. Hence, the sprawling and huge geographic configuration of the former Belgian Congo in the heartland of Africa has been reserved for later consideration. The same can be said of Nigeria [24] and a number of other African states.

THE GEOPOLITICAL FACTOR, REGIONALISM AND PAN-AFRICANISM

Having considered the impact of geography in its broadest sense, including not only the physical aspects but also the cultural, political, and economic aspects inevitably interrelated with size, shape, and location of individual states (chosen for their broader implications), it seems appropriate to conclude the discussion of the geopolitical factor in African nation-building with a brief consideration of the aggregative implications of the problems analyzed and points considered.

The foreign affairs commentator on the editorial page of the *New York Times,* in an article concluding a series on Africa, offers the judgment that the geographically vast area of Africa is also an area of vast political, economic, and ethnic contradictions:

> Africans like to think theirs is a single vast continent but, if geographically true, it is politically, historically, ethnically and economically absurd. One has only to come to this Arab-Berber region [Morocco] from the steaming Indian Ocean and the high plateau of the Eastern Rift to see the contradictions.[25]

Mr. Sulzberger's view of Africa as a mass of contradictions is both revealing and suggestive. In the past, whenever a communist theorist ran into an inexplicable aspect, factor, or practice in capitalist society, particularly a favorable one, such as improved living standards for workers, he found refuge in the catechism *cum* explanation, "a contradiction of capitalism." [26] So too, viewing African diversity in political, historical, and economic conditions as contradictions is a refuge and not an explanation. African conditions are consistent with African geography. The consistency, in fact the causality involved between geography and conditions, is clearly to be seen in East Africa. In the words of a recent study:

If the high land in East Africa had not been quite so high, the modern history of the region would have been very different. . . . The settler problem, for many years diagnosed as the native problem, had its origin in geography.[27]

The same sort of link might be made, in fact has been by African nationalists, in West Africa between the mosquito-infested swamps and the absence of European settlers, in Central Africa between the impenetrable rain forests and their lack of European population, on the one hand, and the mineral-wealthy highlands of Zambia and Katanga with their European populations, on the other, etc.

Thus, the sum of the varied geopolitical situations of the many individual African countries means that taken as a whole the African continent is bound to have a wide range of development and nation-building patterns emerge. This multiplicity of patterns will, in fact already does, have implications for regional development in Africa—in both its political and economic manifestations.

Disputes can be used as an occasion for solving inter-state geopolitical problems by finding solutions in economic and political associations, unions, and federations, which could be designed to accommodate, rectify, alleviate, or balance the geopolitical endowment of nature and the associated legacy of colonialism. For example, the stillborn *Declaration of Federation of the Governments of East Africa*, issued on June 5, 1963, by the heads of government of Tanganyika, Uganda, and Kenya, takes account of this point and concludes: "We believe, in fact, that some of these territorial problems can be solved in the context of such an East African Federation." [28] Disputes can also act to reinforce the geopolitical problems and render them even more intractable and more difficult of solution. So far, unfortunately, the weight of experience has been of the latter type. And in the few instances where political associations or federations have been tried in Africa the net result has been to add to the growing stock of disputes, rather than the resolution of problems. For example,

The psychological shock of the Federation's [Federation of Mali] brutal end resulted not only in a complete severance of all links between Senegal and the Soudan, but in Soudan's estrangement from France; more important for Soudan's subsequent development it spurred the country's leaders to back their defiant and lonely declaration of independence with radical measures designed to prove that, though poorly endowed, Mali could "go it alone." [29]

It is necessary to recall our earlier discussion and emphasize that this result was in large part due to the lack of complementarity of the partners in the proposed unions, among which geopolitical considerations loomed large, but consistent with the related historical, political, ethnic, and economic disparities. It could hardly be otherwise.

Thus, the aggregative implications for nation-building in new African regional geographical configurations extending beyond the inherited boundaries of the new states at the time of independence are but a logical extension of those already identified and considered by us with respect to the individual African states. This then leads to a brief word on nation-building on the largest scale yet conceived of, for the entire African continent. In light of the discussion in this chapter, Dr. Nkrumah's vision of a continental union inhabited by one nation ruled over by one continental-wide government, already discarded by the Addis Ababa and subsequent African summit conference as impracticable, appears not only remote as a goal for African "nationalism" but unwise for any forseeable time period from the point of view of the prospects for successful nation-building and the obstacles interposed thereto by geopolitical considerations.

No matter how many word games are played by Dr. Nkrumah and others of his Pan-African school, the "colonialist devised" barrier of the Sahara does not become transmuted into a "nationalist" bridge as an automatic consequence of accession to independence of territories on both sides of the Sahara and the dispatching of colonialists from the scene. As we have seen in the discussion of Mali, even within the one country the Sahara interposes a formidable obstacle to welding together a nation. As a zone between two and among many states it would seem to be even more of an obstacle to achieving unity and successful "nation-building."

Thus, geography as tempered and shaped by the colonial heritage of the new states provides the physical frame of reference within which nation-building is to proceed in Africa. It sets the limits within which political and economic structures and systems are to be constructed and developed. As we shall see in succeeding chapters, time and again the discussion will highlight basic geopolitical considerations and the limits they place on nation-building. Clearly a resolution of geopolitical problems—particularly the aggregative one involved in regionalism and Pan-Africanism—is an indispensable precondition for successful nation-building. In Chapter 2 it was suggested that at least the aggregative geographic problem raised by the Nkrumahist Pan-African School has been laid to rest, and by and large the inherited colonial boundaries will provide the physical context for nation-building for each independent state. Even regional boundaries, as suggested in Chapter 2, are likely to be the exception over the middle-range future as the locus for African nation-building. What remains then, are the geopolitical considerations, dealt with in this chapter, of size, shape and situs. They constitute a basic factor in African nation-building.

CHAPTER 4

PROBLEM OF STATE STRUCTURE: THE ROLE
OF THE UNITARY ONE-PARTY STATE

Africa is beginning to pay dearly for the insolvency of its institutions. . . . We have said and have repeated without wearying that regimes in which the law is identified with the will of the rulers, and with them alone, only recourse to coups d'état and conspiracies is possible.

BÉCHIR BEN YAMED, *Directeur Général*, Jeune
Afrique *(Tunis), 1964*

By far the largest number of African states belong to the category of unitary one-party state structures. The handful of modernizing oligarchies and multiparty states (unitary and federal) can be treated individually as case studies, as we do in subsequent chapters. In this chapter we are concerned with the structure of unitary one-party states, the centralization of power in such states, and the problems and risks implicit for nation-building in such centralized state structures. For analytical purposes we deal separately in subsequent chapters with the political systems which operate the state structures, although in practice the two—structures and systems—are inevitably closely interwoven. Thus, unavoidably, there will be some overlap with some subsidiary attention to political systems in this chapter.

There is much in the colonial legacy, in the doctrines of the multiplicity of versions of African socialism, and in the realities of present-day Africa which explain or at any rate shed some light on the near universal tendency toward highly-centralized unitary one-party states. Our purpose here, however, is not to study this trend,[1] but rather, as we have already said, to examine its implications for nation-building directly, and also indirectly with respect to its impact on economic development. Thus, we shall confine ourselves in this chapter to an analysis of the key doctrines and practices associated with unitary one-party state structures that are relevant to nation-building.

THE RATIONALE FOR THE UNITARY ONE-PARTY STATE

The central doctrine in the rationale offered for the unitary one-party state structure is that in the given circumstances of Africa it is the most efficacious and practical structure for nation-building and economic development. As Professor Emerson has put it in his monograph on one-party systems:

> The issues involved are relatively simple and straightforward. The single-party system . . . has evident virtues where the people are sharply divided among themselves and unity is the first requisite, where a new political, social, and economic society must be brought into being, and where the hardships and disciplines of development must take priority over private preferences.[2]

On the theory that the convert or aspirant is more ardent than the long-time practitioner, and therefore more revealing, we have chosen to consider a state structure in transition from a multi-party structure to a one-party one. We also believe that the transitional case to which we shall have reference will be most revealing of the implications of various types of state structures for nation-building, because the change is being sought within a federal system, which by definition is likely to be the most decentralized type of state structure. We turn then to the words and actions of an aspiring practitioner of one-party government, who would not only transform a multiparty structure in his own country into a one-party structure, but would do so in a federal system. If he was to succeed, and he seems well along the road to achieving a one-party structure, it would be the first one in a federal context in Africa. What seems more likely in the opinion of the author is that if he does succeed in building a one-party state structure, the federal system will disappear from the scene and reappear as a centralized unitary one, for the decentralization implicit in federalism should prove incompatible with and inevitably yield to the centralization implicit in a one-party structure. President Ahmadou Ahidjo of the Federal Republic of Cameroon gave his views on one-party structures in an interview with a correspondent for the liberal African weekly *Jeune Afrique:*

> For me, the one-party structure is the only way to escape this demagogy ["appeals to tribal, ethnic and religious differences in politics"], the only means to forge national unity, and we are in this domain often misunderstood even by our friends of *Jeune Afrique.* . . .
>
> Our principal objective remains the same, to create with the other parties, notably the friendly F.N.D.P. [the Kameroun National Democratic Party], but also with parties in opposition, a grand unified party

(*un grand parti unifié*), and, why not, even a grand one-party structure (*un grand parti unique*).[3]

Interestingly enough, particularly with respect to the implications for nation-building and development, in the same interview in April 1964 President Ahidjo declared in connection with the country's then pending national elections:

> The position we have taken leaves the door open to the opposition. . . . We would have been able as in other African countries [with one-party structures] to adopt the principle of the one list. We have not done it. The opposition has the possibility of presenting lists separately from the Union Camerounaise [the ruling party]. . . . I do not know if the opposition will present lists. In any case, it has the possibility to do so.[4]

Although in theory the door was left open to the opposition, in practice it was scarcely left ajar. Not too many risks were run with respect to the outcome of the election, and thereafter with respect to the creation of a one-party state structure. The popular will was to be guided along proper lines. The large size of the handful of election *circonscriptions* (districts) into which the country was divided combined with the requirement that each party wishing to contest any seat had to file a complete list of candidates for *all* of the seats to be elected in the *circonscriptions* worked a tremendous hardship on opposition parties with scattered strength in various localities. Although they might have been able to obtain a majority in smaller and more manageable areas for individual candidates, they found it extremely difficult, in fact impossible, to achieve a majority for a list of candidates in the larger areas in which their favorably disposed localities or enclaves had been lodged. These Cameroonian electoral tactics are an interesting, if somewhat special, application of the gerrymandering principle which has been such a familiar feature of the United States election landscape (until the recent decisions of the Supreme Court requiring redistricting).

In addition, lest the best laid plans of mice and men go awry, the government of President Ahidjo took the added precaution of continuing the imprisonment during the election period, *inter alia*, of leaders of two of the principal opposition parties, M. Charles Okala of the Socialist Party and M. André M'bida of the Christian Democratic Party. Finally, there was the ruling party's control of the government machinery, which the *Union Camerounaise* made clear, it was only too ready to use, if, as, and when it might have seemed necessary to insure that things did not get out of hand—that the opposition did not become too effective or successful.

The outcome was an overwhelming victory for the government party.

A one-party structure has been evolving, and *pari passu,* political and economic power has been increasingly centered in Yaoundé, the federal capital.

The Cameroonian experience—words and actions—put in a nutshell what reams of political polemics and innumerable political manoeuvres have proclaimed in one African state after another. The one-party state is required to build national unity, and conversely, national unity is needed to sustain the one-party state. "Both the drive to enforce state unity and the efforts of ruling groups to maintain their dominance contribute to the establishment of one-party states so commonly found in independent African-controlled countries." [5] The first half of the thesis remains to be tested, and is being tested in many parts of Africa, and is our concern in this book. The second half, sadly, has been all too much in evidence and frequently, in practice, seems to have obscured or supplanted the first half. Too often the objective of seeking to forge national unity in the new states has been lost sight of. Too often maintaining the single party in a one-party structure in power has been confused with nation-building.

There is not a one-party state on the continent in which the single party has not used its monopoly of public power to crush actual or potential opposition in the name of unity, which has become synonymous for this purpose with whatever the will or leadership of the controlling party dictates. In fact, the concept of unity in practice throughout the length and breadth of the continent has for the one-party states come to mean uniformity. The late Prime Minister Alhaji Sir Abubakar Tafawa Balewa of the Federal Republic of Nigeria took account of this sleight of hand—the crucial transition from unity to uniformity—when he made the distinction between "unity in diversity" and unity *cum* uniformity in the nation-wide broadcast reporting to the Nigerian people on the Addis Ababa Summit Conference of May 1963, which we quoted in Chapter 2. He said in likening internal Nigerian nation-building to achieving African unity:

> Just as we in Nigeria have been laying down one stone after another in the process of nation-building, thus ensuring that a solid foundation is laid; just as we are determined to preserve our unity in diversity; so the Addis Abada Conference concentrated in those fields where the links between our states can be reinforced and strengthened and where new links can be forged while recognizing the fact that *unity should not be tantamount to uniformity.*[6]

The African predilection for the one-party state structures [7] has found a warm reception in many quarters outside Africa. A striking example of a Western apologia for not only the unitary one-party state structure but also for the authoritarian political system which it seems inevitably to imply (which we consider in Chapter 7) is to be found in the report of an address of a former Deputy Governor of Tanganyika and leading British expert on Commonwealth constitutional issues, Sir John Fletcher-Cooke, to the combined Royal African and Royal Commonwealth Societies in London early in 1964. The applicable paragraphs in the report of Sir John's address follow:

> The party system was not suitable at present. The Western-style legislatures had been retained, unmeaningful trappings and all, for a façade of respectability, but decisions were made within the party machine, which accorded with the concept of the old village council and embraced every political and social activity—farming, youth groups, women's clubs, which could be called real democracy.
> Thus, Julius Nyerere had been able to resign because he knew that the legislature could be controlled by any Prime Minister; he had to control the people.[8]

Stated more directly and more naively by a European writer on African affairs, Erskine B. Childers:

> [The Afro-Asian] country needs stable, uncorrupt government to carry out basic reforms—like land distribution—and development projects. A mild dictatorship has much to its credit if the alternative is partisan manoeuvre, graft, and tension.[9]

A mild dictatorship is like conventional warfare; both are painful and both inevitably "escalate." Mindful of this, the communist bloc countries have also welcomed the one-party trend in Africa. What better preparation for a communist political takeover than an indigenous African one-party structure to pave the way by eliminating all opposition to central authority. All that remains is to capture control of the one-party machinery through externally-supported "progressive elements" in the party. Although not successful as yet, the communist takeover gambit was much in evidence in Algeria and Ghana before the respective *coups* in these two one-party countries, and has been much in evidence in the radical nationalist one-party states of Guinea and Congo (Brazzaville) in their respective internal party manoeuvres. We shall return to the vulnerability of African one-party state structures to communist *coups*.

THE UNITARY ONE-PARTY STATE: VULNERABILITY TO MILITARY COUPS

What does the record to date suggest with respect to the role of centralized unitary one-party state structures in nation-building and economic development?

At the outset, account must be taken of the fact that centralized unitary one-party state structures are so constructed that they are peculiarly vulnerable to military *coups d'état,* no matter how small the military forces in being may be. The two hundred-man Togolese army, which seized power in January 1963, has amply demonstrated this point. Subsequent *coups* in Congo (Brazzaville), Dahomey, Algeria, Upper Volta, the Central African Republic, and Ghana,* and abortive coups in Gabon and Tanganyika (now Tanzania), *inter alia,* have illustrated the vulnerability of unitary one-party states to military *coups,* irrespective of the size of the military and irrespective of the alleged "solidarity," "unity," "mass-mobilized" support of the one-party regime. It may be objected that at the time the coups were perpetrated or undertaken several of these countries were not "pure" one-party states but merely *de facto* or aspiring one-party states. There can be no question, however, about their being centralized or unitary. And for the most part they were one-party states as a matter of law or practice. Certainly this was so of Congo (Brazzaville) at the time of the inconclusive second *coup* in July 1966 and of Dahomey at the time of its second and third *coups* in 1965, if not literally so for both states at the time of their initial *coups.* It was also true of Algeria, Upper Volta, the Central African Republic, Ghana, and Gabon,† and more or less so, of Tanganyika.

It may be argued, however, that it was the absence of total or full one-party state structure in several cases that led to or prepared the ground for these military uprisings, and not, as we suggest, the presence of the one-party structure *per se,* which set the stage for the *coups.* The author does not find this argument persuasive for in all but a handful of one-party states, pure or impure, perfect or imperfect, within or without the sole or dominant party, there are opposition forces, above-ground or underground, before or after the fact, to link up with disaffected, frustrated, or subverted military. For example, the abortive *coup* in Tunisia, a "pure" one-party state, late in 1962, involved both the military and civilians.

And almost as if to prove the point, in June 1965, the *coup d'état* in Algeria, one of the purest of the pure centralized unitary one-party states,

---

* The author certainly would have added Sierra Leone and Mali to this list: Sierra Leone with two army-led *coups,* March 21, 1967, and April 18, 1968; Mali with one coup (so far) led by junior army officers who deposed President Modibo Keita on November 19, 1968, because of his continued promulgation of socialist economic values and his efforts to strengthen the people's militia—a standing threat to the army. J.H.M.

† Vice-President Albert Bongo of Gabon became President upon the death of Léon M'ba in November 1967. (M'ba's government had been saved from an attempted military *coup* in 1964 by the intervention of French troops.) Bongo dissolved the powerful Gabonese Democratic bloc and declared Gabon a one-party state in March 1968. J.H.M.

no matter what its ultimate fate may be, has been the most thorough-going *coup* to date in Africa (with the possible exception of the Ghanaian *coup* of 1966, discussed subsequently).   In one swift thrust the military under Colonel Boumedienne, Chief of Staff, Minister of Defense and Vice-President, arrested President Ahmed Ben Bella and a handful of his closest personal associates in the National Liberation Front (FLN after its French name), the single party, and so "made a revolution."   Only token resistance was offered by an apathetic population.   The political opposition, which had opposed the Ben Bella "personality cult," the trade unions which had been coerced or bribed into the FLN, the professional societies which had been severely circumscribed, the independent entre-preneurs and their interest groups which had been purged or rendered powerless by state regulation or nationalization, etc.—were all too dis-organized or disinterested to offer even token opposition, or were pre-pared to come to terms with the military authorities.   By capturing con-trol of the leadership of the party *cum* state apparatus the military made its revolution.   The lack of national cohesion—notwithstanding the façade erected by the FLN—was clearly demonstrated by the ease of the military takeover and the lack of resistance from the "mass mobilized" society.   Even with the seven years of "blood, sweat and tears" of the Algerian "war of liberation" against France behind the FLN, and the towering personality of a charismatic leader, there was not enough cohesion to achieve a minimum national unity to preclude a *coup*, or if undertaken, to frustrate it.   The future pattern in Algeria seems clear.   The only route to power is extraconstitutional, by *coup*.   In such circumstances, the possibility of widespread public participation and blending to pro-duce a national consciousness and identity seems remote.   And without these, serious nation-building is not possible.

In a sense then, the purer the structure and the more apparently free of formal overt opposition a country, the greater the danger of successful *coups*.   In underdeveloped countries generally, and in authoritarian ones particularly, there are few if any organized bodies to act as countervailing forces to the one-party, which would make the prospects for successful *coups* uncertain and even precarious.   All independent interest groups and sources of power or opinion—trade unions, youth movements, women's clubs, association of traders, chambers of commerce, farmers' alliances, cooperatives, the press, and even religious institutions—which might offer opposition to an attempted *coup*, have already been neutral-ized or sterilized in the one-party states as part and parcel of the creation of the centralized unitary one-party structure.   Thus, the plotters run only one limited risk, the immediate success of the *coup*.   Once accom-plished, all should be serene.   In other societies with different structures *coups* are still possible as evidenced by the January 1966 *coup* in multiparty Nigeria, but their success in achieving and chances of consolidating and holding on to power are far less certain, and this lack of certainty, if nothing else, is likely to have a psychologically inhibiting and deterrent affect.

There are also serious risks of discovery, of leaks, of exposure before a *coup* can be launched in societies with opposing and competing interest groups. In the centralized one-party situation the only real risk of discovery comes from the one vested interest, the one-party incumbents and adherents, who control the structure. And in situations in which the technical capacity for operating a tight, centralized one-party structure is necessarily limited, so too is the capacity to operate its seemingly inevitable and indispensable concomitant, an authoritarian political system, with which to maintain it in power and to sound early warning alarms of conspiracies to overthrow the structure. The very same factors which together add up to underdevelopment, *i.e.*, the lack of national cohesion, of national institutions, particularly an integrated public administration, of national transportation and communication grids, of a market economy, and of all of the infrastructure and superstructure implied and taken for granted in the concept of the nation-state in the twentieth century, limit the capacity of the new African states to operate centralized unitary one-party structures and attendant authoritarian (to say nothing of totalitarian) political systems effectively. "In any case, the African states are far from developed enough, either economically or in the organization of public force, to permit totalitarian rule. The most that can be imposed is authoritarianism." [10] Thus, most abortive *coups* in Africa have failed because of faulty planning or execution by the plotters, and not because of the capability or alertness of the one-party government apparatus, or because the latter was able to obtain external assistance to put down *coups* and uprisings before they consolidated their position, for example, in the abortive uprisings of the military in Tanganyika, Kenya, and Uganda, and the counter-*coup* in Gabon.

THE UNITARY ONE-PARTY STATE: VULNERABILITY TO COMMUNIST COUPS

And what we have said about vulnerability of one-party structures to military *coups* applies, of course, to other types of *coups*, such as "palace revolutions" within the one party and "popular-front" revolutions. "Bourgeois-nationalists" in communist doctrine, when they are supported in their control of one-party structures or as "national liberation" movements to gain such control, are intended to perform the very important function of crushing opposition and, of even greater importance, suppressing all independent well-springs of power, influence, or opinion in a country. This not only paves the way, it plants the seeds of destruction, according to communist doctrine, of the "bourgeois-nationalist liberators" themselves at the hands of the "people's liberators," the communists or communist-manipulated intelligentsia, or proletariat, or peasants, whatever the case may be. This was the unfolding pattern in Zanzibar before President Nyerere's initiative in founding, in conjunction with President Abeid Karume of Zanzibar, the United Republic of Tanzania in April 1964. First there was a "popular front uprising" with an improvised "army"; then there was the beginning of the takeover process by a "palace revolution" within the one party. It may still become the pattern in Zanzibar, dependent on the far from certain fate of the new United Republic. It may also prove to be the pattern that has been unfolding in Congo (Brazzaville), where both the military and the civilian government supported by it, having come to power by a "popular front"-military *coup* and having taken a tactical turn to the left as a ploy for unifying public opinion behind the new government, may find the ongoing pressure too strong to reverse gears and the road too narrow to make a U turn.[11]

President Alphonse Massemba-Débat inherited a *de facto* one-party state structure, which he has been at pains, with military support, to transform into a tighter *de jure* one-party affair. It is not yet clear whether the trade union movement—one of the principal protagonists in the rebellion which brought Massemba-Débat to power—will stand outside and retain its independence, or allow itself to be neutralized by incorporation into the one-party structure. For the present it is the only countervailing force still in being to the military-supported unitary one-party state structure. In an interesting switch, the authors of a recently published study of the 1961 Sekondi-Takoradi general strike in Ghana seem to bemoan the fact that independent trade unions can serve as a countervailing force when they conclude that "the CPP government [Ghana's one-party government] was taking no chances at Sekondi-Tokaradi [in crushing the strike] and the subsequent events in Dahomey and the Congo (Brazzaville) confirmed them in their belief that the action was justified." [12] Obviously the theretofore independent trade unions in Ghana were an obstacle to the creation of a one-party state. The Convention People's Party hardly needed the example of subsequent *coups* elsewhere to convince them of this fact. If the author's conclusion has any meaning, it is to suggest that a stitch in time will save nine for the one-party state practitioners.

If the history of independence movements in other African states is taken as a guide, however, the Ghanaian example has been taken to heart and the chances of the trade unions remaining free of state control are quite marginal. Tanganyika (now Tanzania), which has been held out by many of the Western exponents of one-party structures for Africa as the case *par excellence* of such a structure with moderation, respect for democratic rights, functioning of democratic centralism, mass support of the dominant party, etc., has since achieving national independence transformed a dominant one-party structure into an exclusive legal one-party structure, enacted a Preventive Detention Act, adopted press censorship, and destroyed the independent trade union movement by adopting legislation similar to that of Ghana for controlling its trade unions. The explanations offered are that President Nyerere has acted consistently with his attachment to moderation and democratic concepts in that his actions were necessary to achieve unity and development in his impoverished country, or were necessary to forestall an even more undemocratic and more radical nationalist movement in Tanganyika, spearheaded by the trade unions. Irrespective of motive, there can be little question that the Tanganyika African National Union, the single party, has destroyed all other organized groups and in doing so laid the way for a *coup*—be it military, "a palace revolution," a "popular-front" uprising, or some combination of these. More often than not African *coups* have been an admixture, although analytically we have separated them into categories for ease in examining the principal elements and likely sources of political take-over bids in Africa.

THE UNITARY ONE-PARTY STATE AND NATION-BUILDING

The type of *coup* aside, the recurrent, almost monotonous, reports of abortive *coups* and plots against the government and the former President of Ghana, the government and President of Guinea, and the government and President of the Ivory Coast, all pure one-party states, and intermittently throughout almost all of French-speaking Africa and beyond, illustrate not only the vulnerability of such centralized systems, but the attractiveness and perhaps even more, the inevitability of such repeated attempts in the absence of any legitimate constitutional channel for inducing peaceful change. It also reveals, more pointedly for our purposes, the limited possibility of imposing unity, or inducing it by limiting participation, or where participation is permitted, by manipulating it. "Mass mobilization" or "social mobilization," two of the favorite phrases in the lexicon of the one-party state adherents, has not only proved difficult, it has yet to prove effective in welding together diverse populations or in providing the motivation for economic growth. Perhaps in time this will change, and greater and more tangible results will become apparent. There is, however, little in the structural situation, given the severe limitations in technical capacity already alluded to, which encourages optimism on this score. In fact, at one juncture, in 1965, Guinea, the original "mass mobilizing" society in Africa south of the Sahara, attempted to convert from a "mass party" to an "élite party" because after seven to ten years the threadbare quality of the "mass mobilization" had become evident and apparently an obstacle to development. However, there was neither the technical capacity to convert or to revivify the "mass-party," which remains about where it was at the outset of the effort to change it. The overthrow of Dr. Nkrumah and the CPP regime in Ghana in one swift thrust revealed the fragile façade of unity and cohesion Dr. Nkrumah was said to have achieved in Ghana. On the one hand, the coercion, corruption, and contempt for human rights of the overthrown regime were exposed by a series of investigating commissions; on the other, the rejection of Nkrumahism, Pan-Africanism, radical nationalism, etc.—all the concepts around which the new unity of Ghana was said to have been built—revealed an ordinary African society with many tribal divisions as much in need of national integration as most comparable small African states. With the sound and fury removed, the problem remains of integrating the coast peoples and the "backward" northern peoples, the urban and rural peoples, the Ashanti cocoa growers and all the other country's tribes. The façade removed, the basic task can be confronted. The "mass-mobilizing" CPP apparently had a narrow base of power, limited popular participation, and high manipulation and coercion level.

In addition, the diversion of energy in national crises and the dissipation of scarce economic resources in programs or undertakings designed to consolidate the hold of the one party on the centralized one-party state structure—prestige projects, patronage for the party faithful, military build-ups, propaganda campaigns against the opposition, the suspected opposition, and the "foreign devils," and from time to time, such dangerous and unpredictable foreign adventures, as the "pocket war" between Tunisia and France over the French naval base in Bizerte—combine to accentuate the implicit structural limitations on centralized one-party states achieving the goals of national unity and growth in the difficult geopolitical circumstances of so many African countries. The energy and resources that might have been allocated and utilized for economic growth as a goal and as a means for pulling more and more people into the market economy where the reward is for performance and not a matter of status—traditional, tribal, regional or religious—and is instead used for buttressing the hold of the one-party in power on the one-party structures, must be recorded at least as another question mark with respect to the capacity of one-party structures to build integrated nation-states.

We do not mean to imply that other state structures obviate the misallocations of human energy and economic resources, but merely to emphasize the ease with which one-party structures may fall into this practice in the absence of any checks or fear of opposition criticism, and in fact, in Africa, seem almost universally to have done so. Black Star Square in Accra, intended as a monument to Ghanaian independence, is also one of the most brilliant monuments to this spendthrift practice in one-party states. The practice brought Ghana to the brink of bankruptcy by mid-July 1965, and apparently to a popularly-accepted *coup d'état* in early 1966. The only apparent antidote in a one-party state structure for this ailment is, as always, a *coup* (and recrimination about waste and corruption and nonproductive monument building played a part in the *coups* in Congo-Brazzaville, Dahomey, Algeria and Ghana), or "autocriticism" of the type practiced in Guinea and Mali.

In Dahomey the presidential palace President Hubert Maga built for himself at a reputed cost of three million dollars is referred to as "Maga's tomb," and is recognized as the catalyst that set off the *coup* which ousted Maga from power. A French diplomat was quoted in an article headed, "Empty Palace Symbolizes the Revolt in Dahomey:" "Corruption, low wages and high prices provoked discontent against the President. But it was the palace which brought him down." And in the words of a trade unionist reported in the same newspaper dispatch from Porto-Novo, Dahomey: "Any politician who moved in to 'Maga's palace' would commit political suicide." [13]   In Congo (Brazzaville) the luxury hotel which Abbé Youlou, the deposed President, was building for his own account, reportedly with public funds, has been expropriated, and is pointed out to visitors in Brazzaville, much as "Maga's palace" in Dahomey is, as the symbol of the national rebellion.

In countries of the Guinea (and before the military takeover, Algeria and Ghana) school, public denunciation of suitable individuals usually heralds some startling revelation of dissipation, one way or another, of public funds. These "suitable individuals" are, in reality, mere scapegoats. For, whether implicated or not in the waste or corruption, they have been allowed to remain in office by the one-party structure and its inevitable state police—taut and silent partners—as long as their purposes are served. All of which may for the moment satisfy a short-term emotional need, but which over the long run merely adds one more divisive or disruptive factor to the already formidable reservoir the nation-builders and economic developers must cope with. For how many are persuaded that "X" or "Y" who was ousted was any more corrupt or wasteful or careless of the public purse than many who remain behind in power or succeed to power? If not persuaded, then their lurking suspicion, always just below the surface of tribal, regional, or some other type of discrimination emerges. It is understandable why so many of the cotribalists of the emigré, K. A. Gbedemah, former Ghanaian Finance Minister forced out of office by the Nkrumah regime, suspected that he had to flee because he was a member of the Ewe tribe. Although Gbedemah had been charged with corruption and plotting against the government, his affiliation with the tribe straddling the Ghanaian-Congolese border that had been in the midst of continuing recrimination between Ghana and Togo, led many to believe that the allegation of corruption and conspiracy were mere fabrications. In his testimony before an investigating commission following the overthrow of Dr. Nkrumah, Gbedemah did nothing to disabuse his partisans of any such belief.

In short, the one-party state structure with its centralization of functions and powers, almost instinctively reacts against any derogation of either, and opposition and proposals for change, no matter how well founded, are almost automatically viewed as attempts at derogation. It is therefore extremely difficult for one-party structures to bear criticism, let alone be responsive to it. The understandable reaction of many individuals over time has been to develop a skepticism about government pronouncements about the national interest and a suspicion about government intentions and objectives with respect to such programs as *investissement humain* and forced savings for development. A psychological state of mind that questions government motives hardly seems to be one which is going to be receptive to exhortation, persuasion, or even inducement to make sacrifices for unity and growth. If this be so, then the outlook for centralized unitary one-party state structures to build nation-states and flourishing economies to facilitate and sustain the achievement of national cohesion is anything but promising. Even Tunisia, which has one of the best organized one-party state structures in Africa, and practices a "pragmatic and humane" brand of African socialism—"destourian socialism" or "Bourguibism"—has had difficulty on just this score of mobilizing support for the party. In a well-informed article on "Destourian Socialism in Tunisia" the author concludes:

> The undercurrent of discontent at the time of the Bizerte crisis in 1961 showed then how the party had become stifling in its organization and how insensitive it was to the mood at least of the younger generation. But since that time there has been a reorganization with committees of coordination interposed between local cells and the central party organs. The result has been a much easier two-way flow of ideas between the top and the grass roots, which is essential if a one-party state is to function without the danger of explosive pressures building up.[14]

It is just this "two-way flow," especially the upward flow, that seems so difficult of achievement. Few states have been able to keep these channels unclogged and the traffic upward moving at a fast enough pace to forestall the "explosive pressures" building up, which have been detonating in *coup* after *coup* all over Africa. And it is worth remembering that after the reform in *Néo-Destour's* party structure outlined above, the abortive military—civilian *coup* of late 1962 took place. Thus, the outlook is cloudy, and even Tunisia may have far from clear sailing for its one-party state structure in nation-building and economic development. And if Tunisia has difficulties then the prospects for the remaining one-party structures building national cohesion and modern economies seem even less certain and less promising.

The limitations on one-party state structures in Africa have been summed up by M. Béchir Ben Yamed, Directeur Général of *Jeune Afrique*, in an article which concluded a major series on the strengths and weaknesses of the one-party structure in nation-building and economic development in Africa. His conclusions cogently sum up and round out the points already made in this chapter. In the author's words:

> The one party once installed is the last to perceive the necessity for its disappearance or its evolution. It is practically incapable of democratizing itself or of democratizing the country. Habituated to silencing the opposition, persuaded that it is the general interest, it does not understand the necessity of concessions and fears to give an inch.
>
> In these conditions, what was the motor becomes the brake. The state hardly created, becomes corrupt. Traditions which hardly have been given birth to, rot. The confidence among fellow freedom-fighters disappears. . . . The one party, the leading incarnation of the state and the nation, appears then, for the underdeveloped countries achieving independence, as a kind of historical necessity; animated by men coming from the people and the struggle, the party can, when it sets national objectives, constitute an incomparable instrument of progress during a phase of several years. Beyond this phase, incapable of considering its mission as terminated, it becomes an obstacle to progress.[15]

Hence, even if one were to acknowledge a potential, useful, transitional function for the one-party structure, M. Yamed perceives the danger of centralized power corrupting and becoming muscle-bound, and thus "an obstacle to progress" toward national development. In short, the very social revolution the one-party state system seeks to bring about, must in the end, to prevail, overcome the obstacle to its fulfillment interposed by the self-same one-party structure.

CHAPTER 5

PROBLEM OF STATE STRUCTURE: THE ROLE OF THE MILITARY

For the foreseeable future, as the armed forces of the new countries grow, the taking over of governments by the military will be a more and more frequent occurrence. Although Ayub Khan has endowed Pakistan with basic democracies, for the military regimes as for the one-party one-man governments the return to liberal parliamentary democracy of the Western type is on the whole less rather than more likely to come to pass.

PROFESSOR RUPERT EMERSON, *Harvard University, 1964*

As we have seen in the preceding chapter, the role of the military in nation-building is closely bound up with the type of state structure adopted in the new African states. We have suggested that the one-party state structure is particularly vulnerable to military *coups d'état*, and in a sense prepares the way for military takeovers. This has certainly been the case in Togo, Congo (Brazzaville), Dahomey, Gabon, Algeria, the Central African Republic, Upper Volta, and Ghana. In all these states the military came to power in the context of *de jure* or *de facto* one-party state structures.

Only in the Sudan, the Congo (Kinshasa) and Nigeria did the military come to power in the context of genuine multiparty state structures, and in each of these structures there were particularly acute tribal problems. We have already discussed in Chapter 3 the critical struggle in the Sudan between the Arabic Muslim North and the Black pagan and Christian South. We return briefly to the Sudanese case later in this chapter. The ongoing chaos in the Congo (Kinshasa) with its endemic and epidemic tribal warfare has been before the United Nations and the world since the day of the country's accession to independence, June 30, 1960. We will return to a discussion of the Congo in Chapter 11. The major military *coup* in Nigeria in January 1966 and its second round in July 1966 had an obvious overriding tribal theme—northerner *vs.* southerner, and more Fulani-Hausas *vs.* Ibo. We shall return to the Nigerian case later

61

in this chapter and in our discussion of multiparty states in the next chapter.

Here we are primarily concerned with the role of the military in nation-building generally, and in light of the peculiar affinity between the military and one-party state structures. Professor Emerson in the quotation at the head of this chapter links the one-party state structure with military regimes in still another way. In his view both are likely to preclude a "return to," or one might venture, the development of, parliamentary democracy. And from the vantage point of nation-building, this rules out voluntary, self-motivated, and persuaded participation in political and economic affairs and processes, and means forced, manipulated, and coerced participation. It is the difference between elections and plebiscites. In our view, this is the heart of the matter. The basic precondition for nation-building is true public *participation*, and the problem is how best to achieve it.

ALTERNATIVE VIEWS

As long ago as 1899, Sir Winston Churchill in writing about the Anglo-Egyptian Sudan assessed the role of the military in nation-building and found it wanting. In Sir Winston's words:

> It might seem at first a great advantage that the peoples of the Sudan, instead of being a multitude of wild, discordant tribes, should unite of their own accord into one strong community, actuated by a common spirit, living under fixed laws, and ruled by a single sovereign. But there is one form of centralised government which is almost entirely unprogressive and beyond all other forms costly and tyrannical—the rule of an army. . . . History records many such dominations, ancient and modern, civilised or barbarian; and though education and culture may modify, they cannot change their predominant characteristics—a continual subordination of justice to expediency, an indifference to suffering, a disdain of ethical principles, a laxity of morals, and a complete ignorance of economics. . . . The political supremacy of an army always leads to the formation of a great centralised capital, to the degradation of peaceful inhabitants . . . , to the ruin of commerce, the decay of learning, and the ultimate demoralisation even of the military order. . . .[1]

It is interesting for our purpose that Churchill's dictum on military rule should have grown out of the situation he encountered in the Sudan in the late nineteenth century, for once again in the twentieth century the Sudan was to be ruled by a military government, centralized in Khartoum, and displaying at least insofar as the remote southern Sudanese provinces and their four million inhabitants were concerned, a good many, if not all, of the characteristics set down by Churchill as true of military rule for all times and societies.

The shortcomings of military rule in the Sudan, however, were not confined to the southern provinces. The whole country reaped the harvest—a bitter one in terms of building national cohesion and unity. The military government of General Abboud fell, more or less under its own weight, in 1964, after six years in power. It left the southern problem more acute than ever, with as great a lack of consensus among the Northern Sudanese politicians about national goals and objectives, and as much political instability as obtained at the time the military took over to wipe out the political bickering, to restore order, and get on with the job of unifying and developing the country. In Professor James Coleman's formulation:

> When the Sudanese army assumed power, it did so not just to establish order, but because the latter was a requisite for modernization.[2]

The Abboud government also failed in its temporary incumbency either to build national support for its "non-political" rule or to find a way out, a way back to satisfactory civil government. It fell in a minor student uprising in Khartoum, aided and abetted by divisions within the military, political pressures from the old "pols" who, unlike old soldiers, apparently do not "fade away," and political intrigue by the underground communist party, which almost captured control of the uprising, and incidentally illustrated the converse of the proposition of the vulnerability of one-party state regimes to military takeovers, i.e., the vulnerability of military regimes to communist takeover bids.

The importance of the Sudanese military government experience for Africa cannot be overemphasized because the Sudan was the exception in Africa. In Professor Coleman's words:

> The Sudan is the one African state south of the Sahara to emerge from the colonial period with a modern military establishment possessing the attributes of an independent national army.[3]

And again, Coleman notes:

> When independence was achieved in January 1956, the Sudanization of the officer corps was virtually completed.[4]

When this advanced state of the Sudanese army is taken into account, it is at least pertinent to ask, what nation-building role could be expected of the new, evolving armed forces of other African states, starting from scratch, without the "attributes of an independent national army" and without a *trained* Africanized officer corps. Perhaps the characterization of the Congolese (Kinshasa) army in October 1962 at a meeting of the African Studies Association of the United States, by a former senior UN civilian officer (and a then about to be senior U.S. Embassy and AID officer) in the Congo, as "a rabble" [5] was excessive, even for the Congo. But it is clear that

> with few exceptions, national armies [in Africa] are either non-existent, or they are fragile structures still heavily dependent upon external support for their maintenance and development. . . . African states lack what many other new states of the former colonial world have had, namely, an army which could be a modernizing and stabilizing source of organization and strength in society, a last stand-by reserve which could be called in, or could take over, to prevent external subversion or a total collapse of the political order.[6]

Today, however, in contrast to the Churchill view, there is the new "conventional wisdom" of a popular school of Western advisers on nation-building, which has uncritically transformed its estimate of the nation-building role of the Turkish, Israeli, and Iranian armies, *inter alia*, to the African scene. In this view there has been and there is a constructive multipurpose role for armed forces, aside from their primary military mission, in nation-building through such programs as "civic action," *i.e.*, public-works engineering and building projects, adult education and vocational training, citizenship indoctrination, and administration of relief and "make-work" projects. This rationale for utilizing existing armed forces or marginally augmenting such forces may have some validity in states with established military traditions and forces, and where civil authority over the military is an accepted fact of life and state.[7] In Africa however, all that this conventional wisdom has done has been to provide an aura of respectability and sense of responsibility to military build-ups, *coups d'état* and takeovers, which for the most part have been shabby affairs.

Thus, a prominent British authority writing on the "Armed Forces in New States" tells us:

> An expansion of forces, such as that now taking place in Ghana, may have similar nation-building objectives. National service is likely, whether incidentally or by design, to encourage the development of national rather than regional or tribal loyalties. That is particularly important in federal states like Nigeria and might eventually prove a significant factor in the achievement of stability in Kenya. Alternatively, enforced proximity of this nature may only serve to magnify the differences and tensions.[8]

The alternative result, of a theretofore integrated army fragmenting after assuming power and attempting to discharge the nation-building function, has been the case in Nigeria. There the first *coup* in January 1966 was viewed by the northerners in the country, including the army, as a *coup* engineered by the Ibos of the East. The second *coup* in July 1966 was clearly a counter-action by the northern Hausas in the army against the Ibos.[9] Thus, Lieutenant Colonel Yakuvu Gowon, from the North, who emerged as head of Nigeria's second military government, in his first address after his assumption of power, described the events of January 15th as a *coup* in which "a group of officers [Ibos] in cooperation with certain civilians" plotted "to overthrow the Government . . . by eliminating political leaders and high-ranking officers, *a majority of whom came from a particular section of the country* [the North.]" He then went on to say with respect to the events of July 29th: "The base for unity is not here and has been badly rocked, not once but several times." The Military Governor of Eastern Nigeria at the time of the second *coup*, Lieutenant Colonel Odumegwu Ojukwu, an Ibo, left no doubt of how he viewed the second *coup*. He declared: "The brutal and planned annihilation of officers of Eastern Region origin in the last few days has again cast serious doubts as to whether the people of Nigeria, after these cruel and bloody adventures, can ever sincerely live together as members of the same nation."[10] As an outcome of the second *coup*, the national army was regionalized, with troops serving only in the region of their origin.

The alternative, although somewhat less dramatic, has been the experience in the Sudan too, where southerners were in any event largely excluded from the army, and the in-fighting took place within the closed Arabic Islamic circle. The alternative has also been the repeated history of military events in Congo (Kinshasa). The rebellion of the troops of the former Katanga *gendarmerie* stationed in Stanleyville against the central government and the *Armée Nationale Congolaise* in July 1966, of which it is part, was the latest and most critical of a long series of such tribally- or regionally-based mutinies in that it was directed against the military government of General Mobutu.

So too in Dahomey, the army instead of submerging tribalism became the victim of it. Instead of being above the fray and the nonpolitical arbiter of the nation's internal order and external security, the army became a participant in the nation's political arena. In the words of a sympathetic commentator on the African scene:

> The military are experiencing the consequences of its politization. Thus the army seems to have lost the unity which made it a homogeneous body behind its chief. If appears actually divided into two militant factions

agitating for the return of [ousted President] Maga and [subsequently ousted Vice-President] Ahomadegbe respectively. One fact seems certain: the Dahomeyan army does not seem disposed to confront anew the anguish of power.[11]

And beyond, even where there has not been overt factionalism and strife within the armed forces, they have done very little to build national unity through submerging tribalism or instilling discipline. The Ghanaian army, which was given "social" functions under the Nkrumah regime, particularly with respect to the semimilitary Workers' Brigade for unemployed young people, and a type of national service for "Young Pioneers" can hardly be said to have achieved either of these "social" goals—unity in the nation or discipline in the Workers' Brigade, which became something like paramilitary shock troops for the Convention People's Party. It remains to be seen, of course, whether the armed forces in full control of the government, after the ouster of Dr. Nkrumah, will have any greater success with these "social" functions.

THE AFRICAN EXPERIENCE: MILITARY COUPS AND AFTERMATH

We now turn to an examination of the record of African *coups d'état* * and, where successful, the centralized government they brought in their train, with a view to assessing the military's potential for nation-building in Africa.

The Egyptian and Sudanese military *coups* belong to a somewhat earlier period than the epidemic of military takeovers in the newer African states set off by the January 1963 action of a handful of Togolese soldiers. The result of this action was the assassination of President Sylvanus Olympio and the installation of a civilian government—the Grunitzky government—dependent on and drawing much of its strength from the army, and some would go so far as to say, responsible to the army. It is this latter group of military *coups* we shall be primarily concerned with here. The earlier ones, particularly the Egyptian one, although instructive and relevant, would lead us too far afield, into the Near Eastern milieu of which they are so much a part. We have also already dealt in Chapter 3, and again earlier in this chapter, with the failure of the Abboud regime during its six years in power to integrate the southern Sudanese into a cohesive nation-state, as well as its failure generally in establishing the political and social basis for successful nation-building.

Nineteen sixty-three witnessed in addition to the Togolese *coup* two more successful *coups d'état* by the military—in Congo (Brazzaville) and

* See Appendix for Table of Military *coups d'état* in Africa since 1960. J.H.M.

in Dahomey. In the Congolese case the military followed close on the heels of the trade unions and unemployed in Brazzaville who "made the revolution" by ousting President Abbé Fulbert Youlou. The military "restored order" and sponsored the new one-party government, which initially was beholden on the one hand, to the trade unions, and on the other, to the military. The new one-party regime rests uneasily on the organized strength of the trade unions and the force of the army, and as revealed by the inconclusive uprising by a section of the military in mid-1966 on a cadre of Cuban military advisers to the special Presidential Guard. The government also retains a certain popular appeal deriving from earlier popular dissatisfaction with the Youlou regime. Its attempt to tighten up on *its* one-party power monopoly, based on Youlou's tribal connections, by making the incomplete *de facto* dominance of Youlou's party into a complete *de jure* one, its inability to cope with the wide-spread unemployment in Brazzaville, and its acceptance of, if not complicity in, the brazen corruption which permeated public affairs in the country. Soon after the *coup* the army put down an attempt by tribal followers of former President Abbé Fulbert Youlou to release him from detention and presumably restore him to power. Youlou has since escaped under mysterious circumstances to sanctuary abroad, first in Africa, then in Europe.

In Dahomey the military played a more direct role in overthrowing the Maga government. Unemployed crowds in Cotonou certainly were involved, but so too was the military from the outset. The military set up a provisional government, associating leading political personalities with a military junta, and organized a new national political "front." The opposition to President Hubert Maga, in addition to the military, arose from dissatisfaction of the unemployed, unhappiness among politicians, who were out of power or sharing power with Maga's party, over the President's attempt to create an exclusive one-party structure by transforming the *parti unifié* (a coalition of parties under one umbrella) into a tighter *parti unique* (one-party structure) and a general displeasure with the corruption which was widely known to exist in public life.

A new constitution was promulgated and elections were held in which the new one-party structure organized by the military and its civilian collaborators presented an approved single list of candidates. A civilian government was installed, but there was little question that former Colonel, now General, Christophe Soglo and his troops were the real power in the country. The military in Dahomey also put down a rebellion soon after the *coup* in the north of Dahomey by tribal groups loyal to the dispossessed northerner, former President Hubert Maga.

The civil government proved ineffectual and the military repeated its *coup* in mid-1965 and reorganized the civil government. This too proved ineffective, and several months later, late in 1965, General Soglo led his third *coup*, dismissed the government, gave up the pretext of a civil façade, and installed a military government with himself as President.

Thus, the Congo (Brazzaville) and Dahomey military takeovers, like the Togo one before them, created one-party civilian governments, dependent in greater or lesser degree for support and continuity in office on the military. The Togolese situation differed somewhat from the other two *coups* in origin, however, in that it was nakedly a military takeover, without protective coloration or joint sponsorship, as in Brazzaville of the trade unions, and in Cotonou of the unemployed.

The military in Togo at the outset was also more in evidence—as the base of power for the government, and as the beneficiaries of the revolution. The two hundred man army was quickly expanded to something of the order of fifteen hundred troops, wages were raised, and allowances and living conditions of the army were noticeably improved. However, in Congo (Brazzaville) and even more so in Dahomey the military have come into their own and have emulated the Togolese example with respect to the augmentation of their political roles, the size of their forces, and their material rewards. In fact, in Dahomey, and also in Congo (Brazzaville), the military have caught up with their brethren in Togo and probably have overtaken them.

The *coup d'état* at the outset of 1964 in Zanzibar was radically different from the three in French-speaking Africa in 1963. The Zanzibar *coup* involved anti-Arab nationalists, communists and communist sympathizers, Russian, Red Chinese and Cuban varieties, and a strange, even bizarre collection of miscellaneous African adventurers, nationalists, racialists, and would-be soldiers of fortune under the leadership of the self-styled Field Marshall John Okello, a mystical Ugandan who provided the color and terror of the revolution. The makeshift force was soon dismantled and the Field Marshall repatriated to his more customary rural pursuits in his native Uganda. The one-party structure erected in Zanzibar was a fusion of African nationalists and doctrinaire communist-oriented and outright communist personalities. The Zanzibar *coup* has only limited relevance in this section as its military quality has been largely lost, in fact, was never more than a passing, pragmatic improvisation.

The East African mutinies which followed on the heels of the Zanzibar affairs were abortive and apparently somewhat unfocused and impromptu rebellions by the military in Tanganyika, Uganda, and Kenya. The objectives seemed to be limited to better pay, better allowances, promotions, ousting of European officers (Africanization), and general elevation of the role of the military in public affairs. All three mutinies were quelled by British troops called in by the East African governments. Although the mutinies were all abortive and political power remained with the incumbent civil governments, the military in all three countries have enlarged their roles and improved their material positions, particularly in Uganda. Control of the military was an important factor in Prime Minister Obote's ouster in early 1966 of President Edward Mutesa as President of Uganda and King of Buganda (a largely self-governing kingdom within the republic and in his discarding of the country's quasi-federal constitution and replacing it with a unitary (*cum* one-party?) constitution. Dr. Obote said his was a "preventive *coup*"; he then used the military, after replacing the commanding officer with one friendly to his position, to break up the Kingdom of Buganda into four provinces.

No sooner were the January–February 1964 mutinies put down in East Africa, than a successful military *coup* was launched in Gabon. The government of President Léon M'ba was ousted and replaced by a military-supported, provisional, civilian government. But the new regime was short-lived. French troops intervened within twenty-four hours, and in a counter *coup* overthrew the new government and restored the M'ba regime. Thus, although the Gabonese military *coup* did not result in a new military regime, it did increase the dependence of the restored M'ba regime on the Gabonese military and their French allies.

About a year later, in June 1965, the major military *coup* in Africa up to that time took place in Algeria. The military overthrew the Ben Bella government with little difficulty, and proceeded to purge the one-party, the only other organized group in the country.[12] The military enhanced its power enormously. It took over the party apparatus and the interrelated governmental machinery. It disbanded the separate "Chinese-armed" party militia,[13] and imposed, notwithstanding some limited civilian window-dressing, direct military rule in the country. Earlier the Abboud military government in the Sudan, as we have already noted, also had recourse to direct military rule. In fact, the inability of the military regime in the Sudan to build a civilian base or façade for its power led as much as anything to its downfall. The Boumedienne government in Algiers seems to be heading down the same road, *i.e.*, substituting tightening military control for popular participation, in a situation where the FLN had already destroyed *all* important independent sources of organized power except for some religious bodies.

Late in 1965, there were the two *coups* already referred to in Dahomey,* and a major *coup* in November in Congo (Kinshasa), which brought General Mobutu to power for a second time in five years. The Congo

---

* After General Christophe Soglo's third taking-over of the Dahomeyan government in late 1965, he himself was deposed by young army officers in December 1967. The head of the provisional military government, Lieutenant Colonel Alphonse Alley, installed a military government in June 1968, after the May elections had failed because of a "massive" boycott. J.H.M.

(Kinshasa) is *sui generis*, even in Africa. It is sufficient for our purposes at this juncture to take note of the alleged "civilian conspiracies" to over-throw the military government and the recourse of the military to sum-mary "trials" and execution of prominent Congolese politicians, including a former prime minister and a former minister of defense, as well as the sporadic rebellions that have occurred since the military took over in November 1965.

On New Year's Day 1966, the Central African Republic suffered a mili-tary *coup*, and several days later the Upper Volta followed suit. In January the government of Nigeria was overthrown by a military upris-ing, and in February the government of Ghana fell. All these *coups* emu-lated the Algerian example and have attempted to establish direct military governments. In the Ghanaian case, however, prominent civil servants were associated soon after the *coup* with the military in semiexecutive capacities. In all of the 1966 *coups* economic difficulties, unemployment, corruption, and tribal and regional hostility, and wide-spread popular apathy or frustration were all present as important factors.

In Ghana there were several additional factors. The heavy-handed au-thoritarianism of President Nkrumah and the Convention People's Party had progressively alienated large segments of the population, notwithstand-ing a propaganda barrage to the contrary boasting the unity achieved by the party through its coercive tactics and practices. Increasingly, trade unionists, professional people, civil servants, Ashanti cocoa farmers, intel-lectuals, university students, and authors, became disaffected. Their silence was not acquiescence, and not a reflection of unity, but rather a coerced outward uniformity which readily broke apart when given the chance, as the *coup* and its aftermath have so vividly demonstrated. The toppling of the larger-than-life statue of Dr. Nkrumah, outside Parliament in Accra, was symbolic of the underlying disunity under the façade created by Dr. Nkrumah and the CPP, and all too reminiscent of the toppling of Stalin's statue in Budapest in the 1956 uprising in Hungary.

President Nkrumah, however, as President Ben Bella before him, also made a fatal error in alienating the armed forces' leadership. In both instances, fearful or uneasy about the military they had supported and built up, they had recourse to the Soviet Union and Communist China respectively for aid and personnel to train palace guards or party militia. The "regular" army resented this slur on their honor, as well as the com-petition for status and funds. Colonel Boumedienne acted before the Algerian guard crystallized. The military in Ghana waited, and as a result the only pitched battle and only serious resistance during the *coup* offered to it was by the Presidential Guard under Russian officers at Flagstaff House, the residence of the president.

The *coups* in Algeria and Ghana illustrate the risk involved in dispro-
portionately building up military forces in African states without countervailing or balancing forces in the society. As we have noted, this is particularly so in unitary one-party states where the party as a matter of
doctrine and inevitably in practice proceeds to eliminate or systematically
downgrades all other social, economic, or political institutions or interests,
other than the military. It is not accidental, then, that the Frankenstein's
monster syndrome appears in one-party states—for example, Algeria,
Ghana, and Congo (Brazzaville). Psychologically, as well as pragmat-
ically, the need to create another monster to counter the original one
develops. Interestingly enough, mercenaries are then turned to by the
embattled heads of state, fearful of their own military forces for the delicate task of creating a new balancing force to the military—a palace guard
or party militia. Thus, Algeria turned to Communist China, Ghana to
the Soviet Union, and Congo (Brazzaville) to Cuba for mercenaries *cum*
training officers.

The abortive Gabonese and East African mutinies, the Zanzibar uprising,
and the successful *coups* in francophone Africa, Algeria, Nigeria, and
Ghana all demonstrate the volatile, unpredictable, and, to the author's
mind, dangerous potential of national armies in the underdeveloped states
of Africa. Not only the classic preconditions for nationhood and statehood have been bypassed in the rush to independence and must now be
inserted into the scheme of things as conditions subsequent, but also, particularly in one-party structures, all of the possible balancing or countervailing sources of power to the military have been systematically liquidated. In these circumstances, encouragement of military build-ups for
collateral purposes such as facilitating economic development and nation-
building and finding the rationalization for the build-ups in such collateral
purposes by friendly outside countries can only serve, in the author's
view, to reinforce the already unfortunate tendency for military takeovers, and render the already difficult task of nation-building even more
hazardous and uncertain.

THE MILITARY ROLE IN THE NATION-BUILDING: AN ASSESSMENT

What then has been the role in nation-building of the thinly disguised
military governments, or heavily dependent and beholden-to-the military
civilian governments, in Togo and Congo (Brazzaville), and of the un-
disguised military government in Algeria, and earlier in the Sudan, in
Dahomey, Central African Republic, Upper Volta, Nigeria, and Ghana?
What problems do these quasi-military and direct-military governments
create for the nation-building task?

In Togo the hand-picked civilian government, although ratified in a one-list election under controlled conditions, hardly seems to have been a vehicle for inspiring public confidence and enthusiasm for the difficult nation-, state- and economy-building tasks confronting the country. Yet these are inescapably the priority functions of the government of Togo as of all African governments. The centralization of power in Lomé in the hands of the military-supported civilian government has been going on steadily. Beyond that the country seems to be at a standstill; the center has not been pumping out the life blood of nation-building enthusiasm, esprit and élan, nor does it seem to have a capacity for doing so.

In Congo (Brazzaville) greater emphasis appears to have been placed on building a mass-based, popular-front, one-party state structure, partly as an outward manifestation of support and partly as a façade for the military-dependent government. This was also the case in Dahomey after the first *coup*. Tribal violence, however, broke out in both countries in connection with support for the displaced leaders. In both countries, too, external diversions were manufactured or gratefully seized upon to rally internal support for the new regimes and consolidate the nation behind them.

The controversy of Congo (Brazzaville) with its sister state, Congo (Kinshasa), over the sanctuary provided by the former to rebels seeking to overthrow first the Adoula government and then the Kasavubu-Tshombe government, provided a major distraction from the internal problems and political controversy in Congo (Brazzaville). Congo (Kinshasa) retalliated by providing sanctuary to former President Youlou and to disaffected followers of the deposed President. As a result Congo (Brazzaville) adopted the posture of a beleaguered state surrounded by "imperialist and neo-colonialist governments."

The controversy of Dahomey with the neighboring state of Niger over Lette Island and Dahomey nationals working in Niger came at a most opportune time for the military-supported government headed by then President M. Sourou-Mignan Apithy. A kind of xenophobic antipathy developed in both countries to "strangers," particularly those originating in one another's countries.

The military power in all three countries, Togo, Congo (Brazzaville), and Dahomey, has tried through dependent civilian governments to build support for the regimes and a national consciousness, an essential element in nation-building. The achievement to date in building national unity appears to have been limited. In fact, in Dahomey, the military ripped away the façade and took over. It may even be that the existing divisive tribal, ethnic, religious, and regional factors in all three countries have been accentuated by the *coups* which ousted leaders with special tribal or regional followings. The new governments apparently will be a long time satisfying the suspicions of the followers of the displaced leaders about the disinterested nature and purity of motives of those who made the "revolutions," and particularly of the military who almost inevitably will have been drawn and will more than likely continue to be drawn from tribes and regions other than those "loyal" to the ousted leaders.

If this be so, the tendency to centralize power in the hands of the military, already much in evidence in the three countries, may actually retard the process of welding together disparate groups and achieving national cohesion. It is likely to confirm the worst suspicions of the disaffected groups about the tribal, or ethnic, or regional power motivation of those who have ousted from power their assassinated, imprisoned, detained, or disgraced former leaders.

The position in the direct military governments has differed little from those with a civil or quasi-civil façade. In fact, in the Sudan, Algeria, and Nigeria, *inter alia*, the military has shown even less capacity for political communication with the populace. The very nature of the military has inhibited the development of a representative-constituent relationship mentality. All African states with military governments have been suffering from a political leadership vacuum, on the one hand, and an absence of political dialogue between governors and governed, on the other. No matter how inept or corrupt, this is one task the overthrown African politicians understood—fence-mending and grass-root links. In short, the military has been unable to induce participation, the central precondition for nation-building. Even President Nasser in the United Arab Republic, despite repeated attempts, has been unable to build a continuing political participation of the population through political organizations. He has had to resort to exhortation, mob action, and often plebiscitary-type devices. And in Nigeria, the largest African state to experience a military takeover, the military discovered this problem after a little experience and took steps to meet it after its second military *coup*. In the words of a *New York Times* report:

> It is widely believed here that Nigeria's fierce regional rivalries among the northern Hausas, the eastern Ibos, and western Yorubas . . . can be handled only by the kind of patient horse-trading that is a mark of the civilian politician. When General Ironsi, an Ibo, sought to end these rivalries in military fashion by simply declaring the nation's regions abolished, he aroused fears of the North that led to the takeover by northern elements in the army.[14]

To the same effect is the report of the *Washington Post's* African correspondent:

In their first seven months of military rule, Nigerians learned a surprising thing: as imperfect as their local leaders might have been, there was no other institution in the country capable of maintaining even a partial dialogue between the people and government.[15]

The new military government shares this estimate of the situation when it announced its intention to appoint a civilian advisory group. Lieut. Col. Gowan explained:

This [political advisory] committee is intended to fill the vacuum created by the ban on political organizations.[16]

Similarly, although maintaining the ban of the predecessor military government of General Aguiyi-Ironsi on political parties, Col. Gowan's government's release of all political prisoners, including Chief Obafemi Awolowo, former leader of the Opposition Action Group party at the federal level, could only have been done in the expectation that they would return to "practising their professions and performing their arts." [17] The army in Dahomey had the same experience—a public turning to the ousted politicians in the absence of an effectual rapport with the army.[18]

The militarily-supported as well as the direct military governments have had little success in developing local institutions and local-level government councils and administration that would involve more and more people in public affairs. Nor have they had much success in inducing economic initiatives at local levels throughout the country. The reason for the lack of success is quite clear: either development, the devolution of power to local levels, or the encouragement of independent initiatives and accumulation of economic power at local levels, would threaten the concentration of power at the center, the *sine qua non* for military rule generally and particularly in Africa. Hence, neither development has been undertaken with any serious intention of achieving this self-defeating result. And without building local institutions and encouraging local economic initiatives the chances for fusing plural and diverse populations into a national unit based on shared interests and experience seem remote.

There is also the question of technical capacity, intentions and motivations aside. There seems to be little reason to expect that the new, relatively small, and for the most part indifferently trained, marginally organized, poorly educated, and unevenly disciplined armies of most of the new states are in a position to run their countries or their countries' economies—directly or indirectly through intermediaries. There are, of course, one or two exceptions with respect to the quality of several African armies, but none with respect to their capacity to run their countries' economies. Sir Winston's dictum on this score has been upheld in one African state after another. Within limits the military may "clean up the mess" and restrict the more blatant types of corruption. Thereafter, the creative task of economic development, of encouraging private initiatives, and the growth of the private sector of the economy, has been beyond it.[19] Perhaps in time this picture will alter generally as more and more African officers and noncommissioned officers are turned out by overseas as well as by recently established domestic military colleges and institutions. However, it may also be that any improvement in the capacity of the African military to run things will be outdistanced by the growth of ambitions and stimuli for the military to take over more and more governments, as well as more and more aspects and sectors of national life. In any event, the nation-building potential of the present crop of military and quasi-military African governments south of the Sahara now and for the foreseeable future seems a most limited one, hardly commensurate with the demands of the nation-building challenge.

The conclusions in a recent study of the role of the military in politics in a much wider arena than Africa, *The Man on Horseback*, by Professor S. E. Finer are apposite and congruent with our analysis of the role of the military in nation-building in Africa. In Professor Finer's words:

> In all likelihood, then, those of the new states which are not overtaken by totalitarianism and attracted into the Russian and Chinese orbits, will oscillate for a long time to come between military régimes and civilian restorations. The past patterns of Latin America and the Middle East are likely to occur in the newest states in Asia and in Africa. . . . There are some today who are willing to overlook the despotic nature of any régime providing that it acts or claims to act in the name of the masses; or that it purportedly "raises the standard of living"; or that it serves the cause of anti-colonialism, etc. . . . Four things may however be fairly said. The first is that in a large number of cases the frequency of military intervention is a proof that the society is as yet politically immature and unfit for representative institutions. . . . However, secondly, in a large number of the cases we have cited, the corporate self-interest of the military has itself signally contributed to this political immaturity. If in some cases, like that of Atatürk, military intervention has been tutelary and constitutive, in the vast majority of cases it has not. . . . Thirdly, whatever the motive, the result is some form—direct or indirect—of corporate despotism. Whatever our views on the ends which such régimes may serve, and however desirable these may seem to be, we have the duty, first and last, at least to recognize them for what they are: as despotisms. . . . Lastly one ought to contemplate the more common of the excuses for military intervention in a highly critical spirit: some of them are more than usually specious. A common justification, for instance, is that the intervention was desirable in order to preserve order in a highly disturbed political situation. So it well might be, but one must first inquire whether this result could not have been achieved by the military coming to the aid

of the civil power instead of attacking and supplanting it. . . . Another
common excuse is that the military régime has created greater social
equality and material prosperity than its civilian predecessor.   Again,
this may be true in particular cases; but one ought to bear in mind that
there are few military régimes of which this can be unequivocally asserted,
while there are numerous examples . . . where the effect was the disorder if not the ruin of the economy. *By any world standards military
régimes have shown less than average capacity for statesmanship or economics.*   And yet, even if it could be shown without doubt that the
military intervention had indeed brought material wellbeing and political
stability to a country, it is necessary to ask one final, because transcen-
dently important, question: whether the short-term political and economic
gain is not likely to be overbalanced by a longer-term catastrophe?   For,
in most cases, military intervention has put a stop to constitutional evolution.[20]

CHAPTER 6

PROBLEM OF STATE STRUCTURE: THE ROLE
OF THE MODERNIZING OLIGARCHICAL STATE

*There are many monarchies without kings—autocrats with more
power than kings.*

KING HASSAN II *of Morocco, 1964*

Sir Winston Churchill's stricture on centralization was cast in a military
context. It seems as applicable in other contexts which were not known
or at any rate were not common when Sir Winston was writing on the
Sudan, *i.e.*, "mass mobilizing," authoritarian, African one-party states and
modernizing African oligarchies. The African scene is dominated by
centralized unitary states, predominantly by authoritarian one-party states,
interspersed with a handful of modernizing oligarchical states—the Kingdom of Morocco, the Kingdom of Libya, the Empire of Ethiopia and the
Kingdom of Burundi. We have already considered in Chapter 4 the role
in nation-building of the more typical centralized African states, the one-
party states with presidential systems; before going on to consider the
role of the centralized modernizing oligarchical states, we shall note some
important similarities between the one-party and oligarchical states.

In a recent study on local reform in Morocco, a modernizing oligarchical state, and Tunisia, a unitary one-party state, the author draws the
same basic conclusion:

> The new North African governments have been reluctant to disperse
> their activity and to diffuse power. Every developmental activity is
> highly centralized, however, and even the articulate segment of more
> advanced citizens is sometimes regarded as a threat to development.[1]

The one-party states, as we noted in Chapters 4 and 5, are highly vulnerable to military *coups* and takeovers, and subject to being transformed
into militarily-run states; so too are the modernizing oligarchical states.
One-party states are also in many ways only a somewhat more modern
rendition and masquerade of the modernizing oligarchy growing out of
the more classical royal succession. The leading African monarchical

77

modernizer, King Hassan II, arguing that monarchy can just as successfully lead and develop an underdeveloped state as any other type of state
structure, cogently summed up the position in his statement heading this
chapter: "There are many monarchies [in Africa] without kings—autocrats with more power than Kings." [2]

Thus, the discussion in this chapter of African modernizing oligarchical
states should be read against the background of the analyses of the one-
party unitary state and military regimes. All three-modernizing oligarchies, one-party unitary states and military regimes—share many of the same
qualities and many of the same constraints with regard to nation-building.

THE MODERNIZING OLIGARCHICAL STATES

Oligarchical is used in this discussion in preference to monarchical, as
in all instances, although the individual monarchs play the leading role in
their countries, the very process of modernization implies a certain sharing of power with and reliance on an ever-expanding group of intimates,
colleagues and allies. It also implies the adoption of "constitutional" devices and forms requiring in practice the sharing of some power and
prerogatives with councils, cabinets, and other bodies, perhaps even with
parliaments with circumscribed memberships or powers. For example,
in the first constitution in Ethiopia's 2000-year history, promulgated in
1931 by Emperor Haile Selassie I as an act of grace, the preamble proclaims in lofty terms the goal of modernization and the principle of sharing functions (and power): "It is necessary for the modern Ethiopian to
accustom himself to taking part in the direction of all departments of
state . . . to share in the mighty task which Ethiopian sovereigns have
had to accomplish alone in the past." [3] Thus, we are here confining the
discussion to oligarchical regimes deriving from royal and monarchical
origins, and shall emphasize the two most important instances in Africa,
Morocco, and Ethiopia. For comparative purposes, reference will also be
made to the Kingdoms of Burundi and Libya.

The new constitution of Morocco, adopted in 1962 in a national plebi-
scite, and the relatively new constitution of Ethiopia, promulgated in
1955 by the Emperor, although vastly different in content and style, and
in the degree individual rights are recognized and accorded protection,
are similar with respect to the centralization of power in the hands of the
monarchs and their close associates. There is, as one would expect, in
Morocco given its independence revolution in 1955 (the year the Emperor gave Ethiopia the second constitution in its long history) and the
inevitable unsettled aftermath, a lesser degree and a less obvious concentration of power than in Ethiopia. The latter country has not experienced the nationalist pressures flowing from a long colonial experience

culminating in a successful and relatively widespread movement to oust the colonial power.[4] There has been less cause and motivation in Ethiopia to dilute the concentration of power at the center, or at any rate, to share some of it, as in Morocco with those groups, which frequently have taken the form of political parties, and individuals who helped make the independence revolution.[5]

Morocco got its first constitution as a consequence of its accession to independence in 1955. The Sultan changed his title to King and pledged a constitution to his countrymen as part of the changing scene.[6] Although King Mohammed V died in 1961 before redeeming his independence pledge of a constitution for Morocco, his son and successor, King Hassan II, did make good his father's promise. In late 1962 the King sponsored a draft of what was to be the first written constitution in Morocco's history. It was approved in a national referendum in December 1962 by an overwhelming vote—85 percent of the registered voters cast ballots, and about 95 percent of those voting favored the proposed constitution.

The large participation in the referendum and the overwhelming "yes" vote are intimately tied in with the whole process of achieving independence, seeking to erase the memories of the French protectorate, and building a new national identity. Thus, in Morocco the adoption of a constitution has had important symbolic as well as constitutional implications for nation-building. These aspects reinforce one another and together explain much about the central position of the constitution in Moroccan affairs, and why there is so much more emphasis on modernization and sharing of power in it than in the Ethiopian constitution. The latter was promulgated in 1955 on the occasion of the twenty-fifth anniversary of Haile Selassie's coronation as an act of grace and without any sort of public participation, and commemorates the Emperor's successful return after the brief Italian occupation and the reestablishment of the unchallenged central position of the Menelik dynasty.

In view of the role of the new constitution in economic and political development as well as in nation-building in Morocco, it seems pertinent to consider briefly at this point its major aspects. The constitution establishes a strong hereditary monarchy, disposing of considerable executive powers; the monarch is vested with numerous important prerogatives, including the right of dissolution of Parliament on his own initiative, and the right (in the Gaullist style) to submit a wide range of issues directly to public referenda. It guarantees a broad range of individual and civil rights, and at the same time rules out the institution of a one-party political system. It establishes the first national legislative bodies (a bicameral parliament) in Morocco's history, including a lower house elected by universal franchise and an upper house by a special and more restricted franchise. It also provides for the election of provincial, municipal, and rural community assemblies. The King is also designated as head of the national development planning agency and the *Promotion Nationale,* an agency for initiating and carrying out large-scale public works programs such as reforestation, antierosion and farm-to-country road networks. The army has been involved in the administration of *Promotion Nationale,* as a type of "civic action."

It also seems useful to contrast the Moroccan constitution with that of Ethiopia, where there has been no public participation in the constitution-making or ratifying process and where as yet the constitution plays little role in real or symbolic terms in nation-building. The present Ethiopian constitution spells out with more exactitude than the 1931 constitution it superseded, the distribution of functions—and to some extent, power—the rights of the individual, and the structure of government. As in the earlier constitution power is concentrated in the Emperor. The centralization is more widespread and more apparent than is the case with the centralization of power in the King in the Moroccan constitution. As for the rights of the individual in the Ethiopian constitution they are covered less comprehensively and less precisely than in the Moroccan counterpart. The Ethiopian constitution also provides for the first popularly elected Chamber of Deputies in the country's history, which is to share a very limited legislative power with a Senate appointed by the Emperor. Unlike the Moroccan constitution, it contains no provision for lower level or local government institutions and elections.

Thus, in both modernizing oligarchies, different as they are, and for that matter in the two other instances in Africa of modernizing oligarchies, in Libya and in Burundi, the power focus is the monarchy and surrounding institutions and bodies. The centralization is of a high order, and the devolution of powers almost completely absent. Only in Morocco do we find an awareness of the latter problem and even here there has in practice been no effective devolution or delegation to lower levels of the governmental structure as contemplated in the new constitution.[7] There is, however, at least a contemplated structure, which may in time serve as a framework for the provinces and localities sharing some prerogatives and authority with Rabat.

In Morocco too there is in the constitution a rejection on the one-party system. In practice, there has in fact been a multiparty system. In the May 1963 elections under the new constitution the government party, the front for the Defense of Constitutional Institutions—the King's supporters critics would say, the King's men—held a thin majority when combined with a handful of independents. A period of stress ensued with the country's political forces badly divided between the older and more conservative Istiqual Party, the original Moroccan independence movement, and the newer and more radical National Union of Popular Forces (UNFP after its French name), an offshoot of the Istiqual, on the one hand, and between these two opposition parties and the government party, on the other. In July 1963 many of the leftist opposition leaders were implicated in an alleged plot to subvert the government and assassinate the King and have, after trial, been sentenced to prison; others have gone into exile. As is customary in these situations of alleged conspiracies and plots in Africa, those implicated have claimed that the affair itself was a plot by the government trumped up to rid it of an embarrassing opposition, whereas the government and its supporters have retorted by elaborating the nature of the plot, on the one hand, and by demonstrating the government's fairness and restraint, on the other, through conducting trials and commuting death penalties.

The period of stress has persisted, and in June 1965 King Hassan for the second time became his own prime minister. He invoked a constitutional provision vesting him with emergency powers when he declared, as he did in this instance, "a state of exceptional administration." As his own prime minister, the King became in effect the equivalent of the neighboring heads of one-party unitary states, combining the powers of heads of state and government in a highly centralized structure. In his posture, the King relied increasingly on the power and strength of the military. He became increasingly dependent on the head of the military, General Mohammed Oufkir, who was made Minister of the Interior. So dependent in fact that in the shocking Ben Barka affair, the King apparently had no alternative but to support the General, notwithstanding the latter's apparent complicity in the kidnapping in France in October 1965, of Mehdi Ben Barka, the leading opposition leader in exile, now presumed dead.

In Ethiopia there is no mention or contemplation of parties in the constitution, and in fact, there are still, at this writing, no formal parties in the country. Early in 1966, however, the Emperor talked about the evolution of a "constitutional monarchy" and increasing "public participation" in government affairs. The Emperor, who has brought in Yugoslav planners to advance the country's first and second economic development plans and has made Addis Ababa the "capital of Africa" as the situs of the UN Economic Commission for Africa and the Organization of African Unity, has also relied heavily on the military to sustain his power. Ever since the abortive *coup* of December 1960, when elements of the Imperial Guard and national police, under General Newaye, captured control of the capital, only to lose it three days later when the Emperor returned from abroad and took up leadership of the army and air force, the Emperor has kept a tight reign on government affairs with military support.

The Libyan and Burundese situations are somewhere between the

Moroccan multiparty system and the Ethiopian no-party system. Both countries have emergent political parties, which are in essence primarily groupings with leading personalities and supporting factions, rather than organized modern political party situations. This is so even where the formal structure employs party terminology, as the *Union Nationale du Progrès* (UPRONA), the government party in Burundi. Palace politics and tribal connections have tended in both countries to dominate the political scene and the operation of the nascent political institutions, for example, elected parliaments. Thus, the inner core of the UPRONA party is controlled by the palace, and the opposition party of the mass of the population, *le Parti du Peuple,* is a frankly anti-Tutsi republican party of the Hutu people.

MODERNIZING OLIGARCHIES AND NATION-BUILDING

Nation-building in Morocco, Ethiopia, Libya, and Burundi can hardly be said to have begun, particularly in the last three countries. The centralization of power in all instances has inevitably meant the failure, or perhaps even more accurately, the absence of a serious attempt, to weave together in a coherent national pattern the diverse and plural populations inhabiting the geographical areas comprising the respective countries. The channels of political communication and contact can hardly be said to exist. The geographical limitations imposed on nation-building of the type analyzed in Chapter 3 have been reinforced in the case of Africa's monarchical states by the limitations imposed by the structural requirements of a highly centralized oligarchy in the capital city. At worst, the oligarchy is fearful of sharing knowledge, decision-making, authority, and power. At best, it is unable to do so because of the convergence of tradition and custom with the new rationale of the necessity for the concentration of power at the center as a precondition for modernization and development. (This is noted in the discussion of the one-party state structure, and again in the subsequent discussion of the role of the military.)

The Economist caught the quality of the dilemma of change and centralization in a modernizing African oligarchical state in a despatch from a correspondent in Addis Ababa. The correspondent reported:

> In the traditional Ethiopian view power and authority are indivisible. Change can come only from the top. . . . [Emperor] Haile Selassie continues to work for educational reform. Yet, at the age of 73, he appears reluctant to delegate any of the major decisions to ministers, or any of the royal prerogatives to the crown prince. As a result the atmosphere in Addis Ababa tends to be charged with frustration.[8]

Little needs to be added. The state of frustration gave birth to the abortive *coup*, which we have already noted, in December 1960. It has persisted and is likely to as the people continue to be denied participation in public affairs. This is particularly true of the "new men"—the increasing group of young educated public servants, teachers, and professional people. The Emperor, and in all the other monarchial states of Africa, the sovereigns have been unable to fuse the energies of change and development with the centralization and continuity of ruling monarchies to produce public participation, the life blood of building a sense of national identity, national belonging, and national unity. Thus, the report on Ethiopia already cited concludes: "It is only the extraordinary qualities of the Emperor, his far-sightedness, ruthlessness and realisms, that have headed off their [the 'new men's'] successful revolt so long." [9]

Morocco's "socialist King," who assumed executive powers in June 1965 after dismissing the incumbent government and becoming his own prime minister, announced a month later a program of "Moroccan Socialism" involving the nationalization of large sectors of the export sector and of various foreign-owned lands. Here is an interesting example of a modernizing monarch attempting to ride the wave of change and development implicit in nation-building without losing his country in the process by manipulating the strings of power himself. He has hesitated to allow devolution of power and wide-spread public participation.

In the Kingdom of Burundi there is an example of a traditional monarch, in this case reinforced by a radical nationalist party, UPRONA, concentrating power at the center and attempting to weave together vastly different Hutu and Tutsi populations into a single Burundese nationality. The large Hutu majority, long dominated by the Tutsi minority, to which the Monarch belongs, has been increasingly restive since independence. The Burundese king, Mwami Mwambutsa IV, and his party, having combined the centralization of a traditional monarchy dating back to 1558 with that of an African dominant party structure, substituted an uneasy truce of disparate groups for an actual attempt at drawing more and more people into political and economic decision-making and sharing of power. The fragile structure came apart in the aftermath of the ousting in early 1965 of the Communist Chinese Embassy which had become a factor in internal Burundese politics, first supporting and then conspiring against the Tutsi monarch, as he shifted his "non-aligned" foreign policy from *pro-* to *anti*-Communist Chinese.

In October and November 1965, following on an abortive military *coup* in which the Prime Minister, M. Léopold Biha, a Tutsi from the governing UPRONA party, was nearly assassinated in the Hutu-inspired uprising, there was fairly widespread rioting and killing of Tutsi by Hutu in the rural areas. The Tutsi struck back and the total Hutu leadership of the country was arrested, summarily tried, and executed by the military acting on behalf of the monarch.[10] Then during an uneasy calm, the Crown Prince, Charles Ndizeye, with the assistance of the military took over power in a palace *coup* in July 1966.* The King was out of the country and has not attempted to return, although he has denounced the *coup*.

It is also interesting to note the important role assigned in Ethiopia, Morocco, and Burundi to the armed forces as the mainstay of the regimes. The first two maintain, with the exception of the United Arab Republic and South Africa, both outside the frame of reference of this study, along with Algeria, the largest military establishments on the continent. Although there are many historical reasons for this fact, it nevertheless remains a fact consistent with the existence of highly centralized governmental structures, unable and unwilling to distribute and share power and functions.

It is also pertinent to note the additional functions of the military beyond their central mission of national defense. In Morocco the military have been largely responsible for administering the *Promotion Nationale*. This is perhaps the largest "civic action" program in Africa. In Ethiopia the military have been much in evidence as provincial and regional representatives of the Emperor. In Burundi, apparently as a partner in the July 8, 1966, *coup*, the military now share openly in running the government.

Either way, through fear or inability, there is little disposition and even less capacity in Africa's modernizing monarchies to involve large numbers of people in overall shared national experiences, in decision-making, and in coming together in a larger context than those of the traditional tribal, clan, or extended family. There is also little inclination and ability to build from the local base upwards to the national level through responsible local government, democratic community development, multiple local choices in local, district and regional institutions, and through fostering private institutions, such as independent agricultural cooperatives and independent trade unions.

It is apparently extremely hard to shed power, even where there is a will to do so, particularly when there is a strong tide running the other way, engulfing all one's near neighbors. All that seems to be changing, and this is the burden of King Hassan's comment quoted at the head of this chapter, is the form, not the content. Here, perhaps, is a political explanation for the determination of such monarchs as King Hassan, Em-

---

* Prince Charles became King (Mwami Natare V) on September 1, 1966. He was overthrown by a *coup d'état* led by his Premier, Col. Michael Micombero, on November 28, 1966. Micombero proclaimed Burundi a Republic and became its first President. J.H.M.

peror Haile Selassie [11] and King Idris of Libya,* to retain power and at the same time modernize their countries by economic development. In their view, monarchies can lead and develop underdeveloped states in terms of nation-building and economic growth as well as any other type of state structure. In fact, they feel that they provide in the person of the monarch a more legitimate and enduring national symbol, behind which a nation can be rallied and built, than the new authoritarian leaders of one-party states. The Kingdom of Burundi is perhaps too recent an arrival on the African independence scene to discern any clear lines, but it has to date, notwithstanding its radical nationalist orientation, adopted a course not very different in this regard from the other African monarchies. It has attempted to combine a traditional monarchy with the nation-building and economic development tasks of newly independent (or revivified older states as in Ethiopia) so as to retain the centralized monarchy in the context of a modern nation-state. The repeated recourse to force and strategem by the Hutu, the overwhelming majority of the population, in an effort to gain a proportionate voice and influence in government affairs, underscores the failure of the monarchy to draw the Hutu into full participation. Without such participation, it is meaningless to talk of national cohesion and unity. Yet, as with one-party states, the modernizing but highly centralized monarchies, despite outward seeming plebiscitary demonstrations of public support, have not and cannot entice or allow large-scale public participation and still retain their monopoly of power and functions. This is the dilemma and contradiction of the highly centralized state structure approach to nation-building.

* King Idris of Libya was deposed in early September 1969, and replaced by a group of army officers led by Col. Saad ed-Din Bushweirib. King Idris' son, Prince Hassan al-Reda, who supposedly broadcast his "voluntary abdication" and support of the military regime at the outset of the revolt, was reported four days later (Sept. 4) to have been placed under house arrest in Tripoli. J.H.M.

CHAPTER 7

PROBLEM OF STATE STRUCTURE:
THE ROLE OF FEDERALISM

Under this heading ["Federalism Succeeds"] the example offered by the Cameroun [Federal Republic of Cameroon] to Africa is extremely interesting as it is the only African state building a bridge between English-speaking and French-speaking Africa. The Camerounian constitution is supple enough to respond to all possible development. Perhaps one day it will lead to unity, for the present one can say that federalism has entered into the Camerounian vocabulary—as illustrated by the beauty salon in Yaondé which calls itself "La Beauté Fédérale"!

CHARLES DEBBASCH, *1964*

This chapter will be concerned with federalism or decentralized state structures identified in African doctrine and practice with federalism, which, notwithstanding *la beauté fédérale*, are few and far between. For comparative purposes, we touch on such decentralization as occurs in the unitary state context in Africa, such as Sierra Leone, which tends to be infrequent.

As with so much of the current political folklore of African nationalism, the received doctrine on federalism had its origin in the accession of the Gold Coast to independence. Former President Nkrumah has drawn and generalized the lessons of the Gold Coast's "struggle" for independence, and these have now become part of the African radical nationalist "conventional wisdom." Thus, federalism in radical nationalist circles is a dirty word and frequently viewed as a neocolonialist device to keep newly independent African states weak, divided, and vulnerable to a new colonial intrusion. Dr. Nkrumah successfully frustrated a half-hearted British attempt to incorporate a degree of decentralized regionalism into the constitution of the about-to-be-independent Gold Coast, much as President Jomo Kenyatta of Kenya, a longtime friend of Nkrumah, attempted to do, but with less success in the negotiations leading up to Kenya's independence constitution. Soon after independence, however, in both countries the controlling parties pushed through constitutional

86

amendments to nullify the modest federal-type provisions included in their independent constitutions. The mild element of federal structure proposed for the Gold Coast was equated with tribalism, and that in the end doomed it. The same case against the decentralized regional provisions, which were more inclusive than those in the Ghanaian constitution, was made in Kenya, almost down to the last detail, and with the same result.

The Nkrumahist line of reasoning has evolved. The antifederalist view has been grafted on to the balkanization doctrine. The division or balkanization of Africa into its fifty or so geographic compartments, the thesis goes, was the work of the European colonialist during the "scramble for Africa." This arose from European avarice and competition for Africa's wealth; and also from the European desire to keep the individual units weak and thus submissive to European domination.[1] And now that Africa has asserted itself and has been achieving its independence, the irreconcilable and scheming former colonialists are viewed as seeking through constitutional and political devices, such as federalism, and those institutions commonly associated with it, multiparty political systems, local self-government, and entrenched bills of rights, to prevent the development of strong, unified and economically as well as politically independent African states. Thus, federalism is seen as a refined neocolonialist extension of the colonial balkanization practice, designed to enfeeble or split up independent African states.

It is apposite to note at this point that former President Nkrumah has gone so far as to couple the doctrines of antifederalism and balkanization to produce the doctrine of regional balkanization which opposes as divisive *any* African political grouping or union short of his vision of total continental African union in one step. (See Chapter 2.) Thus, although three African states would have been combined into one federal state, he opposed East African Federation, and thereby, in the view of the author, carried his balkanization doctrine and *antifederalism* to *a reductio ad absurdum*. For, in fact, to achieve Nkrumah's own dream of continental union, regional unions are the only conceivable building blocks available in polycentric Africa and federalism is the only known state structure with which to do it, to say nothing of the possibilities of successfully combining into regional units almost any two, three, or more political units once they have achieved independence. One of the principal reasons for the splitting up of the original "union" of Egypt and Syria in the United Arab Republic was the structural inadequacy of this "union," which although ambiguous and somewhat inchoate, was certainly not federal. And this structural ambivalence—seeking "unions" but backing away from federalism—may well prove to be the Achilles heel of the United Republic of Tanzania, the "union" of Tanganyika and

Zanzibar. It may also help to explain why the Union of African States of Ghana, Guinea, and Mali was stillborn. It eschewed federalism, but could never leap from the position of three highly doctrinaire unitary one-party states to that of total merger into a single unitary union.

THE COLONIAL LEGACY

As for federalism itself, divorced from the questionable doctrine of balkanization, is it a neocolonialist instrumentality for keeping Africa weak? It would hardly seem so from the record.

The French with no background in federalism could hardly be said to have foisted off, or attempted to, any sort of federalism on their African colonies. On the contrary, the charge has been made, originally by M. Senghor, but time and again ever since by President Touré of Guinea, and also by many others, that the French deliberately dismantled the two federal structures that they had organized in the two principal French colonial areas in Africa, French West and Equatorial Africa, when France adopted the *loi cadre* in June 1956. The *loi cadre* conferred on the eight territories in French West Africa and the four in French Equatorial Africa a large measure of local autonomy, established executive councils with a majority of elected members (the forerunner of cabinets with ministerial responsibility), broadened the membership and powers of the territorial assemblies and transformed them into legislative assemblies, to be elected by universal franchise, and generally liquidated the "federal" governments by distributing their functions to the territories.

It has been alleged that the purpose of the seemingly liberal grant of powers to the territories was to fragment, to balkanize the larger federal units so that the resulting twelve territorial units, although somewhat more responsible for their own affairs, would be individually less strong, more malleable, and more vulnerable to manipulation by the colonial power. Intentional or not, the process set in motion by the *loi cadre* resulted in twelve governments developing, with twelve sets of parliamentarians and ministers, and with twelve separate national interests vesting in twelve separate national identities. Thus, ten of the twelve achieved independence only four years later as separate nation-states, and two, Senegal and and Soudan, as the ill-fated and short-lived Federation of Mali. Federation has by and large eluded the twelve, notwithstanding many proposals for union and many initiatives in that direction. Former President Nkrumah also, although somewhat less blatantly since the Addis Ababa Conference, has repeatedly stigmatized ten of the twelve francophone states as "stooges" of France, products of the French Machiavellian *loi cadre* which "balkanized" French Africa.

The British, with no experience of federalism at home, in contrast to the French, did give birth to important and varied federal structures in the United States, Canada, Australia, India, and Nigeria. One is tempted to say that these, like many other British constitutional institutions, have just happened. In fact, with the exception of the American constitution, in the preparation of which the British had no role, they are illustrations of the British penchant for cutting the constitutional cloth to fit the political body, pragmatic responses to existing circumstances and realities. Nevertheless, the general British pattern in Africa has been the unitary state, as in the Sudan, Ghana, Sierra Leone, Tanganyika, Zanzibar, Kenya, Malawi, Zambia, and the Gambia. Uganda, a variation on the unitary theme, is *sui generis*. The overall state was until Prime Minister Obote's "preventive *coup*" in early 1966 unitary in conception, but the Kingdom of Buganda had a limited type of "federal relationship" with the central Ugandan government, and three smaller kingdoms, Toro, Ankole, and Bunyoro, had a "semi-federal relationship" with the central government.[2] And as if this were not enough, the Ugandans in building on their British heritage saw fit to make the King of Buganda, the Kabaka Mutesa II, the first President of Uganda as well, under the style of Sir Frederick Mutesa. Certainly, all one could say about this is that it was British-type improvisation at its best, or worst, depending on one's vantage point. There can be no question about its pragmatism.

This fragile and improvised structure was wiped away when Prime Minister Obote seized the reigns of government in early 1966, and suspended the independence constitution. He forced through a rump session of Parliament, in keeping with African nationalist cant, a constitution providing for a unitary structure, and in effect a one-party state. Thus, the quasi-federal or regional decentralization aspects of the Uganda constitution joined those of Ghana and Kenya on the scrap heap of African independence constitutions.

The Federation of Nigeria, which became the Federal Republic of Nigeria, was the one true federal structure left behind in Africa by the United Kingdom, and is therefore the focus of our study later in this chapter. The attempt to impose, as distinct from negotiate and develop in the Nigerian context, a federal structure in Central Africa of the two Rhodesias and Nyasaland, has proved abortive. It split asunder before Nyasaland and Northern Rhodesia achieved independence as the separate States of Malawi [3] and Zambia [4] respectively, in July and October 1964.

The Belgian legacy to Africa has been anything but federalist. The Belgo-Congolese Roundtable Conference of January–February 1960 in Brussels, which reached agreement on Congolese independence and the terms of a provisional constitution, later enacted by the Belgian Parlia-

ment, the *Loi Fondamentale*, did so in part by avoiding a clear-cut decision on the constitutional structure of the new state. A delicately balanced compromise was worked out in an attempt to accommodate the
multiple, federal, confederal, and separatist tendencies already present at
that time in Congolese political thinking. In effect, the *Loi Fondamentale*
deferred a decision on state structure, and bequeathed the problem to the
new, independent Republic of the Congo to resolve. And ever since
being seized of the problem the Congo has been trying to resolve it.
It has been a critical and vital issue in Congolese development.

No less than a half-dozen conferences have been concerned with the
subject and as many constitutional drafts have been produced which have
tried to cope with it. The problems of relations between the center and
the provinces and among the provinces, including the sharing of powers,
functions, resources, revenue, staff, etc., and of the number and provinces,
have been deeply entangled in, and some would say at the heart of, the
endemic secessionist movements with which the Congo has been be-
devilled since birth. It is sufficient for our purpose here to characterize
the problem of the Congo's state structure by quoting briefly M. Moïse
Tshombé, deposed President of Katanga (and subsequently for a time
Prime Minister of the Republic of the Congo), on the subject of federalism. Describing the issues discussed at the conference in the spring
of 1962 between a Katangese government delegation and a central government delegation in Léopoldville (now Kinshasa) on the terms for terminating the Katanga secession, M. Tshombé said:

> The Katanga delegation did not defend merely one province but the
> institutional aspirations of all the provinces, each of which wanted a large
> measure of autonomy within a federal Constitution. These conversations
> in Léopoldville led to the U Thant Plan in the following August. . . . The
> plan, which caused the Katanga Government to renounce what has been
> called the secession, became law when it was accepted by the Katanga
> Government, and the Central Government. . . .[5]

Irrespective of one's appraisal of the role of M. Tshombé and of his
juridical opinions, there can be no question that on the constitutional and
political questions involved in deciding on a state structure for the Congo
he reflected a very widespread view. In fact by early 1963 the Congo
government had altered its structure drastically through a combination
of parliamentary actions and executive decrees. The six provinces in
being on independence day, June 30, 1960, became twenty-two by the
end of 1963,[6] and their autonomy was markedly increased over what it
had been under the colonial regime. Thus *de facto* federalism replaced
the ambiguous, centralized unitary structure with quasi-federal features

bequeathed by the Belgians. The *de facto* federalism gave way subsequently after considerable controversy and wrangling in 1964, under the terms of a new constitution to formal *de jure* federalism.

In Ruanda-Urundi, the UN Trust Territory administered by the Belgians since the end of World War I, the Belgians were unable or unwilling to evolve some sort of federal structures, which might have brought these territories to independence as a single unit. Instead one became independent as the Republic of Rwanda and the other as the Kingdom of Burundi. So bad have been the relations between the two ever since independence that all the connecting links—a common market, a common currency, a shared central bank, joint research institutions, etc. —have been terminated. And from time to time during 1963–65, Burundi provided privileged sanctuary to and served as a base for incursions of Tutsi émigrés into Rwanda, and for good measure as a base for Congolese "National Liberation Committee" émigré raids into Central Kivu Province of the Congo during the 1964–1965 rebellion.

Thus, there is nothing in the Belgian legacy to Africa that adds up to a federal structure. More basically, however, and not in the way implied by Dr. Nkrumah and the African nationalist antifederalists when they argue that federal structures are neocolonialist in design, Belgium has left a legacy which is fertile ground for federalism. And the same may be said, in one degree or another, about all the European colonial powers in Africa. To the extent the colonial powers integrated geographic areas into colonial territories and at the same time failed to integrate the populations of these areas into nations and the separate economies of the areas into complementary and unified structures, then to this extent the objective conditions have been created for constitutional structures responsive to the pluralism that has been built into the territorial agglomerations of Africa. This in the author's judgment means, as we shall see, that in many contexts, particularly in the Congo and the other more diverse geographical units with plural populations, such as Nigeria and probably the Sudan, federal structures are not only the most promising ones for nation-building and economic development, but also inescapable if these large states are to have a hope of holding together as national units.

We now turn to a brief consideration of the colonial legacy in a key area for nation-building, local government, from the dual perspective of federal and unitary structures.

The Colonial Legacy: Local Government

It must be recognized that at least in principle decentralization is possible in a unitary state context as well as in a federal one, and does exist in unitary structures in various parts of the world. The United Kingdom is perhaps as good an example as is to be found. In Africa, however, the examples of decentralized government and administration in a unitary state framework are hard to come by. And the reasons for this are clear enough.

For the most part states with strong local governments and decentralized administrations have a heritage of the consolidation of political power at many governmental levels before achieving consolidation at the national level. In the words of a leading British Africanist:

> Africans are attempting almost the exact reverse of our British experience. First we had a coagulation of our separate tribes and kingdoms. Then some centuries of development of central government. . . . Africans have taken over this end product before any of its necessary antecedents have been achieved.[7]

States with decentralized governments and administrations also frequently have a heritage of "town hall" democracy or something akin to it, which antedates the growth of and provides the underlying base for public participation in central institutions and power. For De Tocqueville the secret and strength of American democracy flows from this fact. Writing his classic study in the early 1830's, De Tocqueville started with "the necessity of examining the conditions of the states before that of the union at large." He observed:

> The form of the Federal government of the United States was the last to be adopted; and it is in fact nothing more than a summary of those republican principles which were current in the whole community before it existed, and independently of its existence.
> . . . The great political principles which now govern American society undoubtedly took their origin and their growth in the state. Their political or administrative life is centered in three focuses of action, which may be compared to the different nervous centers that give motion to the human body. The township is the first in order, then the country, and lastly the state.[8]

De Tocqueville then proceeded to an examination of the American township and concluded:

> . . . Municipal institutions constitute the strength of free nations. Town meetings are to liberty what primary schools are to science; they bring it within the people's reach, they teach men how to use it and to enjoy it. A nation may establish a free government, but without municipal institutions it cannot have the spirit of liberty. Transient passions, the interests of an hour, or the chance of circumstances may create the external forms of independence, but the despotic tendency which has been driven into

the interior of the social system will sooner or later reappear on the surface.[9]

Over 130 years ago De Tocqueville thus perceived and laid down some basic political principles, many of which in the author's view remain equally valid today, and also apposite to Africa today. The absence of viable and modern local government institutions throughout the larger part of Africa is perhaps the single most important gap in building stable states, cohesive nations, and flourishing economies. In the absence of such institutions, public participation is severely circumscribed and public opinion has no outlet. This in turn means that the central task of nation-building and economic development, the drawing-in of more and more people into the modern political and economic sector from the stagnant traditional subsistence sector, and developing a sense of national consciousness and identity, will be frustrated. The chasm between no participation in modern sector activity to full participation at the national level with no bridges or ladders to help span the gap is too great. The result can only be nominal, empty, and *pro forma* participation, and not the free and willing participation that successful nation-building demands.

The nature of the colonial relationship militated all too long against the evolution of independent sources of power in a multiplicity of areas. The control function—maintenance of "law and order"—of the colonial administration did not allow much room for the growth of genuinely independent and open sources of local power and free expression. Such growth would have complicated the task of a handful of colonial administrators in vast and frequently difficult geographic areas.

Thus, on the one hand, the status, power, and authority of traditional rulers and institutions where they existed were almost uniformly denigrated, if not destroyed, by the colonial authorities in much of Africa. In a particularly frank and thoughtful book, M. Delavignette, a long-time French colonial administrator in Africa, records the crucial, overwhelming importance of the colonial power's *Cercle* and its *Commandant* in French colonial administration, to wit:

> . . . The territorial colonial administration is charged with introducing a new political and economic régime into the country; it is concentrated in the hands of a few Europeans who can only communicate through intermediaries with the masses they govern, and from whom they are separated by ways of life, forms of thought and method of work. How could this administration be anything but revolutionary and authoritarian? To contest this is to be afraid of words and hypocritically to leave the way open for a parade-ground militarism, a caricature of military command. On the contrary, in order to humanize this authority, it is necessary to bring it into the light and entrust it to responsible people. There

is an inner principle proper to territorial colonial administration: the personal authority of the administrator and, in final analysis, his personal character expressed in the exercise of authority.[10]

And on the other hand, where the colonial authorities embraced traditional authorities and retained the façade of their office and perpetuated the traditional institutions, at least in their outward manifestations, they succeeded for the most part only in compromising the integrity of these rulers and institutions so that the new nationalists, as soon as they acceded to power, undertook to complete the job and do what the colonial authorities left undone, the liquidation of the remaining traditional centers of power. There are, of course, here and there important exceptions to this general sweep. The British practice of "indirect rule" initiated by Lord Lugard [11] in Northern Nigeria has resulted in the preservation of the status and power of the traditional rulers in much of the Northern Region, and the British protectorate over Buganda in Uganda has had until recently much the same effect with respect to the status and power of Kabaka of Buganda. In the words of one of the United Kingdom's distinguished colonial administrators, Sir Andrew Cohen, former Governor-General of Uganda:

> Indirect rule, governing in local affairs through the customary institutions of the people in the area, fits into the general British conception of relying on local institutions rather than a centralized bureaucracy.[12]

But these legacies of indirect rule are islands of tradition and stability in a churning sea of centralizing forces, which has by and large not yet found its limits or organized its ebb and flow. It remains to be seen whether any of these Native Authorities, as they have frequently been called by the British, can or will survive outside a congenial federal structure. As we have already noted in this chapter, all decentralized or quasi-federal features grafted onto the unitary states of Ghana, Kenya, and Uganda, have already disappeared, within a few years of their achievement of independence. The centralizing drive of African unitary states, aided and abetted by the one-party state structure mentality, are not able or willing to sustain local and regional government institutions, or in power terms, independent bases of political or economic power at local or regional levels. It has also certainly been the judgment, as we shall see later in this chapter, of the Sardauna of Sokoto, that for the survival of local and regional power and initiative in Northern Nigeria federalism was essential.

The modernizing oligarchy of Northern Nigeria, it should also be noted, has been confronted with many of the problems and issues already discussed in Chapter 6 with respect to Morocco and Ethiopia. On a lesser scale the Kingdom of Buganda has also had much the same experience. Ironically, because these areas and others like them have a kind of continuity and stability, they have come to be viewed as backward, conservative, traditional—as obstacles to change and progress—by the state-builders and nation-builders leading most of the new states. And in a sense they are resistant to change; but in another sense, they provide some of the little structure and shape, some of the few established links between otherwise disparate and unrelated peoples, some of the few supporting walls available to hold things together, while new ones are being designed and put in place. One of the crucial questions, all too frequently ignored, for modernizing societies is how to retain a balance, a juxtaposition of the old and the new, so that a discontinuity is not created between what is in process of being destroyed and what has not as yet come into being to take its place. For, it is this prolonged interregnum now confronting so many of the nascent African states that makes their tasks so intractable.

Once again, to return to our principal point, the importance of local government institutions, the words of Sir Andrew Cohen are apposite:

> In areas where there was a firm traditional foundation to build on, indirect rule served the territories well. Because it functioned through machinery broadly familiar to them, it was a good means of contact between the people and the Government. . . . Indirect rule, moreover, laid the foundation of local government and sometimes more than the foundation.[13]

But the exceptions aside, by and large, local rulers and institutions fell prey to colonial practice, and the new ones that have been introduced have seldom taken root. In most instances they came too late to survive the central, and centralizing institutions created by all the colonial powers, including those practicising "indirect rule," which the new nationalists have fallen heir to and now exercise with even more determination, buttressed as they frequently are by the centralizing tendencies implicit in one-party structures. This is why, as the author views it, unitary structures with inherited, semideveloped, local institutions and administrations are not likely to tolerate them for long as genuinely independent foci of power, in contradistinction to and as a counterbalance to power at the center. For the most part centralization of power has meant a concentration of governmental and party power at headquarters in the capital city. The pattern in Ghana and Guinea has been for the central government to preserve the shell and remove the authority and power of all independent sources of power and authority through use of government machinery or through party takeovers. In Tanzania, and more recently in Malawi, the one-party has in many places openly supplanted local government. In Upper Volta, Niger, Chad, and the Central African Republic, among others, little or nothing has been done to create local government and institutions where none exist, and this has generally been the pattern—little interest in, and perhaps even less ability for building local institutions.

There has been little motivation for unitary states with one-party structures or dominant-party structures to seek new problems in the form of local pools of interest and power. And, as always in the African unitary one-party states, the problem of limited competence and capacity to stimulate and mobilize local initiatives arises in this connection as in all state, nation, and economy-building tasks.

Only in the rare instances in Africa of a unitary multiparty structure, such as in Sierra Leone, does one find a situation where local government and institutions have been tolerated, but where the colonial legacy in this regard has not been particularly different from that common in most of British Africa. (Sierra Leone had its share of indirect rule but did not start with the strong traditional local government units to be found in the emirates of Northern Nigeria.) It is difficult in the absence of existing institutions and in the circumstances of underdevelopment to see how a sufficient number of sufficiently strong local institutions can evolve *before* the processes of centralization at work in all unitary states take hold so firmly that the opportunity for creating such local institutions has been lost. In any event, there is nothing in the unitary structure that can be viewed as a built-in regulator of the trend toward centralization comparable to that which exists in federal structures. Thus, we note that increasingly the government party in Sierra Leone, the Sierra Leone People's Party, has used its position at the center to interfere in the operation of the Freetown City Council, which for a time was in control of the opposition political party, the All People's Congress. Under the control of the SLPP, the City Council has lost much of its role as an independent local government for the nation's capital city. Public participation has declined and cynicism about the effectiveness of such participation has grown. Public opinion has become *sub rosa* or inchoate. The Council no longer serves as an outlet or meeting place.

It is not accidental that the decline of the City Council in Freetown as an independent local government has coincided with the drive of Sir Albert Margai, Prime Minister of Sierra Leone, to transform his multiparty and relatively decentralized unitary state into a one-party state.*

---

* The same drive on the part of Sir Albert Margai to create a one-party state led ultimately to his downfall. Entering the March 17, 1967, election in the wake of widespread criticism, Sir Albert's People's Party lost by a slight margin to the All People's Congress led by Siaka Stevens. Stevens was ousted by an army-led *coup d'état* a few minutes after being sworn in as Prime Minister on March 21, 1967. A year and one month later (April 18, 1968), the eight-man National Reformation Council headed by Lt. Col. Andrew Juxon-Smith was deposed by a *coup* led by non-

They are part and parcel of the centralizing authoritarian approach to nation-building.

Two Case Studies

In light of our discussion of nationalist doctrine and colonial legacy in the field of federalism, we now turn to case studies, the Cameroonian and Nigerian, which illustrate very different types of federal structures. The first case is one of a postindependence federation, involving former British and French territories, with a strong bias toward the development of a one-party state. Are they compatible—a federal structure and a one-party state? The second is one of a preindependence federation, involving vastly different regions, but all of them former British areas, in a state of crisis growing out of regional and tribal conflicts reflected in conflicting attitudes toward continuation of the federal structure or transforming it into a unitary one. The examples are revealing of the role that federalism can play in nation-building in varying circumstances.

"La Beauté Fédérale": The Cameroonian Case

Federal-state structures are as we have already noted the exception rather than the rule in Africa. Nevertheless, in many ways the future of Africa is tied up with federalism. If ever there is to be a combination, association, or grouping of African states involving organic political union, then federalism seems the only feasible structure available. It is precisely for this reason that the experience of the Federal Republic of Cameroon has important implications for Pan-Africanist designs.

Although too soon to assess the probable success of the Cameroonian federation, it seems quite clear already that any other structure would have been out of the question. A centralized unitary state structure would have created an appearance of unity that would have belied the actual situation. As the opening quotation to this chapter states: "The Cameroonian constitution is supple enough to respond to all possible development. Perhaps one day it will lead to unity, for the present one can say that federalism has entered the Cameroonian vocabulary. . . ."[14] If President Ahidjo succeeds in his program to transform the Federal Republic into a one-party state, as we suggested in Chapter 4 he was well on the way to doing, then we believe the federal structure too will yield to a unitary one, with unfortunate consequences for national unity.

These are the crucial characteristics of a federal structure: flexibility,

commissioned army officers. One week later Stevens was again sworn in as Prime Minister, and this time he formed a cabinet of civilians. Sir Albert Margai had long since sought the safer climate of London. J.H.M.

accommodation, responsiveness, adaptation, pluralism, and inventiveness. All these characteristics are urgently required to make a going concern out of the Cameroonian federation, to build simultaneously "national" cohesion within each of the two regions and national unity between the two regions. One of the constraints—and it is real, important, and too often ignored by Pan-Africanists—on building political unions, federal or otherwise, in Africa is the superimposition of a new and formidable nation-building task in the larger unit—forging cohesion between the separate "national" populations of the component parts—on the already existing and difficult nation-building task of developing "national" cohesion of the disparate population groups *within* the separate component parts. It is this dual nation-building task that renders the prospects for success of so many projects for African political unions so very doubtful. Before "unity" has been achieved in any of the parts, or states of the union, they are to be combined, and the task of achieving unity not only has to confront a larger terrain and a broader canvas, but also the complications, frequently unpredictable, which evolve from the amalgam of nation-building problems at two distinctly different levels.

Thus, the problems of nation-building in the former Republic of Cameroon, the former French-administered UN Trust Territory, have been commingled with those of the former Southern Cameroons, part of the former British-administered UN Trust Territory, in the framework of the Federal Republic of Cameroon. Can there be any doubt that fostering bonds, forging unity, and founding a concept of Cameroon nationality among the total population as well as in the separate units of the enlarged geographic area has not been rendered all the more difficult by the combination of tribal groupings, with differing French and British cultural, social, juridical, administrative, philosophical, economic, and political legacies inevitably accompanying the respective peoples of the two units into the larger federation?

And a comparable set of questions may be asked about economy-building in the Federal Republic of Cameroon. Have the two units developed economies in their respective areas that are complementary? Are their economies sufficiently cohesive and evolved so that they will add strength to one another and reinforce one another? Will the nation-building task, multiplied as it is by federation, weigh heavily on the economy? Will the economy of the stronger unit suffer as a result of spreading its strength over the weaker unit? [15] Will the economy of the weaker unit really benefit at the cost of the economy of the stronger one [16] or will the total effect be a little bit like spreading the butter so thin that it loses all its flavor? Finally, will the stronger unit benefit at the expense of the weaker one? [17]

Answers to all these questions await the unfolding of the Cameroonian experience. However, the very act of formulating and posing the questions suggests the author's concern over the easy assumption that somehow Africa's problems can be disposed of by the simple process of putting together more and more units under one political roof. The Cameroonian experiment may prove out, but so many of the proposals so lightly thrown about for African political unions, up to and including Dr. Nkrumah's continental union, have been launched without serious analysis and assessment of the problems involved and the probable impact of union on them, and as a consequence their prospects for success have been badly compromised, and in the process the possible benefit to the component units severely circumscribed.

Unconscious and unthinking acceptance of the doctrine of the automatic benefit of bigness can and already has led to premature and unsound unions in Africa, with the sad repercussions alluded to in the discussion of the Federation of Mali in Chapter 3. In the economic field, as suggested in footnotes 15, 16 and 17 of this chapter, the results have not been entirely happy either for the poor member(s) of a union, as is generally assumed will automatically be the case, or always a bed of roses for the wealthy member. Thus Tanganyika (now Tanzania), the poor unit in the East African common market area, has come out considerably less well than Kenya, the wealthy member, and Northern Rhodesia, the wealthy member in the Central African Federation, has come out less well than Southern Rhodesia, which although not poor in the same sense as the other member of the federation, Nyasaland (now Malawi), was, it did not have the mineral wealth of Northern Rhodesia. In short, Tanganyika subsidized Kenyan industrial development at the expense of its own development, and Northern Rhodesia subsidized Southern Rhodesian industrial development at the expense of its own development.

The point being made here is not that all federations or common markets have to have the results experienced in Tanganyika or Northern Rhodesia, but that bigness, federations, and customs unions *per se* are not necessarily and *ipso facto* the panacea that so many Africans and their foreign advisers seem to think they are. They can be, but experience, in Africa at any rate, suggests that they have to be analyzed, planned, structured, and carried through with far more caution and skill than has yet been evidenced.[18] We return to a consideration of economic factors in nation-building in Chapter 10.

"UNITY IN DIVERSITY AND DIVERSITY IN UNITY": THE NIGERIAN CASE

In so many ways Nigeria has been a unique state in Africa.[19] This has of course been implicit in much that has already been written in this book, and will become explicit in much that will follow. This has also been the judgment of many leading Africans with respect to Nigeria's structure and system and the interplay of the two. For example, and particularly pertinent to our discussion, is the following report from Lagos on the Nigerian radio on a recent state visit of President Léopold Sédar Senghor of Senegal:

> Senegalese President Senghor . . . strongly appealed to Nigerians to maintain the unity of their country, not only in their own interest or that of Africa but also for world peace. The Senegalese President added that African unity is the cornerstone of African development, and Nigeria, he declared, has a great role to play, mainly as an ideal constructor of African unity. That is why Nigerians must not allow the federation to disintegrate.
>
> Dr. Senghor then recalled his visit to Nigeria in 1961 and said that between then and now [1964] he has been deeply impressed with the country's development within the framework of African unity. This, he said, is the ideal he had dreamed of for French-speaking West Africa, but he observed that where he had failed Nigeria had succeeded.
>
> . . . African unity, President Senghor said, is the challenge of the industrial world. It is therefore necessary he went on, that the Nigerian Federation should endure as an amazing and exciting example of what Africans with many cultures could be.[20]

President Senghor, in singling out Nigeria, linked state structure, nation-building, and economic development. What are the ingredients of the Nigerian story that evoke such admiration from one of French-speaking Africa's most distinguished spokesmen, and one who had such a disillusioning experience first with the dissolution of French West Africa under the loi cadre and then when he took the independent state of Senegal out of the Federation of Mali?

Significantly, Nigeria has been the only state in Africa to date to come to independence as a single unit with a fully operating federal system, opted for by the democratically-elected political leadership of the country and successfully negotiated for by them with the colonial power before independence. The structure was not determined by the United Nations [21] or imposed by the colonial power [22] or negotiated among independent or near-independent states.[23] It was the considered decision of the leadership of three regions administered by the United Kingdom collectively as Nigeria. The leadership of each region decided, after weighing the merits of the case, to adopt federalism as the only principle under which independence could be achieved by Nigeria as a single political entity. The likelihood is that Nigeria would not have come into existence within its present boundaries (its former colonial boundaries) if agreement had not been reached on a federal structure. Two or more states would probably have emerged and the timing of their independence would possibly have been delayed, at least for one of the new states.

Chief Obafemi Awolowo, one of the early Nigerian nationalist leaders from the Western Region, former Premier of the Western Region, former leader of the Opposition in the Federal Parliament, and leader of the Action Group, was also one of the early advocates of federalism for Nigeria. In his autobiography "Awo" he devotes two chapters to the subject, the "Evolution of a Federalist." [24] According to Chief Awolowo, "Until 1951, when the Action Group proclaimed its slogan of Unity through Federation, the question as to what type of constitution Nigeria should have was not at all an issue in the country's politics." [25] Chief Awolowo also approved of the federalist beliefs of Dr. Nnandi Azikiwe, an even earlier nationalist leader from the Eastern Region, former Premier of the Eastern Region, former leader of the National Council of Nigeria and the Cameroons, former President of the Nigerian Senate, first and only Nigerian Governor-General of the Federation of Nigeria, and former President of the Federal Republic of Nigeria. Chief Awolowo had this to say in his autobiography on Dr. Nnandi Azikiwe: "At our first joint meeting [between the leadership of the Action Group and the NCNC in March 1953] we took up the question of federalism. It did not take us any time to persuade Dr. Azikiwe. It must be said to his credit that he is himself a believer in federalism." [26]

"Zik," as Dr. Azikiwe has long been called, deferred to nobody in his dedication to federalism, not even his contemporary, "Awo," who as we have seen, accorded "Zik" the accolade of "believer in federalism." This is what Dr. Azikiwe has written in his collection of speeches entitled Zik of the London Conference on the revision of the Macpherson Constitution during the summer of 1953:

> Our second major proposal was that the form of government in Nigeria should be federal with the residuary powers in the Regions. We based our argument on the ground that such form of government would preserve our unity and guarantee common nationality in view of the large area of the country and its heterogeneous population factors which make federalism imperative.[27]

Dr. Azikiwe then went on to say: "Our third major proposal was that parliamentary democracy should be practiced in Nigeria." [28]

This connection between the two, federal structure and democratic political system, has been a recurrent theme in Nigerian political thinking, and has even appeared to be inevitable, a point which has long struck the author as one of distinctive aspects of Nigerian political thought and

practice, and one of the factors that goes far in explaining why and how
Nigeria remained for so long an island of relative democracy in a surrounding sea of authoritarianism. Thus Dr. Azikiwe has said:

> To put it in classic phraseology, we can achieve what the Greek philoso-
> pher, Heraclitus, described as "unity in diversity and diversity in unity." [29]

Finally, to make it unanimous, we turn to the third of the "big three"
in Nigerian politics and constitution-making in the critical preindependence period. The late Alhaji Sir Ahmadu Bello, Sardauna of Sokoto, and
former Premier of the Northern Region, in his autobiography has made
it clear that only federalism permitted Nigeria to achieve independence
as a unit. This is what he had to say about the position of the Northern
People's Congress at the crucial London Conference of 1956 on the Nigerian Constitution:

> The first and most important point was to clear up the relations between
> the Central Government and the Regions. The British Government had
> already said it would agree to changes. . . .
> It was agreed that the Regions should be as independent as possible,
> and there was a long argument as to whether specific functions should be
> allotted to the Centre or the Regions.[30]

And in the concluding chapter of his autobiography the Sardauna sums
up his view (and it was, and in light of subsequent developments remains,
a key one in Nigerian political life) on federalism in these words:

> That is why we are so keen on our Regional self-government. This is
> the only guarantee that the country will progress evenly all over, for *we*
> can spend the money we receive, and the money we raise, in the directions
> best suited to us. To show what I mean, you have only to consider the
> former backwardness of our educational and medical provisions, compared
> with that of areas near Lagos. As I have suggested elsewhere, if it had
> not been for the Native Authorities the North would have been left com-
> pletely standing in these and other important developments.[31]

Thus the Sardauna made the connection between the two, federal structure and economic development, which like the link between federal structure and a democratic political system, has been a recurrent and insistent
thought in Nigerian political thinking, and an important background factor to be borne in mind when considering, as we subsequently shall, the
Nigerian experience with economic growth.

The perceived theoretical rationale underlying the choice of federation
before independence continues to exist and appears, if anything, to have

gained strength with practice and the passage of time. It is this rationale, the specifics of which we now turn to, which makes federalism the *sine qua non* for Nigeria's existence as a single country.

First, the three regions (which became four when the Mid-West Region was founded in the area of the Western Region) recognized their cultural, social, religious, ethnic, linguistic, political and economic differences. Only a structure that faced up to this pluralism could, as the Nigerians are wont to say, achieve "unity amidst diversity." In the words of Chief Awolowo:

> A unitary constitution with only one central government would only result in frustration to the more pushful and more dynamic ethnic groups, whereas the division of the country into regions along ethnic lines would enable each linguistic group not only to develop its own peculiar culture and institutions, but to move forward at its own pace. . . .[32]

Second, the three regions recognized their economic complementarity. The landlocked Northern Region needs the ports of Apapa and Port Harcourt in the Western and Eastern Regions respectively to evacuate its exports and receive its imports. The Niger and Benue Rivers, the railroad, the road system, and the air network all tended to emphasize the interlocking nature of the transportation grid of the country. The value of the economic diversity achieved by putting together the Western Region's (including the newest Mid-West Region) cocoa, palm kernels, rubber, and tropical hardwoods, the Northern Region's groundnuts, cattle, cotton, and tin, and the Eastern Region's palm oil and kernels, foodstuffs, and coal, was already demonstrated during the colonial period. This complementarity of resources has been reinforced since independence by the increasing commercial production of crude and refined oil in the Eastern Region, and the associated discovery of natural gas, and the discovery of additional oil and natural gas deposits in that part of the Western Region which became part of the new Mid-West Region. Similarly, the importance of the large market constituted by a single political unit with a population then estimated at between 35 and 40 million people (and since the 1963 census said to be over 55 million),[33] in providing a base for industrial development and in attracting foreign private investment was not lost on the Nigerian leadership. The postindependence experience, although still not conclusive, suggests that this judgment remains valid.

Third, the desire to play a major role in African affairs and beyond had its attraction too for many of the Nigerian leaders, and size, population, and wealth would all obviously be relevant factors in making such a role possible. Nigeria's role in African affairs, as we have already noted, has been a major one, starting with the Monrovia Conference of May 1961, which led up to the Addis Ababa Conference of May 1963. The triumph of the Nigerian position was in calling for economic, cultural, scientific, social, and political cooperation among African states in contradistinction to the Pan-African position of immediate political union, without forging all of the links Nigeria believes essential before even considering political union.

Finally, and by no means last in importance, a series of unifying factors, carrying over from the colonial period in various degrees in all three regions—common language, university education, concepts and practices of modern jurisprudence, including the fundamental concept of the Rule of Law, a common system of administration, a common currency, an expanding market system, a uniform system of weights and measures, a telecommunications system, and one could go on—have all tended to tie together the three regions collectively constituted as Nigeria by the colonial power. Thus for years Ibos from the Eastern Region with their considerable mobility have helped staff the public service of the Northern Region (although this practice has increasingly been discouraged by the Northern Region policy of "Northernization"), and the even more mobile Hausa traders from the Northern Region have carried their wares far and wide throughout the Western and Eastern Regions. And the federal capital of Lagos, formerly part of the Western Region, has become a microcosm of the ethnic composition of the country—with large populations of Western Region Yorubas, Eastern Region Ibos, and Northern Region Hausas, and with smaller populations from many of the other Nigerian tribes.

The Nigerian federal structure was thus built on a solid foundation of shared common interests, traditions, and experience. The years of independence since October 1960, including the launching of Nigeria's first postindependence economic development plan,[34] have if anything deepened and broadened the common interests, enhanced the common traditions and enlarged the common experience. This does not mean that there have not been problems.

On the contrary, there have been serious problems, but—and this seems to be the important thing—until the military *coup* of January 1966 they were handled constitutionally within the existing federal framework. For example, although economic planning and development as such were within the scope of power of both the Regions for regional matters, and the Federal Government for federal functions and the federal territory of Lagos, the Federal Government was able with the cooperation of the Regions to develop a National Framework for Development within which first the four and then the five development plans of the Regions and the Federal Government were for the first time correlated. Similarly, national machinery for consultation and coordination of the development plans and other economic policy was established in the National Economic Council, in which all four regional governments as well as the federal government participated. In the same vein, although agriculture and primary and secondary education were regional functions, through a system of federal grants and grants-in-aid the Federal Government was able to play an increasingly important role.[35]

In a different vein, but of striking importance, a fourth region was carved out of the Western Region in accordance with existing constitutional provisions and procedures involving a complicated series of steps to safeguard all concerned against the capricious establishment of new regions. The new region—the Midwest Region—came into being and its regional government was elected. Also, as the result of the political agreement of the leadership of all of the regions, the relevant constitutional provisions were invoked and Nigeria, which was a dominion in the Commonwealth with Queen Elizabeth of the United Kingdom also Queen of Nigeria, was transformed into a republic, with Dr. Azikiwe as the country's first president.

The ability of the Federation of Nigeria to evolve institutions and techniques on the one hand, and to undergo basic constitutional development on the other, of such fundamental importance as those just alluded to, suggested that the Nigerians had found the way to adapt their complicated federal structure to their needs and make their federation responsive to the imperatives of their political and economic development. (As we have noted in the opening quotation of this chapter, the distinctive quality claimed for the constitution of the Federal Republic of Cameroon is that it too "is supple enough to respond to all possible development.") Thus, for Nigeria, as with other cases of successfully operating federal states— such as the United States, Canada and Australia—federalism has served as a congenial and congruent context for the evolution of a plural society and operation of a democratic political system (discussed in the next two chapters). It is for this reason that we expressed serious doubt earlier in this chapter and in Chapter 4 about the compatibility of a federal structure with a one-party political system, which President Ahidjo apparently intends to establish in the Federal Republic of Cameroon. Federation tolerates difference, whereas one-party systems abhor it.

Notwithstanding this seeming ability of Nigerians to adapt their federal structure to their evolving needs and to undergo basic constitutional changes peacefully, something has gone radically wrong. The Nigerian capacity to go to the brink time and again over the five years between independence and the military *coup* of January 1966 with its political crises, but at the last possible minute to pull back, to compromise differences and find a political solution within the constitutional framework, faltered in late 1965 in the crisis over the Western Region elections and then failed with the military *coups d'état* of January and July 1966 (discussed in Chapter 5), which carried Nigeria over the brink.

What happened? Did federalism fail? Or is it a case of underlying divisive regional and tribal factors proving too strong for the particular Nigerian federal structure? Would any other nonfederal structure, such as the typical one-party unitary structure, have done any better? What responsibility for the failure attaches to the actions and policies of those who wanted to replace the federal structure with a unitary one, and precipitated a confrontation between federalist and unitary forces in the national election campaign of 1964? What responsibility attaches to the actions and policies of those who attempted to manipulate the structure for regional and partisan purposes?

We can only begin to sketch in an answer on the major points that affect any judgment about the role of federalism in African nation-building. For the rest, it would take us on an exploration far beyond the scope of this book.

The two *coups*, rather than diminishing the case for a federal structure in Nigeria, have served to emphasize the fundamentally federal and plural character of Nigerian society. Thus, the *coup d'état* of January 15, which overthrew the then existing federal structure of Nigeria, did not alter the basic imperatives of Nigerian life which make inevitable a type of decentralized governmental structure responsive to the country's size, diversity, and pluralism. Almost inevitably this means a type of federal structure; the crucial question seems to be not whether to adopt a federal or unitary structure of government but rather, assuming Nigeria remains a single state, how to distribute power and functions within a federal structure to achieve a balance between the realities of Nigerian pluralism and regionalism, on the one hand, and the necessities of central policy-making and direction, on the other.

Obviously, the last time out the Nigerian constitution vested too many powers and too much authority in the then Regional Governments, and too few powers and too little authority in the then Federal Government. For example, the power of the Federal Government over the principal sector of the Nigerian economy, the agricultural sector, was severely circumscribed, in effect largely confined to research. However, as we have noted, in practice through the use of federal funds, this role was enlarged. A Ministry of Agriculture at the federal level was apparently not contemplated at the time the constitution of the federation was adopted, and was only established a short time before the overthrow of the government, and then only in blueprint form.

In addition to an unbalanced distribution of powers between the Federal and Regional Governments, the compromise which permitted Nigeria to emerge as a single state, unfortunately for the future of the federal

structure, contained another serious imbalance, the entirely disproportionate size (and related power) of the Regions. The south was divided
into two relatively small regions, the Eastern and Western Regions, and
the north, overshadowing the two southern regions in size, population,
and representation in the national legislature, emerged as a single region
which could by itself dominate the federal structure. Unfortunately too,
the state of development of the Northern Region was in many ways—
economically, politically and educationally—less advanced than that of
the two smaller southern regions, which it could in theory, and, in large
part, did in fact, dominate at the federal level. Thus, not only were the
regions too strong *vis-à-vis* the center, but one region was able to dominate the Federal Government and, through this domination, to exercise
significant pressure and influence in the other regions.

In addition to the foregoing two significant structural flaws—imbalance
in the distribution of powers between the center and the regions and
disproportionate concentration of power in one of the then three regions
—there was an unfortunate psychological miscalculation built into the
federal constitution. It was unfortunate, indeed, to designate the heads
of the Regional Governments as premiers and the heads of regional departments as ministers. If the Regional Governments needed any additional incentive to act as independent entities, and their leaders to act as
heads of independent governments, the ill-advised selection of terminology certainly provided the added push. Thus, when regional premiers
traveled abroad they behaved like, and expected to be received as, heads
of government. The Sardauna of Sokoto, the late Premier of the Northern Region, in effect carried on an independent foreign policy with the
Islamic States of the Near East. He did not "recognize" Israel although
the Federal Government not only recognized Israel but also had important foreign aid arrangements with it.

The interesting and in a way remarkable thing about Nigeria's first five
years of independence is how close the Nigerians came to making their
unbalanced federal structure work. A lack of patience in the southern
regions with the pace at which national institutions were evolving, particularly the pace at which the Northern Region was becoming effectively integrated into the national state structure; unfortunate political
dissension and violence in the Western Region deriving from crude attempts to manipulate the governmental structure of the Region on behalf
of one faction, which was allied with the Northern power structure;
unwillingness on the part of the Northern Region leadership to share its
power more rapidly with the southern regions; and an unfortunate
amount of personal aggrandizement on the part of political leaders in all
of the regions and at the center—all combined to bring the Federal Government to the brink of disaster late in 1965. On other occasions, most

noticeably during the initial phase of the political crisis in the Western Region in 1962–63, the general strike of June 1964, and the federal election crises of December 1964–January 1965, the Nigerian capacity for ordering their own affairs through negotiation, compromise, and basic awareness of the overriding advantages to all sections of the country of remaining a single state prevailed. In January 1966, however, months of violent disorder in the Western Region relating to and resulting from the highly manipulated regional election in October 1965, created a crisis situation to which the Federal Government was unable or unwilling to respond. Nigeria went over the brink. A group of young army officers resolved the crisis by overthrowing the government, and in the process created a new crisis, an ongoing one, and one which may in the end turn out to be more critical than the one that was resolved. In fact, so critical that the patient may not survive as a single unit but fragment or "balkanize." For now the issue is not only how to rearrange the distribution of power and functions in a federal structure, but how to attain a new constitutional balance during a period of military rule in such a way that there will be a peaceful and orderly transition from what all believe to be a temporary interval of military government to a successor civil regime.

The first bitter fruit of the processes set in motion by the January *coup* was the decree of the National Military Government of May 24, which purported to abolish the Federal Government and establish in its place a unitary government with a single national public administration. The decree tended to consolidate the view that the federal constitution was the villain of the piece—the cause of Nigeria's political difficulties—and tended to deny what the dispossessed politicians understood and subsequent events have in fact borne out: "regional suspicions, jealousies and antagonisms" were and are the root of the trouble.[36] The decree in question was rapidly followed by two violent week ends of riots in various parts of the Northern Regions, particularly in the capital city of Kaduna and the principal cities of Kano and Zaria. The riots were directed generally against southerners, but particularly against the Ibos from the Eastern Region resident in the North. The National Military Government acknowledged a death toll of ninety-two in the riots. Unofficial observers place the toll considerable higher.[37] There has also been a substantial exodus of Ibos from the Northern Region back to the Eastern Region.[38] As a consequence of the outbreaks, in response to the demands of the traditional rulers in the Northern Region, who convened and presented a petition to the Military Governor of the North, the National Military Government backed away significantly from the implications of its May 24th decree. In its response to the petition of the Northern Emirs, the National Military Government explained that all changes in government structure which it introduced were temporary and only intended to reflect the necessities and actualities of military government; that nothing it had done or would do would prejudice the outcome of the deliberations of the Constitutional Commission drafting a new constitution for the country; and that any new constitution would be adopted only after a national referendum. Given the North's official population, assuming the vote was extended to women, a referendum would insure that the North's interest in retaining a federal structure with considerable regional autonomy would be safeguarded.

In addition, the original decree was interpreted so that the various regional public administrations and the central public administration would be consolidated only at the highest levels of the civil service. And in practice even this limited unification of civil services was not carried through. Thus, officially and publicly, the national military government recognized the reality and existence of "regional suspicions, jealousies and antagonisms."

The *coup* of July 29th was the second harvest of bitter fruit from the January *coup*. The July *coup* carried the protest of Northern Nigeria in May against a unitary state and the concomitant fear of Ibo domination in such a state to a shattering climax. The assassination of Ibos by Northern Hausas reached frightful proportions in the July *coup*, and the flight of the Ibos from the North, and also from the capital city of Lagos, to eastern Nigeria accelerated to panic proportions.

And now the shoe was on the other foot. The momentum for the original federal structure came as we have seen in significant degree from all the regions of Nigeria, but from none with more steadfast insistence than the North. Now, the Eastern Region was to become a leading exponent of federalism. The recent momentum for centralizing power at the center came from the East. Dr. Michael Okpara, the former Premier of the Eastern Region and President of the National Convention of Nigerian Citizens (NCNC), the government party in the Eastern Region, forced the confrontation between federalist and centralist forces when he broke the alliance of the NCNC with the Northern People's Congress, the government party in the North and the senior partner in the NPC-NCNC coalition government in Lagos. The NCNC teamed up with the opposition party in the Western Region, the Action Group (AG), to contest the federal elections of December 1964. The NCNC-AG alliance compaigned on a platform which could only break the delicate balance of power among the country's regional forces. It sought not only electoral victory at the expense of the North, but also a corresponding centralization of power in Lagos at the expense of the regional government, particularly of the Northern Region. In fact, a centralizing unitary-leaning state, behind a façade of federation.[39]

The January *coup* seemed to stand for just such a policy—elimination of the federal structure and replacement of it by a unitary one. But none could be too sure. The Northerners waited, and the May 24th decree fed their worst suspicions and fears. There was to be a unitary state, the regions were abolished, and the military regime and its civilian associates seemed to be predominantly Ibo.

The July *coup* struck out at these threats. The Northerners sought to redress the balance (as well as exact a measure of vengeance for the fate dealt out to northern leaders by the original *coup*). Lieutenant Colonel Gowan, the head of the second military government, quickly made it clear that Nigeria would either remain a federal structure or break up into several states. There was to be no Ibo-dominated unitary structure. Colonel Gowan's initial despair about maintaining Nigeria as a single state within a federal structure yielded to a mild hope that a loose federal structure for a single Nigerian state could be revived or devised.

Then it was the easterners turn. Fearful of a new northern-dominated federation after the "blood-baths" of May and July, they lost hope for preserving a single Nigerian state and talked increasingly of Eastern "secession." Lieutenant Colonel Ojukwu, Military Governor of Eastern Nigeria and the principal force in the Ironsi government for a unitary state, despaired of keeping the country together and negotiated with Col. Gowan a "repatriation" of Ibo soldiers to the East and Hausa soldiers to the North. He talked of separate Ibo and Hausa military forces.[40] And so the most that the easterners seemed prepared for in the way of a unified state was a loose federal one. It became the only alternative to outright secession,* or association in an attenuated confederation.

Thus the failure, if one probes, has not been one of federalism *per se;* no other structure could have contained any more effectively the centrifugal forces at work. The failure was rather attributable to the underlying "regional suspicions, jealousies and antagonisms." Only federalism and an appropriate federal structure had a hope of containing these forces in the past, and has a chance of doing so in the future. Those who pushed too far too fast for unity may well have contributed most to precipitating the confrontation between federalists and centralists before sufficient national cohesion was achieved and sufficient economic momentum engendered for the federal structure to hold the ring for so fundamental a contest.

In the words of Colonel Ojukwu after the second *coup:*

---

* "Outright secession" finally was chosen by Colonel Ojukwu on May 30, 1967, when he declared that the former Eastern Region henceforth should be a separate state known as the Republic of Biafra. By July 6, 1967, troops of the Federal Republic of Nigeria invaded Biafra with the hope of quickly crushing secession. The massive land, sea, and air blockade set up by the Federal troops has caused widespread starvation in Biafra, but there has been no indication up to the end of June 1969 that the Biafran government would capitulate. J.H.M.

> I grieve for the failure of national unity, which we in the army tried so hard to forge. But we did fail and we have to face it.
>
> We mustn't discard the things that still bind us: Our railroads, our airline, our commercial links and our common currency, our national image. Anyone who looks at the cold, hard consequences of a total break-up must see this.[41]

In addition to Colonel Ojukwu's frank admission of the army's failure to "forge national unity," his words had the measured cadence of reason and enlightened self-interest, which has so often been characteristic of Nigerian politics in moments of crisis. He put the "cold" case for national unity *after* being disabused of the possibility of a unitary structure forging such unity in Nigeria. The case for federalism, coming as it did from Colonel Ojukwu, "who had been the foremost apostle of a unitary state under the deposed military regime of General Johnson Aguiyi-Ironsi," [42] for nation-building in Africa, particularly in its larger, sprawling, pluralistic states, could probably not have been put more effectively or authoritatively.

CHAPTER 8

PROBLEM OF POLITICAL SYSTEMS: THE ROLE OF THE RULE OF LAW

The Rule of Law is not a Western idea, nor is it linked up with any economic or social system. . . . As soon as you accept that man is governed by law and not by whims of men, it is the Rule of Law.

Sir Adetokunbo A. Ademola, *Chief Justice of Nigeria, 1961*

There can be little question of the central importance of the Rule of Law to state structures, political systems, and types of economy that African states are now concerned to build, or of the fundamental link between the nature of these structures and systems and the principal focus in this study—nation-building. The presence or absence of the degree of respect for or infringement of, and the coincidence of practice with precept in regard to, the Rule of Law relate in a basic way to the level of centralization or decentralization of authority and functions in state structures, the degree of coercion or voluntarism in political systems, and the scope or lack of it for private initiatives in economic development. Our concern in this chapter is the pivotal importance of the Rule of Law to African political systems, and thus to nation-building. We shall start with contrasting views of the Chief Justice of Nigeria, quoted at the outset of this chapter, and of a spokesman for the "modern" school of thought that believes or accepts that "the need of national unity and economic development" in Africa requires "one-party democracy," with its admitted "illiberal," "non-democratic tendency" and disregard of the "independence of the judiciary."

ALTERNATIVE VIEWS

Sir Adetokunbo A. Ademola, Chief Justice of Nigeria, struck the keynote of the African Conference on The Rule of Law at Lagos, in January 1961, when he identified the Rule of Law administered by an independent judiciary and a public-spirited legal profession as the pivotal and universal element in determining the nature of a political system—in Africa as well as elsewhere. He rejected the notion, so conveniently fostered in some African circles, and concurred in by some western circles, that the Rule of Law, like bills of rights, independent judiciaries, and the concept of political opposition in parliamentary systems are western ideas, either alien to or beyond the grasp of Africans and their governments. Typical of the latter approach is an ironically titled volume, *Africa: The Politics of Independence*, in which the author asserts:

> The assessments of the degree of democracy in African states must be based on the appreciation of the alternatives that exist. The choice is not between a one-party system and a multi-party parliamentary system. The structural prerequisites for the latter do not yet exist to a sufficient degree in Africa. The effective choice for the newly independent states is between a one-party (or one-dominant-party) system, which allows for some real popular participation in, and control over, the government, or anarchy. . . .[1]

In sharp contrast are the words of Sir Adetokunbo at the African Conference on the Rule of Law commenting on the countries "around us," which the proceedings of the Conference make unmistakable, refer *inter alia* to Ghana, the prototype of Professor Wallerstein's "one-party system, which allows for some real popular participation in, and control over, the government." The Chief Justice's estimate was made at the very time the book in question was being published. The Chief Justice declared:

> It has been said that the Rule of Law is merely an Anglo-American institution, that the concept of "Government under Law" and such phrases as the "Supremacy of Law" and the "Rule of Law" are all purely Western inventions.
>
> The Communist analysis maintained that everything is legal which is good for the State and the problem of adjusting the legitimate claims of the individual and his society has no place.
>
> But the Rule of Law is not a Western idea, nor is it linked up with any economic or social system. As soon as you accept that man is government by Law and not by whims of men, it is the Rule of Law. It may be under different forms from country to country, but it is based on principles; it is not an abstract notion. It exists not only in democratic countries but in every country where the law is supreme, where the dignity of man is respected and provisions made for his legitimate rights. Today, around us we see countries where basic principles are disregarded; where there are cases of arbitrary arrests and detention without trial; cases of denial of the right of individuals to prepare their defence when charged; cases of repression of the opposition in parliamentary government; cases of negation of social and political rights; cases of the Judiciary stifled and

paralysed by fear of dismissal of the judges. When we look around we find some of these encroachments of the Executive on the rights of individuals, which I have mentioned, in countries ostensibly practising parliamentary democracies, but in actual fact the individual is subject to such restrictions which deprive him almost completely of his freedom. . . . An independent Judiciary and a public-spirited legal profession are absolute necessities in every country to keep untrammelled the basic principles of the Rule of Law, so that the world may be built up into a temple wherein dwells the spirit of liberty and justice.[2]

Perhaps the clearest way to demonstrate the link and pivotal importance of the Rule of Law to political systems is to contrast the conception of and practice in applying the Rule of Law in Nigeria with those of Ghana before the military *coups d'état* in both countries at the beginning of 1966. We start with the Nigerian precept and practice.

THE RULE OF LAW: PRECEPT AND PRACTICE IN NIGERIA

At the same opening session of the African Conference on the Rule of Law, at which the Chief Justice of Nigeria delivered the address we have quoted, Alhaji Sir Abubakar Tafawa Balewa, the then Prime Minister of the Federal Republic of Nigeria, stressed the importance of the Rule of Law in Nigeria and the Nigerian determination to safeguard the rights of the individual by entrenching those rights in the country's constitution. Sir Abubakar, who almost exactly five years later was to be assassinated in a military *coup* which seriously compromised his country's commitment to the Rule of Law, put his government's attitude in words which were to prove sadly prophetic:

> Perhaps you will wonder at these [constitutional] precautions; it is not that we mistrust ourselves but that elsewhere we have witnessed all too frequently the ease with which Governments representing only a sectional interest have been able to twist and change the shape of their laws, and to deprive even a majority of their citizens of their rights. In some cases this deprivation of rights has been carried out methodically and in cold blood, but in other cases resort has been had to the excuse that Government security justifies the action. Well, you are going to discuss this second aspect and I must not steal your thunder but I warn you that I shall study very carefully every word which is spoken in this Conference and I reserve the right to come and address you again. Gentlemen, I do really wish that I could be present and take part in the whole of this Conference. It is a subject very dear to my heart and I am always mindful of that terrible saying that power corrupts. We, who find ourselves in positions of authority, have a responsibility to preserve law and order and

at the same time to guard the laws of eternal justice even while we are being guided by them—and how difficult it can be in practice as opposed to theory.[3]

Chief Arthur Prest (barrister-at-law and chairman of "Liberty," the Nigerian section of the International Commission of Jurists), the Nigerian representative at the Rule of Law Conference of the third element in the tripartite equation * implicit in practicing the Rule of Law, made the important connection between the Rule of Law and African state structures and political systems. He stated:

> There are some doubts still in the minds of those who see us from afar, whether we could achieve unity in diversity. I think we can, because we Nigerians have always believed in the Rule of Law which springs from our respect for human dignity.
>
> Before the advent of western civilization various communities of the vast country now known as Nigeria, have always maintained a code of behaviour which is embedded in our unwritten diverse native laws and customs. We believe, for instance, that a man's property cannot be taken away from him without adequate compensation. We also believe that a man cannot be deprived of his liberty, without due enquiry by the elders of the community in which he lives. . . . We have always cherished and protected individual human rights and civil liberties.
>
> In the last few decades, many nations have come to regard the unwanted interference with human rights as a violation of the Rule of Law and have dedicated themselves by various resolutions and declarations to establish justice under the Rule of Law. . . . The Nigerian Constitution, for example, contains many of the provisions of this Declaration of Human Rights proclaimed by the UN General Assembly in 1948 and of the European Convention of Human Rights of 1950.
>
> Despite these instruments we have seen in some parts of the world today how the liberty of the citizens is being sacrificed on the altar of political expediency, and how some nations are descending to the rule of the jungle. We have seen in Africa how so-called civilized nations are inciting newly emergent states to disregard the most elementary principles of human rights. We have known of cases recently where the decrees of the courts have been treated with utter contempt; where systems based on the Rule of Law have been arbitrarily destroyed with the connivance of great powers.
>
> Judges do not make the law. They only interpret the law. They have no means of enforcing their decrees—that power is vested in the instruments of the state, i.e., the police and the army. Where these instruments

---

* The three elements are: a public-spirited bar, an independent judiciary applying and interpreting the law, and a democratic government making and executing the laws. J.H.M.

are controlled by a tyrant or a group of tyrants, the power of the court to uphold the Rule of Law is of no avail.

If we believe, and I am sure we all do, that the Rule of Law is a living concept which applies not only to rules of substantive and procedural law but also to the requirements of a social and economic system that enables the individual to fulfill his aspirations and uphold his dignity, then it is our duty to take up the challenge.[4]

The philosophical precept which governed the Nigerian commitment to the Rule of Law was no accident. It was consistent with, and more, it was part and parcel of the general Nigerian outlook on building an open, plural society; hence, Nigeria's pre-*coup* federal structure, multi-party system, constitutional entrenchment of individual rights, insistence on an independent judiciary and free bar, incorporation of the Rule of Law at the heart of the country's political system, and commitment to the policy of building a nation around the concept of "unity in diversity and diversity in unity." Even Professor Wallerstein had to concede of pre-*coup* Nigeria:

> The one important exception [to the "nondemocratic trend"] thus far has been Nigeria. In Nigeria, there are three regions, each with a dominant party. Were those regions independent states, there is little reason to suppose that each would not have evolved along the lines of its neighbors. Because they are in a *federal structure* without any effective national party in existence, no group has been able to engage in electorial manipulating, expulsions, deportations, and detentions—at least not the extent of other states. Because no one has a clear majority at the federal level, each party can protect its friends in the other region.[5]

What more effective, if grudging, recognition of the difference between the federal state structure and the unitary one-party state structure and the democratic and "nondemocratic" political systems associated with the respective structures in Africa, could be made. And what more per-suasive justification could, because it is inadvertent, be offered for federal state structures in Africa.

Nigeria's then Minister of Justice and Attorney General summoned up the Nigerian outlook in contrast to "totalitarian regimes" in his "General Report" to the Rule of Law Conference. Dr. T. O. Elias observed:

> And yet, it is precisely to prevent the State from imposing the jugger-naut on sections of the community for the benefit of a ruling few that the concept of the Rule of Law has been pressed so much and so often into the service of moral philosophy and of political democracy.
>
> . . . Political emancipation is desirable, but willing respect for law and order is the corner-stone of democratic self-government.

. . . Our earlier analysis has shown the different attitudes towards human rights and fundamental freedoms which States adopt according to whether they are liberal democracies or dictatorships.

Totalitarian regimes regard judges and lawyers purely as instruments of State policy and the courts as set up to justify the excesses of the Executive in the name of what has been called "revolutionary legality." Judges and lawyers who fail to put loyalty to the Party in power above loyalty to the principle of the Rule of Law lose their position or practice soon enough.[6]

Nigeria's commitment to the Rule of Law has been severely tested by a series of major political crises, and although stretched and scarred, until the 1966 coup, and the events leading up to it, it could be said the Rule of Law remained substantially intact.

The Western Region crisis which started in the summer of 1962 severely pulled at the very fabric of the state structure. Nevertheless, despite recriminations and charges and countercharges, *all* parties had recourse to the courts and contested their complicated allegations and argued their rights, and in the end accepted the Nigerian court rulings on fundamental constitutional issues.

Aside from the complicated issue as to which faction of the disrupted Action Group had the legal right to govern, and the constitutional issue of the power of the Governor (the then representative of Queen Elizabeth of Great Britain) to dismiss a regional premier or recognize a successor, the crisis involved for the first time the suspension of a regional government by the federal government and the appointment of a federal administrator during the period of declared "emergency" in accordance with constitutional procedures. In the event, the federal government did not prolong the emergency under one guise or another but withdrew in the specified time and constituted a new majority government from elected members of the Western Region parliament. The temptation to usurp regional power or at least drag heels in the withdrawal process must have been a strong one for important elements of the federal coalition government.

What remained to be done after the emergency was the prompt calling and conducting of new regional elections to give a new popular mandate to a postcrisis regional government, the one emerging from the crisis or another not yet constituted. A fair election in the Western Region, free of coercion and manipulation, would have been an overwhelming testimonial to Nigerian acceptance and practice of the Rule of Law. Unfortunately, this was not to be the case. The election was not held until October 1965, and then it was anything but fair. The result was an outbreak of lawlessness and intratribal warfare among two factions of the Yoruba tribe. The disregard for the Rule of Law in the electoral manipulation and its aftermath led directly in January 1966 to the first military *coup*.

The indictment and trial of Chief Awolowo and twenty of his Action Group associates in 1963–64 for "treasonable felony" and what amounted to conspiring to overthrow the government of Nigeria by force, although a sad and trying episode in Nigeria's postindependence life, was handled with due regard to procedural safeguards and substantive rights afforded by the law to the accused in the grave circumstances involved.   The Awolowo incident, notwithstanding defense contentions of political plots to destroy the leader of the opposition, Chief Awolowo, and his party, the Action Group, was not a theatrical performance, a trumped-up affair, a "political trial," or a kangaroo court.   Due process was by all responsible accounts adhered to with members of the bar prosecuting and defending without fear or hindrance.   Three of the defendants were acquitted.   Chief Awolowo was convicted and sentenced to ten years imprisonment; his seventeen convicted codefendants were sentenced to lesser terms.   Four defendants had their convictions reversed on appeal to the Supreme Court on the ground that the evidence adduced on the trial did not support the verdict of guilty.   Interestingly enough, the Chief Justice of Nigeria, Sir Adetokunbo, acting for an unanimous court of five, handed down the court's opinion dismissing the four defendants, and its subsequent opinion upholding the conviction of Chief Awolowo and the remaining codefendants who had joined in the appeal.[7]

In general, on constitutional issues the Nigerian courts tended to act with vigilance and impartiality, to the extent of holding unconstitutional an act of the federal Parliament passed in 1961 at the initiative of the Prime Minister himself in attempting to set up an inquiry into corruption in the government of the Western Region.   The federal structure and the separation of powers between the executive and the judiciary precluded the particular approach the Prime Minister sought.   In another instance in a private civil case a leading federal minister was found guilty of illegal entry and seizure and required to make restitution.   Before the law the plaintiff was found to have the same right to protection of the Rule of Law as the defendant minister of state; they were equal before the law, an integral part of the Rule of Law.

In addition to the actual practice of the Rule of Law in the courts, the atmosphere in the country, until the events leading up to the 1966 coup, was by and large conducive to its practice.   In August 1963, the independent judiciary, the Nigerian bar, Nigerian newspapers, and leading Nigerian political personages banded together in defense of the Rule of Law and rendered abortive an attempt by a group of leading politicians in power in the federal government to adopt a preventive detention act. In the words of the *New York Times* correspondent in Lagos at the time:

The defeat of a proposed preventive detention act here this week would appear to confirm Nigeria as one of Africa's democratic countries.

Nigeria has long been conspicuous for not having succumbed to the trend toward authoritarianism so prevalent elsewhere on this continent.[8]

A year later the then President of the Federal Republic of Nigeria, Dr. Azikiwe, in a major address at the University of Nigeria, which he founded, unmistakably made the connection between pluralism and federalism, and between political systems and the Rule of Law. The following brief extract from the report of Dr. Azikiwe's address, which interestingly enough was entitled "Tribalism, a Pragmatic Instrument of National Unity," links the major points of concern:

> President Azikiwe today declared that the answer to tribalism in Nigeria is a federal system of government which will concede existence to all linguistic groups and accord them the right to coexist on the basis of equality within the framework of political and constitutional rights that will protect their individual freedom under the rule of law. The President said that transferring of the lower loyalty to the tribe to a higher loyalty to the nation will depend upon the rigidity or flexibility of such guarantees [of individual rights and welfare], the temperament of the people concerned, and the caliber of the leadership of the country. Dr. Azikiwe said that, since tribes are so linked with the human society, they cannot be exterminated without committing wholesale genocide of a section of the human race. He added that without an individual there can be no community; without communities, no tribes; and without tribes, no nation. He ended by appealing to the people to make the atmosphere of our nation conducive to the maintenance of law, order, and good government, so that tribalism will be harnessed to become an instrument for forging our national unity.[9]

As we have noted, the second round of the Western Region crisis in October 1965 grew out of a disregard for the Rule of Law by the heavy-handed manipulation of the electoral machinery by the incumbent NPC-supported Nigerian National Democratic Party government against the opposition Action Group, and the latter's recourse to violence to nullify the result of the manipulated elections. The military *coups* followed.

In its seven months' regime, the first military government proved to be a rather special type of military government. There were various reasons for this: important among these were the training of the military, police, and civil service leadership and the society which threw up the military government and which it sought to govern. For the most part the integrity of the judiciary was respected and the courts operated without interference and applied for the most part the existing law. There was no wholesale "preventive detention"; due process continued to be re-

spected.   A considerable degree of freedom of assembly, speech, and press
continued in effect.   There was considerable freedom of movement, and
by and large freedom of economic activity.   There were restrictions and
limitations in some areas, but in a comparative sense in the African context
there was probably still more freedom in Nigeria under the military government than in most any other African state with a civil or military
government.   Thus, although badly compromised, there was still a significant degree of respect in many quarters of Nigeria for the Rule of
Law.   Whether or not this respect will be enlarged or diminished remains
uncertain.   The second *coup* makes the prospects even more uncertain.
The future of the Rule of Law in Nigeria appears to be closely bound
up with the speed with which there is a peaceful transition to civil government and the future structure of that government.   A reasonably
decentralized structure in the *prevailing* Nigerian circumstances seems the
only one compatible with the maintenance of the Rule of Law; clearly a
highly centralized unitary structure is not only incompatible but out of
the question.

The Contrasting Case: Ghana

In Ghana, both in doctrine and practice, the Rule of Law was so badly
eroded that little remained at the time of the February 1966 *coup*.   The
processes of law and order were severely circumscribed by the rise of the
Nkrumah personality cult and the elevation of the Osagyefo and the
Convention People's Party to dominant roles.   Under a Gaullist-type
constitution the President of the Republic and the "Life President" of the
CPP substituted his will for that of the elected parliament, the party
hierarchy, the civil service, the executive branch, the judiciary, and,
through the party apparatus and the machinery of the government, and
for the will of the people and their nominal "interest groups," such as
trade unions, cooperatives, farm groups, women's clubs, and youth
groups.   The reality was in sharp contrast with Professor Wallerstein's
dictum that "the national hero is not a dictator who reigns by whim
and fiat." [10]
The principal instrumentality employed by President Nkrumah and
his party associates to establish their formidable roles was the preventive
detention act.   This barometer of uncontrolled state authority over the
individual increasingly recorded the erosion of procedural due process
and substantive rights of individuals.   The original preventive detention
act was extended, and its scope expanded, while at the same time such
safeguards as originally existed gradually disappeared.   It became apparent that the act was no longer, if in fact it ever was, an "emergency"
device to forestall a "clear and present" danger.   It became a control

technique for governing on a daily basis. Thus, not only the political opposition was incarcerated, but also trade union leaders, professional people, traders, independents, and the "disloyal" among the CPP and government elites. The Ghanaian "revolution" became in the time-honored way actively engaged in feeling on its own; devouring those suspected of too much ambition ("conspiracy"), too much initiative ("subversion"), too much independence of mind ("disloyalty"), too much status ("corruption"), too much moderation (*"bourgeois* mentalities").

It is relevant to note the judgment of Dr. Elias, Nigeria's Attorney General, on the Ghanaian preventive detention act in his *General Report* to the African Conference on the Rule of Law. The *Report* states:

> Ghana often claims in self-defence that her Preventive Detention and the Deportation Acts are largely hangovers from British colonial administration. The British can probably retort that in their day a comparatively small ruling group had need of such measures in governing Africa's and Asia's teeming millions. This might no doubt be alleged in favour of the often tight laws on seditious or criminal libel, or those banning certain associations as illegal, or those governing the opening and the running of newspapers. These were generally stricter than their equivalents in the United Kingdom. It is an interesting commentary, however, that the ex-British and the ex-French colonies have yet to show a softening of these laws; they have, rather significantly, made some of them even tougher. Perhaps the problem lies partly in the nature of the case.[11]

The nature of the case: one-party unitary states with growing authoritarian governments have found the repressive colonial devices useful; they have found less useful the colonial legacy of parliamentary government.

It is also appropriate to compare this measured judgment of the Ghanaian practice with the general conclusion of the African Conference on the Rule of Law about when the circumscribed use of the preventive detention instrumentability may be legitimate and consistent with practising the Rule of Law. In the words of the International Commission of Jurists:

> The Conference stressed a number of points "having regard to the particular problems of emerging States," and emphatically declared that "in a free society practicing the Rule of Law it is essential that the absolute independence of the judiciary be guaranteed" and that "except during a public emergency preventive detention without trial is held to be contrary to the Rule of Law. . . . Both the declaration of public emergency and any consequent detention of individuals should be effective only for a

specified and limited period of time (not exceeding six months)." These are the principles laid down and accepted by African jurists for application in Africa. Neither specious references to what is supposed to have happened in other countries nor the shibboleth that African conditions require different principles can override the fundamentals of a free society in any place in any time.[12]

The gulf between Ghanaian doctrine and practice and the accepted view of Africa's leading jurists, lawyers, and judicial officials was thus a vast one. It proved to be unbridgeable. The Ghanaian government went on in 1963–64 to destroy the independence of the country's judiciary, the last constraint on the indiscriminate use of arbitrary arrest and imprisonment without review in pre-*coup* Ghana. There were no remaining constraints left; the judiciary became but one more cog in the control machinery of Osagyefo, the President, his party apparatus, and his centralized governmental structure.

The melancholy story starts and ends with the preventive detention act. An attempt on the life of Osagyefo (one in a seemingly endless series) during 1963 led to the arrest of a substantial number of Ghanaians under the preventive detention act. Eventually a handful, five in number, were brought to trial, including the second ranking official of the ruling party, the Convention People's Party, and two government ministers, the minister of foreign affairs and the minister of information, who was also a key official of the ruling party. There was a note of poetic justice, if no other kind, about the Minister of Information Adamafio's fall from grace. At the time he was the leading spokesman on issues of doctrine for the regime and an outspoken apologist for the party. In fact, his growing ambition to control the party machinery has been assigned by close observers of the Ghanaian scene as the principal cause of his undoing. He let his aspirations get out of hand and he became something of a "left deviationist." The trial was conducted under a special law concerned with conspiracies to overthrow the government by force, commit treason, or engage in subversion, by a Special Court established pursuant to said law, from whose decision no appeal could be lodged even though the court could impose the death penalty. The court convicted the two lesser defendants, who were in effect witnesses for the prosecution and "confessed" their guilt, but acquitted the two government ministers and the party official for lack of evidence.

The reaction was stunning. When Dr. Nkrumah's shock dissipated, his rage knew no limits; and the CPP and the controlled press went on a rampage seeking culprits in high places and low. The Chief Justice of the Supreme Court, who presided at the trial, was an obvious target. He was dismissed out of hand by the President. However, under the constitution he remained a justice, as a two-thirds vote of the legislature was required to remove a justice of the Supreme Court, and so the country's laws and constitution had to be amended too. In the meantime the ex-Chief Justice resigned his judicial position *in toto*. The country's laws and the constitution, nevertheless, were amended, and thenceforth all justices were to serve in effect at the pleasure of the President. The venerable and distinguished former Chief Justice, Sir Arku Korsah, was villified beyond description in the party press, along with his judicial associates who joined in the court decision of acquittal. They have since also resigned or been removed.

The International Commission of Jurists attempted to forestall the final plunge of Ghana from law administered by an independent judiciary to law administered by party officials; subsequently, when it became apparent that Dr. Nkrumah was intent on reprisals and depriving the judiciary of its professional independence, the International Commission went on to record the melancholy story as an object lesson of what happens when the Rule of Law and its impartial administration are sacrificed to political control in the name of national unity.

The first attempt of the International Commission of Jurists was embodied in a cable from its Secretary General John MacBride to Dr. Nkrumah:

> Shocked at the news of removal of Sir Arku Korsah from post of Chief Justice stop As a friend of yours of Ghana and African nationalism I appeal to you to review this action which is bound to shock the whole world and damage the name of Ghana.[13]

Mr. MacBride also addressed a letter, dated December 12, 1963, to Dr. Nkrumah on the subject:

> The removal of a Judge from office, let alone the Chief Justice, by a Government which is displeased with a legal decision strikes at the very foundation of the Rule of Law. It is hard to conceive of a more grievous blow to the administration of justice in any jurisdiction.
>
> The action of the Ghana Government sets a highly dangerous headline for the future ordered development of Africa and the application of the Rule of Law in the African continent. Furthermore, it makes our task in seeking to secure the application of proper legal standards in South Africa all the more difficult.
>
> I can only hope that this was a hasty decision taken in a moment of temporary irritation and that wiser counsels will prevail before further damage is done to the good name of a leading independent African State.
>
> No one who knows Sir Arku Korsah, the deposed Chief Justice, could suggest that he was even remotely antagonistic to the Ghana Government.

He was just a conscientious lawyer discharging his sacred duty as a Judge, without fear or favour or affection. Every lawyer in the world will regard him with admiration and, until he is re-instated, will condemn the Government that removed him from office.[14]

The tale of the decline and fall of the Ghanaian judiciary, with its object lesson, was then recorded in the Commission's monthly *Bulletin* under the heading "Ghana—Towards Dictatorship." Pertinent extracts follow:

> The International Commission of Jurists has on a number of occasions drawn attention to disturbing trends in the laws of Ghana and in particular has commented on the system of preventive detention in operation there (*Journal of the International Commission of Jurists,* Vol. III, No. 2, 1961) and on the Act creating a Special Court in 1961. Briefly, preventive detention in Ghana admits of no recourse to a judicial tribunal and applications for habeas corpus have been unsuccessful. In other words, preventive detention is a matter of executive discretion.
>
> Unfortunately, President Nkrumah has gone even further in the same direction. The Ghanaian legislature voted him powers at his urgent request to set aside verdicts of the Special Court, and this he did without delay.
>
> There are further chapters in this melancholy story. A law recently approved by an overwhelming majority in a referendum will enable the President to dismiss judges of the High Court and the Supreme Court as freely as he has been able to dismiss the Chief Justice. The battered remnants of organized opposition in Ghana have received another blow by the acceptance of the principle of a one-party State. After the recent attempt on the President's life, there was a further group of arrests under the preventive detention legislation and once again Dr. J. B. Danquah, President Nkrumah's defeated opponent in the presidential election, is languishing in custody. The climate of free and legitimate opposition to the Government, a prerequisite in any democratic society, African or otherwise, is scarcely propitious. If there is to be a trial for offences against the safety of the State, it will be by a special court consisting of judges dismissable at the discretion of the President, the judgment of the court being equally at the President's discretion. Should this not be sufficient, there remains preventive detention until November 1968 and no guarantee that the 1963 Act will not be renewed. The high hopes that were aroused when Ghana led the way as an independent African State in 1957 have been sadly shattered.
>
> The principles laid down by the African Conference on the Rule of Law held in Lagos in January 1961 under the aegis of the International Commission of Jurists are opposed root and branch to the recent changes in the law of the Republic of Ghana.
>
> Ghana has now unmistakably chosen the path of centralized personal

rule. The mechanism of dictatorship is now in place, and supreme power over all organs of state is now in the hands of one man—power which, as usually in the case of a dictatorship, is said to derive from the people.[15]

It is clear that pre-*coup* Ghana had by precept and practice wandered into the uncharted areas of authoritarian rule, having abandoned the Rule of Law and destroyed the independent judiciary required to administer it, and intimidated the public-spirited bar needed to practice it. (Ghana's leading barrister-at-law and opposition candidate for President against Dr. Nkrumah, Mr. Danquah, was twice detained under the preventive detention act and in fact died while "in detention.") And insofar as there was any lingering doubt about the road Ghana had chosen, the country came full circle, and the point of departure, the "emergency" adoption and administration of the preventive detention act, also became the point of no return, the end of the road. For under the new act the three acquitted defendants were first retained in indefinite detention, and then retried and convicted by a Nkrumahist court, notwithstanding their acquittal of the charge of conspiracy by the duly constituted court with exclusive jurisdiction in the matter. Thus, the initial court's action was nullified, with the aid of special *ex post facto* legislation, permitting the President to set aside verdicts of the Special Court. The prisoners were put in "double jeopardy" and were penalized retroactively in disregard of the original court ruling. The three justices involved were purged. The judiciary was made completely dependent on the will of the executive. The Rule of Law had no further meaning in Ghana under the Nkrumah regime.

"Power corrupts, and absolute power corrupts absolutely." The regime of Dr. Nkrumah without any legal or political restraints on its behavior, carried the logic of the one-party unitary state in Africa to its ultimate conclusion, a regime so capricious and so repressive that only recourse to a military *coup* was left for those who would have change. And as we have suggested, the one-party structure planted the seeds of its own destruction at the hands of the military. Whereas the military *coup d'état* in Nigeria might have been avoided, there could have been no other outcome in Ghana. It is just possible that in Nigeria the federal structure and related political system would have in time, if it had been available, forged sufficient national cohesion to contain and tame the micronationalism of tribalism. In Ghana, and other states that destroy or preclude the very citizen participation that nation-building requires, in their attempt to face and coerce unity, there could only be recourse to force—to *coups*—to obtain change, which is the indispensable ingredient of growth. And in any event, as a pragmatic matter, it is not at all clear aften ten years of Dr. Nkrumah and the CPP, how much tribalism

has been denigrated in Ghana. Compared to the damage inflicted by
Nkrumahism on the promising Ghanaian economy, the one effective en-
gine for nation-building in being in the country, it may well be that the
whole exercise was counterproductive, that on balance nation-building
was retarded more than advanced.

The Western partisans of one-party state structures and authoritarian
political systems for nation-building in Africa, unable to accept the failure
of their prescription for nation-building in their prototype state of Ghana,
took refuge in the irrelevant and shopworn Marxist rationale of an externally-supported *bourgeois* counterrevolution. Thus, Professor Hodgkin has concluded:

> Although General Ankrah is no Louis Napoleon, the Ghana *coup d'état*
> of February 24, 1966, was a counter-revolution of a classic type. . . . The
> coup . . . was "popular" in the sense that it was approved by the *bour-
> geoisie*. . . . But there is no evidence that the coup was "popular" in the
> deeper sense that it was generally supported and welcomed by the mass
> of the Ghanaian people.[16]

Apparently "popular" support "in the deeper sense" was not a necessary precondition for imposing "unity" under the CPP's "socialist revolution," but is a precondition for the rejection of the imposed unity.
Aside from the obvious inconsistency of ignoring popular participation
in achieving unity under the one-party authoritarian approach and requiring it for dispensing with the one-party approach, it is irrelevant and
self-defeating doctrine to view the *bourgeoisie* as an "enemy" rather than
as the vanguard for nation-building and economic development. What
after all is the *bourgeoisie* in the typical African state if it is not the
small professional and technical cadres, the politicians, the civil servants,
the traders and emerging entrepreneurs, the schoolteachers, and the small-
holder agriculturists (where they exist as in Ghana and Nigeria)? In
short, the very people who have entered the modern sector and are indispensable as community leaders for nation-building and development.
If popular participation is sought for building national cohesion and unity
in the new African states, then the so-called *bourgeoisie* are needed as
catalysts and leaders.

TANZANIA'S DILEMMA: RULE OF LAW
IN ONE-PARTY POLITICAL SYSTEMS

In Ghana, the alternative to destroying the judiciary—accepting the
court's ruling, even if disapproved of—might have preserved what little
remained at the time, 1963–64, of the Ghanaian commitment to the Rule

of Law, and deferred the day of reckoning. This is precisely what Tanganyika (now Tanzania) and its President, Julius K. Nyerere, did in far more critical and far more understandable circumstances. As an aftermath of the January 1964 mutiny of the Tanganyikan army, a special mixed civil-military court tried the ringleaders and imposed sentences which were widely disapproved of in Tanganyika because of their mildness. President Nyerere made a national broadcast designed to calm disquiet, and not to whip up mob enthusiasm. Pertinent extracts from the report on President Nyerere's address follow:

> A statement by the president of the republic, Mwalimu Nyerere, said today that the government shared the feeling that the penalties imposed by the high court judge and the two army officers bear no relation to the seriousness of the offenses and damage which was done to the country. Despite this criticism, the government does not intend to vary the sentences, because by doing so it would be abrogating the rule of law, a theory for which the mutineers were being condemned.
>
> The soldiers knew, the statement added, that there were laws about the way they were supposed to behave and that there was machinery to deal with any grievances they had. "By leading a mutiny," the President's statement went on, "the convicted soldiers invited people to break the peace and abandon law. We saw something of the results of the absence of law in the succeeding hours. The rule of law is the basis on which rests the freedom and equality of our citizens. It must remain the foundation of our state. We must not allow even our disgust with the mutineers to overcome our principles." [17]

Thus, President Nyerere recognized, perhaps in view of what has since happened in Tanzania unwittingly, the dangers implicit in the situation prevailing in his country—and in the author's view, in all African states with authoritarian one-party governments operating in highly centralized state structures. The need to perfect the monopoly of power precludes the existence of independent sources of power or functions or checks and balances, or impartial arbiters. And this ultimately must mean the destruction of the Rule of Law, which by definition stands for the procedural and substantive protection of individual rights and their expression through groups of their own choosing. The destruction of the Rule of Law means, *inter alia*, the absence of legally constituted and recognized channels for registering protest and inducing change. The only road left is force and violence, which means *coups*. There is no need for invoking the Marxist doctrine of "counter-revolution" to explain the *coups*, which are made inevitable if there is to be change—in short, the Ghanaian case. Can Tanganyika stop short of this fate and extricate itself before there is no turning back? Obviously President Nyerere does not

consciously want to destroy his country's judiciary and the practice of
the Rule of Law. But does he have any alternative given the road of
one-party, centralized, authoritarian rule he has chosen to travel? If his
calculated campaign to subordinate the country's civil service (a subject
considered in the next chapter) to the control of the Tanganyika African
National Union (TANU), the single party permitted in Tanganyika, is a
case in point, the answer would seem to be "no." Many of the same
compulsions are at work in both cases, the destruction of the impartiality
of the civil service and the independence of the judiciary.

Nowhere perhaps is the dilemma likely to be more painful than in
Tanzania where the President is obviously seeking to combine contrasting, and, in this writer's opinion, incompatible, goals. Thus, President
Nyerere established a Constitutional Commission to advise on the creation of a "democratic one-party state" and laid down a set of principles
to guide the Commission, including the principle that "the Rule of Law
and the independence of the Judiciary shall be preserved." [18] Almost
simultaneously Mr. Christopher Tumbo, former Tanganyikan High Commissioner in London and leader of the Tanganyika railroad union, was
taken into custody under the country's preventive detention act.[19]

There is something patently inconsistent between democratic concepts
and arbitrary arrest in peacetime, and between the Rule of Law administered by an independent judiciary and an executive branch with unre-
strained power, and, in practice, a compulsive need to stifle the opposition, using the machinery of government, including a preventive detention act, to do so.

The losing nature of the fight to establish a "democratic" political system in a unitary one-party structure is perhaps no more poignantly
illustrated than in Tanzania, which, as we have seen, has been confronted
with the dilemma of trying to reconcile the Rule of Law and the democratic practices associated with it, with a one-party structure and system.
It is obviously too soon to make a definite assessment of the new Tanzanian one-party system, but what has been hailed as a new departure
in African democratic one-party practice,[20] a popularity contest between hand-picked and certified pure candidates running for office without platforms, seems hardly revolutionary, or hardly democratic. The
overall context remains one-party, centralized, and authoritarian. In
fact, in the words of a leading Western partisan of the Tanzanian contribution of "something new and valuable in the art of democratic government in Africa."

> These [electoral] rules circumscribed quite sharply the area in which
> the candidates might challenge the government or each other. In theory
> at least, candidates were not to question such domestic issues as the alloca-

tion in the development plan, the role of the military, or the position of Asian or other middlemen in the economy. They did not question the foreign policy of nonalignment in relation to the Soviet Union, China, the United States and the two Germanys. Union with Zanzibar was also outside the debate, as was the government's decision to replace the East African common currency with a national one.[21]

The catalogue of exclusions reads like the table of contents of this book. Every subject central to public participation in nation-building was carefully excluded: economic development, which Professor Morgenthau herself in the article just quoted makes central to the success of the "new democratic system"; the role of the military, in a state that was saved from a military takeover by timely British intervention in January 1964, and where the size, quality and training of the military is still a vital issue; the position of Asians and other middlemen in the economy, in a situation where the fate of the Asian minority and "other middlemen in the economy" is a volatile as well as critical one for both nation-building and economic development; the "policy of non-alignment" in relation to the principal external powers involved in Tanzania's foreign affairs, and in significant degree in its internal affairs, if one has regard to economic assistance and its role in development, military assistance and its role in military posture of a country, etc.; Union with Zanzibar, the key issue in nation-building as it goes to the geopolitical problem of size, shape, and situs of the area in which the state is to be constructed and the nation built; the government's policy of dismantling the East African currency area, and one could add common market, a basic issue in geopolitical and economic terms, with important implications for nation-building.

In short, everything and anything that had any connection with genuine public participation in national political and economic activity and decision-making was excluded. The people would have no voice in what was to happen in those policy areas most directly relating to nation-building and their *interests* in the process, and little more than the voice of a chorus in *who* would make it happen. And thus, if the "Rule of Law is [viewed as] a living concept which applies not only to rules of substantive and procedural law, but also to the requirements of social and economic systems that enables the individual to fulfill his aspirations and uphold his dignity,"[22] then the new Tanzanian one-party system can hardly be thought of as compatible with the Rule of Law.

Elsewhere in Africa the warning signals are also flying. The Rule of Law is in mortal danger. Guinea has adopted "socialist legality," and the opposition and discontented, the black-market practitioners, and the political patronage dispensers, and whatever other categories may fall into disfavor at one time or another are *dehors la loi*—outside the law—and not entitled to its protection or its privileges. For them the Rule of Law has no applicability.

In Uganda, the recent convert to a unitary one-party state structure, the inevitable authoritarianism and disregard for the Rule of Law has followed:

> In Uganda, five former Ministers detained by President Obote's Government succeeded when their writ of Habeas Corpus came before the Court of Appeal for Eastern Africa. The Appeals Court set aside an order of the High Court which had dismissed their Habeas Corpus writ—and ordered that they be released from detention immediately.
>
> What happened? The Uganda Government merely flew them into Buganda, where they became subject to Emergency legislation, rearrested them under this legislation, and flew them off again to an undeclared destination.
>
> Uganda Government spokesmen may argue that their rearrest was necessary in the interests of public security. But to the man-in-the-street the law was made to look foolish and the rule of law something capable of adaptation to political expediency.[23]

In the long list of authoritarian one-party states, in Upper Volta, in Congo (Brazzaville), in Chad, and a score of other countries, special courts exist to safeguard the state against its "enemies" and to hand down a stern "justice," which raise innumerable questions and doubts about procedural due process and substantive rights of the accused, and ultimately about the fundamental stability and unity of the state. For one-party structures inevitably spawn authoritarian political systems to sustain them. They are vulnerable to military coups and "palace revolutions." Those in power today can be ousted tomorrow, and be subjected to the same excesses—the very excesses the Rule of Law is designed to guard against. How could nation-building, dependent as it is on increasing active public participation, be carried on in this context? President Nyerere recognized the danger when he said: "The rule of law is the basis on which rests the freedom and equality of our citizens. It must remain the foundation of our state."

But in the nature of things, can this indispensable principle coexist with uniformity, enforced by the executive branch, as must inevitably be the case in our view in unitary, centralized, authoritarian, one-party states? Certainly the experience to date in Africa has given no cause for optimism on this score. And if our analysis in this and preceding chapters is valid, then there is little reason to expect a change from the unfolding pattern, exemplified by Ghana, and increasingly emulated in a score of other new one-party African states.

CHAPTER 9

PROBLEM OF POLITICAL SYSTEMS:
THE ROLE OF INDEPENDENT INSTITUTIONS

The one-party system in the African countries is often a significant step toward the liberal state, not a first step away from it.

> IMMANUEL WALLERSTEIN, *African Studies Program, Columbia University, 1961*

The International Commission of Jurists sees in the one-party system the beginning of totalitarian rule and holds it to be inconsistent with the Rule of Law.

> *The International Commission of Jurists, 1964*

State structure and political system are determinant of one another, and in practice, reinforce one another. Certainly this has been the case in Africa. Without exception, the one-party structure has led to the evolution of authoritarian political systems, differing only as to degree of comprehensiveness of government control over the individual and capacity to exercise that control, and varying only as to where on the ideological political spectrum their authoritarianism places them. As we have seen, the federal structure is a rarity in Africa. In the one state where it has had any sort of a trial run, Nigeria before its recent *coups*, there was one of the very few political systems on the continent that could be described with anything approaching accuracy as democratic. We have examined in the preceding chapter the role of the Rule of Law in determining the nature of a political system; in this chapter we consider the related question of the role of independent institutions. Together the two chapters should provide us with an overview of the two principal deteriorating routes to nation-building in Africa.

THE COERCIVE MODEL: INDEPENDENT INSTITUTIONS AND GHANA'S ONE-PARTY SYSTEM

The clearest expression of the one-party trend in Africa has been in pre-*coup* Ghana. In the preceding chapter we considered the growth

131

of authoritarianism in Ghana with respect to the erosion of the Rule of Law and the impairment of the integrity of the judicial system, particularly of the independence of the judiciary to administer the Rule of Law. We now turn briefly to Ghana's systematic destruction of the other two principal supports of free public participation in nation-building efforts in Ghana. First, we consider the attack on the spirit of free enquiry and academic freedom in higher education, particularly at the University of Ghana, and the related harnessing of all levels of education in the country to propagating the CPP party line; thereafter we turn to the campaign against a professional and independent civil service in the country. We shall then have the full picture of how, with the abrogation of the Rule of Law and the destruction of an independent judiciary and bar, the institution of thought control throughout the educational system, the attack on an independent teaching profession and independent academic institutions, and the systematic attempt at infiltration, control, and takeover of the civil service by the one-party machine, Ghana perfected its one-party structure and completed the development of the accompanying one-party authoritarian political system. There were no independent or free institutions or sources of opinion left untouched in Ghana; all had been purged, taken over, or were under bitter attack. The revolution had started, as we have already seen in the preceding chapter, to devour its own. This, of course, was in keeping with the classic pattern elsewhere, and not a surprising outcome, except to those who persist in the belief that "African conditions are different" and that a one-party system can be "democratic" or even "work" in the interests of African nation-building and development.

The military *coup d'état* that overthrew the structure and system reflects the technical limitations of an underdeveloped African country organizing and administering such a complex with the scientific efficiency of a modern totalitarian state, and not, as the one-party apologists, seeking to make the most of a job badly done, a "Fabian moderation," or a "democratic spirit." [1] There is an obvious contradiction between underdevelopment and the level of efficiency and infallability required to run the machinery of an authoritarian or totalitarian regime. If for no other reason, the unitary one-party structure and system are poor choices for African nation-building. And as we have had occasion to note elsewhere, the one-party state system in obliterating all independent institutions and vital interests outside the party and the army prepares the way for the latter in proportion to its zeal for entrenching the former.

ACADEMIC FREEDOM IN GHANA

In language reminiscent of that of Sir Adetokunbo Ademola, quoted at the beginning of the preceding chapter, the then Vice-Chancellor of the University of Ghana, Conor Cruise O'Brien, decried the propaganda line of the apologists for one-party systems about "African values" being different and compatible with authoritarianism, particularly in the educational sector. Before proceeding to Vice-Chancellor O'Brien's significant comments in a major address (which in the event turned out to be his swan song), it is pertinent to note that O'Brien was hand-picked for his post by President Nkrumah after he had been withdrawn from his post with the United Nations in the Congo (Kinshasa) and had quit the United Nations with a blast at alleged British intrigue in the Congo on behalf of M. Tshombé. The designation of Dr. O'Brien to head the University of Ghana served a dual purpose—first, it was a repudiation of the British "values" exemplified by the "neo-colonialist mentality" of the preceding British administration of the university, and second, it was a self-serving act in support of Dr. Nkrumah's own position in the Congo crisis, which, *inter alia*, disapproved of the way the United Nations had up to that time treated with Moïse Tshombé, supported Cyrille Adoula, and contained certain external intrusions such as Ghana's various initiatives.

It is also pertinent to take account of the background to Dr. O'Brien's speech to realize that it was not merely an abstract expression of concern for academic freedom, but rather, on the contrary, a pointed and challenging declaration in a volatile political context. On February 8, 1964, with notice of something like 48 hours, the Ghanaian Government deported six University of Ghana faculty members for "subversive activities." The following account is quoted verbatim from *Africa Digest* as it gives in cogent fashion the principal facts without comment, and in doing so records the xenophobia and authoritarianism that had taken hold in Ghana. The report states:

> They were Professor W. B. Harvey and Mr. R. B. Seidman, Americans, of the Faculty of Law; Mr. G. Greco of Guadeloupe, and Mr. W. Jean-Pierre, an American Negro, of the French Department; Professor L. H. Schuster, an American, of the Institute of Administration, and the Rev. J. V. Stewart, a Briton, of the Department for the Study of Religion.
>
> According to a Government statement all were involved in "recent events" and their activities were prejudicial to the security of the State. Their presence in Ghana was "not conducive to the public good."
>
> The deportations came after strong attacks in the pro-Government Press here on both students and some members of the University staff.
>
> The Ghanaian Times said: "According to the newspaper the time had come to uproot the little pockets of subversion which Busia [former head of the opposition party who fled from the country several years ago] left behind and which are being sustained by agents of neo-colonialism and internal reaction."
>
> On his arrival in Britain, the Rev. J. V. Stewart denied categorically that

he had engaged in subversive activities. He said that: "At the University there is almost universal unhappiness and uneasiness. The present feeling of the Government seemed to be that the University is modelled too much on British and Western lines and should be redirected to suit the needs of a socialist State." Dr. Conor Cruise O'Brien, Vice-Chancellor of the University, tried to intercede, he said, "but no Ghanaian authority was prepared to give a reason for our deportation."

On the day the deportations were announced a crowd of about 2,000 people marched through the University campus demonstrating against the students and the professors. They bore slogans such as "Down with the arrogant students," "CIA students," "Saboteur intellectuals," and marched through the halls of residence, watched by students and staff.

This incident came shortly after an English professor at the University of Ghana, Dr. Dennis Osborne, had been detained from January 17 to January 24.[2]

The pertinent comments from the Vice-Chancellor "Address to Congregation," on March 4, 1964, just one month after the deportation incident follow:

. . . The values to which we adhere have nothing in common with colonialism or with any other system of oppression, nor have they anything in common with neo-colonialism or any other system of deceit. They are forces of their nature hostile to such systems as colonialism and neo-colonialism, and they have served to bring about the downfall of the first system and the exposure of the second. Respect for truth, intellectual courage in the pursuit of truth, moral courage in the telling of truth: these are the qualities essential to the life of learning and teaching, these are the qualities of a real, of a living University. Since the days of Socrates in Greece and Mencius in China these values have been asserted, and have been attacked. . . . This is not, as is sometimes suggested, curiously enough, by both colonialists and some of their adversaries, a question of "introducing European values into Africa." These are not European values: they are universal values. Mencius taught in China very much in the same spirit as Socrates taught in Greece. They were almost contemporaries. The geographical and cultural gap between them was the widest possible, yet it is clear that they would have understood one another.

. . . In this country, we are fortunate in this degree that our Chancellor, Osagyefo Dr. Nkrumah, has gone on record with a statement which categorically and in strong terms denies any doctrine that would encroach on the proper sphere of the teacher's freedom. I should like to quote this important passage from a speech made by our Chancellor a little more than a year ago, on 24th February, 1963: "We know that the objectives of a University cannot be achieved without scrupulous respect for academic freedom, for without academic freedom there can be no university. Teachers must be free to teach their subjects without any other concern than to convey their students the truth as faithfully as they know it.

Scholars must be free to pursue the truth and to publish the results of their researches without fear, for true scholarship fears nothing. It can even challenge the dead learning which has come to us from the cloistral and monastic schools of the middle ages. We know that without respect for academic freedom, in this sense, there can be no higher education worthy of the name, and therefore, no intellectual progress, no flowering of the Nation's mind. The genius of the people is stultified. We therefore cherish and shall continue to cherish academic freedom at our universities."

. . . In times of rapid social and political change, such as those in which we are living, centres of critical and independent thought seldom enjoy unalloyed and universal favour. In the long run, the survival of such centres is secure, for it is in the nature of the human mind to question, and to check and to test the answers to the questions. In the short run, however, at any given point in space and time, the future of a particular centre of critical and independent thought may be in doubt. What of the future of this particular centre now? If the spirit of those noble words of our Chancellor's which I have just quoted will prevail in all the practical relations between the University and the authorities, as surely it ought to do, then this University's future will be as secure as any institution has a right to expect. The constitution of the University, the Act and our Council, enshrine principles of academic freedom which are very old, will be respected, and our academy will flourish. We must hope that this will be so. We cannot, in the light of some recent events, and the comments of certain publicists, simply take it for granted that our intellectual freedoms are unchallenged.

. . . Whatever the language used, however, the nature of the operation remained the same, and its motive the same; the need to overawe and, if possible, inhibit the working and expression of a free intelligence. People driven by this impulse of coercion are heard from in disturbed times, and it would be surprising if we did not hear from them; we have heard from them, and we have recognised what they represent. What we do not know is to what extent their voices may prevail. For the University it is vital that they shall not prevail but that the enlightened policy proclaimed by our Chancellor in the passage from which I have quoted, should stand firm.

We hope naturally, that this will happen and that we shall enjoy a resumption of the pleasant and fruitful conditions of work which characterised the last academic year. But even if we face, as well we may, a time of difficulties and of painful silences, we should not allow ourselves to become despondent. Respect for learning, for truth, for justice and for intelligence are enduring human qualities which are present in ample measure in the people of Ghana. These qualities may be obscured for a time, but in the long run they are tougher and more resourceful than their impatient adversaries. It is a reasonable faith, therefore, that the flame of free learning which has been lit on this hill will not be suffered to die out.[3]

Dr. O'Brien's points, embedded as they were in a diplomatic utterance, took on added meaning because of the circumstances in which they were made. The quotation of Chancellor Nkrumah's words sharpened the cutting edge of the Vice-Chancellor's words, for Chancellor Nkrumah was also President Nkrumah, whose government deported the six professors over the Vice-Chancellor's protests, and Life Chairman Nkrumah of the Convention People's Party, which called for the heads of the professors and engineered the invasion of the campus by a mob led by party thugs to intimidate the "anti-government" student body. As for Dr. O'Brien's protestation of faith, it seemed necessary to keep him going, but like so many protestations of faith in similar contexts elsewhere, it was sadly doomed to disappointment, for the incident of the six teachers was but one of a series, and part and parcel of the pattern of Ghanaian, and we would generalize, African, one-party authoritarianism.

Almost as if to illustrate the inexorable nature of the political processes of authoritarianism and the "wheels within wheels" quality of the Ghanaian variant, but also incidentally the rather hopeless quality of Dr. O'Brien's "faith," two brief reports from The Times of London cogently link up the Ghanaian purge of the judiciary, the abrogation of the Rule of Law, and the purge of the educational system. First:

> The Times (February 3, 1964) commented that the removal of the three judges showed that the President meant to make full use of the power over judiciary given him by the recent constitutional amendment. All three of the recently dismissed judges were in the past associated with the political Opposition. It was possible that the party zealots were turning their attention to the bench, after their recent successful campaign against the "bookish" teachers in the university.[4]

Second:

> A recent report on the deportation of the Ghana University staff, the International Commission of Jurists pointed out, indicated that even legal education was being interfered with by the Government, further endangering the rule of law (February 28, 1964).[5]

The principle of state control of education not only at the university level but at all levels to indoctrinate the party line was made clear in frequent pronouncements of Mr. Koduro Addison, a former member of the President's Commission and former Director of the Kwame Nkrumah Ideological Institute. Typically, he declared those responsible for training of youth would be expected to instill in the youths "the true meaning of nationalism . . . the ideals and principles of Nkrumahism. . . ."[6] When translated, nationalism cum Nkrumahism meant indoctrination in the

CPP philosophy of one-party authoritarianism.   This was but one more type of coercion—the denial or withholding of knowledge and the adjustment or slanting of it, with a pinch of "brain-washing" thrown in for good measure.

THE CIVIL SERVICE IN GHANA

The civil service story in Ghana can be related even more briefly. Ghana achieved independence with a cadre of some of the finest trained and experienced indigenous civil servants in Africa, and one of the largest pools of educated, indigenous personnel qualified for public service positions.   Hence, Africanization—replacement of foreign personnel by indigenous personnel—although a disturbing and unsettling process in Ghana as elsewhere in Africa, was probably less so than in most other countries, with the possible exception of Nigeria.   Nevertheless, within five years of independence, the Ghanaian civil service had undergone a drastic transformation.

As with the judiciary and the university, so too with the civil service. It collided with the party, and it had to yield. The list of self-imposed exiles from the Ghanaian public service, of whom Ambassador Daniel Chapman, first Ghanaian ambassador to the United States and the United Nations, was one of the earliest, was a steadily lengthening one; and in many ways became a sad measure of the turn of events since a year or so after independence.   The issue that arose was clear; it was inevitable. The British concept—and one might say as with the Rule of Law and academic freedom, the universal concept in democratic society—of a professional, impartial, and dedicated public service, indifferent, or as nearly so as human behavior allows, to the political composition of the government of the day, was anathema to the one-party authoritarianism of the CPP government in Ghana.   And so the party exerted its will, and the civil servants bowed under or fled to the hills—in many instances to the sanctuary of jobs with the United Nations and its many specialized agencies.[7]   Those who resisted or were slow to respond to the new order had serious difficulty—dismissed, passed over for promotions, relegated to occupational *culs-de-sac*, or accorded even worse treatment.   For example, a senior civil servant, Mr. Ebenezer T. O. Ayeh, Acting Principal Secretary at the Ministry of Information and Broadcasting, was summarily removed from office, and tried on the ground that he had "published a false rumour that President Nkrumah had shot a soldier at his official residence.   Ayeh was alleged to have mentioned the rumour to William Coleman, head of Ghana Radio, who checked it with Attorney-General, Mr. Kwaw Swanzy."[8]   Ayeh pleaded not guilty, was convicted and sentenced to nine months' imprisonment.   Aside from the nature of the statute under which Ayeh was tried and the character of the evidence presented by the prosecution, the fact that his case "is one of a series of legal actions brought by the Government in its drive against rumour-mongering" [9] was not lost on his Civil Service colleagues. What is a rumour in a controlled society? And more, what is a rumour in the mouth of a senior Civil Servant in the Ministry of Information and Broad-casting? The extent of the demoralization of those who survived in the Ghanaian civil service only became fully apparent when the façade of unity was lifted after the fall of Dr. Nkrumah. The successor National Liberation Council inherited a spiritless and largely leaderless group, which as a matter of urgency it had to try to reinvigorate.

The Ascendancy of the Party in Ghana

In commenting on the new status of the CPP in the amended Constitu-tion of Ghana, adopted in 1964, as "the one national party which shall be the vanguard of the people . . . and which shall be the core of all organizations of the people," *West Africa*, the well-informed weekly journal, noted that "while in the past the party had identified with the State, the State was now to be identified with the party. Party officials would be regarded as state officials, just as much as Civil Servants were. The party's governing body would be as important as the Cabinet." [10] This would seem to have been the final word on a professional civil serv-ice, free of political manipulation; and for that matter the final word on the representative quality of "a one-man, one-vote" government in Ghana, subject as it was by the amended constitution to manipulation by a party apparatus which in no sense was responsible to the voters, but only to the controlling clique in the party, headed by the Life Chairman.

Thus, when the demise of an independent judiciary, educational profes-sion and civil service, are added to the earlier take-overs of the trade unions, agricultural organizations, youth groups, women's clubs, news-papers and other channels of communication by the government and the party apparatus, the structure and system of one-party authoritarianism was entrenched in Ghana. Coercion by the government and party to create and perfect the structure and system was supplanted by coercion by the government and party to manipulate the structure and system to induce the "mass-mobilization" performance required for nation-building under the doctrines of Nkrumaism,[11] the name given to Ghana's brand of "socialism" by the CPP and the party press. Coercion was clearly the technique chosen to build a cohesive Ghanaian nation with a "socialist society and economy." And force met counterforce in the February 1966 *coup*, and the "entrenchment" of the one-party structure and system in Ghana proved no more enduring than the entrenched "bill of rights" in so many of the British-drawn constitutions of independent African unitary one-party states.

THE COERCIVE TREND: ECHOS FROM OTHER AFRICAN STATES

The Civil Service in Tanzania

We have already made reference to the Tanzanian dilemma of creating a "democratic one-party state" consistent with the Rule of Law.   The civil service issue as we have already noted also arose in Tanganyika (as the country then was).   President Nyerere disposed of one part of it to the satisfaction of the party, TANU, when he rejected late in 1963 the concept of an impartial and professional service as "British" in concept and not African.   He announced that henceforth party ideals (rather than merit) and party supervision (rather than that of a public service commission) would prevail in the public service.   And since every vice can be made a virtue, Professor Morgenthau has written, "In 1964, the government had already departed from the British model by permitting [requiring would more nearly describe the situation] civil servants to join TANU so as not to deprive the party of the most educated citizens." [12] This of course gets the "democratic" priorities exactly right.   The party must not be deprived of "the most educated citizens"; the government and its public service could do without.   In fact, the government and the public service are instrumentalities of the party, which is run by its National Executive Committee.   And since TANU is not synonymous with the totality of the electorate, and since the NEC is not responsible to the totality of the electorate, it is indeed difficult to reconcile a party-ruled "civil service" with the skilled professional role it should play in nation-building and economic development.   A one-party state spoils system is even less attractive than a multiparty one, and both, of course, have far less to offer to a national effort to build cohesion and achieve development than a professionally-trained, impartial public service with continuity and pride of tradition, after the British model.

However, in part, Dr. Nyerere did not satisfy the party when he announced in late 1963 that citizenship rather than color would determine basic eligibility for public service positions, and quality of performance rather than "skin pigment" of Tanganyika (as the country then was) citizens would govern.   In addition to TANU, the trade unions and the army were not satisfied with this declaration of policy.   The unions consistently opposed the Nyerere doctrine of "localization" as contrasted with "Africanization."   Prominent among the reasons assigned for the army mutiny in January 1964 was opposition to the President's declaration, which was understood to mean a slow-down in Africanization of the officer corps of the army. And the one-party, TANU, with which President Nyerere had previously had trouble over this issue, in this instance was discreetly absent from the scene—and in the ensuing army mutiny offered no opposition to the uprising. Here too, there was another dilemma for President Nyerere: how to reconcile a party-dominated civil service, affording preference to true believers, with, on the one hand, the doctrine of merit, and on the other, nondiscrimination on racial grounds. In fact, Europeans and Asians have left the Tanzanian civil service in large numbers. The coexistence of the two goals seems as unlikely as that of the Rule of Law and a one-party system.

A comparable development took place in the army. As an outgrowth of the January 20, 1964, military mutiny the army was disbanded and a new army recruited. The then second Vice-President of the United Republic of Tanganyika and Zanzibar (now Tanzania), Rashidi Kawawa, emphasized that for the new army "the recruitment criterion would shift from physical fitness to loyalty and political affiliation. He told the House that it had been decided to make TANU or Afro-Shirazi membership the basic qualification for entrance into the army." [13] Thus, to combat military indiscipline and unreliability, which was but a reflection of the serious lack of social cohesion and national consciousness in the country, and the lack of group organization outside the one-party structure, TANU, Tanganyika had embarked on what appears to be an even greater evil, a political army. Almost as if intent on its own destruction, the civil government has added to the risk of unbalanced military power in a society precluding organized expression of interests, the risk of a politically-conscious army which could become disaffected for doctrinaire reasons as well as for imagined or real personal grievances. The control of TANU too was rendered all the more attractive, as the prize would carry with it by extension at least initial control over the army. The state structure and the public administration seem destined in Tanzania to become even more of an empty shell than had existed before. In these circumstances, growing reliance on party coercion as the technique for nation-building becomes inevitable.

THE JUDICIARY IN THE IVORY COAST

The Ivory Coast which has a strong one-party structure and system occupies a position on the one-party spectrum far removed from that of pre-*coup* Ghana. Yet the pattern in the plunge toward right authoritarianism has not been appreciably different from Ghana's toward left authoritarianism. Coercion to force performance rather than persuasion to induce it has been very much the rule. The spate of plots and conspiracies against the government of President Félix Houphouët-Boigny has also been typical of the reaction to the authoritarian pattern. The Rule of Law has been going much the same way as in Ghana. For example, a presidential decree in early May 1964 dismissed several judges from the Ivory Coast State Security Court, which was the counterpart of Ghana's Special Court for trying security cases. Among the justices dismissed was M. Jean-Baptiste Mackey, the President of the Court, who had been held under house arrest since September 1963, when an alleged plot to assassinate Houphouët-Boigny was uncovered. Another judge who fell afoul of President Houphouët-Boigny was M. Ernest Boka, President of the Supreme Court, who was dismissed in January 1963 after being implicated in an earlier plot against the life of President Houphouët-Boigny. Boka was not arrested, however, until April 1964, after his alleged complicity in the September 1963 plot was reported by a commission of inquiry. Boka was reported to have committed suicide April 6, 1964, while under arrest.[14]

Preventive detention, a special security court, impairment of the independence of the judiciary, and the elimination of all opposition to the one-party in power—all of the ingredients of authoritarian one-party systems—have been much in evidence in the political chain reaction which now appears well under way in the Ivory Coast. The resultant public apathy, the antithesis of the required public participation for nation-building, has been massive.

TRADE UNIONS IN MALAWI

Elsewhere in Africa the clearest focus of the coercive drive of one-party systems has been on the trade unions. This is not to suggest that trade unions have fared any better in Ghana, Tanzania and the Ivory Coast, *inter alia*, but rather, because some of the newer states have not yet caught up with the pace-setters, the constraints imposed on the trade union movements are still in process of being imposed or only recently completed, and the mechanics being or recently employed still discernible and not yet covered over by layers of rationalization, propaganda, and time. In addition, in the newer states attention has not yet been diverted from the fate of the trade unions by still more exciting issues or dramatic incidents.

Thus, in Malawi, one of the newest African states, on the eve of independence in mid-1964, the "liberal" *Central African Examiner* reported (not without sympathy):

> In the absence of big industry and in the atmosphere of stringent economy, trade unions and wage claims are obviously a luxury too. At pres-

ent, Government labour officers deal with disputes, so far very effectively, by consulting both employed and employers, thus by-passing trade unions which have been steadily losing what little power they had.[15]

How familiar the rationale: trade unions, like opposition parties, are a "luxury," and the state can do it better anyway. Dr. Banda, then Prime Minister and now President of Malawi, has on other occasions pronounced his views on trade unions in his country—they need "have no fear" as long as they act in a "responsible" way, i.e., follow Malawi Congress Party directives on what they may do. And of the one-party structures in Africa, the Malawi Congress Party is one of the more formidable. Thus, Malawi has come to independence with an exclusive one-party structure and political system to match and without an effective independent trade union movement. So formidable, in fact, was the one-party, that in the last elections scheduled prior to independence for the spring of 1964, the arrangements never got beyond the registration of voters and nomination of candidates by the Malawi Congress Party, notwithstanding the continuing British presence at the time. And the *Central African Examiner* gave us the explanation for the nonelection before it was decided not to hold it when it approvingly proclaimed:

> It looks as though Nyasaland is to be deprived of elections forever. The most important occasion as far as the National Assembly is concerned was the mass rally at Luchenza airstrip when Dr. Banda named his 50 candidates from the Malawi Congress Party. After the registration campaigns and this, the election on April 28, if it happens at all, will be an anti-climax. . . . In these efforts of nation-building, political unity is essential for all sections of the population. Malawians should perhaps be grateful there will probably be no elections—there are so many other things to do.[16]

Here we are given a bit more of the rationale for the one-party system, carried in this case, the first in Africa, to nonelections (which in fact did not occur) as a technique for nation-building. In the words of the *Malawi News* it was a "matchless victory." [17] Elections are divisive, take time from the "many other things to do," and are expensive. The title of the article from which this extract and the preceding one on *non*-trade unions has been taken is: "Nyasaland: Stringent Economy in Nation-Building."

And so, independent trade unions are deemed a luxury which must go with independence and the establishment of the single-party structure operated by a single-party system. Dramatically, within the confines of the same article, in the same week, and in the same country, we find the beginning of the end of free trade unions acknowledged and hailed as an achievement, and the contemplation of dispensing with elections welcomed as an equally promising achievement. For our purposes in this chapter, no more vivid demonstration of the intrinsic, inherent, and inexorable nature of the one-party structure could be forthcoming than the juxtaposition and linkage under the heading of "nation-building" of the two above-mentioned events. Especially is this so, inasmuch as the one-party structure requires a one-party system, which in turn, in defending its exclusivity must become authoritarian. With the trade unions, the press, and the farming groups already in hand, Malawi after independence turned its attention, in keeping with the teachings of the preceptor, Dr. Nkrumah, to the judiciary, the educational profession, and the civil service. All of this in the name of nation-building. In the words of Ngwazi Dr. H. Kamuzu Banda, in an address to the Malawi Congress Party:

> It is the leadership that decides. I have to decide. If I leave you to choose, you will choose someone because he is your brother, uncle, brother-in-law or anyone who has a beautiful sister. That is why I alone must choose for your own good.
>
> I am not going to allow you to do what you like. Anybody who does not like that must get out of the M.C.P. Anybody who is a true Malawian must obey the laws and regulations of the party.[18]

As always, Dr. Banda's declarations are characterized by forthrightness, even bluntness. Here, stripped of ideology and apologia, are the basic ingredients of the coercive route to nation-building, the one-party system at work. And the most damaging postscript of all must be added: within two months of independence Malawi was confronted with a governmental crisis, when Dr. Banda ousted three ministers for allegedly plotting to overthrow the government in collaboration with the Chinese Communist Embassy in Dar-es-Salaam and "to murder" him in the process. Three more ministers resigned, leaving only Dr. Banda and two other ministers in office. The outgoing ministers, in turn, complained of Dr. Banda's authoritarian behavior, his proposal for a preventive detention act, his foreign policy of friendship with Southern Rhodesia and Portugal, his failure "to Africanize" quickly enough, his policy of budgetary austerity, etc. Civil strife ensued, the MCP was purged and its authoritarian grip on the country tightened.

More perhaps than any comparable crisis in African politics since 1960 the Malawi crisis revealed and demonstrated the inadequacy of "democratic centralism" and one-party rule. The only possibility for change for those who fell from power seemed to be a *coup*, and the temptation for them to turn to outside "friends" seemed nearly irresistible. At any rate, Dr. Banda has reportedly charged the fallen ministers with plotting to overthrow his government by force, and Tanzania with complicity in providing a sanctuary, base, and arms to the alleged plotters.

In Malawi there was no overt, admitted, or apparent opposition outside the one-party. The party was "blooded" in the events of 1959 and the "struggle against federation." There were no obvious tribal or sectoral differences. There was a charismatic leader at the helm. And yet there was no unity. There remained important differences of view, opinion, and policy, notwithstanding the one-party partisans who smugly proclaim that Africans have nothing to differ about and that multiple parties are merely the vehicles for self-seeking personal ambitions of politicians out of power.

The Malawi crisis, seen in perspective, is but one more manifestation of the basic pluralism of African society. It is all the more striking because of the advertised impossibility of things falling apart in Malawi under the leadership of Dr. Banda.

INTERNATIONAL AFFILIATION OF TRADE UNIONS

Before going on to consider the role of independent institutions in voluntaristic political systems, it seems important to note that a concomitant of coercive political systems in their approach to nation-building has been the development of carefully cultivated xenophobic and isolationist attitudes with respect to the affiliation of national institutions with international bodies, such as international trade unions. Thus, states like pre-*coup* Ghana went on from the stage of controlling unions and making them state or one-party auxiliaries to a campaign to subvert the independence of all trade unions on the continent. The technique has been to isolate unions from all outside contacts in the name of "African unity." Thus, the All-African Trade Union Federation (AATUF), composed initially and in large part of trade unions of Ghana, Guinea, Mali, Morocco, Algeria, the United Arab Republic, and Tanzania made membership contingent on cutting ties with all trade unions outside Africa.

The tactic was clear. The communist-dominated World Federation of Trade Unions lost out in Africa, partly because of its own ineptness, partly because of losing control of important unions in Africa to "revisionist" African Marxists, and partly because of competition from the International Confederation of Free Trade Unions. Thus, there was no percentage in any African unions maintaining formal, public WFTU affiliation. On the other hand, many African unions, particularly in Kenya, Tunisia, and Nigeria, at various times found the ICFTU affiliation valuable. To impair and destroy this affiliation with free trade unions, which militates against authoritarianism, parochialism and the one-party mentality, and provides an alternative focus to looking inward, the former

Casablanca bloc states, plus Tanzania, with the blessings of the WFTU, have been intent on disrupting all international trade union affiliations. The pressures have been mounting for breaking away from the ICFTU.

Many one-party state leaders, irrespective of their views of the Casablanca bloc powers, have found, as part of the monopoly of power they seek and seem to require to run a one-party system, that it was self-serving and opportune to forbid outside links. For example, pre-*coup* Upper Volta passed a law in May 1964, which gave its unions three weeks to "disaffiliate" from non-African or international bodies reaching beyond Africa on penalty of dissolution for noncompliance.[19]

Other African states, such as Kenya in 1964, found themselves the target of considerable pressure to "disaffiliate." The then general secretary of what was the principal Kenyan labor organization, the Kenya Federation of Labor, Mr. Lubembe, charged in 1964 that the Kenya Federation of progressive Trade Unions was being financed by the Ghana Trade Union Congress as part of the Ghanaian drive to disrupt the Kenya Federation of Labor's affiliation with the ICFTU. Mr. Lubembe added for good measure the charge that the Ghana Trades Union Congress was being "heavily subsidized by the WFTU."[20] Irrespective of the degree or the precise role of Ghana involvement in the Kenya controversy,[21] it seems clear that Ghana and the All-African Trade Union Federation then located in Accra were in Kenya, and elsewhere in Africa, the basic source of inspiration and support for the anti-ICFTU affiliation movement.[22]

Thus, there exists the double thrust to isolate trade unions in Africa from outside contacts, overtly, by suggestion to receptive one-party governments (as in Upper Volta) and covertly, by pressure, infiltration and subversion (as in Kenya) where a one-party system had yet to emerge, and where the trade unions had yet to be fully absorbed into a one-party mechanism.

The danger authoritarian one-party states perceive in affiliation of African unions with the ICFTU was illustrated by the curious dialogue between a head of state, President Sékou Touré of Guinea, and the leadership of the Tunisian trade unions during President Touré's state visit to Tunisia early in 1964. President Touré's advice to the Tunisian unions to "disaffiliate" from the ICFTU was rejected out of hand by the Tunisian Trade Union leaders. They in turn offered some unsolicited advice in return to President Touré about the need for world-wide trade union solidarity and working-class unity, and the way ICFTU affiliation could and did buttress the strength and resources of African unions. Needless to say, it was just this buttressing of the strength and resources of trade unions, which could make them an independent force in Guinea, and for that matter in all other African states, to which President Touré objected. Independent trade unions insisting on the rights of labor to organize and strike for economic purposes—and perhaps for political objectives—and to resist coercive labor practices under one or another guise of *investisse-ment humain* are the very thing that authoritarian-minded African governments cannot afford to tolerate.   Independent trade unions would impair the one-party monopoly of power.   So bitter did the exchange become between the President and the trade unionists that President Bourguiba of Tunisia felt called upon to explain away publicly the impromptu exchange and exact a public apology from the trade unionists to his guest, President Touré.

It is pertinent to note the concern articulated at the Fourth Annual Meeting of the African Regional Conference of the International Confederation of Free Trade Unions on the growing encroachment of African governments on the freedom of the trade unions in their countries. The Conference put on record its "grave concern and apprehension at the tendency in some countries in Africa to control by legislative or administrative action trade union organizations" and urged African governments to insure the existence of trade unions "free from political control and other forms of external domination." [23]

At the same meeting the outgoing Conference chairman, Alhaji H. P. Adebola, a leading Nigerian trade unionist, tied together the independence of African trade unions, their right to affiliate with international trade union federations such as the ICFTU, and the Nigerian concern with unity amidst diversity.   Alhaji Adebola declared:

> Efforts to achieve [trade union] unity have been hampered by the controversial question of international affiliation.   This issue has been made the scapegoat.   It is not affiliation which has brought about the present controversy.   The friction centers around whether trade union leaders are prepared to accept international principles and standards entrenched in the I.L.O. conventions and the United Nations Declaration of Human Rights before moving towards the desired unity, which can be found in the . . . respect for fundamental rights and autonomy of each national center, however large or small.[24]

Alhaji Adebola's words have received confirmation, unintended but nevertheless confirmation, from a most unlikely source, a British journal on African affairs which approves the philosophy of the radical nationalist African states—the core of the All-African Trade Union Federation. In its leading article, entitled "Nigeria's Unity," the journal declared:

> Trade union legislation in Nigeria under British rule has been aptly described as a "guideline to anarchy"; it was largely responsible for what seemed like the irreconcilable differences between the ICFTU and WFTU. They have met the present crisis [the June 1964 general strike] by form-

ing a joint action committee whose call for a general strike met with a nation-wide response and extremely effective results.[25]

Alhaji Adebola, who was one of the leaders of the Joint Action Committee (see below for discussion of the Nigerian general strike), and worked to make it a success, could only be intrigued by this transparent recourse to what he had already termed a "scapegoat" as background for explaining the formation of the JAC. He may also be intrigued by the journal's apparent characterization of the two principal wings of the Nigerian Trade Union movement as "the ICFTU and WFTU," as the non-ICFTU affiliated unions have long maintained that they are non-WFTU affiliated too! The former wicked colonialist power, the United Kingdom, might also derive some comfort from this oblique admission that it permitted a free trade union movement to development in Nigeria, and did not impose a "unified" state union. It is also interesting to note the recurrence in yet another African context of the issue: "unity amidst diversity" or "unity in uniformity"?

THE VOLUNTARISTIC MODEL: INDEPENDENT INSTITUTIONS AND NIGERIA'S MULTIPARTY SYSTEM

We have already dealt with important aspects of the Nigerian political system at some length in previous chapters in the discussions of Nigeria's pre-*coup* federal structure and commitment to the Rule of Law. We shall therefore confine ourselves in this section to considering those distinctive aspects of the Nigerian attempt to build a nation without recourse to coercion, which we have not already explored in the earlier chapters. Our emphasis will thus be on those rare, almost exotic institutions in tropical Africa—a free press, free trade unions, academic freedom, an independent civil service, and freedom to organize political parties and groups. A free press and multipolitical parties were not discussed in our consideration of the coercive model. By definition, they are excluded in precept and practice in unitary one-party African states. The states, however, do have institutions which are generically related to free trade unions, academic freedom, and an independent civil service in voluntaristic multiparty states, and can be fruitfully compared and contrasted with them. In effect, that is what we shall be doing in the ensuing discussion.

NIGERIA'S FREE PRESS

Almost alone on the continent Nigeria has enjoyed a free press. Frequently sensational, even irresponsible, but obviously and proudly free, the Nigerian press reveled in its ability to comment on every and any aspect of public life and governmental affairs. All major political parties have at one time or another published or caused to be published newspapers friendly to their cause, aspirations, programs, and candidates. Even during tense periods when passions were running high, the press has been left more or less to its own devices. Only after the 1966 military *coups* was there any serious effort to censor the press, and even then it tended to be postcensorship, or recrimination and penalty *after* the publication of "offensive" material, rather than *prior* censorship. There was also relative freedom for the foreign press and its correspondents until the military *coups*. Thereafter, there was a series of ousters of foreign correspondents for sending critical or "offensive" despatches to their newspapers.

No political personality entirely escaped the wide net of political commentary thrown out by the national and regional newspapers. For example, the running dispute between the then Ministry of External and Commonwealth Affairs, the Hon. Jaja Wachuku, and a large section of the press, went on intermittently over the years, heating up and dying away. The former Minister's penchant for the provocative act and the extravagant statement was matched by one or another of the Nigerian newspapers at different times. There have been many other instances of this sort, but perhaps none as persistent or as entertaining for the electorate as this one.

National policy on a range of issues has been clearly influenced by press comments and editorials. We have referred to the participation of the press along with the Nigerian Bar Association and others in the successful campaign against the enactment of a preventive detention act. In the words of a *New York Times* press despatch from Lagos at the time:

> An all party conference of Nigeria's top political leaders rejected today a proposal for a preventive detention act.
> This was viewed as a decisive victory for Nigeria's free press, which waged a vigorous campaign against the proposal.[26]

The press was divided on the issue of the establishment of a national coalition of political parties in a structure which would have approximated the French-speaking African countries' *parti unifié*. However, a significant portion of the press opposed such a movement and played a discernible role in turning back the attempt to launch the movement. There have been many other instances of the Nigerian press playing a vigorous role in formulation of national policy.

The press has also been characterized by highly partisan behavior. Exposés of the activities or alleged activities of political personalities in opposing parties have been a constant ingredient of the daily press. The same may be said about revelations concerning the activities or alleged activities of opposing political parties. At times political editorials have verged on the scurrilous.

There have also been government-published newspapers in Nigeria, the *Outlook*, published by the Eastern Region government, *The New Nigerian*, published by the Northern Region Government, and the *Nigerian Morning Post* (also the *Nigerian Sunday Post*) published by the federal government. Although, like most "house organs" these newspapers have tended to be tamer, they have from time to time acted up, and the *Post* has been known at times to bite the hand that fed it. Nigeria has also, even after the military *coups* of January and July 1966, been one of the very few African countries to permit the publication of an independent foreign-owned newspaper, *The Times*.

All in all, the Nigerian press has been rambunctious, truculent, vigorous, partisan, exciting, uninhibited and above all, free. In many ways it has mirrored the rough and tumble of Nigerian politics, and some of the more visible aspects of Nigerian society.

FREE TRADE UNIONS

The pluralism that characterizes so much of Nigerian life also has characterized its trade union movement. There is both a diversity and multiplicity of trade unions in the country, frequently at odds with one another on labor policy, political issues, foreign affairs, affiliation with international trade union federations, and leadership of the country's growing number of wage earners. Nevertheless, much to the surprise of the federal government, and one suspects to themselves, the Nigerian unions were able to unite for two weeks in June 1964 in a Joint Action Committee, which waged an effective and successful nationwide general strike against the Government white paper on the Morgan Commission Wage Structure Report.[27]

First, the JAC struck to force the hand of government with respect to publishing the Report and the Government white paper on the Report, and then persisted in the strike because of the government's only partial acceptance of the Report as well as its equally significant rejection of parts of the Report. The 155-page report was handed down by the Morgan Salaries and Wages Review Commission, as the review commission came to be known after its chairman, Mr. Justice Adeyinka Morgan, on April 30, 1964. The government did not turn over copies of the Report officially to the unions until the beginning of June, although many of its principal recommendations had become quite widely known. The Government White Paper was not issued until June 3.

After thirteen days and an abortive ultimatum by the Prime Minister to the strikers to return to work in forty-eight hours or be "sacked," the Government reversed its position and agreed to negotiate, not on the basis of the Government's white paper which offered considerably less than the Morgan Commission Report, but on the basis of the Report's recommendations. The final settlement, a short time later, went some way towards compromising the differences between the recommendations of the Morgan Commission and the original position of the government white paper. For example, the Morgan Commission recommended a £12 per month minimum wage for Lagos and the federal territory and the government white paper stipulated a £9.2 minimum. Final agreement was reached on a £10 minimum.[28] The very serious economic and possibly inflationary impact of the Morgan Commission awards aside, which is beyond the purpose of our discussion in this chapter, the Nigerian general strike more than most any other event in pre-*coup* Nigerian history demonstrated the open, democratic nature of the society and the real freedom and independence of the trade union movement. One need only contrast the army's union-busting tactics in a series of other African countries: in the Congo (Kinshasa), where in early 1964 the army broke the strike for higher wages of some 13,000 miners at *Union Minière* in Katanga which threatened the government's "hold-the-wage-line" policy; and earlier on in Ghana, where the army broke the strike of dock, railroad, and other workers against a forced levy of the government requiring the workers to purchase government bonds up to a fixed percentage of their salaries, and arrested and held in preventive detention all of the strike leaders; and also earlier on in Guinea where the army broke the strike of a teachers' union and subsequently put down with considerable force a sympathy strike of relatively young students protesting the arrest and imprisonment of their teachers in a detention camp.

The absence of violence after one local minor initial clash in Lagos the day before the strike broke out; the ability of the conflicting unions to unite and organize so effective a strike; the restraint of the then federal government in refraining from using the army or the police to break the strike in what has now become more or less the prevailing style in Africa; the corresponding use of the army and the police to maintain order and provide limited emergency communications, such as priority government cable traffic; the good-natured acceptance of considerable inconvenience and even hardship by the public at large (and the writer who was strikebound for the entire two weeks in Nigeria can personally testify to this); and the willingness and ability of the parties on all sides to negotiate and bargain, distinguished the general strike from most others in recent years in Africa and provided a dramatic illustration of voluntary participation in public affairs by an economic interest group of growing importance.

Regionalism, tribalism, and sectarianism generally yielded to an alternative interest—a shared concern about wages and living standards. *Nigerians* were sharing an interest, not as Hausas, Yorubas, Ibos, etc., but as members of free trade unions, and were uniting in their mutual interest. Here then, is the essence of forging national cohesion and building unity—the submerging of parochial interests in larger national political and economic ones, the creation of a sense of national identity based on vesting interests in the national entity, and the existence of legal channels for the articulation of the interests.

In the words of John Bulloch, correspondent for the conservative London *Daily Telegraph* writing from Lagos:

> The whole stoppage was conducted calmly and sensibly. Only once, right at the beginning, did police and workers clash in anything resembling a riot. . . . This absence of violence could have occurred in no other African country. In the Congo, the threat of a strike by one union leads to road blocks, tanks and troops. In South Africa strike is synonymous with violence. Here, things are arranged very cordially. In the middle of the strike the Labour Minister, Chief J. M. Johnson, saw nothing odd in joining strikers celebrating a traditional annual carnival, and strike leaders happily confessed that the fact that telephone engineers were still at work "made their job a lot easier"! In an odd way, the 13-days of the Nigerian general strike has enhanced the country's stature and given a *sense of identity* notably lacking before. But that is something that can happen only once, and it is to be hoped that the union leaders realize this.[29]

And the opinion of *West Africa* was much to the same effect:

> To Nigeria's reputation abroad, the strike has done little damage. The comparative lack of violence, the purely industrial nature of the unions' demands, and, if not its earlier and much criticized handling, the Government's firm use of police and armed forces, have even impressed some observers with the country's maturity. But this could scarcely survive a repeat performance.[30]

ACADEMIC FREEDOM

The Nigerian educational system has been noted for its freedom of expression, particularly at the university level. The University of Ibadan in Western Nigeria and the University of Nigeria in Eastern Nigeria have animated and articulate student bodies and variegated faculties drawn not only from Nigeria, but from many other nations around the world. The federal government and the regional governments have by and large kept hands off the universities. The newer universities, the University of Lagos, Ahmadu Bello University in Northern Nigeria, and the University of Ife in Western Nigeria have, however, had problems in their relations with government. The Universities of Lagos and Ife presumably have had teething problems, and these have been largely of a political character, reflecting the generally distraught political state of mind which prevailed in the Western Region as the aftermath of the 1962 "emergency," and spilled over into federal affairs in Lagos.

There has been nothing in Nigeria, however, reminiscent of the systematic drive in Ghana to control education, particularly at the university level, in the interests of perpetuating the hold of the Convention People's Party on the country, and to indoctrinate the youth of the country in CPP doctrine through the school system. There has been nothing of the type of indoctrination in the principles and doctrines of the sole party in Guinea, the *Parti Démocratique de Guinée*, and the equivalent of the personality cult of President Touré, which has characterized the education system of Guinea. There has been nothing of the type of the "Arabization" program which has characterized education in the Sudan, particularly in the Southern non-Arab regions, and more recently in Mauritania, particularly in the Southern non-Arab Senegal River Valley. And one could cite other contrasts. The fact is that in education, as with the press and unions, Nigeria has accorded so much more freedom of thought and action than any other country in Africa as to represent a difference not only in degree but also in kind.

INDEPENDENT CIVIL SERVICE

The Nigerian civil service has escaped the Ghanaian, Guinean, Tanzanian one-party state trend of openly as well as overtly subordinating the civil service to the manipulation and control of the one party in the country. The Nigerian public service has absorbed a good deal of the tradition of professional, independent behavior and performance so intimately associated with the British civil service.[31] There has been relatively little party influence exercised on the civil service. Unfortunately, the civil service, particularly in some regions, has not always been able to escape local and tribal influences. But this has been an unfortunate problem in all Africa; a manifestation of the lack of national identity and an attribute of underdevelopment. In short, just one more symptom of the pluralism of Africa which nation-building must take in stride if it is to be successful.

Nigerianization has proceeded in the public service as Africanization has in every other African country, but in a more systematic way than in most other countries in Africa, and without the racial overtones implicit in parts of East Africa and discussed earlier in this chapter in connection with Tanzania.

Interestingly enough, the military *coup* which overthrew the civil government found in the Nigerian civil service the one continuing professional mainstay, which could give the country administrative continuity and whatever stability was possible in economic and technical sectors of national life. Although not free of tribal and personal recrimination, the post-*coup* civil service was not torn by partisan political vendettas or purges. It has remained largely intact to administer the government. What has been lacking is the political leadership and decision-making that the military have found so difficult to supply.

FREEDOM TO ORGANIZE POLITICAL PARTIES AND GROUPS

Unlike pre-*coup* Ghana, Algeria, Malawi and Tanzania (Tanganyika plus Zanzibar) where constitutionally and legally only the CPP, FLN, MCP, TANU (in Tanganyika) and the Afro-Shirazi Party (in Zanzibar) could exist, and take precedence over government, pre-*coup* Nigeria, Sierra Leone, and the Gambia have had multiparty systems. In addition to major parties in the latter three countries, minor parties, splinter parties, political pressure groups, etc., have appeared and disappeared with the political seasons. In short, organized, pluralistic political activity has flourished. This is not to suggest that from time to time opposition groups have not run into difficulties and even discrimination at the hands of the controlling political party or parties. But this has tended to be sporadic, episodic, and scattered, and in a comparative sense, relatively minor, if one takes Africa at large as the unit of comparison. Nevertheless, in Nigeria the heavy-handed treatment of the Action Group by the controlling party, the NNDP, with the support of the NPC, was a key factor in the political crisis which led up to the military takeover of January 1966. The departure from the obviously required political pluralism of the country, and the attempts to substitute coercive political action for voluntary action had the anticipated result—the resort to force to meet force. How deeply the commitment to the Rule of Law and to voluntaristic political and social institutions has been impaired in Nigeria remains to be seen. What has clearly emerged from the recent Nigerian experience is that coercion as a technique of nation-building cannot be readily substituted for voluntarism in a country of Nigeria's size, diversity, and pluralism.

A CONCLUDING WORD

Freedom of organized open political activity in support of or in opposition to the ruling party and the government of the day is rare on the African continent. It has been no accident that in the few societies where it has occurred, there have also been decentralized political structures, respect for the Rule of Law administered by an independent judiciary, pluralistic interests openly held and proclaimed, and independent institutions—free presses, free trade union movements, academic freedom, and independent civil services—and as we shall see in the next chapter, open economies with decentralized decision-making, and a significant role for multiple private initiatives. These are together the voluntaristic approach to nation-building and development. It is in sharp contrast, as we have seen throughout our discussion, to the coercive approach, where the absence of all of the foregoing conditions and characteristics has been the *sine qua non* of that approach.

CHAPTER 10

PROBLEM OF ECONOMIC DEVELOPMENT: PRIORITIES, PATTERNS, AND PURPOSES

Growth is not automatic and cannot be achieved without sacrifice. Planning for growth means, essentially, using our present resources from wherever they may be derived in such a way that in the end the total resources of our nation will be increased. But it is a great mistake to imagine that economic growth can be achieved merely by producing programmes for spending massive amounts of capital. The total to be invested is important, it is true, but of even greater importance is the need to ensure that the investments are channeled into productive and profitable uses. Our people would doubtless welcome at once far more schools and hospitals than the Development Plan envisages, but without heavy investment both by the Governments and by private capital in the productive sectors of the economy to increase the resources of the nation, they would be insufficient to pay for the teachers, doctors and nurses required to staff these schools and hospitals. But investment must not only be productive, it must also be profitable. It is of little use pouring capital into enterprises which require heavy subsidies in one form or another. The resources which are drained away into providing these subsidies could be far better employed creating new enterprises, new opportunities for employment and opening up new vistas for our people. In short, one way leads to stagnation and a decline in the standard of living, despite the illusion created by massive expenditure. The way we have chosen is very different from this, and involves a present sacrifice for our future well-being.

> The HON. CHIEF FESTUS SAM OKOTIE-EBOH,
> late Minister of Finance, Federal Republic of
> Nigeria, 1962

Economic growth depends on a large proportion of the country's inhabitants—farmers, wage-earners, professionals, entrepreneurs—responding to opportunities for improving their economic conditions. Incentives are the key to economic growth.

> SIR ARTHUR LEWIS, *economist, professor, former university principal, former economic adviser to the President of Ghana, and consultant and author on economic development, 1966*

155

Nation-building and economic development in Africa are twin goals and intimately related tasks, sharing many of the same problems, confronting many of the same challenges, and interrelating at many levels of public policy and practice. In an earlier volume the author had occasion to explore the interdependence and interaction of the quest for economic growth and the search for political stability—the development nexus: growth and stability.[1] In this chapter the existence of the development nexus is accepted and emphasis will be placed on the dual role of economic development as a joint goal (*i.e.*, as a precondition for, factor in, and consequence of nation-building) and as an instrumentality for nation-building.

In the same way that geopolitical factors, the degree of centralization or decentralization of power and functions in the state structure, the admixture of coercion and persuasion and penalties and rewards in the political system, and the degree of respect for individual and group rights accorded in a society, influence, affect, and determine the path, the pattern, and ultimately the fate, of nation-building, so too the overall priority envisaged, the sectoral priorities assigned, the techniques and methods used, and the purposes and goals established for economic development, have been shaping and influencing not only the choice of types and structures of the economies of the new African states, but also their prospects for successful nation-building.

PRIORITY FOR DEVELOPMENT *

African leader after African leader has proclaimed that economic development is at least a priority objective of the newly independent states, and many have declared it to be *the* priority objective. In practice the performance has been somewhat different. Few states have got down to cases. Only a handful have worked out serious economic development plans; among them, Nigeria, Tunisia, and the Sudan. Others have merely gone through the motions or adopted what are essentially *pro-forma* plans; among them, Mauritania, Ethiopia, Sierra Leone, Malawi, Upper Volta, Niger, Dahomey, Togo, and Guinea. Many, too many, of the "plans" are in reality little more than "shopping lists," looking for finance without clear priorities and "hard" projects, without serious provisions for mobilizing internal resources, without correlation of social overhead and infrastructure investment with investment in the productive sector, without provision for meeting recurrent expenditure, without action programs of surveys, studies, and projects, and without appropriate provision for administrative and implementing machinery.

* See Appendix for "Population and Gross National Product Per Capita (U.S. Dollars)." J.H.M.

Some too, have been pretentious social documents, reflecting the government's political doctrine, such as Nkrumahism in Ghana, with little or no relation to African realities or capabilities. Thus, in Ghana the *Programme of the Convention People's Party* (published by the Ministry of Information and printed by the Government Printer) for the country's new Seven-Year Plan states:

> Nkrumahism, which is based on scientific socialism, is all-pervading, and while its theory in full can only be developed in and around the Party leadership, it must influence in some form all education and indeed all thinking and action.[2]

Here in a nutshell is the coercive technique of development through a controlling party elite and indoctrination of the masses. Coupled with party *élitism* was Party *cum* State control and ownership of the major means of production:

> The Party is firmly of the view that the planning of the national economy can only be really effective when the major means of production, distribution and exchange have been brought under the control and ownership of the State.[3]

The predictable result: "major and minor lunacies"; "Dr. Nkrumah increasingly shifted responsibility for development contracts from professional civil servants to party hacks, most of them both inexpert and corrupt"; "Ghana's development this past decade seems in many ways to have been incompetently planned, incompetently coordinated and incompetently carried out"; and "his [Dr. Nkrumah's] mismanagement of economic development and his Pan-African ventures almost broke Ghana." [4]

In many African states development plans can be said, at least in principle, to exist. Few of them have been able, and, in some instances, willing to follow through with plan administration and execution, including the difficult and sometimes costly and tedious task of project preparation and evaluation, and the making of difficult political choices among projects contending for limited resources, drawing inescapable and even invidious distinctions between prestige projects, make-work projects, busywork projects, patronage projects, and the ones that really count, payoff projects. Few have been willing to take the tough decisions involved in mobilizing internal resources for development—limiting and even cutting back on public sector consumption, including the living standards of ministers and the salary and fringe-benefit scale of civil servants, and the size, shape, and scope of the armed forces, and increasing revenue through administrative reform, wiping out corruption, adopting more equitable tax structures, and imposing and collecting taxes, license fees, and charges for public services provided for by statute or ordinance.

Besides to the inadequacy of what passes for plans or ordered development programs, and the absence of plan administration and economic coordination machinery and the associated will to carry through with proclaimed national development programs, in many states, preoccupation with Pan-Africanist, irredentist and prestigious goals or objectives, of the types and varieties discussed in earlier chapters has in practice, and in some instances, even in theory, shifted or diverted the priority in the use of national resources from economic development to other "national interests." Thus, pre-*coup* Ghana, in pursuit of Dr. Nkrumah's Pan-Africanist goals, subordinated its economic development to foreign policy objectives. It financed "national liberation" movements in both dependent and independent African areas. It subsidized "All-African" bodies such as trade union federations, press associations, and women's clubs, as a means of propagating the Nkrumahist Pan-African line and bringing pressure to bear on those individuals, organizations and governments who resisted it. It invested in prestige projects for the international stage as well as for domestic consumption, such as international conferences and assemblies on any and all subjects. It operated unprofitable international air routes, such as those between Accra and Warsaw and Accra and Moscow, where not only the airline, Ghana Airways, had to be subsidized but also the passengers. It developed a military jet air force, constructed "Africa's longest runway" at Tamale, which has been abandoned, built a nuclear reactor "despite American offers to supply isotopes free," built a $20-million dry dock "for 120-ton ships," and $25-million "cocoa silos condemned as impractical by the World Bank." It established a marble works "employed almost exclusively [for] paving the homes and patios of Dr. Nkrumah's fat cats," a meat-canning factory and a leather factory which were "virtually inoperative because there are not enough cows," and a glass factory while simultaneously importing "two years' supply of Czech glass." [5] One could cite many more such expenditures, utilizing scarce resources of capital, time, energy, and personnel which could have been applied to productive investment and serious economic development.

The tragedy of Ghana is that unlike so many of its sister countries, it had substantial reserves, of the order of $500 million, and a relatively high per capita income by African standards, about $170, at independence,[6] which could be drawn on for development investment. In less than ten years, however, the economy was brought to the brink of bankruptcy with *all* its reserves dissipated, and a staggering foreign debt of the order of one billion dollars substituted for the comfortable reserve of foreign exchange.

Mali too, in its drive for "total independence," has taken political decisions without regard to their economic implications, and to the detriment of the growth of the economy. We have already discussed instances of this in Chapter 3. Elsewhere, as in Guinea, the pursuit of doctrinaire goals, in part associated with achieving "economic independence" have led to decisions in obvious conflict with the needs of the economy, and at the expense of it. The nationalization, subsequent denationalization, and renationalization of much of the country's import, wholesale, and retail trade and the construction of nonpaying state sector industrial enterprises, are cases in point. The nature and scope of Guinea's policies and practices in this regard are cogently summed up in an article highly approving of Guinea and its leader, President Touré:

> Sékou Touré did not content himself with making resounding speeches in favor of socialism, but carried out a number of basic reforms which spoke for his serious intentions to lead Guinea along a path of development contrary to capitalism. He has begun nationalisation of enterprises, has created the state sector of the economy, initiated the development of cooperatives and taken all-out measures to restrict the operations of foreign companies in the country.[7]

To round out the picture the commentator might well have added that President Touré withdrew his country from the franc zone, and substituted Guinea's own currency, which immediately became inconvertible and generally unacceptable as legal payment in world trade; President Touré also withdrew Guinea (or made inevitable its exclusion from the European Common Market and its important Overseas Development Fund;[8] he attempted to compensate for these self-abnegating financial and economic actions by having Guinea conclude a series of extensive, expensive, and unproductive (for Guinea, and probably in the event for the Soviet Union and Communist China) aid and trade agreements with the Sino-Soviet blocs. These doctrinaire and ideologically-induced actions clearly affected Guinea's economy adversely and consequently compromised its development prospects.

In such instances as those of Ghana, Mali, and Guinea, it is hard to maintain that economic development has been *the* priority objective of government, or even *a* priority objective. With but limited and scarce resources available, the diversion and allocation of them to nonproductive uses could only mean less for productive investment growth. In these cases too the impact of economic development as an instrumentality for nation-building has been sharply reduced. The allocation, or from the vantage point of nation-building, the misallocation, of resources to other national "interests"—foreign policy goals, prestige, purposes, "economic independence," doctrinaire goals—has meant the denial of these resources to growth projects. Cumulatively this has meant less growth, and hence, less of the nation-building effects of economic development. The result generally has been that fewer people have been drawn into the market economy than might have been or should have been. This has in turn caused the prolongation of the difficult and unsettling transitional period from subsistence to market production, with Africans left straddling the line between the subsistence sector and the market sector, a foot uneasily planted in each. Inefficiency and uncertainty were induced in both sectors by a constant stream of labor migration, labor turnover, absenteeism, lack of proficiency in acquiring skills and experience, wastage, and imbalance in population. The important psychological transition to modernism, with its new technology, reliance on one's own efforts instead of acceptance of one's lot as preordained by fate or imposed by the powerful juju of an enemy or evil spirit, and emphasis on breaking out of the confining tribal shell surrounding subsistence society, has inevitably been retarded, and at times even frustrated. Almost in direct proportion to the retardation of growth or stagnation of African economies, the cause of nation-building has been adversely affected, for both economic development and nation-building share the problems of modernization and the need at the heart of the modernization process for change in methods, attitudes of mind, and ways of thinking, in order to achieve their respective and inextricably related ends, national growth and cohesion.

Thus, the late Dunduzu K. Chisiza, the youthful collaborator of Dr. Kamuzu Banda in the Malawi Congress Party, and the first African to hold the post of Parliamentary Secretary to the Ministry of Finance in Nyasaland, in what may be considered his political testament, wrote with considerable perspicacity:

> The question thus arises: shall the meager resources of the new states be used for waging war on neighboring states, for subduing the traditional rulers, for economic development, or for meeting the expenses of social, political and legal reform? Better still, what line of action should receive emphasis?
>
> The strategy which this suggests is not so much that reliance should be placed on any element as that the dominant elements in the State should be sold on the need to concentrate on the task of economic modernization.
>
> In this selling job, Western leaders can do a great deal to influence the attitude of African leaders. . . . Western leaders can make it clear to African leaders that while in non-self-governing countries the leader who is admired is the one who struggles for the liberation of his country, in independent countries the leader who wins the respect of Western nations is the one who is bent on reform and economic modernization.
>
> But the people who are most likely to succeed in selling African leaders

on the necessity of according priority to modernization are men from the ranks of the African leaders themselves. Some of the leaders are already sold on modernization. These leaders should be given facilities for communicating their convictions to their counterparts in other countries.[9]

Mr. Chisiza would thus accord economic development *the* priority among Africa's contending and competing needs and aspirations, and realistically concludes that an important "selling job" is still needed to focus many African leaders on economic modernization in preference to the other national goals he identifies as competitive.

IMPLICATIONS FOR NATION-BUILDING

Mr. Chisiza also linked economic modernization and nation-building in his paper, when he listed among the objectives of what he termed a "pragmatic pattern of development" the following two points:

Promotion of a sense of purpose and participation among the masses [and] encouragement of a sense of fellowship and belonging among the races. . . . Promotion of a sense of purpose and participation among the masses requires: popular indigenous leadership dedicated (after the attainment of independence) to economic and social modernization, a mass nationalist movement, and initiation of development programs in which the masses (*i.e.,* rural populations) can participate.[10]

Thus, Mr. Chisiza intimately related nation-buiding, in fact, tied it, to development and growth. The sense of purpose and participation and the sense of fellowship and belonging referred to by Mr. Chisiza, are in fact preconditions for as well as consequences of development; they are also important as factors in development, in building consumer demand, developing a stable labor force, increasing productivity, and making incentives effective. These factors are also the very essence of nation-building—in forging national cohesion, in encouraging cooperation among disparate populations, and in replacing xenophobic tendencies by unifying ones. The process is circular: economic growth facilitates nation-building, and nation-building sustains growth, and both go on in unison and in interacting and interlocking stages. There is a clear correspondence between the stages of growth and the levels of nation-building. Priority for economic growth clearly implies a priority for nation-building, and, less recognized or perhaps less conceded, impairment or reduction of the priority for development in practice or in theory means a consequential and corresponding impairment or reduction of the priority for nation-building.

If this thesis is valid, then those African states paying only lip service to development or concerned with "national interests" other than development at the expense of the latter, are consciously or unconsciously injuring their efforts to build national cohesion and national unity. To the extent African states retard nation-building through diverting energy and resources from development, the reaction (or reflex action) seems to be to compensate by increasing coercive measures to force unity. In the process of imposing rather than achieving unity, they preclude even more the voluntary participation in economic development, which Sir Arthur Lewis views as the key to growth, as well as voluntary participation in political processes which we have identified as the key to nation-building. Thus, the type of political system an African state chooses converges with as well as reflects the approach of that state to nation-building and, inevitably, also circumscribes the choice of priority which is likely to be accorded by it to economic development.

DEVELOPMENT PRIORITIES [11]

A country's basic choice of priority among economic development, military power, doctrinaire political goals, such as Pan-African leadership, and prestige goals, once made will then establish the sociopolitical priorities of a society, and in so doing determine and perhaps even dictate the planning priorities for economic development, the sectoral priorities. In the ensuing discussion we cannot anticipate, and even to the extent we might be able to, cannot accommodate all the possible variations and patterns of basic decisions by African states on their national interests and the resultant priorities accorded by them to these interests with regard to the use of limited national resources. Instead, we have selected two principal themes on which to focus our analysis and to illustrate the close links between political decisions, economic choices, and nation-building, once the basic decision as to the priority to be accorded economic development and other national interests has been taken, or committed in practice. We shall thus be concerned in the ensuing discussion first with priorities among sectors, and then with priorities within the productive sector. Common to any consideration of intersectoral priorities and intrasectoral priorities in the productive sector is the fact that by definition development resources in underdeveloped countries are scarce and limited. The choices made in the allocation of these resources are therefore crucial.

> In the short run any government assistance given to one sector of the economy is at the expense of other sectors; in the short run each sector competes for limited resources against all others. In the long run the matter is not so clear-cut. The different sectors of an economy are inter-

related, and growth in one sector may not only raise the level of resources available generally but may also more directly promote growth in other sectors.[12]

Alternatively, because the different sectors are interrelated, lack of growth in one sector or disproportionate growth in one sector may not only waste resources but may also more directly inhibit growth in other sectors. Thus, "the unemployment of educated people in backward areas often represents the over-supply of particular types of trained labour, that is, it is the result of misdirected investment of capital embodied in human beings." [13] Also, "to over-emphasize industry, as some countries have found out to their cost, leads paradoxically in the end to a slower rate of industrialization." [14] And "if capital is being put into developing manufacturing industry while a country's agriculture remains stagnant, the result is bound to be distress in the manufacturing sector, as factory and cottage workers compete for a limited demand." [15]

Hence, what is invested or expended in one sector is not available for another; moreover, what is overinvested or overexpended in one sector, may and probably will create conditions which will impose other limitations on growth or development in other sectors beyond those arising from the direct denial of the overinvested or overexpended resources.

It is well to note here that for our purposes in this chapter investment priorities might better be termed *development* priorities as they relate not so much to the allocation of capital as to the importance and preference a particular sector should be accorded in the total scheme of economic activity, *i.e.*, the assignment of preference with respect to utilizing the limited pool of skilled manpower and to establishing training institutions for producing more manpower. In this connection therewith, the assignment of preference in using available teachers, and in using existing but limited facilities such as buildings, equipment-maintenance facilities, transportation facilities, etc., could and frequently are in the first instance as important or more important than the allocation of capital to a sector or a project within a sector. For example, it may well be that in most African countries, as in a good many other underdeveloped countries, agriculture would and should be the primary sector, but the absorptive capacity of traditional subsistence agriculture is so limited that it cannot immediately absorb large injections of capital. Nevertheless, if agriculture should be accorded the first priority, it would follow that breaking the bottlenecks or surmounting the obstacles to greater absorptive capacity should be given preference over all other endeavors. This could and usually does mean that developing trained agriculturalists, involving an extension service and developing the acceptance for such a service in the traditional farming areas, should be undertaken first and have a superior call on the enthusiasm, energy, *élan*, and other noncapital resources of the country. This does not mean that adequate and growing capital allocation to priority sectors will not be desirable or necessary. On the contrary, the very objective at hand is to render the sector of priority importance but with limited capacity for absorbing capital investment better able to do so. Thus, it is conceivable in a development plan that agriculture with an allocation say of 12–15 percent of the capital resources may be a first priority whereas transportation with an allocation of perhaps twice as much may be a second or third or less priority.

The important indicators of change, of establishing the preconditions for growth, would be the improvement in the performance of a priority sector or significant part thereof, which may or may not be quantifiable, but ideally of course would be the increasing of productivity and production; and second, the trend in capital allocation over a reasonable period of time. If, for example, a priority is maintained in practice in an area like agriculture, the likelihood is that in the first instance, largely within the present framework, changes in technique, practices, systems, seeds, etc., would produce increasing output, and that thereafter or perhaps even *pari passu* capital allocations to agriculture would also steadily increase as the framework alters and absorptive capacity expands.

First Theme: Priorities Among Sectors

The following analysis of overinvestment and excess expenditure of public resources—to say nothing of private resources—in the education sector of more and more African countries is intended to illustrate the diverse aspects of our first theme, the intersectoral priorities and related allocations: the importance and impact of the political decisions on economic choices, the implications of overinvestment and overexpenditure for other sectors—particularly the productive sector; the resultant burden imposed by the pattern of investment and expenditure on the overall economy, and again, particularly on the productive sector; and the heritage of social problems accruing from the wrong priorities and the misallocation of resources. In other words, the direct and indirect implications for nation-building resulting from priorities accorded to various sectors and the impact of these on growth.

Keeping in mind that the political decision already made on the priority to be accorded to economic development will in many ways and for many purposes establish the framework and limit the area of subsidiary political decisions and economic choices, the first set of questions that should confront the economic development planner in African countries would be concerned with the assignment of sectoral investment priorities. Should investment in the productive sector take preference, or investment in economic infrastructure, or in social overhead?   (Through-out the discussion, in addition to the limitations imposed on economic planners by political and economic realities, the dictum of Robert Burns on the best laid plans of men and mice going awry needs keeping in mind.)

Frequently, the situation in many African countries has been one of heavy investment in social overhead, public administration, and basic economic infrastructure with very limited investment in the productive sector.   Some African countries are already in this position and others are rapidly approaching it.

In Nigeria for example, in the former Eastern and Western Regions, between 40 and 45 percent of the ordinary budgets was expended in recent years on education.   Of this amount, between two-thirds and three-quarters probably went for primary education.   A relatively large portion of the balance went to higher education, and what remained had to cover intermediate education—secondary education vocational and technical training, including teacher training, and all other miscellaneous educational needs.   With the continuing emphasis on education in the Nigerian Six-Year Development Plan (1962–1967), intended in part to meet the obvious gaps revealed by the above composition of recurrent expenditure for education, and in part to respond to political drives, to provide universities in the three original regions of the country, and also in part to expand primary education, particularly in the Northern Region where it had lagged badly, the result has been a continuing high level of educational expenditure, making major demands on the recurrent budgets of the former Nigerian regions and the federal government, to say nothing of the demands on the development budgets.

If one adds to educational expenditure the recurrent expenditure for public administration, maintenance of internal law and order, defense, public health, debt service, and a few other fixed charges, very little was left for economic services and objectives, such as training and staffing an agricultural extension service, an agricultural credit supervisory service, an advisory service for cooperatives, an investment advisory service, and research staffs.   Little or no surplus was available for transfer to eco-nomic development budgets for investment in the productive sector.

In the Congo (Kinshasa) one finds an even more extreme example: approximately 35 percent of *all* government expenditure has in recent years gone to education and of this approximately 70 percent was allo-cated to primary education.   In addition, almost all the expenditure on education was to meet current salaries and a very limited amount of main-tenance, with little or nothing for new or improved facilities or buildings. When other "normal" expenditures of government are added in the Congo, there was nothing left for economic services and objectives and certainly nothing for investment in the productive sector or basic infra-structure, or for that matter, for anything else.

What these two examples point up is the extremely difficult political dilemma facing the new African states. How much can a new African state allocate for education and other social purposes and still have enough left for economic services and for investment purposes in the productive sector? How many African states are destined to find themselves in the situation of Nigeria and the Congo, where the political decision assigning a major priority to the educational sector with commensurate allocation of funds imposed serious constraints on economic planning choices?

The two countries have been producing hundreds of thousands of young primary school-leavers and dropouts with fragmentary education and little or no capacity to make a contribution to society, let alone an economic one, uprooted from their rural communities and flooding into urban areas where they lead a relatively aimless existence. In Nigeria in the former Eastern and Western provinces alone there were under the 1962–68 Development Plan some 150,000 school-leavers (to say nothing of dropouts) a year from 1963 onwards. Henceforth, it is quite clear that the Nigerian economy, even if it meets its development plan target of a growth rate of 4 to 4.5 percent per annum in the GNP, could not productively absorb in the industrial sector and in urban areas this stag-gering number of ill-trained, inexperienced young people. The result has been something approaching a panic reaction with the political leadership in both Regions grasping for any way out of the dilemma that offered any promise at all.

All too often the "solutions" adopted under pressure have compounded the problem of overinvestment in nonproductive sectors. For example, the former Western Region of Nigeria, which expended a vast sum on creating the problem, has since engaged in spending another significant sum in attempting to meet the problem by setting up extremely costly farm-settlement schemes which at best could only absorb a very small fraction of the people involved and, in any event, involves a per capita cost which it could not long hope to sustain. Elsewhere, in Kenya, for example, where the magnitude of the problem has not yet reached the proportions it has in southern Nigeria, it has nevertheless become acute. For although the numbers involved have been smaller, the resources available have also been smaller and the range of economic activities into which young primary-school leavers (and dropouts) could be absorbed has been far more limited. The "solution" in Kenya has been an informal agreement with European employers to maintain larger staffs than would otherwise be needed, on the understanding that the Government would do the same. In effect both of them would be buying a type of insurance to forestall the worsening of the unemployment situation in urban areas and the inevitable political instability that it brings in its train. The initial "revolutions" in Congo (Brazzaville) and Dahomey, already discussed in Chapter 4, involved, in fact were characterized by, riots of unemployed young people in the capital cities.

These, then, are very expensive short-term improvisations and palliatives to meet a continuing and growing problem, which was simultaneously being aggravated by the policies being pursued by the governments concerned in allocating ever increasing resources to primary education.[16] The political decisions according primary education its priority have thus not only circumscribed economic choices, but also have initiated a chain reaction leading to further political decisions—ill-conceived farm-settlement schemes, payroll padding, "feather-bedding," etc.—which in turn have acted to limit even more the possible economic planning choices.

SECOND THEME: PRIORITIES WITHIN THE PRODUCTIVE SECTOR

In this section we are concerned with our second principal theme: priorities and allocation of resources within the productive sector of an economy.

"The secret of most development problems is to maintain a proper balance between sectors."[17] "One might consider the industrialization of these countries as one chapter of agrarian reconstruction, or one might treat the improvement of agrarian production as one chapter of industrialization. What matters is to remember that the two tasks are interconnected parts of one problem."[18] "Paradoxically, the best way for government to foster industrialization may be for it to use more rather than less of its resources to encourage the enlargement of agricultural output and the improvement of agricultural techniques."[19]

Too often, development has been equated with industrialization, first in Asia, and now in Africa. Too often, the time factor and the related development sequence have been lost sight of in making comparisons between the developed and largely industrialized economies of today and the underdeveloped and largely nonindustrialized economies of today. It seems quite clear, however, as we have already suggested, that agriculture has been and is likely to be the leading sector of most African economies. In those few cases where mining predominates, agriculture still remains of major, and perhaps decisive importance.[20] In fact, extractive industry, mining, partakes in many ways of the characteristics of the agricultural sector, in that it involves production of primary products, and, to the extent processed, semiprocessed products, for sale in world trade.

There seems to be a near consensus of opinion on the historical role of agriculture as the springboard for most, perhaps all, economic development in the countries now commonly thought of as developed. The economic historian, Professor W. W. Rostow, has summed up the crucial role of agriculture in what he has termed the "transitional stage" of economic development. In his words:

> There are . . . three distinct major roles agriculture must play in the transitional process between a traditional society and a successful take-off. . . . First, agriculture must supply more food. . . . And, in most cases, increased agriculture supplies are needed as well to help meet the foreign exchange bill for capital development: either positively by earning foreign exchange . . . or negatively, to minimize the foreign exchange bill for food. . . . Put another way, the rate of increase in output in agriculture may set the limit within which modernization proceeds. . . . Agriculture may enter the picture in a related but quite distinctive way, from the side of demand as well as supply. . . . Let us assume that some of the potential leading sectors are in consumer goods—as, indeed, has often been the case: not only cotton textiles—but a wide range of import substitutes. . . . In addition, the modern sector can and often should be built in part on items of capital for agriculture: farm machinery, chemical fertilizers, diesel pumps, etc. In short, an environment of rising real incomes in agriculture, rooted in increased productivity, may be an important stimulus to new modern industrial sectors essential to the take-off. . . . There is a third distinctive role for agriculture in the transitional period which goes beyond its function in supplying resources, effective demand or tax revenues: agriculture must yield up a substantial part of its surplus income to the modern sector. . . . It is thus the multiple, distinctive, but converging consequences of the revolution in agriculture which give it a peculiar importance in the period of preconditions. Agriculture must supply expanded food, expanded markets, and an expanded supply of loanable funds to the modern sector.[21]

Bauer and Yamey, starting from a completely different point of departure—debunking "the mystique [which makes] manufacturing industry . . . a panacea for economic stagnation and poverty"—make many of the same points as Rostow.[22] They also make an additional point of considerable importance to the African scene—the employment effect of industrialization. In their words:

> The United States, Canada, New Zealand, and Sweden all have an appreciably larger proportion of their population in agriculture than the United Kingdom and yet their real income per head is larger. In the United States it was not until towards the end of the nineteenth century that manufacturing industry became generally prominent in the economy; and not until 1910 did the size of the labour force employed in agriculture

cease to increase. And it is especially noteworthy that it was not until 1941 that manufacturing employment exceeded agricultural employment in the United States, by which time it had for many decades been the richest or one of the richest countries in the world.[23]

Thus, declining employment in agriculture should not be automatically equated with development, and in any event, it is important to note that such decline as takes place does so over a long period of time, and in a sense, is a consequence of development rather than the point of departure. The intractable problem challenging the political stability as well as the economic growth prospects of many of the African states—growing unemployment in urban areas—has of course been one of the goads to indiscriminate emphasis on industrialization in African development planning. Frequently there has been a lack of appreciation of the limited employment capacity of industry for a very long time, in fact until many of the intermediary and consequential offshoots develop in the service and administrative areas. When viewed in light of the growing *volume* of unemployed young school-leavers and dropouts in Africa, industrialization as a solution has very limited short or medium-term promise.

Thus in Africa, agricultural and rural development is intimately related to achieving political stability as well as economic growth, and to the prospects of the many states for successful nation-building. Drawing into the market economy and the modern sector of national life, and to provide, in Mr. Chisiza's phrase, a sense of purpose, participation and belonging to, the estimated 75 to 90 percent of African populations to be found in the rural areas would seem to be a precondition not only for development but also for nation-building. Otherwise, as all too often has been the case in Africa, nation-building efforts will not touch the mass of the population. Lacking incentives to participate in development, and hence in nation-building, the rural masses have been viewed as apathetic or recalcitrant. Too often, coercion rather than inducement has been the formula. The choice of priorities therefore, the emphasis accorded agriculture vis-à-vis industry, has a direct relation not only to development but also to nation-building. If participation in modern sector activity is the goal, then agricultural modernization and rural reconstruction are keys to national growth and cohesion.

PURPOSES AND GOALS

Economic development purposes and goals vary among African states; they are not all seeking the same thing in the same order, or in the same way. There are obviously many roads to African socialism and many more roads to economic development. The preceding discussion of the

overall priority being accorded economic development by African states
and to the various sectors of their economy to a substantial degree fore-
shadows the purposes and goals to be found in the specific development
plans of different African states.

Thus, Nigeria's objectives were put succinctly in its first postindependence plan as follows:

> To achieve a modernised economy consistent with the democratic, polit-
> ical and social aspirations of the people. This includes the achievement
> of a more equitable distribution of means both among people and among
> regions.[24]

These purposes and goals are, as we know from earlier analysis, consistent with the Nigerian outlook on state structure, political system, the
Rule of Law, and economic structure. They also reflect the Nigerian
attitude on development of the private sector and encouragement of
widespread Nigerian participation in the private sector.

Equally consistent with its outlook and sharply contrasting with the
stated Nigerian objectives are those of Ghana, set out in the following
statement from the *Programme of the Convention People's Party*, which
established the terms of reference for Ghana's Seven-Year Plan:

> The basic aim of our economic development is to free our economy
> from alien control and domination. To achieve this, it is necessary for
> the State to participate in the wholesale and retail sectors of trade through-
> out the country. . . . The Party is firmly of the view that the planning
> of the national economy can only be really effective when the major means
> of production, distribution and exchange have been brought under the
> control and ownership of the State.[25]

It is interesting to compare this definition of Ghanaian socialism with
that of the Hungarian Marxist who served as economic adviser to the
Ghanaian government and produced a "planning paper" for Dr. Nkrumah
"for the consideration of the Planning Commission" at about the same
time as the CPP Program appeared.[26] The Planning Paper of Dr. Joseph
Bognar is curiously in many ways less socialistic and more capitalistic
than the *Programme of the Convention People's Party*. Thus, when
stripped of the convoluted language of Marxist economies and the intellectual flying buttresses which obscure much of what is being said,
one finds the following reasonably clear statement in the chapter of the
Bognar essay entitled, "Prospective Economic Tasks Arising from the
Political System and the International Situation of the Country":

In organizing an up-to-date economy and in industrialising the country the state plays in many respects an initiating and determinating part. . . . *This role of the state arises from its anticolonialist character* and therefore it is an essential role, which will be strengthened in the future. . . . The whole social and economic life of Ghana is inspired by the policy of the ruling C.P.P. incarnated in the person of Osagyefo. . . . In order to concentrate the national resources in a planned economy and to consolidate economic independence, it is necessary to ensure that the Government: retains the initiative and the controlling role in the State's economic life without endangering the part played for foreign capital in the economic development of the country. . . . Every possibility in the State for investment ought to be used whether by its own enterprise or in partnership with private capital, without hindering possible cooperation with foreign enterprise.[27]

And again in the conclusion to the chapter we find the following words, which can be read as a prescient observation, as a sophisticated counsel to accept the inevitable, or as a forecast of things to come.

It is necessary to take into consideration the behaviour and reaction which we may expect from persons and groups participating in economic activities. . . . A realistic approach to this question of behaviour is that once a man has acquired a certain position, attained a certain standard of living or adopted certain customs of consumption he will do all he can to evade our measures in order to retain what he has.[28]

The shift in Dr. Nkrumah's view of African socialism, from the common African Marxist (deviationist) view that there are no classes in African society, and therefore no class struggle, and consequently no need for a "dictatorship of the proletariat," to a more conformist Marxist view, dropping the African prefix, and reinstating the doctrine of the class struggle, suggests that the reading of Bognar's conclusion as a forecast of things to come may well have been the correct one. In any event, starting in late 1963 and with mounting furor, until its downfall in February 1966, the CPP and the party press campaigned against "bourgeois elements" and "capitalists" as the "enemies of the state" and its effort to build socialism.

Differing from both the sharply contrasting Nigerian and Ghanaian purposes and goals, are those of the Congo (Kinshasa). In a state paper published in July 1963, the Ministry of Plan and Industrial Development of the Congo published a set of *General Principles for a Five-Year Economic and Social Development Plan.*[29] Under the heading, "Directing Principles for Economic and Social Planning of the Republic of the Congo," the following brief statement of purposes and goals appears:

A development plan—even one conceived in a period of troubles and confusion—is always an element of stabilization and order.

The restoration of political order, which has been practically realized, is inseparable from the restoration of order in the economy.

The restoration of order in our economy must be accomplished in the framework of planning on new bases. Former planning no longer responds to the new imperatives.

Planning will have a considerable psychological impact on the nation. It will channel toward concrete goals the attention now focussed on political passions. It will harmonize the efforts of all who—in the given situation—are looking for the salvation of the country in a policy of work and progress. It will give the people the confidence of hope.

The plan will permit the coordination of policies, undertakings and measures formulated by the Government for domestic purposes, and in doing so afford more weight to the Government's foreign policy.[30]

Here, then, M. Cléophas Kamitatu, the then Minister of Plan, imaginatively perceived the many possible implications and ramifications of economic development for his strife-torn country. The use of economic development planning as a rallying point for the divided and fragmented Congo, beset by secessionist and separatist tendencies and movements from the date of its birth, June 30, 1960, is an extreme, but highly illustrative, application of the concept of economic development as an instrumentality for nation-building.

Although purposes and goals of economic development are not necessarily mutually exclusive, the emphasis and the nature of the various purposes would seem inevitably to lead to very different development results and patterns. Thus, the unrelenting Ghanaian emphasis on "economic independence" and "state control and ownership" have led Ghana down a path of public investment which the successor military government has found not easily reversible. Ghana widely substituted government investment for already existing private investment in shipping, aviation, gold mining, diamond marketing, and wholesale and retail trade. The government also invested in hotels, a laundry, related service industries, state farms, manufacturing plants, a steel mill based on turning out ingots from scrap iron, and other commercial enterprises. In all instances Government involvement in operations and management accompanied the investments.

The evolving Nigerian pattern, although not without public investment in what has frequently been thought of as private-sector fields, has been marked by its encouragement of private investment, domestic and foreign, its acceptance of free trade unions, its nondoctrinaire approach to development problems, and its recognition of the role of economic growth in uniting its pluralistic society. Finally, the Congo's statement of principles, if translated into a plan, could well lead to an investment pattern stressing development in agriculture where the bulk of the population still resides and in transportation and communications to weld the vast, sprawling, and unconnected country into a cohesive national unit.

Economic Development and Nation-Building

If the thesis in this chapter is valid, if participation and initiatives by a mass of individuals in economic development affairs is important in nation-building; if the economic incentives and rewards of increasing wages, salaries, profits, and dividends are important factors in drawing more and more people into the modern sector of the economy; if identifying independence, statehood, and nationhood with economic development is thought to be useful as well as an accurate appreciation of what in fact has been happening in Africa, then the conclusion seems clear that the voluntaristic approach to economic development has a greater possibility of being a positive factor in effectuating nation-building and serving as an instrumentality to facilitate it than the coercive approach; it also seems the more likely way to induce economic growth *per se*.

Pursuing an entirely different field of inquiry, the role of education in political development, Professor James Coleman has formulated a central conclusion of his work in language that is not only consistent with the foregoing conclusion on the link between economic development and nation-building and the crucial role of voluntary participation in both processes, but also synthesizes many of the themes developed in our analysis in Part II. It is therefore fitting to quote Coleman at some length as a summation of Part II:

> Comparisons of historical development of educational systems in modern societies strongly support the proposition that where alternative channels of mobility exist, a politically dysfunctional intellectual proletariat is less likely to appear. . . . The Japanese and Philippine course of evolution . . . strongly suggests the crucial importance of a vigorous and expanding private sector in coping with the dysfunctional consequences of educational expansion. Alternative careers outside government employment can provide status, as well as political influence. Moreover, in highly competitive, achievement-oriented societies, the blame for educational and career failure can be projected against one's self rather than against the system or the government. These and other factors help to create a societal capacity to manage politically destabilizing tensions, a capacity demonstrated by both Japan and the Philippines, but lacked by most new states because of the weakness of the private sector of their economies, and the consequent absence of alternative channels for upward mobility. Moreover, in most new states the private sector is likely to remain weak, not only because of

the strong statist orientation of the governing elites, but also because of the habituation of the masses to a bureaucratic and statist policy. *The real dilemma confronted by the leaders of such societies is that they possess neither the disposition to emulate the Japanese or Philippine pluralistic example, nor the organizational and administrative capacity to pursue effectively the totalitarian alternative.*[31]   [Emphasis supplied.]

PART III

NATION-BUILDING IN AFRICA: PROSPECTS

From these general observations it becomes apparent that the task of nation-building in traditional societies is peculiarly complex and difficult. . . . In sum, the issues of national unity represent basic constitutional problems. Only as they are resolved can society develop its policy and create the means for grappling with the social and economic problems of modernization.

. . . Politically the guiding interest is that chaos, tensions, and failure do not lead people to accept a repressive concentration of power in the hands either of a traditional elite or of a revolutionary dictatorship. This means that as increasing numbers of people become politically conscious they must see opportunities to exert some influence on the political process and on the decisions that affect their lives. . . . Where traditionally the individual has had little opportunity to shape his own destiny, what is required is the development of a wide range of activities that bring home to each group a sense of its responsibility for building its own future in the context of a wider loyalty to the society as a whole. For constructive political evolution to occur, these new activities must touch all aspects of life, not only politics. Public and private institutions of all sorts must be established.

. . . Finally, there is the economic dimension. If the economy does not move forward, the prospects for progress in other areas will not appear bright. Economic progress must be regarded both as a result of a movement toward modernization on other fronts and as a force making for further change. . . . Economic progress requires a dispersion of initiative and decision-making to a growing number of groups throughout the society. . . . Economic progress itself also generates both

175

the new attitudes and the new resources which permit such progress to continue. Finally, the phase of take-off, if successful, not only consolidates the capacity of the society to grow regularly but also tends to consolidate the political, social and psychological benefits of modernization.

MAX F. MILLIKAN *and* DONALD L. M. BLACKMER, *Director and Assistant Director The Center for International Studies, Massachusetts Institute of Technology, 1961*

CHAPTER 11

THE SPECIAL CASE OF THE CONGO (KINSHASA)

We remain the enemies of federalism and regionalism and oppose splitting the nation into a multitude of provinces.

> GASTON SOUMIALOT, *former Congolese rebel leader in North Katanga, Central Kivu, and Haut Congo, 1964*

General Mobutu sees the army as a main factor in nation-building and is particularly keen that his men should be drawn from all tribes.

> *"Congo Strong Man?"*, West Africa (*London*), *1964*

It is essential that a stable system of government and public service be established in Africa in this post-independence period. Hopefully, this can be accomplished without the sort of confusion which has ensued in the Congo, where independence was achieved with the minimum of preparation and thus resulted in in a complete breakdown of government as we know it, with catastrophic costs in manpower, money, and the energies of the rest of the world. If the Congo is to be the common experience, then I'm afraid that Africa will be the problem continent for a couple of generations.

> SAM S. RICHARDSON, *The Evolving Public Service in Africa, 1964*

The Congo is indeed a special case for nation-building, and has been since the Belgians took their fateful decision in January 1960 to abandon the country to its fate. Less than six months later, unprepared and ill-equipped, the Congo backed into independence and promptly fell into chaos, from which it has never extricated itself. And its prospects for doing so are almost devoid of promise.

The introductory quotations offer a kaleidoscopic view of the principal obstacle to Congolese nation-building—the geopolitical problems of size, shape and situs; a lack of national consensus on the physical perimeters of the country, involved with and reflected by the unrelenting struggle

177

over the state structure (confederal, federal, decentralized unitary, centralized unitary, and multiple separatist units); the role of the military, and the relation of the military to civil authority; the absence of trained and skilled cadres, involved with and reflected by the form, size, and power of the state structure and the political system to operate that structure; and finally, the geopolitical problem, after Addis Ababa as well as before, of direct intervention and extension of political sanctuary to disaffected factions and émigré groups by neighboring states to subvert the political stability and government of the Congo. We shall briefly consider these obstacles in the following sections of this chapter, emphasizing their ramifications and implications for the prospects of successful nation-building in the Congo.

Needless to say, many of the points considered in the ensuing exploration could be read into the situations existing in some of the countries alluded to in Chapter 13. Obviously, many of these points would fit, for example, the situation which has long existed in the Sudan in former British Africa. We have already noted elsewhere the divided racial and religious blocs and conflicting geographical areas in that country, the problems of guerrilla warfare and external sanctuary, and the special role of the military. And in the neighboring state of Chad, for example, in former French Africa, many of these points would also obviously apply. A brief extract from a report on a major address by President François Tombalbaye will suffice to show how much of the Congo nation-building drama has been reenacted elsewhere—fortunately with less vigor and less thoroughly, and fortunately without all of the Congo's ailments breaking out at the same moment. The report from *West Africa* reads:

> President Tombalbaye has also disclosed that a group calling itself "the Committee of Northern Chad" has sent a letter to General de Gaulle on March 14 [1964] criticising the attitude of the present Chad government. . . . "The authors of this letter," the President went on, "violently attacked my attitude and that of my Government toward Muslims. I am accused of having had numerous Muslims killed or imprisoned, notably following the events of March 22, 1963." He said that "these are pure lies emanating from our most incorrigible enemies. Those people—we must get rid of them quickly." [1]

It's all there—the disaffected, restless minority population group, without legal recourse in a one-party state, casting about for outside support to redress its plight. In this instance the father confessor to whom the disaffected and disenfranchised turned was General de Gaulle, patron saint of large parts of former French Africa. More recently, the Muslim minority has sought solace and aid closer to home, from the neighboring

Sudan. The result has been a worsening of the festering relations between the Sudan and the Chad.[2]

The lack of national consensus, the awkward size and shape of the elongated piece of real estate called the Chad, the divided population, the unitary one-party structure, the coercive political system, and a nearby sympathetic sanctuary for disaffected elements—all are present in the case of the Chad, and one could read in, instead of the Chad, Mali, or Mauritania without straining too much.

Thus, the special case of the Congo has implications for much of Africa. It seems that in the Congo *all* the problems of nation-building are all present at once and in more acute form than elsewhere on the continent (intensified by the abrupt withdrawal of Belgium in 1960, followed four years later by an only slightly less abrupt withdrawal of the United Nations); the evolving situation has resulted in such a classic text-book case of the problems and perils of nation-building in Africa that we think it useful to devote a full chapter to its analysis and appraisal.

BACKGROUND AND CONTEXT FOR CONGOLESE NATION-BUILDING

A few days after achieving independence on June 30, 1960, the Republic of Congo entered into a state of crisis from which it has yet fully to emerge. In rapid-fire succession the Congo experienced a series of serious army mutinies, with attendant strife, looting and disorder; intervention by Belgian armed forces, involving a series of military engagements, including the bombing of the port of Matadi; and then intervention at the request of the Congolese government by a multinational United Nations military force, which remained in the country some four years. (UN civil operations on a declining scale still remain in the country.) Accompanying and interwoven with these events were at least three major secession movements in Katanga, South Kasai, and the Stanleyville area of Oriental Province (the last of which terminated in Katanga in early 1963); the fall of the first Congolese government (the Lumumba government); a *coup d'état* of Colonel (now General) Mobutu; major tribal warfare in various parts of the country, particularly between the Baluba and Lulua in Kasai Province; widespread civil disorder and breakdown of local government, particularly in the Maniema and Kivu; major famine, particularly in South Kasai; large-scale refuge movements of Balubas from rural areas to the comparative safety of urban centers; disruption of the *Voie Nationale* (the national rail-river) transportation system for copper from Katanga to Matadi); banditry, and innumerable minor crises.

At the constitutional and political level the Congo came to independence more as a geographic expression than a national political unit. The

Belgians governed the Congo with no thought of independence, and with no contemplation of building a Congolese nation. More than in the British and French areas of Africa, the Belgian territories in Africa were run from the capital of the colonial power. The six Congolese provinces were administrative divisions administered for convenience as a unit. There was no organic fusion of the provinces of the type necessary for nation-building. In short, the Congo, at independence, was little more than a large sprawling area reaching from a narrow neck at the mouth of the Congo River on the Atlantic to the mountainous highlands of Central Africa on Lake Tanganyika. In this context the dispute for power among the many Congolese parties, factions and leaders emerged abruptly with independence and led to the constitution and reconstitution of weak governments in rapid order, the capture and assassination of the dismissed Prime Minister, Patrice Lumumba, and several of his ministerial collaborators. There ensued a series of seemingly endless, sporadic political negotiations among Congolese political leaders and factions seeking a compromise constitutional formula for the country between, at one extreme, a weak confederal system with limited powers vested in the confederal government, and at the other extreme, a relatively centralized unitary government. Interspersed throughout this period, aggravating and distorting the political focus, was a variety of military engagements, which lasted through December 1962 into early 1963, involving UN troops, elements of the Congolese National Army, and the armed forces of the secessionist provinces of Katanga and South Kasai. The Katanga secession led by the provincial president, Moïse Tshombé, was the most serious of the secessionist movements, and was only ended by UN forces after three rounds of fighting. Thereupon, Tshombé quit the Congo until he was to be called back in July 1964 to become Prime Minister of the whole country.

Four years after independence, at the end of June 1964, the UN military forces departed without having restored any degree of security, stability, or unity to the country. There were twenty-two provinces in existence in place of the original six at the moment of independence, each with a relatively new and inexperienced provincial administration struggling to organize itself and assert its authority. In addition to the twenty-two provinces, there were at the time in dispute some twelve to fifteen areas in the country claimed by neighboring provinces or seeking separate status as additional provinces. Violence in these disputed areas, often between forces of the competing provinces laying claim to the areas, was a common occurrence. At any one time, anywhere from four to five of the provinces were under martial law (*état d'exception*) declared by the central government in Kinshasa. Within the provinces there was frequent conflict and violence between political factions in power and those seeking power. In addition, in important areas of the country, particularly in the former Katanga province, banditry outside the large cities was widely practiced.

Starting in early 1964 with the Kwilu Province uprising, the Congo was afflicted by a new series of major rebellions in Central Kivu, North Katanga, Maniema and Haut-Congo (Stanleyville area), in which the moving parties were disaffected Congolese factions. Of these the National Liberation Committee, based in Brazzaville and Bujumbura (Burundi) was the most important, in association with local tribal groups and external Communist advisers (both Chinese and Russian varieties, particularly the former).

The government of Prime Minister Cyrille Adoula, which had the longest run of any Congolese government, resigned at the end of June 1964 (with most of these uprisings already under way), when its mandate under the provisions of the expiring provisional Congolese constitution, the *Loi Fondamentale*, ran out. The Adoula government was followed by a "caretaker government," which became the "government of national reconciliation" under Prime Minister Moïse Tshombé, in a most remarkable turn-about which even for Congolese politics must have seemed bizarre. Shortly thereafter, the national referendum on the new Congolese constitution was completed and the results announced. Thus, on August 1, 1964, a new federal-type constitution came into effect in the Congo. It provided, *inter alia*, that incumbent President Kasavubu would rule for another six months, by decree, after which a new Parliament and President would be elected. In the event, a new Parliament was elected with a wide spread of parties, President Kasavubu dismissed Tshombé as prime minister, and charged Evarist Kimba [3] with forming a new government. Kimba's attempt to find a Parliamentary majority was blocked by Tshombé. A deadlock ensued between the forces of President Kasavubu and those of ex-Prime Minister Tshombé, whereupon, on November 24, 1965, General Mobutu for the second time seized power and instituted a military regime. Mobutu assumed the presidency and declared the military would govern for a five-year period.

Tshombé is once again in exile.* His major achievement during his regime was to suppress the violent and widespread foreign-supported rebellions in the northeastern and central-eastern parts of the country. He did this in large part by relying on a small army of white mercenaries recruited in South Africa, Rhodesia, England, Belgium, and France (of

---

* Tshombé, in exile in Spain, was kidnapped aboard a private plane over the Mediterranean in 1967. He was flown to Algeria, incarcerated and held for extradition to the Congo, where he had been condemned to death *in absentia*. Tshombé, still a prisoner in Algeria at the end of June 1969, died suddenly, according to report, of a heart attack at the age of forty-nine. J.H.M.

the type he relied on earlier to sustain the Katanga secession). Ironically, in mid-1966, mutiny and minor secessionist tendencies broke out again in the Stanleyville area, with serious tension and division between the former Katanga *gendarmerie* stationed there and other troops of the central government. Although physically absent, Tshombé's presence remains a factor in Congolese politics.

The legal writ of the central government has thus never been fully established across the entire country. In practice, the central government's authority has been openly and repeatedly rebuffed. None of the Congolese governments—the original Lumumba government, the short-lived Iléo governments, the Mobutu-inspired "college of commissioners," the Adoula government, the Tshombé government, or the successor military regime of General Mobutu—has been able to establish an acceptable state structure, organize a suitable political system, or launch an economic development program. None has been able to establish the preconditions for nation-building or development. Why?

To answer, we turn to an examination of the principal nation-building problems confronting the Congo at independence, and unfortunately, as elsewhere in a large part of Africa, still confront the country years later in much the same form.

THE GEOPOLITICAL AND STATE STRUCTURE PROBLEM [4]

In their clearest form and in their most extreme manifestation, the absence of an accepted governmental structure and an adequate public administration to operate it, in the geopolitical circumstances of the Congo, and the consequences of this absence for nation-building and development, are most vividly illustrated by the continuing events in the Congo.

Although there are many converging reasons for the absence of a workable governmental structure and an adequate civil service to man it, these are beyond the scope of this chapter. It is sufficient for our purpose to note that the Congo came to independence on June 30, 1960, with an interim constitution, the *Loi Fondamentale*, promulgated by the Belgian government after the hastily convened Belgo-Congolese Round-Table of January–February 1960.

The conferees, in order to avoid a clear-cut confrontation on the crucial issue of the basic structure of the Congolese government and the distribution of powers between the center and the regions, devised a formula which permitted every Congolese leader, no matter what his point of view, to return to the Congo and claim a victory for his view, his party, or his region. The writer vividly recalls the heady atmosphere and the triumphant welcomes accorded one Congolese leader after another as he stepped from an airliner at Ndjili airport outside Léopoldville (now Kinshasa). The Congo was to be a unitary, federal, and confederal state all at one and the same time.

In short, to avoid making a decision among the unitary, federal, confederal, and separatist tendencies evident in the thinking of the new Congolese leadership even before independence, the *Loi Fondamentale* created an uneasy state structure, delicately balancing, or at any rate compromising, these various tendencies in the distribution of power and functions between Léopoldville and the then existing six provincial capitals. The result, already apparent before formal accession to independence, has been endless dispute and intermittent conflict, and a series of major secession movements and rebellions, interspersed with a seemingly never-ending series of constitutional and political conferences seeking to resolve the problem of governmental structure. Any number of draft constitutions emerged from the conferences but none was adopted until late July 1964, when the constitution hammered out by the Constitutional Commission of Luluabourg was approved in a national referendum. Prior to the adoption of the new constitution, as we have already noted, the original six provinces of the Congo fragmented into twenty-two more or less autonomous provinces with attenuated links to the central government in Léopoldville. The inevitable accompaniment of this outpouring of energy, resources, and wealth in dispute, conflict, and negotiations was a near breakdown in intergovernmental relations between the center and the provinces, and at the center itself, a kind of administrative *immobilisme*.

The new federal-type constitution recognized the proliferation of provinces and attempted to formalize and systematize it in the new federal structure. The parliamentary system of the *Loi Fondamentale* was replaced by a "semi-presidential" regime, suggestive in important aspect of the new Moroccan constitution and also the constitution of the Fifth French Republic. The major power was vested in the President. The Prime Minister and the cabinet were to be chosen by and were made responsible to the President and not to Parliament. The Parliament could not censure the government.[5]

The new constitution hardly had a chance to come to grips with the geopolitical problems of the Congo. The constitution was adopted and came into effect at a time when the Congo was torn with rebellion and external intrusions, and in practice, could not be put into effect in a large area of the country. Soon thereafter, the Mobutu military coup took place and the constitution was suspended for the whole country. Hence, an assessment is not possible of the suitability of the new constitutional structure for containing the many secessionist and separatist tendencies that have flourished in the Congo, and for establishing a state structure, and related thereto, a political system that would be able to attract the public participation and support required to operate the state structure effectively.

With the mutinies in the *Force Publique* in early June 1960, roughly 10,000 of the 12,000 Belgian civil servants in the Congo departed abruptly, and in doing so created a near vacuum in public administration. Although a number of Belgians have returned and other personnel has been made available by the United Nations and under bilateral aid programs, in fact the foreign contingent in the Congolese public service has probably not exceeded 3,500 since the troubles of July 1960. As a direct consequence, in the absence of trained and experienced Congolese staff in many critical sectors of the public administration, the level and quality of performance has deteriorated seriously and has had a ramifying effect throughout the entire public service.

The total impact of this dual institutional gap—the absence of a defined governmental structure and an appropriate public administration with trained manpower—has had a decisive and overriding impact on all Congolese nation-building and development. The Congo experience provides an all too perfect illustration of the negative effects that flow when a new state is unable to fulfill the minimal role of a nation-state—the provision of basic services, and the maintenance of law and order as well as the basic framework within which all else takes place in organized society. The impact on national unity and development prospects has been devastating.

More specifically, the limited capacity of the government to insure internal security and minimal political stability for over six years has not only inhibited the growth of a sense of Congolese nationality and nationhood and of national development, it has led to retrogression: secessionist movements, tribal warfare, rebellions, disaffection, disinvestment, flight of capital, decline in production, inflation, deterioration of infrastructure as well as of productive facilities, disruption of established marketing systems, and a general series of economic and financial dislocations, many of which are unfortunately becoming embedded in the economic structure. The lack of capacity of the government for maintaining effective relations with or control of the provincial and lesser governmental units has led to a serious lack of public order, an absence of control over tax collections and public expenditure, and a dissipation of the country's rich patrimony of natural resources.

THE PROBLEM OF THE MILITARY

The ongoing Congo crisis started with *les événements*—the series of military mutinies in July 1960. The thread of continuity in the Congo crisis has since been provided by the military. More perhaps than any other single institution in the country the army, contrary to the conventional wisdom on the role of the military in nation-building, has reflected the total lack of a sense of national identity which pervades the vast area collectively designated as the Democratic Republic of the Congo. The army has reflected the absence of an accepted geopolitical-constitutional format; the lack of an accepted state structure and political system; the lack of an effective and purposeful public administration, in fact, the absence of a national *raison d'être*.

The army, as many other Congolese institutions, has been a force without purpose, without allegiance, without definition. Thus, the repeated efforts to reorganize and retrain the Congolese army have been doomed to failure. It is extremely difficult, if not impossible, to create an effective, disciplined and obedient army in the absence of some accepted power or force to which the army is required to be responsible. Even mercenaries require an authority structure—civil or military—to perform in an acceptable manner. In the Congo certainly there has been no such national civil authority since independence. And there has been no equivalent military authority to command loyalty or demand performance. There has been no sense of legitimacy to lend authority to the new Congolese officer hierarchy. There has been no general identification among the Congolese people with the National Army. On the contrary, more than its predecessor, the *Force Publique*, the Congolese National Army (ANC, after its French initials) has not been accepted as part of the national structure. Its potential for nation-building, General Mobutu's aspirations recorded in the quotation at the opening of this chapter notwithstanding, has been and remains for the most part nonexistent.

The resolution of the constitutional dispute and the interrelated struggle for political ascendancy are preconditions for solution of the military problem. The army has not been particularly responsive or responsible to constituted civil authority, such as it has been. Nor has it been particularly responsive or responsible to its military hierarchy under either a civil or military regime. It has in turn been mutinous, rebellious, disorderly, predatory, and generally irresponsible. It has also been unable or unwilling to perform against ill-equipped, undisciplined, and disorganized rebel forces. Training and equipment may have improved the performance of this or that officer, or this or that unit, but only as a transitory matter, and not affecting the whole. Improved equipment appears only to have escalated rebellions or mutinies or foreign intervention, and not improved the comparative effectiveness of the ANC. And so, one of the principal objectives of the United Nations in the Congo, reorganization and retraining of the ANC, after four years of the UN presence in the Congo still remains unfinished business.

In his official report in late June 1964 on the withdrawal of the UN forces from the Congo, UN Secretary General U Thant states that the future of the Congo "must depend on two major and indispensable conditions:" "the retraining and reorganization of the National Army" and "the achievement of national reconciliation among the contending political leaders and factions of the country." [6] Both tasks, over two years later, still remain.

Thus, there can be no serious law and order, territorial integrity, and orderly government in the Congo until the ANC has been transformed into a national force responsible to and taking its orders from an established military hierarchy commissioned by and owing allegiance to a nationally accepted constitutional structure and government. And only then can training and modern equipment become significant. In many ways then the preconditions for nation-building are also preconditions for the creation of an effective military; and also in many ways, a circular relationship exists, in that the absence of a minimally effective military has been a serious obstacle to successful nation-building in the Congo.

Although, not deliberately linking the two—nation-building and reshaping the Congolese army—U Thant did so in effect in his report on the departure of the UN forces from the Congo when he enumerated the two outstanding tasks remaining, and then went on to say that the "failure to overcome [these] present dangers would no doubt bring disintegration and ruin" to the country. There can be no quarrel with U Thant's assessment, except to note that his tense may be wrong. Failure to achieve the reorganization and revamping of the Congolese army and to make progress in developing national cohesion during the UN period in the Congo may mean that the "disintegration" had already occurred, and that it has only been the discovery of the extent of the "disintegration" which has remained to become apparent.

EXTERNAL INTRUSION AND SUBVERSION

The Congo more perhaps than any other African state has suffered repeated external intrusion in its affairs. Almost from the beginning of its appearance on the world scene as an independent state, the Congo has been beset by outside interference. This has come not only from afar, but also from within Africa. Hence, not only the Soviet Embassy, but also at various times the Ghanaian, Burundese, Congolese (Brazzaville), and United Arab Republic embassies were asked to withdraw for interfering in the country's internal affairs. All of this, of course, was in addition to the towering Belgian presence.

Two important instances in the post-UN period illustrate the continuing nature of the interference and its adverse affects on internal cohesion and nation-building. The first of these relates to the activity of the Chinese Communists in Africa and the apparent willingness of the Burundese government to permit the "Communist-Chinese [to] turn the small kingdom into Peking's main Central African base." [7] The rebel activity launched from Burundi by Gaston Soumialot succeeded at one point in enveloping no less than four provinces of the Eastern Congo in serious strife. The externally-supported uprising had a serious impact on Congolese prospects for developing national unity and renewing its preindependence economic development. The excesses on both sides—particularly the terrorist activities of the rebellious forces—resulted in the liquidation of almost all local leadership and educated Congolese in one-third of the country, the widespread destruction of property, the waste of scarce resources, the disruption of production, and the exacerbation of the divisive and separatist tendencies in the large area involved in the fighting and destruction. The implications for nation-building and development of this legacy are obvious.

The second instance was Africa-wide. The Council of Ministers of the Organization of African Unity, at the insistence of the heads of state of Algeria and Ghana, inter alia, requested President Kasavubu not to permit the new Prime Minister of the Congo, Moïse Tshombé, to attend the OAU Heads of State Conference at Cairo in July 1964, as part of the Congolese delegation. Kasavubu reacted by refusing himself to attend the meeting, and by appointing Prime Minister Tshombé to head the Congolese delegation. Tshombé subsequently arrived and was placed under "house arrest" and forced to leave Cairo without attending the Conference.

The incident had serious repercussions at the time with any number of African heads of state and government taking exception to the "interference in the internal affairs of the Congo." They all noted that irrespective of what opinion one might have of M. Tshombé, he was duly appointed Prime Minister in accordance with the constitutional procedures of his country. Among the most outspoken were President Grunitzky of Togo,[8] then President Apithy of Dahomey, then Prime Minister Balewa of Nigeria, and President Tsiranana of the Malagasy Republic. The latter uttered some of the harshest words, on this point, at a Conference where harsh words were not rare. President Tsiranana declared, according to the French text:

> We are not all angels and if M. Tshombé goes to hell, there will be others among us to go there with him.[9]

The more dramatic version recorded in the English version follows:

Tshombé won't go to hell but if he does there will be many of you there to receive him.[10]

The significance of the Tshombé incident was recognized at the time and pointed out in *West Africa*, in a whimsical mood, in an article entitled "Tshombé or Not Tshombé?" The article commented:

One of the principles of the Charter of the Organization of African Unity which gained most support at Addis, just over a year ago, was that of noninterference in the internal affairs of member states. Though the ex-Casablanca powers—with Mali rather out in the cold, and Guinea, so far, silent—are so opposed to Mr. Tshombé as to make this principle of non-interference of secondary importance, a significant number, of whom Nigeria is certainly one, believe that this is of prime significance.[11]

External pulling and pushing, externally-inspired or supported subversive movements, and even open rebellions, and external intrusion in Congolese domestic affairs have obviously detracted from and complicated the prospects of the Congo achieving internal stability and security, restoring law and order and the Rule of Law, resolving the problem of the fundamental constitutional structure of the country, and relaunching the dislocated economy. Thus the prospects for building any sort of national identity and forging any sort of national cohesion have been drastically reduced.

A CONCLUDING WORD

Although the Congo must be viewed as a special case, as we observed at the outset of this chapter, many and in some instances most of the problems in one degree or another have been confronting the nascent African states as they seek to develop national identities and structures, and as they seek to expand and develop their economies. The Congo, however, has all the problems, and has them all more acutely. Consequently, its prospects for successful nation-building can only be viewed as dismal at present and over the foreseeable future. And this has serious implications for nation-building and development elsewhere in Africa, for as *The Economist* wryly observed: "Without the Congo, Africa is like a doughnut—it has a hole in the center." [12]

CHAPTER 12

OTHER SPECIAL CASES: RWANDA, BURUNDI, SOMALIA, LIBYA, ETHIOPIA, AND LIBERIA

Somalia is the only nation in Africa trying to become also a single state.

Dalka (*Mogadishu*), *an independent monthly journal, 1966*

In this chapter we shall treat briefly with the nation-building prospects of a handful of cases outside the former French and British African empires. The prime case of nation-building in a new state outside the two former major African colonial empires, dealt with in the preceding chapter, that of the Congo (Kinshasa), leads to a consideration of the prospects of the only other former Belgian area in Africa, the UN Trust Territory of Ruanda-Urundi. After consideration of the former trust territory, which came to independence in 1962 as the Republic of Rwanda and the Kingdom of Burundi, we shall turn briefly to another former UN Trust Territory, Italian Somaliland, and then to the strange case of Libya, which became a state and independent almost by accident. Thereafter, we will examine, again briefly, the nation-building prospects of two older states, which have taken a new lease on life as part of African independence revolution, Liberia and Ethiopia, and analyze their nation-building prospects.

RWANDA AND BURUNDI: BALKANIZATION, AFRICAN STYLE

The abrupt Belgian withdrawal from the Congo, as we have seen, left its mark on much that has since happened in that sadly befuddled country. The Belgian withdrawal from the UN Trust Territory of Ruanda-Urundi was only slightly less precipitous, and has had a continuing impact on the fate of these two strangely contrived states lying between the Democratic Republic of Congo and Tanzania.

Although conceived of as a single trust territory and in overall terms—such as trade, banking, currency, and research—administered as a unit by the trustee power, Belgium, no attempt, as in the Congo, was made to achieve organic unity between the two areas, and at the approach of independence, the two areas insisted on coming to independence as separate sovereign states. African states directly and through their representation in the United Nations vigorously opposed the emergence of two states as "balkanization." Nevertheless, the Rwandese and Burundese insisted and had their way.

Brought to independence with no more preparation than the Congo, and with far fewer developed economic resources, the two states have had to launch their nation-building efforts from scratch. Strangely enough, Rwanda has come to independence as a republic with a multiparty system, and friendly ties with the former metropole, Belgium, and close links to the African states of French expression, whereas Burundi has emerged as a kingdom, also with a multiparty system, but with only attenuated links to Belgium and the francophone states, and close relations with Communist China.

We shall first consider the Republic of Rwanda. Shortly before independence Rwanda had a far-reaching social revolution. After generations of control, the Tutsi monarchy and feudal aristocracy which governed Rwanda were overthrown by the Bahutu.[1] Belgium played the role of midwife in bringing about this drastic transformation and some would go so far as to say that Belgium was the designer as well as executive agent of the revolution.[2] Either way, there can be little doubt that after some four decades of accepting the overlordship of the minority Watutsi tribe over the majority Bahutu tribe, the Belgians, taking account of growing Hutu opposition to the Tutsi aristocracy, switched their political patronage,[3] sponsored the country's first elections for a national parliament, and permitted the African nationalist doctrine of "one man, one vote" free reign.

In the words of a recognized authority on the area, Dr. Benoît Verhagen:

> After November 1959, the two sides ranged themselves in opposing camps. The weight of the trustee power and the game of electoral arithmetic tipped the balance in favor of the Hutu.[4]

The inevitable outcome, with the Bahutu accounting for some three-quarters or more of population, was a Bahutu victory.[5] It was but a step to replacing the monarchy with a republic.

The revolution took place over a period of years starting in November 1959, with the outbreak of a bitter civil war several months after a *coup d'état* by *"les dures"* of the Tutsi aristocracy put Kigeli V on the throne, following the death of Mwami (King) Mutara, a moderate Tutsi king, who was reputed to be concerned about reforming the country's social

and political structure, and culminating some three years later with independence. The revolution was characterized by some of the most violent
and bloody tribal warfare in recent African history. And the aftermath,
the 1963–64 incursions into Rwanda of exiled and refugee Watutsi from
Burundi and Uganda, and the fierce and frenetic Hutu response, visited
not only on the "invaders" but also on the still remaining Watutsi in the
country, has been a crucial factor in Rwanda's attempt at nation-building.

The Hutu takeover not only displaced the Tutsi monarchy, it also
broke the socioeconomic pattern through which the Tutsi aristocracy
reigned. The Tutsi monopoly of the country's wealth, particularly the
exclusive ownership of cattle, the principal symbol of wealth in the country, was destroyed. The Bahutu, who had been relegated to the local
version of hewers of wood and drawers of water, rose up from their
lowly status as agricultural cultivators to become cattle-owners as well as
political rulers.

As with all social transformations of so basic a character, there are
obviously refinements which could be added to render the picture more
precise. For example, one would have to take account of the small Twa
pygmy population and its role in the civil war, the Tutsi "radicals" who
attempted to make common cause with the Hutu "moderates," the policies of the Belgian administration, and the various interventions of the
UN Trusteeship Council and other external forces. But for our purpose
the broad picture outlined above provides the principal ingredients for
understanding the nation-building politics, problems and preconditions
(primarily the absence thereof) of the Republic of Rwanda.

From what has already been said, it seems clear that Rwanda has a long
and difficult road to travel to build a state structure, a concept of nationality, a stable social structure, and a supporting economy, before really
launching out on a conscious effort at nation-building. Central to all
these preconditions for nation-building is the question of the position of
the Tutsi population. Is it to be part of the new nation? If so, on what
terms can it be integrated into the state structure, social structure, and
economy? What too can be done and by whom to restore the production of the principal export cash crop, coffee, which has suffered badly
as a result of the political turmoil and armed clashes and as a result of the
limited capability of the largely inchoate public administration which the
republic relies on for overseeing the economy?

As if the lack of national cohesion were not enough, the formidable
geopolitical problems of an oddly shaped sliver of mountainous land,
densely populated (220 inhabitants per square mile),[6] and without known
mineral resources, sandwiched between an unfriendly neighbor to the
south, the Tutsi-dominated Kingdom of Burundi, the strife-torn Congo
to the west, and two English-speaking states with which it has little in

common, Uganda to the north and Tanzania to the east, must be thrown into the scale. The outcome is overwhelmingly weighted on the low side with respect to nation-building possibilities.

The Kingdom of Burundi shares many of the problems of Rwanda. There, however, no social revolution comparable to the Rwandese has occurred. A Tutsi monarchy continues in power. The history of the country is this regard has been sufficiently different,[7] so that the present dispositions may persist for a time.

However, the Bahutu have been increasingly active in seeking political power and achieved a better than 2-1 majority in the Parliament in the 1965 elections. The Hutu majority was frustrated when the King named a Tutsi Prime Minister. An abortive military *coup d'état* involving Hutu soldiers in October 1965 was then used by the Tutsi-dominated regime to liquidate *all* the Hutu leadership in the country. Military courts summarily condemned to death a reported 130 civil leaders, who subsequently were executed.[8] The International Commission of Jurists publicly condemned the disregard for the Rule of Law in the way the trials and executions were handled.[9]

Unrest and uneasiness have characterized the scene ever since the King was ousted by a palace *coup* of his son, Crown Prince Charles, and Tutsi officers in the army in mid-1966. The Crown Prince assumed power as Mwami (King) Ntare V on September 1, 1966.

The background of tribal division and repression suggests that the basic preconditions for nation-building are absent in Burundi. There is no agreement on the shape and structure of the country. There is increasing agitation for discarding the monarchy and becoming a republic,[10] but there is no consensus on who should rule, let alone how. The dominant role of the military, purged of its Hutu element, is hardly a force for bringing about a climate in which the issues could be resolved by decisions of the population. In the meantime, there has been little time or energy to devote to economic development.

In place of a social revolution such as the Rwandese, the Burundese monarchy has, like the new regime in Congo (Brazzaville), taken a turn to the left,[11] offering a more or less stereotyped menu of African radicalism. Externally, this has taken the form of providing a base and sanctuary to antigovernment Congolese émigré and rebel forces on the ground that first the Adoula and then the Tshombé governments were pro-Western and neocolonialist. Comparable facilities were also provided the Tutsi émigrés and refugees *vis-à-vis* Rwanda on much the same ground with the Belgians being cast as the villains in the piece. Its policy toward Congo (Kinshasa) and Rwanda had the expected result—relations between the two countries and Burundi were severely strained and even for a time disrupted.

As a concomitant of this studied hostility toward alleged neocolonialism, "a lively little" Communist Chinese Embassy was given a warm welcome and allowed for a long time—until a temporary internal shift back from the left, led to the ouster of the Chinese Embassy in 1965—to intervene quite openly in the various Congolese rebellions in adjacent Kivu province and beyond.[12]   In addition to the part-time marriage of convenience of the Burundese Kingdom with the People's Democratic Republic of China, Burundi has remained aloof from the Union of African and Malagasy States and its successor organizations, the Union of African and Malagasy States for Economic Cooperation, and the Common Organization of African and Malagasy States, with all of which Rwanda has affiliated.   Burundi, however, along with Rwanda, Congo (Kinshasa) and sixteen other French-speaking African states, is an Associate Member of the European Economic Community.

In sum then, Burundese nation-building prospects do not differ markedly from those of its erstwhile sister in the former UN Trust Territory. If anything, in light of the internal situation and the country's external posture, they may well be poorer.

A Note on Political Parties in Rwanda and Burundi

In the circumstances of Rwanda and Burundi, as in the Congo (Kinshasa), political parties have tended to be factions centered on a leading personality, frequently a tribal personality, or outright tribally based groups.   The government party in Rwanda, the *Paramehutu*, is clearly the party of the dominant Bahutu tribe.   The majority party, out of power, in Burundi, *le Parti du Peuple*, is equally clearly the party of the Bahutu tribe.   The governing party in Burundi, *l'Union Nationale du Progrès* (UPRONA), is controlled by the Watutsi tribe, but includes some Hutu moderates seeking a bridge with the Tutsi moderates in the party.

The dethroned monarch attempted before the victory of the *le Parti du Peuple* in the 1965 elections to foster a one-party approach to nation-building.   UPRONA was the vehicle, and it provided an umbrella for a collection of factions—the traditional Tutsi feudalists, a group of Tutsi moderates seeking a rapprochment with the Bahutu, and a group of Hutu moderates.   However, internal competition for control in the party and marked differences among the factions was a principal characteristic.   In the words of a party declaration at a "summit conference" of the party in Kitega in September 1964, its principal tasks were:

> Complete reconciliation among the leaders of UPRONA . . . and the complete suppression of the two factions, namely the Monrovia and Casa-

blanca, from the midst of the party, the Parliament and the government
. . . and the relentless struggle against all divisions and the adoption of
measures to be taken against all instigators of division. . . .[13]

It is all there—the divisions of opinion, the attempt to contain them
all within the structure of one party, and the seemingly inevitable pitch
for suppressing the differences. It is interesting to note too the characterization of the internal differences in the party as "Monrovia and Casablanca," in light of the analysis in Chapter 2 with respect to the per-
sistence of these two general postures in the Organization of African
Unity.

THE KINGDOM OF LIBYA: A VERY SPECIAL CASE

The Kingdom of Libya will be treated here only to the extent of noting
that the peculiar circumstances surrounding its creation and accession to
independence on Christmas Eve in 1951 are in reality more a part of the
story of the Italian peace settlement and the immediate post-World War
II manoeuvering of the great powers in the United Nations, than a chapter in the African independence revolution. A detailed consideration of
the Libyan experience would take us far afield from the main lines of our
analysis of nation-building in the new African states (and the two renewed states) and lead us into the fascinating but highly particularistic
story of how the United Nations put together three former Italian territories in North Africa—Tripolitania, Cyrenaica and the Fezzan—and,
being unable to work out a great power agreement on a UN trusteeship
for the area, cut it adrift as an independent state.[14] Also, a detailed consideration of Libya would take us into the strange and special world of
poor underdeveloped countries suddenly transformed into oil-rich powers.
This was the fate of Libya some ten years after independence. It has all
the problems of nation-building we have been concerned with here, but
its new vast wealth and the special history of its accession to independence
are such important distinguishing factors as to give its experience limited
applicability to the large bulk of African states, particularly those south
of the Sahara.

The nation-building prospects of this large sprawling country—a
goodly portion of which is desert—with a population of just over a million
people, is extremely hard to assess. It was brought to independence as
a monarchy, with a federal governmental structure. The centralizing
tendency of the monarchy, which for our purpose here, is not unlike
that of a one-party structure, led to the disappearance of the federal
structure early in the 1960's. King Idris I has been able, first with large
foreign aid from the United States and the United Kingdom, and then

with the country's oil wealth, to hold the ring and achieve a degree of national unity. There is considerable concern over what will follow after King Idris. There has as yet been relatively limited participation by the bulk of the citizenry in public affairs or the modern sector of the economy. There has also been intermittent external interference in the country's affairs from the neighboring state, the United Arab Republic. The outlook is thus uncertain, and might be assessed as fair.

SOMALIA: DIASPORA AND GATHERING-IN, AN AFRICAN VERSION

Somalia, unlike the special case of the Congo, with its heterogeneous multitribal population, and the special cases of Rwanda and Burundi with their sharp population cleavage between Watutsi and Bahutu, has a relatively homogeneous population. It has been estimated that 90.5 percent of the population is composed of Somalis, and the remaining 9.5 percent of "Negroid groups" (6.2 percent), and Asians, including Arabs, (3.3 percent).[15] In addition, there has been frequent intermarriage between Somalis and Arabs, "at least since the eighteenth century."[16] Finally, Islam is the universal religion and Islamic culture is ubiquitous.

Contrasting with these favorable factors for national cohesion in the new state of Somalia which came into being in 1960, are the large size of the country, 246,000 square miles, over which two million people are scattered, two-thirds of whom are nomads; the thin elongated shape of the country with its flying northern wedge; few natural resources; one of the lowest per capita incomes in Africa, estimated at $22 in 1960,[17] and the Somali version of the diaspora.

Dominating all else in Somalia is the drive to gather in the fragmented Somali people (with the land they occupy) in the Haud and Ogaden areas of the Empire of Ethiopia, in the Northern Frontier District of Kenya, and in French Somaliland. British Somaliland has already been incorporated; by agreement of the local government in British Somaliland with the colonial power, the United Kingdom, the British protectorate was terminated and the territory acceded to independence in time to combine with Italian Somaliland when it acceded to independence on July 1, 1960, as the Republic of Somalia.[18]

The story of Somalia's running conflicts with Ethiopia and Kenya is long and complicated. In response to Somalia's design for a Greater Somalia, by the gathering-in of territory and population now included within the geographic borders of their two states, Ethiopia and Kenya have entered into a mutual defense pact. Both sides have also been undergoing military build-ups. And both sides have also displayed their willingness to use their arms.

For our purpose, it is enough to note the serious and overriding concern of Somalia with this irredentist issue. In the context of what has already been said, the following quotation from then Prime Minister Abdirashid Ali Sharmarke of Somalia demonstrates the pivotal nature of the issue that overshadows all else, including the staggering problems of economic development and the formidable problems of nation-building within the existing territorial limits of the Somali Republic. The then Prime Minister wrote in 1962:

> No! Our misfortune is that our neighboring countries with whom, like the rest of Africa, we seek to promote constructive and harmonious relations, are not our neighbors. Our neighbors are our Somali kinsmen whose citizenship has been falsified by indiscriminate boundary "arrangements." They have to move across artificial frontiers to their pasture lands. They occupy the same terrain and pursue the same pastural economy as ourselves. We share the same creed, the same culture and the same traditions. How *can* we regard our brothers as foreigners?
>
> Of course we all have a strong and very natural desire to be united. The first step in this direction was taken in 1960 when the British Somaliland Protectorate was united with Somalia. This act was not an act of "colonialism" or "expansionism" or annexation. It was a positive contribution to peace and unity in Africa and was made possible by the application of the principle of the right to self-determination. We adhere most rigidly to this principle which is linked to our pledge in Article VI of our Constitution that we shall promote "by legal and peaceful means the union of Somali territories." [19]

The same volume, published by the Somali Government, in which the Prime Minister's words appeared, quotes with obvious approval the declaration of Lord Rennell:

> For one brief period during the war, World War II, nearly the whole of Somaliland was under British administration. . . . But the world was not sensible enough, and we were not interested enough, and so the only part of Africa which is radically [sic] homogeneous has again been split up into such three parts as made Caesar's Gaul the problem and the cockpit of Europe for the last two thousand years. And Somaliland will probably become the cockpit of East Africa. . . .[20]

And not to be outdone by their Somali adversaries, the Ethiopians too have their British champion, whose answer to Somali nationalism is "union of the Somalilands . . . within Ethiopia." This is what Mrs. Sylvia Pankhurst, the famous British suffragette leader and long-time friend of Ethiopia, wrote in her early voluminous work, *Ex-Italian Somaliland* ("*The Benadir*"), in 1951:

At the time of the Italian defeat many forward thinking Somalis foresaw that union of the Somalilands could only be successfully realised within Ethiopia, the Somalilands being a part of a great entity comprising the whole Horn of Africa. They saw that to divide the Somalilands from the grain-producing Ethiopian highlands would be economically a most serious act of unwisdom, to which the people of Ethiopian Somaliland would never willingly assent; they had not ceased to protest against being administratively divided from Ethiopia during the seven years of British military occupation.[21]

The author goes on to conclude:

One would suggest that the policy of segmenting into separate states the great area comprised by the Horn of Africa is from every aspect retrograde. . . . The economy of the territories surrounding Ethiopia is not based on a separate territorial existence, these colonies depend on Ethiopia and form with Ethiopia an economic entity. . . . The sentiment of hostility and estrangement towards the people of free Ethiopia in the great land mass of which the seaboard colonies are geographically a part was intrinsically opposed to the interests of the people in the seaboard colonies as well as the interior. It was in the main artificially imbibed from the foreign rulers of the colonial territories.[22]

The jousting of the English romantic school of foreign policy aside, the fundamentally conflicting postures of Somalia and Ethiopia, Somalia and Kenya, and in the wings, Somalia and France[23] (denounced by Somalia as an ally of Ethiopia) have adversely affected the development and nation-building prospects of all the African states concerned. As the leading protagonist, Somalia has probably diverted proportionately more of its scarce resources (taken in a literal sense as well as an economic concept) than the other states have of theirs. In fact,

Somali anger and bitterness over the failure of the West to supply the republic with military support commensurate with that accorded to Ethiopia . . . may have caused the Somali leaders to get themselves in deeper with the USSR and Communist China than is prescribed under the country's traditional policy of "balance." . . . Total Somali indebtedness to the Soviet Bloc by the end of 1963 could total over $100,000,000, including military equipment. Indeed, there were some indications that the major Soviet effort to gain a springboard in Africa may have been transferred from West Africa to the Horn.[24]

Written in 1963, the foregoing assessment would be brought up to date by taking account of Chou En-lai's peregrinations through Africa in 1964, and his solicitude for and support of the Somali campaign of "national liberation" against the "neo-colonialists and their lackeys." In Chou En-lai's words, as he terminated his African tour in Somalia: "Revolutionary prospects are excellent throughout the African Continent." [25]

In addition to the diverting and unsettling effect of Somalia's grand design for Greater Somalia, there are other pressing problems of internal nation-building. The absorption or fusion of British Somaliland into Somalia has obviously thrown up problems. Our earlier discussion of the problems of merging the British Southern Cameroons with the Republic of Cameroon into the Federal Republic of Cameroon and of the difficulties in the way of a merger of Gambia and Senegal are at least in part apposite here. The fusion of the smaller British Somaliland with the far larger former Italian Somaliland has raised a host of problems involving the reconciliation and blending of cultural, linguistic, political, administrative, judicial, economic, financial, and other differences. Only one overt manifestation of the problems has been of sufficient magnitude to gain outside notice *i.e.*, "a brief uprising of British-trained officers in the Northern Region in 1961." [26]

There are several political parties in the country which actively contest national elections. The Northern Region, the former British Somaliland, tends to have its own parties, and the Somali Youth League (SYL), the principal party in the country, is predominantly based in the south, in former Italian Somaliland, where it was founded during the British occupation in World War II. In addition, there are apparently several major clans or tribal groupings in the country which seem to receive special recognition in the distribution of appointments and other public awards.[27]

Economically the country is dependent on outside grants from Western countries of as much as $10 million a year for ordinary budget expenses. Its dependence on subsidized Italian imports of its principal export crop, bananas, makes the economy particularly vulnerable. Development assistance has come from the European Common Market with which Somalia is associated, Italy, the United States, and other western countries and the Soviet Union. The country's Five-Year Development Plan belongs to that group characterized in Chapter 10 as "*pro forma*." The plan was recently characterized in Somalia in these words:

> The unbelievably fantastic aspect of the Plan is that it so plainly contemplates that 60 per cent of the funds necessary for its execution will never be available. It was no Plan, but a big fraud. The sooner it is officially buried the better.[28]

In sum, then, this potentially homogeneous country in which nation-building ought to be off to a good start is so beset by the geopolitical problems of size and shape,[29] the problems involved in integrating two separate territorial units with different colonial heritages and serious problems of economic growth, that the outlook for successful nation-building is quite poor.

EMPIRE OF ETHIOPIA: ODD, BUT NOT OUT

Addis Ababa, as the headquarters of the Organization of African Unity and the UN Economic Commission for Africa, has come to be thought of increasingly as the capital of Africa as well as the capital of Ethiopia. It is at once strange but somehow fitting that this oldest of independent African states, with its ancient civilization, historical continuity, traditional society and imperial rule should house the capital of recently independent, modernizing, republican Africa. It can no longer be said of Ethiopia that it is in Africa but not of it. We have discussed Ethiopia in some detail, particularly in Chapter 6. We now turn briefly to additional points.

Ethiopia is a large (400,000 square miles) and variegated country. Its terrain varies from a high plateau of 8,000 to 10,000 feet in the central part of the country, which descends to a low plateau of 4,000 to 5,000 feet, and then tapers off into scrubland and desert on its borders, particularly those shared with Somalia and Kenya.

Its population (estimated at 22 million) is no less variegated. The central ruling group comes from the Amharic nobility on the highland plateau. Allied by marriage, conquest, and joint interest are the Galla, Shoa, Tigre, and other principal tribes dwelling in the plateau areas. The Amharic are thought to have come from the Near East, probably from the Arabian peninsula. In the Haud and Ogaden areas are Somali peoples. In the south, and on the border with Sudan, there are Negroid tribes. The population is also divided between adherents of the two principal religions, the Ethiopian State Church, an offshoot of the Egyptian Coptic Church, and Islam. There are also practitioners of traditional animistic religions of the type found elsewhere in Africa. There are also many vestiges of the declining feudal system which still characterize the social and economic status and role of much of the population.

Integrating this diverse population scattered across a vast, mountainous country, with very limited means of transportation and communication, would by itself present a major challenge. When the limited governmental structure and, until recently, largely inchoate public administration are taken into account, it becomes an overwhelming task. Yet, this task and the related one of modernizing the economy with its low per capita income and heavy reliance on a single cash crop, coffee, must be successfully confronted if Ethiopia is to become a modern nation-state.

In the absence of political parties, the political process takes its impetus from the Emperor. He has broadened the political participation somewhat, sharing some authority with close associates as he inevitably must as part of his program to modernize the economy, build the nation, and win a central place for Ethiopia in African affairs. There is also a Parliament with nominal powers, and a growing formal civil service, which inevitably has been assuming more functions, and consequently authority, as a concomitant of the economic development plans launched by the Emperor. The modern and relatively large army, by African standards, has had an increasingly important role since it put down in December 1960 an abortive *coup d'état* of a portion of the Imperial Guard in league with some disaffected noblemen. As an outgrowth of the attempted *coup* the Emperor has tended to bring more of the recently returned, university-educated young men into the newly established civil service and into minor ministerial posts as "assistant ministers."

The State Church with its clergy and various orders has also played an important role in Ethiopia's political, social, and economic evolution. As powerful and privileged parts of the changing feudal structure with vast land holdings, the Church and clergy have tended to resist modernization, involving as it must a shift in power, or at least a dilution of it. As large landholders they have tended to resist land reform, including a new land measurement system, a land tax system, and a new income-tax schedule on income deriving from land, to say nothing of land redistribution.

Unlike most of Africa, then, Ethiopia in its nation-building is confronted not only with the many problems common to all the new African states but also with the problem of overcoming serious entrenched or vested interests. The royal family, nobility, the landed gentry, the State Church, and the clergy all tend to resist changes that mean revamping of the traditional system which affords them their privileged positions. This resistance interacting with the forces for change determines the pace for nation-building.

The divisions in the population deriving from the traditional system also seriously militate against a sense of Ethiopian nationality. The lack of identity between the top and the bottom of the social structure, the stratification of society based on tribe and religion as well as on social rank (inherited or accorded by the Emperor), the maldistribution of wealth and economic opportunity, and so on, built into the established system, all throw up added obstacles to growth and change, to economic development, and to nation-building. At the same time, as we have suggested elsewhere, the traditional structure does have elements of strength which could sustain modernizing tendencies and innovations. Will it

prove to be sufficiently yielding and sufficiently adaptable in accommo-
dating the changes now in the offing?

Uncertainty as to what will follow after Emperor Haile Selassie, the
modernizing reigning monarch, now in his seventies, departs the scene, has
also tended to have an inhibiting effect with respect to national cohesion
and growth. Will the Crown Prince, compromised to a degree in the
abortive 1960 rebellion, succeed to the throne? If he does, will he continue, as the present Emperor, to command the support of the Army,
the nobility, the Church, the younger generation in the civil service, the
bulk of the population scattered in remote rural areas? The overhanging
uncertainty has tended to impart a note of caution to the actions of those
who should lead in the nation-building and development efforts. Offense
given today may be regretted tomorrow; better wait and see. Such
caution and hesitancy are hardly the qualities for launching imaginative
ventures to transform and develop traditional, divided, and subsistence
communities into a cohesive, modern nation-state.

Nevertheless, Ethiopia is on the move after generations of near stagnation. This has been in significant part a reaction, shared with Liberia
(considered next), to the African independence revolution. The Empire
of Ethiopia can no longer be dismissed as the *opéra bouffe* kingdom so
amusingly and satirically projected in the novels of Evelyn Waugh.[30]
Its nation-building prospects are not particularly bright. The outlook is
for a difficult, complicated, and relatively slow fusion of the country
and its population, with economic development and a related social revolution as the prime movers in the process.

LIBERIA: "THE LOVE OF LIBERTY BROUGHT US HERE"

The Seal of the Republic of Liberia proudly proclaims: "The Love of
Liberty Brought Us Here." The preamble of the Constitution of Liberia
also proclaims:

> We the People of the Commonwealth of Liberia, in Africa, acknowledg-
> ing with devout gratitude, the goodness of God, in granting to us the bless-
> ings of the Christian religion and political, religious and civil liberty, do,
> in order to secure these blessings for ourselves and our posterity, and to
> establish justice, insure domestic peace, and promote the general welfare,
> hereby solemnly associate, and constitute ourselves a Free, Sovereign and
> Independent State. . . .[31]

The story of transplanting freed African slaves from pre-Civil-War
United States on the Liberian Coast, starting in 1820 with Sherbro Island

(now part of Sierra Leone) and slowly spreading along the coastal areas of the mainland, is reflected by the legend on the seal of the new republic and in the preamble to the country's Constitution, with its phrasing and cadence so reminiscent of an earlier preamble to the constitution of the country from which the ex-slaves had returned to Africa. And, as in the United States, the promise of the new preamble did not always reach in practice to all the inhabitants. The "people of the interior"—the indigenous Africans, who had not been displaced by slavery and made immigrants in their own land, or "colonists" as the Americo-Liberians have come to call themselves—long remained outside the élite circle and the web of protection the Americo-Liberians understandably wove around themselves to insulate them from the "tribal peoples."

From this historical sequence of events comes Liberia's major nation-building problem, how to unite the coastal ruling class and the multi-tribal peoples of the interior, many of whom have been victimized or feel that they have been by the Americo-Liberian oligarchy. In the words of a well-known Liberian writing a straightforward primer on his country as recent as 1959, we find:

> The people who live in the Liberian interior are tribal people with their age-old customs and ways of life.
> Therefore it is to the coast and a few hundred miles in the interior that we must look if we wish to learn about Liberia. . . .
> Along the coast and in the interior several tribes dwell side by side with the descendants of the colonists. The task of joining up or uniting these tribes and the descendants of the colonists has been a great one. For many years little was accomplished in this direction, but the administration of President Tubman has done much and is doing all that is possible to unite all Liberians.[32]

Mr. Yancy's brief but revealing statement covers cogently the story of almost 150 years of colonization during which the indigenous people remained for the most part outside the structure, except as in all classic colonial contexts, as the source of labor when needed, and as the source of external threats which served, when needed, to induce cohesion within the colonizing group. Mr. Yancy's account also reveals the classic ego-centricity of colonizers and their descendants in their view that history and culture only began with their arrival. Beyond that, the account concedes that little was accomplished prior to President Tubman's administration (now in its fourth term) to unite the bulk of the inhabitants of the country—the tribal people—with the descendants of the colonizers on the coast. This lack of cohesion—"unity"—remains the number one problem of Liberian nation-building today.[33]

In addition, Liberia has the classic problems of nation-building in

Africa.   They are perhaps more acute in Liberia than some of her West Coast neighbors because Liberia's reawakening in a sense came later.   The spillover of the African independence revolution is what by and large catapulted Liberia into its current efforts at nation-building and economic growth.   In the latter category Liberia's vast and rich resources of iron ore, her established and expanding rubber industry,[34] and the related development of other resources, all have injected into the society in recent years a dynamic force for change.   The impetus for internal national unity derives in part and flows inevitably in part from the relatively new and forceful flow of economic activity, incentives and income.   However, the narrow social and political power base, the *de facto* one-party or dominant party, the True Whig Party, and the concentration of wealth among the Americo-Liberians—all have tended to offer resistance to the pressures for change, which have come in the train of the evolving market economy, and to the sharing of influence, affluence and power implicit in the ongoing change.   There are, thus, aspects of the Ethiopian situation present in Liberia.

On the one hand, Liberian prospects for successful nation-building are complicated by "the interior peoples" problem and the entrenched interests problem.   Liberia's small population, estimated at between a million and a million and a half people, needs to overcome the typical obstacles to nation-building, and these two additional problems only add to the difficulties of an already formidable task.   On the other hand, Liberia's long experience of independence, the promise of its economy,[35] if managed in a reasonable way and not dissipated by prestige expenditure, corrupt practices, or bad resource planning,[36] and the increasing number of returning university graduates and trained young people, all are hopeful factors.   Much will depend on the quality of Liberia's leadership and its ability to evolve a structure allowing for peaceful change and modernization so that there is neither a sharp break nor an enforced *status quo* after the aging incumbent President William V. S. Tubman departs the scene.   If Liberia can manage its post-Tubman transition well, then its nation-building prospects would appear fair.   In no event, however, will it be a short or painless experience.   The adjustments required are major but many of the ingredients for making successful adjustments are present in the evolving Liberian situation.

A Concluding Word

The special cases in this chapter as well as the more general ones in the preceding chapter have been offered not as definitive country studies, but as applications in specific contexts of the analysis and assessments made in Parts I and II of the book.   Our purpose has been to be suggestive rather than conclusive or dogmatic about the prospects of the nascent African states for successful nation-building. Although on the whole the prospects, as we have already noted, are not brilliant, they are not in individual cases without hope. In a few instances they hold promise. Eventually, of course, all will build nations.

What we have been concerned with is the outlook over the next several decades—given the nature of the African revolution and the characteristic of being "a continent in a hurry" which it has imparted. Economic development, the handmaiden of nation-building, and nation-building itself, are likely to be more difficult of achievement and take more time than anybody would like, and definitely more time than most Africans appear to expect. The "revolution of rising expectations" has happened, as part and parcel of the independence revolution, or is happening in the aftermath of the independence revolution. On the other hand, economic development and nation-building have only just begun, and these are inescapable preconditions to satisfying the expectations already engendered by independence. This state of affairs—of expectations outrunning capacity—is likely to make the next several decades in Africa highly unsettled and render the already uncertain nation-building and development prospects even more hazardous.

CHAPTER 13

PROSPECTS IN THE FORMER BRITISH AND FRENCH AREAS

I would like to conclude my remarks by reiterating my position on the issue of whether or not the single-party tendencies in Africa today are authoritarian. My inclination is to consider a single-party system as authoritarian and not as a meaningful form of political participation on the part of most of the people most of the time. It is interesting to note, by the way, that the ruling elites in Africa have been unwilling to rationalize the single-party process as an authoritarian process; they are concerned about defining it in democratic terms.

MARTIN KILSON, *Center for International Affairs, Harvard University, 1964*

The discussion up to this point suggests that the prospects for successful nation-building in Africa are not brilliant. The discussion also suggests that the politics of nation-building are complicated, the problems many and varied, ranging from manageable to seemingly intractable, and the preconditions not only absent but in many ways as difficult of achievement as nation-building itself; and in any event their achievement is intimately interrelated with the successful achievement of nation-building.

Up to now, too, the discussion has tended to view the efforts of African states in nation-building in terms of their attitudes, approaches, and actions with respect to the size, shape, and situs of their geographic configurations, their evolving state structures, their developing political systems, and their emerging economic development systems. What the analysis suggests is a continuum with poor nation-building prospects for centralized, unitary, one-party, authoritarian-oriented, large public-sector states at one end of the continuum, and somewhat better prospects for decentralized, possibly federal, multiparty, democratically-oriented, relatively large private-sector states at the other.

In earlier chapters we have refined and elaborated our analysis by taking account of the special cases the African independence revolution has thrown up—special in that they come from outside the two principal colonial systems, with differing colonial heritages, and more, special in the sense that they tend to be more or less *sui generis* in their developing nation-building patterns. We have treated briefly the two special cases of long-independent African states, without a colonial heritage, which have only recently taken a new lease on life, more or less in response to the African independence revolution—the Empire of Ethiopia and the Republic of Liberia.

In this chapter an effort will be made to add perspective with which to appraise the outlook for the various nation-building patterns that have emerged from our analysis of the problems and preconditions of African nation-building in Part II. We shall assess the prospects for successful nation-building from the vantage point of the comparative possibilities of states that have shared *common* membership in one or another of the two former principal European colonial systems in Africa—those of the United Kingdom and France—and also from the vantage point of the comparative possibilities of states deriving from the former British and French African areas. Thus, we shall view the nation-building prospects of, say, Ghana and Nigeria, as units deriving from the dismantled British African Empire, and of Guinea and the Ivory Coast, for example, as units deriving from the liquidated French-African Empire. We shall also briefly view the comparative prospects *en bloc* of the former British and French areas. The two principal African empires have provided Africa with more independent units than we could possibly have accommodated individually in our analysis, and so we shall draw our evaluation of the prospects for African nation-building in this chapter primarily from the general tendencies and limitations discernible *en bloc* in the decolonized units of these two principal former African empires.

PROSPECTS OF FORMER BRITISH AFRICA

Prospects for successful nation-building in former British Africa vary from fair to very poor. The average prospect, however, for successful nation-building in English-speaking Africa is, in the author's judgment, somewhat better than the average in the areas of any of the other former European colonial systems in Africa. The comparative prospects should emerge from the discussion in this and subsequent sections.

In former British Africa the best prospects occur in West Africa. Here the processes of nation-building, state-building, political system-building, and economy-building have been uniformly more advanced and more integrated than in any other part of Africa. Nevertheless, there are dramatic differences in this single area.

WEST AFRICA

The contrast between pre-*coup* Nigeria, and to a degree Sierra Leone, and also Gambia, on the one hand, and pre-*coup* Ghana, on the other, as we have seen, has been a sharp one. The first group of West African states have represented an exception to the general trend of one-party authoritarianism engulfing the continent, whereas the remaining British former West African state, Ghana, has long been among the pace-setters for those intent on establishing one-party authoritarian states.

The three states that have proved so far to be exceptions to the general one-party trend in Africa have fair prospects for successful nation-building. The prospects of Nigeria, Sierra Leone,* and the Gambia cannot be rated any higher. As we know from our earlier discussion, all three have attempted—in the African context—to follow a pluralistic approach to nation-building. They have not had ready success in coping with the problems of nation-building, nor with establishing the necessary pre-conditions. Nevertheless, if our analysis in Part II is valid, their approach seems the only one with a hope of success. Nigeria's impatience with its federal multiparty approach has largely compromised its prospects, and the consequence has been the two 1966 military *coups d'état*, which have further compromised the country's prospects. Future nation-building prospects will turn on the capacity of the military to turn back power to a civil constitutional order in a peaceful and orderly way, and to do so after a succession of events—the two *coups* and their aftermaths—which ironically exacerbated the very centrifugal forces of tribalism, regionalism, and particularism which the *coups* set out to overcome. The task is obviously a formidable one, and the outcome by no means certain. If a reasonable federal structure emerges, the country's prospects for nation-building should be fair, which is better than the prospects of most of its neighbors.

Sierra Leone has flirted with the adoption of a one-party structure and its future has been put in doubt by the internal dissension precipitated by Sir Albert Margai's one-party structure gambit. Gambia alone remains intact as a multiparty state, but because of its intractable geopolitical problems faces a difficult nation-building task.

Ghana has to start anew, but with the heavy legacy of dissension, despair, and debt bequeathed it by the regime of Dr. Nkrumah.† The

---

* See note on the new status of Sierra Leone, Chapter 7, pp. 96, 97. J.H.M.

† After Nkrumah was deposed by a military-led *coup d'état* while on a visit to Peking in 1966 (and sought refuge in Guinea), Ghana was ruled by the National Liberation Council, headed by General Joseph A. Ankrah. Young army officers made an unsuccessful attempt to overthrow the Ankrah regime in April 1967. Just two

authoritarian one-party structure and system, in terms of the analysis offered in Part II, inexorably arrived at the only possible conclusion—failure in its nation-building efforts. Its attempts to coerce national unity failed. National cohesion cannot be coerced. And even to the extent it could be, the capability to coerce it—to run an effective authoritarian or totalitarian regime—did not exist. Whether the successor military regime will fare any better remains to be seen. If our analysis in Chapter 5 holds true, it will not fare any better if it attempts to develop a military government for anything but a brief transitional period. Assuming that the military regime is to serve only as a transition to a new civil constitutional order, the moment of crisis will occur when the military attempts to hand over power. Until then, the future nation-building prospects of the country cannot readily be assessed.

EAST AFRICA

The rest of former British Africa appears to have taken the pre-*coup* Ghanaian example as its model. Thus, we find in former British East Africa, a definite cut or two behind former British West Africa on all accounts—nation-building through economy-building—striving to emulate the pre-*coup* Ghanaian pattern. Although not there yet, Kenya, with its deteriorating multiparty system, seems intent on doing away with it.

In Kenya the already watered-down eve-of-independence version of regionalism, originally sought by the now defunct Kenya Africa Democratic Union, has already disappeared. Prime Minister (now President) Kenyatta decreed the end of what little regional autonomy was left in the country's constitutional arrangements after the last preindependence constitution conference in London in 1963.[1] In July 1964, just six months after Kenya's accession to independence, Prime Minister Kenyatta started to rally public support for a one-party system. In the Prime Minister's words: "From today we shall work toward a one-party system in Kenya."[2] The Kenya Africa Democratic Union, the opposition party, disintegrated soon after independence as the result of a combination of raids, pressures, and blandishments by the controlling Kenya African National Union, and as a result of the internal factionalism that minority groups under this sort of combined pressure seem to develop. KADU only offered sporadic and spasmodic resistance to the apparently in-

years later (April 1969) Ankrah resigned under a cloud of scandal, after confessing to NCL representatives that he had accepted, for political purposes, money solicited from a foreign concern. Ankrah was followed in office by thirty-three-year-old Brig. Gen. Akwai A. Afrifa, former Minister of Finance, who promised the lifting of the three-year ban on political parties by May 1, 1969, and pledged the elimination of corruption, economic blunders, and suppression of freedom. J.H.M.

evitable KANU take-over of the total political life of the country to the exclusion of all other organized legal political activity.*

The KANU monopoly of political power lasted about two years. Then, in April 1966 the inevitable division in the single party occurred, and the left wing of KANU split off to form a new party, the Kenya People's Union, under former Vice President Oginga Odinga. The survival potential of the new party remains uncertain, but if past performance is any indication it is none too bright. The one-party state mentality of KANU is likely to make life exceedingly difficult—if at all possible—for the new party.

Uganda with inherited constitutional structural factors militating against it, including the quasi-federal elements discussed in an earlier chapter, has only recently crossed the White Nile into the controlled world of African one-party systems.

Tanzania too has recently managed the passage to a one-party authoritarian structure, but not without stresses and strains. Tanganyika was beset in its transition by difficulties arising from President Nyerere's internal conflicts—between attempting, as we have seen, to retain the Rule of Law and inaugurating a one-party monopoly of power; between attempting to retain an impartial merit system with respect to race in the public service, and embracing a system of recognized preference for party loyalists dedicated to party goals, which are viewed by TANU as *the* national interest.

It seems increasingly clear that President Nyerere's internal conflicts must be resolved against his remaining democratic tendencies, and also in derogation of the country's public administration, and thus at the expense of the country's nation-building and economic development prospects. The authoritarianism of one-party state structures, as we have seen in earlier chapters, makes it impossible for all independent institutions and sources of power outside of the party's control to exist. An independent judiciary and a professional civil service must yield to the imperatives of party doctrine and control. This has happened in both component parts of the United Republic of Tanzania. It has been most apparent in Zanzibar, where the Afro-Shirazi Party (ASP) is the one party in control, corresponding to the Tanganyika African National Union (TANU) in Tanganyika. In the words of Thabit Kombo, the Secretary-General of ASP:

---

* Tom Mboya, Kenya's Minister of Economic Affairs, Secretary of KANU, and possible successor to the aging President Jomo Kenyatta, was killed by an unknown assassin in downtown Nairobi on July 5, 1969. The tragic death of the thirty-eight-year-old Mboya, a member of the Luo tribe, precipitated scattered tribal clashes. Kenyatta's automobile was stoned by Mboya followers when the President attended funeral services for the deceased official. J.H.M.

We would not like to see a person of any type, color, or religion without a membership card of the Afro-Shirazi Party. Such a thing would be impossible. If one is a commissioner of police, he must have a card. If he is a police superintendent, he must also have a card. How long are we going to have soldiers outside politics? Why should they be outside politics? Everyone must be in politics. A clerk must have a card. If he has no card, then why should he work in an office? Why should he benefit from an office if he has no card. If you do not want an Afro [ASP] card, then resign your post and go away and if you are in Dar-es-Salaam and refuse to have a TANU card, then resign your post. A number of people are taking out cards and those who are not will go.[3]

A sympathetic American political scientist formulated the problem confronting TANU as follows:

Within its pervasive organizational network, numerous conflicts arise and are handled at the national level by a process of compromise and adjustment among TANU's collegial leadership. The political task facing party leadership is to build a new concensual ideology which will give meaning and purpose to organizational membership and so permit intra-party pluralism to flourish without jeopardizing the organizational structure.[4]

By definition, this formulation excludes extraparty opinion. Pluralism in this view is confined within party perimeters. And within the one-party, "intra-party pluralism" has in practice yielded in this instance, as it has in most and perhaps must in all instances in Africa, to the will of the controlling party clique. The "consensual ideology" is to serve the machine, and not vice versa. The machine has not been established to carry out the ideology, and therefore preservation of the machine (the one-party) takes precedence over policy or "consensual ideology" (nation-building). Thus, as we have seen in an earlier chapter, "elections" are essentially popularity contests, for the "consensual ideology" has already been arranged by the controlling party clique, and issues are not at issue in the election contests. Dissenting opinion within the party has been obviated or nullified. An indoctrinated civil service, a politicized military establishment, a larger than life-sized charismatic leader, and an inner-directed party—all make it extremely difficult for a would-be dissenter to surface. The control of trade unions and preventive detention acts should take care of the potential sources of dissension as well as the party deviant who might somehow emerge. The stage has been set for the struggle of party factions—"intra-party pluralism"—and the palace *coup* or the military *coup d'état*.

The prospects for successful nation-building on the foundation of a one-party state structure and an accompanying authoritarian political system in Tanzania seem anything but bright. Manipulated participation is not an effective substitute for free participation; the supremacy of the party machine means inevitably compromises at the expense of the objectives of nation-building and economic development; and subordination of the state structure and its public service to the party means constraints on economic development and its contributions to nation-building. Moreover, Zanzibar has refused to merge its single party, the Afro-Shirazi Party with TANU. Thus, the situation that led as much as any other to the break-up of the Federation of Mali obtains in Tanzania—two exclusive one-party systems, each dominant in its own geographic area, and each supreme vis-à-vis the governmental structure in its respective area. In these circumstances fusion of the two "states" into one nation-state, a prerequisite for Tanzanian nation-building, is not possible. So, in Tanzania, often singled out as the most promising East African country for nation-building success, the prospects, measured by the criteria developed in this book, are poor.

Uganda's prospects, without a party apparatus approaching the organization and experience of TANU and with many more basic tribal, religious, regional, and economic divisive forces to cope with, seem even poorer. Kenya's prospects are most uncertain, especially in the light of its apparent drift toward one-party authoritarianism.

A federal structure with multiparty competition at the federal level, and over time increasing multiparty competition at the territorial level— e.g., Tanganyika and Zanzibar—might, as in pre-*coup* Nigeria, provide a possible workable alternative to the present Tanzanian alliance *cum* state structure. Coalition government as practiced in pre-*coup* Nigeria was a different species from alliance government in the former Federation of Mali, the former United Arab Republic, and the current United Republic of Tanzania. In the latter group of "union" states, the monolithic one-party structures in each of the component parts of the new "unions," insisting on exclusivity, have resisted free participation across territorial lines and open competition at the national level, and in so doing have inhibited the very cohesion indispensable to nation-building. As soon as the one-party in former state A has tried to win friends and influence people in the one-party former state B, it has been considered a breach of "union" etiquette and an attempt at infiltration and subversion of the one-party monopoly in former state B. This, of course, was the allegation leveled by Syria at Egypt at the time of its withdrawal from the UAR, and by Senegal at the Soudan at the time of its withdrawal from the Federation of Mali.

The former Anglo-Egyptian Sudan, the Republic of Sudan, was, as we already have seen in Chapter 5, the first state in former British Africa to be run by the military. It had all the strengths and all the weaknesses of such a system, with the balance on the side of weakness insofar as inducing widespread popular participation in nation-building and economic development programs was concerned. We have already analyzed the reasons for this in Chapter 5, and have noted the sad aftermath of the military period of rule, the dissension and strife which have dominated Sudanese public affairs since the fall of the Abboud regime in November 1964. We have also explored the serious geopolitical problems of the Sudan in Chapter 3. The attempt to construct a cohesive national government in a badly divided country—an Arab Muslim North and a black pagan and Christian South—with an active guerrilla campaign being conducted by southerners from neighboring states, makes the nation-building prospects of the Sudan something less than promising.

There has also been considerable question under the military regime and the successive civil regime about the government's capacity or willingness to carry forward effective economic development in the southern provinces of the Sudan. On the one hand, partisans of the South have alleged discrimination in the allocation of resources and "colonization" and "exploitation" by the "Arabizing North." On the other hand, the government has repeatedly asserted that it has not only been fair to the South, but has given it priority in the allocation of resources. Either way, the prospects for successful development in the Sudan are likely to have been compromised and even retarded by this basic racial and religious strife. To the extent there may have been discrimination, willing and productive southern participation in development is likely to have been impaired and may even have been precluded. To the extent there may have been a priority accorded for political reasons, this too may not have been effective in view of the apparent belief of southerners that they have been discriminated against, and even to the extent that the priority may have proved to be effective, it may not turn out to have been a valid priority in terms of maximum economic pay-off from investment of scarce resources. The Sudanese experience illustrates how the lack of national cohesion can divert, and even distort, what have been analytically and technically determined to be the economic development priorities of a country. Distorted priorities also tend to reduce the contribution that successful economic development could make to nation-building. Thus, once again, the intimate and circular relationship of nation-building and economic development emerges. The Sudanese case also illustrates how this relationship leads to coercion in one sector (political) inevitably spilling over into the other (economic). Increased coercion in the political sector, which has been the trend over the last half dozen years, can thus be expected to be reflected in the economic sector and *vice versa*. This in many ways is the dilemma that has been confronting Sudanese nation-building and development. The country's nation-building failure has compromised the country's otherwise relatively promising prospects for economic development, which has in turn meant a smaller contribution than a dynamic economy might have made to the country's nation-building effort.

CENTRAL AFRICA

In former British Central Africa too, Ghana rather than the democratically inclined trio of Nigeria, Sierra Leone, and Gambia seems to have been the model. In Malawi there is a full-blown one-party setup, as well organized and as effective as any in former British Africa. Within months of achieving independence, a struggle between Dr. Banda and the younger, more radically inclined founders of the Malawi Congress Party broke out. Civil strife, purges, flight, and a tightening party dictatorship by the controlling faction supporting Dr. Banda have been the result. The political disunity in the country—with the half-dozen key organizers of the party and the anticolonial campaign against the British in 1959–60, which resulted in British withdrawal from Nyasaland, in exile—has been covered over by increasing coercion and party control. Less rather than more public participation has been the result. Similarly, economic development, disrupted by the internal political struggle, has done little more than keep pace with the country's population growth. When the fanciful geographical situation of the country is added to the picture, the prospects for successful nation-building are clearly not good.

In Zambia the picture has had some shadings. UNIP—the United National Independence Party—which controls the government, has in substance a monopoly of power. But there has been opposition, particularly in trade union circles, and some still remains. And President Kenneth Kaunda seems personally to share some of President Nyerere's misgivings about an unqualified, naked, one-party authoritarian structure and system. He appears to be concerned to retain some of the safeguards of a democratic system, but like his colleague, President Nyerere has been under constant pressure of the more extremist elements in the dominant and emergent *de facto* party, UNIP. These elements in the controlling party have not been bothered by President Kaunda's scruples, and have pressed for going the whole way down the authoritarian road. Thus, Sikota Wina, Minister of Health in the first UNIP government, the last government before the attainment of full independence, pressed as early as June 1964, months before independence, for a one-party structure.[5] Another Zambian Minister, Minister of Lands Solomon Kalulu, three months before actual independence, spoke in the authoritarian terms that seem indispensable to one-party states, when he warned that criticism of [then Prime Minister and now] President Kenneth Kaunda would be considered a "conspiracy against the state deserving severe penalties." The Minister then approvingly noted that Malawi, which had only become independent on July 6, 1964, had already adopted punitive measures to teach "these fools" that "no one is allowed to speak ill" of Prime Minister Banda.[6] The Zambian case appears to be but one more application of the rule of behavior in African politics, a kind of Gresham's law, which makes it impossible for democratic and authoritarian concepts, decentralizing and centralizing tendencies, and pluralism and uniformity, to coexist within the same state. The authoritarian centralized one-party system tendency seems inevitably to drive out the democratic pluralistic multiparty tendency. If Zambia goes the whole way down the one-party state road to nation-building and development, its prospects for success in both endeavors are poor. More perhaps than many other former British territories, more certainly than the former British West African territories, Zambia lacks the organizational ability, managerial skill, and trained manpower, to run an effective one-party state and economy. If, on the other hand, Dr. Kaunda is able to resist the internal party pressures for a one-party authoritarian approach, which have been strengthened immeasurably by the Rhodesian rebellion and the intransigence of the Ian Smith regime in Salisbury, and a quasi-democratic pluralistic political structure and system evolve, with the significant private sector already in being, retained and expanded, then the prospects for successful development and nation-building should be fairly good. Zambia has one of the more promising economies in Central and East Africa with which and on which to build.

The final assessment suggested by our analysis is that the trio of heretofore democratically-inclined West African states—Nigeria, Sierra Leone, and Gambia—and possibly Zambia, still have the best relative prospects for obtaining *"meaningful political participation"* by a larger cross section of people than is likely to obtain in former British Africa where other techniques are being employed, and also a larger participation of individuals in modern economic activity than is likely to obtain elsewhere in former British Africa under state-dominated economies. These states have thus the best prospects, circumscribed as they may be, among all former British African territories for successful nation-building. The voluntaristic, pluralistic approach offers the most, perhaps the only, promise for achieving national cohesion and unity, for building new African nations.

PROSPECTS IN FORMER FRENCH AFRICA

By and large, in former French Africa we do not have the division between types of political structures and systems encountered in former

British Africa.   Here the major difference seems to be between, on the one hand, left-oriented radical nationalist centralized one-party states— Guinea, Mali, and pre-*coup* Algeria, and most recently Congo (Brazzaville)—and on the other, right-oriented centralized one-party states, either *parti unique* or *parti unifié*—most of the remaining states in former French Africa.   Tunisia and Senegal seem to be somewhere in between these two major categories of one-party states.   Morocco stands alone in former French Africa with a multiparty system, compromised, however, by the favored position accorded in practice to the parties supporting the monarch.   Many of the one-party states have sustained military *coups*, and are now under military regimes or mixed one-party-military regimes. On the left, Algeria and Congo (Brazzaville), and on the right, Dahomey, Central African Republic, and Upper Volta—all fit into this category. Gabon only narrowly escapes it.

All the points developed in Chapters 3 through 10 apply here, as well as the points just made in connection with the prospects of the one-party coercive approach of many English-speaking African states.   However, the differences in colonial inheritance and in the respective post-independence syntheses developed in the structures and systems of the former French and British territories seem to make the French-speaking states' nation-building prospects even less certain, and, by and large, even less promising than those of the English-speaking states.

RADICAL NATIONALIST STATES

Organizationally, the radical nationalist French-speaking African states —particularly Mali and Guinea, and also pre-*coup* Algeria—carried the concentration of power vested in the single party at the expense of the state structure, and in practice, if not theory, at the expense of broad-based public participation in *making* and *deciding* policy, further than all other French-speaking African states, and probably further than most other African states.

The description of *The Times* (London) concerning Mali could be read to apply equally to Guinea:

> Mali is a socialist state, organized deliberately and as far as one can judge effectively on orthodox Communist lines.   Policy is decided by the party, Union Soudanaise.   The Government is the executive arm carrying out the decisions taken by the nineteen-man *bureau politique*.   President Modibo Keita is not only the Head of State and Government, he is also *primus inter pares* in the politburo.   The party organization is repeated, exactly, at district and subdistrict level.[7]

The situation in pre-*coup* Algeria was more unsettled and volatile. The following account from *The Economist* records it well:

In the third year of independence—a year that began on July 5th—
Algerians look like finding themselves more divided than ever before.
There is certainly a "counter-revolution"; but it is less against President
Benbella than against the extreme leftists who are powerful in the central
committee of the FLN [the National Liberation Front] and who in mid-
June demanded a purge of the party's less doctrinaire socialists.

In the past year, through travelling abroad, and through paying too
much attention to the European socialist advisers (who do not understand
Moslems), the president has tended to get out of touch with his people.
And since he offers them little outlet for free expression it is not to be
wondered that opposition bursts out in lawless ways.[8]

One year later *The Economist's* assessment of the Algerian situation
proved out. A *coup d'état* ousted Ben Bella and the military took over
the state and party apparatus.

What then are the nation-building prospects of the best organized of
the left-oriented unitary one-party French-speaking African states?

In Guinea, the nation-building prospects seem limited but perhaps not
so poor as in Mali, with its heavy burden of geopolitical problems discussed in Chapter 3; nor so uncertain as in Algeria, where the problem
of imposing uniformity—the apparent goal of the pre-*coup* dominant
faction in the FLN as well as the Boumedienne military regime—on a
divided population (Arab-Berber) is clearly intractable and formidable.
The difficulty in Algeria stems partly from the attempts to apply FLN
doctrine on the supremacy of party control, centralization of powers, the
desirability of extensive state ownership, and partly from efforts to govern the widely scattered Arab-Berber population in the context of a
sophisticated European-type economic structure and public administration badly suffering from the hasty exodus of almost a million Europeans.

Also in Algeria, the problem of containing a large military establishment, which was eventually to take over power, was from the outset a
complicating aspect of the country's nation-building. In many ways
Algeria is a classic example of the limitations of both centralized one-
party systems and of successor military governments, discussed in earlier
chapters. For in many ways the one-party FLN regime paved the way
for the military *coup* of Defense Minister and Vice President Colonel
Houari Boumedienne, the representative of the dominant army faction
in the government and party apparatus.

Starting with a decree published in late July 1964, President Ahmed
Ben Bella put in motion the forces which a year later were to prove his
undoing. He established a special military court to try secretly army
personnel and civilian "accomplices" for plotting against the government.
"Several hundred foes or suspected foes of the regime . . . secretly
arrested in a new policy and army crackdown that began at the end of
June," [9] were to be tried by the new court. The special court's president

was chosen by the Minister of Justice, but the five other members were chosen by the Minister of Defense.   There was no appeal from the court's decision.   And "the accused, according to Justice Ministry sources, [would] not have the right to defense counsel." [10]

Military "purges" were substituted for civil judicial processes.   The Rule of Law, both procedurally, as regards secret arrests, special tribunals, and lack of defense counsel, and substantively, as regards the definition of "crimes against the state" (*i.e.* the party), was flagrantly disregarded.   Having yielded significant power to the army under Colonel Boumedienne, with respect to "state security," in the context of balance of power (and terror) politics of one-party rule in a pluralist situation, President Ben Bella turned around and appointed a national commissioner of a newly organized, party-controlled "people's-militia," "in what some observers regarded as a move to curb the influence of the 50,000-man regular army." [11]   Clearly, the competition for power between party and army was initiated.   It only ended when the military ousted Ben Bella a year later, purged the party apparatus, and instituted a military regime which found the one-party structure not only an easy route to power, but a useful mechanism for staying in power.

The implications of these developments for nation-building in Algeria are obviously grave—an absence of independent institutions, concentration of power, disregard for the Rule of Law, coercion, repression of initiatives, absence of constitutional channels for change, diversion of resources, energy and attention to power politics.   "Where," one might ask, and "when," is there to be time for nation-building and economy-building?

So far there has been little time for either, and the prospects of finding time in the near future are not promising.   Apathy and lack of channels and capacity of the military for stimulating public participation make the outlook for successful nation-building and development quite poor. This outlook is particularly sad in view of the seven-year struggle Algeria waged for independence, which it was thought would have had the effect of forging national unity in the crucible of war, and in view of the considerable national income deriving from the rich oil fields developed by the French in the last years of their colonial presence.

As for Guinea's prospects, we have already dealt with Guinea's economic policies and their adverse effect on development and nation-building.   All that need be added is that the economic policies have been a consistent application of Guinea's one-party authoritarian political structure and system.   The outlook is for more of the same, and hence for limited public participation in nation-building and development. Guinea's prospects, despite considerable natural wealth—bauxite, iron ore, agricultural potential—are also quite poor.

And Mali's are poorest of the three.   We have already dealt at length with Mali's nightmare geography and hinterland position, and her authoritarian one-party state structure and economy to match. All that need be added is that without the natural wealth of Algeria and Guinea, Mali has even less of a base on which to build than either of the other two like-minded states.

RIGHT-ORIENTED STATES

Of the right-oriented, one-party states, the prospects in the Ivory Coast seem limited too, although perhaps better than those of all the states in this category. The *Parti Démocratique de la Côte d'Ivoire* (the PDCI) is probably the best organized and the most broadly-based of the parties in the right-oriented *parti unique* and *parti unifié* states of French-speaking Africa. The Ivory Coast also has a more evolved economy with more participants in the market economy, and better development prospects. The Ivory Coast also has had the advantage of a favorable coastal location, and serves as an outlet to the sea for its land-locked neighbors, Niger and Upper Volta, and to a lesser degree for Mali. As leader—political and economic of the *Entente* states—the Ivory Coast has provided limited economic support, first through a Solidarity Fund and more recently through a Guaranty Fund—to her less fortunate neighbors, Niger, Upper Volta, Dahomey, and Togo. Thus, the Ivory Coast's prospects are better than the other states in this category; they are also probably better than those of Guinea.

The lack of effective public participation and political outlet occurs in both, and the use of the one-party to preclude criticism from without the party ("plots") and criticism from within the party ("deviationism," "revisionism" or "treason"), is common to both the Ivory Coast and Guinea. The Ivory Coast lacks something of the dynamic and hortative quality of Guinea, and also lacks something of Guinea's early missionary zeal, which apparently is on the wane. It probably has less public participation and less sense of national purpose, and hence less conscious nation-building objectives than are to be found in Guinea. There has been criticism of the relatively slow rate of Africanization of the public service and the private sector in the Ivory Coast and of the expanding French presence. Balanced off against this is a more developed, expanding, and dynamic market economy than is to be found in Guinea, with more people already engaged in the market sector. There has also been less xenophobic and bureaucratic interference by the state and party machines in the economy in the Ivory Coast than in Guinea. The Ivory Coast has sought to develop its private sector, whereas Guinea has sought to control its private sector and develop its public sector; not surprisingly, the volume of external private investment in the Ivory Coast has been steadily growing and, unlike in Guinea, has not been confined to one or two major mineral exploitation developments.

The Ivory Coast has also escaped Guinea's predicament of an inconvertible currency and trade, barter, and aid arrangements with communist countries, which have in no sense compensated for the loss of development and other financial assistance from France and the European Common Market. The Ivory Coast has had recourse to compulsory "national service," which for the most part has been quasi-military in character, and largely related to young people working the land. Guinea, for its part, has emphasized *investissement humain*, a type of coerced "voluntarism," related to community development projects for building roads and schools and keeping the capital city, Conakry, and major towns clean and presentable-looking. Both programs border on what in the colonial period was labeled "forced labor." It is not clear that either of the two forced participation systems has been particularly successful in contributing to nation-building or economic development.

Gabon, which might have been thought of as having in the right-oriented one-party state category promising nation-building prospects only second to those of the Ivory Coast, experienced a *coup* and counter-*coup* in February 1964. The clay feet underpinning Gabon's one-party or dominant-party state structure with respect to its underlying stability and popular support crumbled. The military *coup* and French-led counter-*coup*, which we discussed in an earlier chapter, have exposed the glaring lack of national cohesion and unity in the country. And there is every reason to believe the situation is little different in the other French-speaking Equatorial African states to emerge from the dismantled colonial regional federation—in the Chad, the Central African Republic and Congo (Brazzaville). In fact, as we know from our earlier discussion, too, of the Congolese and Central African Republic *coups*, there has to date been little more national cohesion and unity in either of these two states than in Gabon. In an attempt to provide such cohesion and unity, Congo (Brazzaville) has moved over to the radical nationalist side of the one-party state ledger. None of the three states that have sustained *coups* has materially improved its position, with regard to public participation in public affairs or economic activities, and their prospects for successful nation-building are poor. Gabon, because of its natural wealth—tropical woods, manganese, iron ore, petroleum—probably has the best prospects, and stands in relation to Congo (Brazzaville) as the Ivory Coast appears to in relation to Guinea. The Chad, with its geopolitical problems, manifested by the clashes between a minority Arabic-Berber north and a majority black "pagan" and Christian south, and a lack of known resources, appears to have very poor prospects for either nation-building or economic growth. The prospects of the Central African Republic are only slightly better.

The remaining French-speaking state in former French Equatorial Africa is the Federal Republic of Cameroon. We have already dealt at length with Cameroon, particularly in Chapter 4. As we have suggested, the problems of nation-building in the Federal Republic are considerable. The drive toward a one-party state is likely to render the federal quality of the state obsolescent, and should this happen, the already difficult task of nation-building in a state with a French-language area and an English-language area, with the two areas totally disproportioned in size, population, state of development, wealth, customs, colonial legacy, etc., would be made even more intractable. In fact what might otherwise be a fair prospect for success in its nation-building and development tasks is likely to be diminished to something less—poor to fair.

SENEGAL AND TUNISIA

Senegal and Tunisia, the in-between one-party states in former French Africa, seem also to have in-between prospects for successful nation-building. Their less openly heavy-handed authoritarianism, their less doctrinaire one-party state systems, and their somewhat more developed economic base may provide greater opportunities and meet with more success in creating a sense of national identity and purpose on the part of their populations. This seems somewhat more the case in Tunisia, where the Neo-Destour Party, under the leadership of President Bourguiba, has apparently had more success in blending its one-party structure and political system with a mixed economy, and preserving individual initiatives in the private sector. The critical juncture in both states in nation-building and development is likely to occur with the problem of succession, if and when there is change of leadership. For the delicate balance in each state has been maintained in large part by the personal role of a charismatic leader. A change in leadership, through natural causes or as a common occurrence in one-party states, could easily lead to one-party situations prevalent elsewhere in French-speaking Africa, with a consequent derogation of their relatively fair nation-building prospects.

MOROCCO

Morocco stands by itself with somewhat limited prospects for fusing its highly divided rural and urban populations, its Arab and Berber populations, and its ideologically-divided political movements, ranging from pro to antimonarchy, into a cohesive unit. The prospects are not less good than those of many other French-speaking African states, and in some ways are distinctly better.

The monarchy, the continuation of which has been much in dispute among the members and adherents of the left-inclined opposition party *Union Nationale des Forces Populaires* (UNFP) and the closely related trade union group, the *Union Marocaine du Travail* (UMT), was during the "independence struggle," and has been ever since, a rallying point and a symbol of the nation, an unbroken link with the old Cherifian Kingdom or Sultanate. It is also incidentally one of the most successful French applications of the doctrine of "indirect rule." The Lyautey doctrine in Morocco, like the Lugard doctrine in Northern Nigeria, carefully preserved selected customary and traditional institutions around and through which the colonial powers exercised authority and administered their areas with only nominal commitment of their manpower. We have discussed in Chapter 6 the role of the country's constitution as a national symbol and unifying force. The active adherence of the bulk of the population to the Islamic religion, of which the King is the recognized national head, has also acted to strengthen the role of the monarch as a unifying force in the country. Finally, the country's economy, which with independence has tended to stagnate, is still one of the most developed in Africa, and has been a source of national strength.

On the debit side of the country's nation-building prospects, there has been only limited public participation in state affairs and in the economy, control of a large part of which has been in the hands of French companies and *colons* and a small associated group of Moroccans, on the one hand, and, on the other, in keeping with French policy in Africa, in the hands of public corporations such as the phosphates monopoly. The techniques, too, employed for nation-building have been mixed, with perhaps more reliance on constraints and coercion than on voluntaristic and persuasive means. The army, the *gendarmerie*, and the police have had a larger role to play in support of the monarchy. The army has been active too in carrying forward the work of the *Promotion Nationale*, which the King heads. The prominent role of the military, including the significant portion of the recurrent budget which goes for its support, has undoubtedly contributed to the maintenance of the King's position and to internal law and order. It is doubtful, however, how much it has contributed to inducing voluntary and effective participation by the mass of the Moroccan people in national, political, and economic activities.

There are, however, in Morocco multiple parties which contest elections and when permitted constitute not only the ruling party, but also the recognized official opposition in the parliament. There is also a relatively independent press, with a fair proportion of it in the hands of the political opposition. In some ways the Moroccan press is suggestive of the pre-*coup* Nigerian press, although far less influential and far less free of constraints.

Morocco thus seems to have both elements of strength and elements of weakness in its search for a viable political structure and system, and in its quest for national cohesion. One thoughtful assessment of Morocco's prospects in *Jeune Afrique* in mid-1964, which in large part remains apposite two years later, focused on the role of King Hassan II, and gave this rather favorable assessment of the position:

> Where does he stand [King Hassan II]? For the present at a crossroads. By training and taste, he has made Morocco a country, where democracy is not an empty word. For those who know Africa, this multi-party system and total freedom of expression is astonishing. One detail: The French language Moroccan press belongs entirely to the opposition, the parties in power disposing of only one small journal in Arabic.[12]

The outlook is thus fair for only a handful of states in former French Africa—the Ivory Coast, Tunisia, Senegal and Morocco, and possibly, in an even more attenuated way, for the Cameroon, and the uncertainties in all five cases are considerable. Much depends, as we have noted in the cases of Tunisia and Senegal, on the peculiar qualities of the heads of state. This too is in large degree true of President Houphouët-Boigny in the Ivory Coast and King Hassan in Morocco. The delicately balanced and nuanced approach in both states to nation-building and development revolves around the personalities and personal standing of the two leaders in their respective countries.

It is not too difficult to envisage a sharp change in policy and therefore in prospects should there be an abrupt change in leadership. This is always a risk in the one-party state context. It may also be in the special circumstances of Morocco, with the major role accorded the military.

For the rest, the prospects are poor to very poor.

COMPARATIVE PROSPECTS: FORMER BRITISH AND FRENCH AFRICA

The general position would seem to be a greater element of self-reliance and a greater capacity for survival by their own efforts and under their own steam in the new states in the former British area than in those in the former French area. The differences may in practice turn out to be less decisive than they seem to be in our analysis at this juncture in Africa's development. Only time will provide the evidence on which to base a final judgment. For the present, our interim conclusion is that the

British legacy provides a more promising base for nation-building and development.

It would be beyond the scope of this book to attempt a thorough comparative analysis of French and British colonial practices and the legacy they have bequeathed to their respective ex-territories. In the opening chapter we sketched in the broad outlines of the respective nation-building legacies of the main African colonial powers. Here, we shall touch on a few critical aspects of the respective French and British legacies in the economic sector, to reinforce the differences already noted in Chapter 1 concerning their approach in the political sphere to internal development.

In French-speaking Africa the colonial heritage of generally limited participation of the African population in modern sector economic activities, particularly with regard to individual initiatives and private decision-making, and the widely and uncritically accepted French doctrine of the need for dominant public sectors in the economies of African states, makes particularly difficult the task of developing modern economies with broad-based public participation. The absence of the opportunity for private participation and the normality of a large bureaucratic role in the economy has been the general heritage in French Africa. There did not have to be a break with the colonial past when the new states in former French Africa opted for large public sectors. They merely continued what had been—and public participation in the modern sector, a critical element both directly in economic development and indirectly in nation building, has been slower in evolving in francophone Africa than in former British Africa.

In the latter the heritage generally has been, and particularly in West Africa, of increasing participation of the African population in modern sector economic activities. Cash-cropping by individual small-holders was by far more widespread in Ghana, Nigeria, and even Sierra Leone, than in any of the French-speaking neighboring states. This was also increasingly so in Uganda, Kenya, and Tanganyika, compared, say, to the former French Equatorial African areas.

Closely related to the volume of African economic activity is the quality of that activity. In almost all French-speaking states the principal cash-crop agricultural exports have long been and will continue on a declining scale to be subsidized by payment of *"surprix,"* or above world market prices, by France, and in lieu of France quite recently, to a certain extent, by the European Common Market. In fact, in the Yaoundé *Convention of Association* of 1963, of the Eighteen African States, the bulk of whom are former French African areas, with the European Economic Community, there is a special provision establishing a new $230 million fund to increase the productivity and diversification of the agriculture of the African Associate States, so that they will be better able to compete in the world market, without subsidies. It is also intended to compensate them for the planned reduction in the payment of *surprix* for their agricultural output during their transition from high-cost protected production to competitive non-protected production.

By contrast, in the former British territories, the African area producers received only limited trade preferences under the Imperial, and later Commonwealth, Trade Preference Scheme. By and large, the African producers in British Africa had to be competitive with other producers in the world market. As a result, the structure and nature of agricultural production in English-speaking Africa tended and tends to be more economic, more adaptable, and more able to sustain itself in the unpredictable crosscurrents of world trade. For the economic development of *independent* states in the African context, where, as we noted in the discussion of economic development, on an average between 75 and 90 percent of the population is dependent on agriculture, the difference between highly protected agriculture largely dependent on outside states for its protection and relatively competitive agriculture is crucial.

The implications of the *quality* of the participation in the national economy and in public affairs in these differing situations certainly must be considerable. The comparative private sector activity in former French and British Africa is revealing on this point. In the former, African participation is limited, and in the interior states such as Chad and Upper Volta, almost unknown. In ex-British Africa, although African participation in the private sector is still not large, it is generally considerably larger than in the francophone states, and quite well known even in such isolated countries as Malawi. And in some states, as we have already suggested, in West Africa, African participation is very large.

Similarly, in British Africa, the limited size of the public sector and the emphasis on the productive function being located in the private sector, has left a heritage offering considerably more opportunity for the increasing participation of industrial entrepreneurs than in French Africa, where the public-sector nature of much economic activity made the transition to state-sector economies after independence extremely easy. Only in Tunisia and the Ivory Coast has the private entrepreneur made an appearance in any strength.

The dead weight of heavy recurrent expenditure to sustain and maintain large state sectors and other nonproductive investment has been built into all too many economies of the former French African area. In former British Africa this factor is not entirely absent, but in French-speaking Africa it is more sharply defined, more markedly present, and more commonplace. For example, so many more French African territories during the colonial era, and, since independence, former territories, have required and received substantial budget support from France to meet ordinary budget deficits of a recurring nature than has been the case in the British area before and since independence. As late as 1964 no less than twelve former French African territories were receiving direct French subsidies to help cover their ordinary governmental current expenditures.[13] Although this number has fluctuated in the past year or two, and generally has declined, it still outdistances the comparable situation in former British Africa. Only in the special cases of Malawi, deriving in large part from the dissolution of the ill-fated Federation of Rhodesia and Nyasaland, and in Gambia, the oldest British holding in Africa and the last to achieve independence in geopolitical circumstances that make it untenable for this enclave in Senegal to become a viable state, has the British government resorted to budget-supporting grants in Africa in the postindependence period. And in the preindependence period, except for Kenya in the Mau Mau emergency and postemergency periods, the British government's granting of budget-supporting aid has been a relatively rare phenomenon in Africa. Gambia was one of the few nonemergency recipients in Africa of colonial budget-supporting grants. Even such poverty-stricken territories as Bechuanaland and Basutoland received very little British budget-supporting aid, and as the recently independent states of Botswana and Lesotho are not expected to receive very much budget aid.

Without judging the wisdom or unwisdom or the generosity or lack of generosity of the respective policies and practices, the self-reliant nature of the British legacy is clear; equally clear is the dependency nature of the French. The implications for economic development are also clear. The motivation for participation on a basis of self-help has certainly been stronger and more in evidence in the former case than in the latter.

Finally, the colonial heritage in the former French areas has been generally one of elaborate and costly public administrative structures (without related African trained personnel to staff and operate them), of costly public infrastructure in the shape of capital cities, public buildings, and prestige installations, of ill-conceived and inappropriate social welfare programs, such as the family allowance system, and the paucity of institutions in the financing, banking, agricultural, educational, and other fields for raising funds and training people.

The colonial heritage in the former British areas has been generally both qualitatively and quantitatively better for the most part with respect to the foregoing points. In any event, the general British rule of thumb, requiring the colonies by and large to pay for themselves, precluded much of the costly and elaborate infrastructure and superstructure of the French African area. Also, it generally stimulated the British to do more in the way of institution-building for raising funds locally as well as training local people. The general result has been less burden on the resources of the new states in the British area to maintain disproportionate or inappropriate investments and programs, on the one hand, and more capacity or willingness in the new states in the former British area to shift for themselves—and in the process to rely more on their own resources, human and managerial, to develop. There has been more motivation to attract and induce general public participation.

Thus, if the view taken in this book of the interaction between development and nation-building is valid in any serious degree, then the former French areas have a far more difficult nation-building task confronting them than the average run of former British areas. Their prospects for successful expansion of the market sectors of their economies, for enlarging public participation, and in the process for breaking down parochial and traditional status and ethnic attachments and replacing them by generally accepted systems of incentives and rewards as the motivation for behavior and belief, would seem accordingly to diminish in keeping with the added difficulties of the development task. And thus, their nation-building prospects seem less likely or more difficult of achievement.

PROSPECTS OF THE NEW STATES: SOME CONCLUSIONS

The burden of our analysis has centered on the likelihood and capability of the growing number of authoritarian one-party states in former British and French Africa to build integrated nation-states and modern economies. We have tended to be dubious about the suitability of the authoritarian choice for the purpose at hand, and about the capacity of the embryonic states to make the most of their choice and utilize the coercive approach effectively to realize in practice whatever advantages the one-party authoritarian system may be thought to have. With respect to the capacity of the new African states to utilize the coercive approach effectively to obtain widespread public participation we quote briefly from Dr. Kilson, whom we also quoted at the outset of this chapter with regard to the authoritarian nature of African one-party states. In Dr. Kilson's words:

> The mass-type parties [in the author's typology, the PDG in Guinea, the CPP in Ghana, and TANU in Tanganyika] were the first to show tendencies toward single-party rule. This is due to their high degree of centralization of organization. Despite the claim that an internal democratic centralism is operative in this kind of party, the lines of communication are pretty callous and are mainly from the top to the bottom. What comes up from the bottom to the top is predetermined by the very structure, the very process of organization.[14]

Participation of this sort is participation in name only. It results in 99 percent polls in favor of the single candidate of the one-party.[15] It is in no sense the participation which is the *sine qua non* of nation-building. The cynical belief, or worse, the sad self-delusion, that such *pro forma* participation can lead to national cohesion and unity, imposes one of the more serious constraints on the prospects for successful nation-building in former British and French Africa.

Summing up, although the overall prospects for building sound and cohesive nation-states in former British and French Africa are far from brilliant, they are not entirely without hope, and, in some instances where the voluntaristic approach is being tried, not without some promise. It is perhaps too soon to emulate the young African boy, who, in a speech in 1903 bemoaning the decline in the status of the Creole population of the coastal area of Sierra Leone, "apostrophized the glorious past from a present without prospect of a future, ending with the piteous cry, 'Alas, poor Africa.' " [16]

CHAPTER 14

COMPARATIVE PROSPECTS OF AFRICA, ASIA, AND LATIN AMERICA

The whole of Latin America until recently has been on the margin of world history. But the gap is narrowing; and most Latin Americans who have thought about it believe that when they are—or are compelled—to play a really active part in world affairs, their intervention will somehow be distinctively Latin American.

GEORGE PENDLE, A History of Latin America, *1963*

The accomplishments of this program [of economic development] *in the next few years will largely determine India's political future and will have a heavy bearing on the future of other Asian and African countries.*

JOHN P. LEWIS, Quiet Crisis in India, *1962*

I endeavor to show [in my book] *that in Latin America—unlike central Africa and certain countries of Southeast Asia—there exist more positive than negative factors. Nevertheless, in order to emphasize the achievements, it is occasionally necessary to call attention to the many powerful forces working against progress, which can and must be defeated.*

VÍCTOR L. URQUIDI, The Challenge of Development in Latin America, *1964*

Africa south of the Saharas is populated mostly by a large variety of African negroid races and tribes. There has apparently not been any unifying common history until the European powers' penetration of Africa in the 19th century. The colonial area [sic] *introduced western civilization and this laid an essential, if fragmentary basis for the present striving towards nationalism. The latter coupled with consciously desired economic growth and development is the first really unifying influence to which that part of Africa has been subjected.*

ERIN E. JUCKER-FLEETWOOD, Money and Finance in Africa, *1964*

This chapter employs the comparative approach to highlight, once again, the nation-building and development prospects of the new African states. In the earlier parts of the book the politics, problems, and preconditions for nation-building and development were approached functionally, and the prospects were treated, or at least inferred, from the analysis and consideration of geopolitical, political and economic factors. In the preceding chapters of Part III we turned to an appreciation of the prospects of the African states from the point of view of their former colonial relationships—primarily French and British, but also Belgian and Italian—and, in the rare cases of Liberia and Ethiopia, the absence of colonial relationships. Now we approach the prospects of the nascent African states from still another point of view: their comparative prospects *vis-à-vis* other major portions of what has loosely and variously been described as the underdeveloped world, the "third world," and even "the southern half of the world" in some supposed division of the world into wealthy northern countries and poor southern ones to replace the more common east-west ideological division. With the seeming relenting of the cold war and the growing impatience of the underdeveloped world to develop, vividly illustrated at Geneva in 1964 at the UN Conference on Trade and Development, the latter characterization has gained currency.

Needless to say, the comparisons are intended to be suggestive rather than definitive, schematic rather than comprehensive, and focused on Africa rather than Asia and Latin America. If the comparisons serve to throw into bolder relief African prospects for successful nation-building, then the purpose of this chapter will have been served, even though the consideration of the prospects of the other areas of the third world may seem to have been given relatively short shrift.

Although exaggerated, Lord Keynes's dictum that "the world is ruled by little else" than by ideas is not without application to the nation-building and development efforts of the newly independent African states and more generally to those of the underdeveloped world at large. There is sometimes a tendency to denigrate the importance of ideas—or more structured collections and systems of ideas, in short ideologies—in the nation-building and development processes selected, followed, rejected, and synthesized by the underdeveloped states. Although structural factors may impose perimeters and limitations, and although pragmatic adaptation rather than preconceived notions and mathematical formulae may more often than not prevail, it would be a serious mistake to fail to take account of the beliefs, ideas, and concepts held at various times by the leadership of these states; and also to fail to take account of those of the populations of these states, to the degree that they may influence policy by articulating their convictions, and, negatively to the degree they can obstruct policy by resisting change, even when their ideas remain inchoate.

This is not the place to review the history of the development of political philosophy and economic thought in Africa, Asia, and Latin America. Suffice it to say that there appears to be a central core of ideas shared to a greater or lesser degree by all three areas today. Beyond that there seems to be a wide divergence of ideas and varying assessments as to where this central core of ideas leads. These differences may in large part be attributed to the differences in prevailing conditions—*les réalités*—among the three areas, which are discussed in the ensuing sections of this chapter. At this point we are concerned only with the content of the shared central core of ideas.

Professor Hirschman, writing of the eminent Peruvian leader Haya de la Torre, summarized Haya's views on Latin America's search for an "Indomerican Way" of economic development as follows:

> Attribution of backwardness to imperialist exploitation, direction of economic development by the state, avoidance of the excesses that have marked the early stages of capitalist development in the West, and the community of interests of all of Latin America—these are the basic ingredients of Haya's thought which . . . have left a deep mark on Latin American economic thinking.
>
> A final element is the search for elements in the Indian or primitive past of Latin America that are not only worth preserving but that can be used in building a better social and economic order.[1]

Haya was writing in the 1930's of his own Peru and to an extent more generally of Latin America. Much of what Hirschman attributed to Haya in the foregoing quotation remains applicable today, and with little or no emendation is now also applicable to the new states of Africa. With regard to much of Asia, the quotation, with one important difference, also appears in large part applicable. The counterpart of the Pan-Africanism of the newly independent African states does not occur in Asia. The Sino-Indian rivalry, the Pakistani-Indian dispute over Kashmir, the Indonesian policy of "confrontation" with Malaysia, the Communist Chinese "big brother" posture towards its smaller neighbors, the Japanese island aloofness (as well as the residue of bitterness remaining from Japanese aggression in the 1930's and early 40's), the two-Chinas problem, the divided Korean peninsula, the Vietnamese situation, the separateness of the Near East from the rest of the Asian continent, and in the Near East the Arab-Israeli problem, the special position of Russian Siberia and Outer Mongolia, and so on—all militate against the current Latin American and African preoccupation with regional and continental associations and organizations—frequently, if misleading, lumped together under the heading of "unity."

In the following sections we shall consider specific factors which differentiate as well as characterize the three areas, and, where pertinent, will relate these factors to the central core of shared ideas described above.

THE TIME FACTOR

The time sequence has been markedly different for the three areas. One can hardly describe the Latin-American states, most of which have been independent for some 150 years as newly independent, nascent, or emergent. Even as between Asian and African states one must distinguish carefully. Many Asian states are old ones with long histories unbroken by colonial rule or only interfered with but never fully submerged and occupied for long periods of time, e.g., Iran, Afghanistan, Nepal, Thailand, and Japan. Others, although more recently independent are composed of areas with long unbroken histories, which notwithstanding colonial occupation, have retained intact much of their own historical and cultural development, e.g., Korea, India, Pakistan, and China.

Africa, with the exception of Ethiopia and Liberia, and perhaps Egypt, has come to independence very late in the day—effectively starting in 1957 and gaining momentum in 1960—after a colonial occupation, which in significant degree interrupted the historical and cultural continuity of the continent, and in the process created the boundaries for new states artificially and with little concern or awareness of their antecedents. With respect to the new African states one can employ the terms "nascent" and "emergent" to describe them with considerably more precision than one could in the case of most Latin-American and many Asian states.

Thus, African states start later, considerably later than the Latin-American states, in their nation-building and development efforts, and in point of time, only yesterday, with respect to revivifying and consolidating national cultural traditions and recapturing their historical continuity, particularly in comparison to many Asian states.

Before going further it would be well to rebut any possible inference that our comments on the discontinuity of African cultural and historical development are intended to suggest that Africa has no history or that its history and culture remained in a state of suspended animation during the European occupation. For this has certainly not been the case. Rather, the intention is to suggest that the natural evolution of culture and history had been diverted and frequently impaired to a point where many of the threads have become badly unraveled and many of the structures wholly dismantled. Strictly speaking, this may be viewed as acculturation and historical synthesis. However, because of the magnitude and the aftermath of the European presence, we prefer to talk of discontinuity and interruption. To avoid any misapprehension on this score we quote the following brief passage:

> It is because Nyoro are historians, not because we are, that this historical section has been included; a book about Bunyoro [a kingdom included in the present day independent state of Uganda] which neglected its history would be like *Hamlet*, if not without the Prince of Denmark, at least without his father's ghost.[2]

Hence, many African states have with independence embarked on the "rediscovery" and "reinterpretation" of their history. Too often, it has been with a view to rationalizing and justifying present policies and actions, rather than with the purpose of uncovering the actual state of affairs which existed before they became obscured or covered over by the European presence.

In sharp contrast to the general African experience of historical and cultural continuity, we turn briefly to the Japanese experience. Thus we note "the strong sense of continuity the Japanese continue to derive from their own history. The 1,200-year-old view of history—indeed, the 3,000-year-old prehistory, protohistory and history of Japan—still casts a spell over the Japanese mind. . . . And, disregarding for the moment the plodding process of proving or disproving the legends, Japan is beyond doubt the country with the oldest continuous government in the world." [3]

Since the eighth century the Japanese have consciously been using written history—historiography—"as a significant political instrument of the state itself." [4] The modern Japanese state houses a nation which over the centuries has been fused together, sharing, with little more than passing interruption, a common historical and continuous cultural development. The difference between the Japanese pattern at one end of a continuum, and such African states as the Chad, Central African Republic, Gabon, and the two Congos at the other end, makes a world of difference in their prospects for successful nation-building and economic development. In fact, so much difference, that Japan can no longer be thought of in either sense—nation-building or economic development—as belonging to the underdeveloped world. Nevertheless, in order to emphasize our point, Japan has been included in this discussion. Other Asian states such as Iran and Thailand, which have in no sense achieved the Japanese standards of national cohesion and economic growth, still share many of the aspects of Japanese continuity, and on a continuum, are much closer to the Japanese end than that of the African states.

There may be other—less favorable—attributes of this historical and cultural continuity, which we shall discuss in subsequent sections. But for our purpose in this section, it seems clear that the central cohesion imparted by a more or less shared continuous cultural evolution among a given people over long centuries gives them an important advantage in their nation-building and economic development efforts. Notwithstanding inequities and divisions which may be inherent in these ancient but largely intact cultures, they do provide a type of cohesive and sustaining quality—akin to the institutional support alluded to earlier in the case of the Moroccan king and the Ethiopian emperor—to bind and hold together a society while it is modernizing its very nature and reconstituting itself in the framework of a modern nation-state. To invoke the Japanese analogy again: "Modern Japan has inherited a remarkedly integrated ethos which, despite rapid changes, has always provided a source of stability." [5]

Thus, interlaced with the timing of a state's accession to independence is the related factor of the timing of the historical and cultural experience of its people. Together, they compose the time dimension for viewing a state's nation-making and economic growth prospects today.[6]

Africa's late start in the third world's nation-building and development sweepstakes is thus in a temporal sense a handicap. Africa must compete not only with the developed world but also frequently with the more developed parts of the underdeveloped world. So too, Africa comes late to stake out its claim to developed world investment, trade, and aid. On the other hand, coming late to the race, Africa has the benefit of the cumulative experience of others in comparable circumstances and of a kind of psychological compulsion "to catch-up," which frequently characterizes the attitude of the youngest member of the family with respect to older brothers and sisters.

THE GEOPOLITICAL FACTOR

H. T. Buckle declared that nowhere else in the world were natural obstacles so formidable as in Brazil. Even today his remarks apply to many parts of Latin America. "The mountains are too high to scale, the rivers are too wide to bridge [he wrote]. The progress of agriculture is stopped by impassable forests, and the harvests are destroyed by innumerable insects." [7]

This quotation, as we know from our earlier consideration of the geopolitical factor in Africa, could for the most part be applied equally to much of Africa, and for that matter to much of Asia too. One could in the case of Africa probably add, or perhaps substitute for the reference to "mountains," the following phrase, "the deserts and wastelands are too vast to cross or irrigate," and recast the reference to rivers to read "the rivers are too formidable to navigate." The point is that all three geographic areas—Asia, Latin America and Africa—have major geopolitical problems, even barriers, to cope with in their nation-building and economic growth efforts.

The African and Latin American situations particularly have been rendered even more formidable by the legacies bequeathed them on the dissolution of the European colonial empires in their respective areas—legacies characterized by the artificiality of geographic boundaries and, in fact, by the artificiality of their total geographic configurations. The states in both areas were accidental by-products of colonial history, strange and variable in size and shape (and also in population makeup, discussed next). Brazil and Chile rival the Congo (Kinshasa) and Mali for oddness of size and shape, and Bolivia and Paraguay rival Malawi and Upper Volta for awkwardness of form and landlocked isolation. Nor has Asia escaped this legacy of colonial artificiality—e.g., the geopolitical juxtaposition of Pakistan and India in the subcontinent, the string of islands which compose Indonesia, the awkward composition of the Federation of Malaysia, and the strangely contrived succession states in the Indo-Chinese peninsula. However, the Latin-American countries have had a considerably longer time than the African and many of the Asian countries as independent states in which to try to come to terms with their geopolitical problems.

THE HUMAN FACTOR

Size and density of population are obviously significant elements in the dual processes of nation-building and economic development. Their importance is dramatically and cogently illustrated by noting that the population of India alone is larger than the total of the combined populations of Africa and Latin America, whereas the land space it occupies is only a fraction of that of Africa and Latin America. The implications of this staggering concentration of people in the Indian sub-continent for nation-building and development are enormous. Welding together the destinies of over 450 million people within the borders of a single state at the low level of development prevailing in India is a task of gigantic proportions.

This weight of population means running hard, almost at the outer extreme of any pace conceivably attainable, to remain abreast of the needs engendered by the normal growth of the Indian population. There is not likely to be very much left over for further investment to renew the growth process, let alone augment it. Thus, during the Second Indian Plan a national growth rate of 3.7 percent per annum was achieved, whereas population increased by 2.1 percent per annum. On a per capita basis real income grew only on an average of 1.6 percent per annum.

During the current Third Indian Plan population is assumed to be growing at an increased rate, namely 2.4 percent a year. This would mean, assuming a 3.7 percent annual growth rate, a per capita average real income increase of only 1.3 percent. If one contemplates a modest increase in per capita personal consumption, say 1 percent per annum, this leaves only .3 percent for increases in public consumption and investment. This seems hardly enough to accommodate normal growth in governmental recurrent expenditure and at the same time provide a modest margin for investment to continue the growth cycle.[8]

There would seem to be little doubt that excessive population impairs economic welfare and development, and thus, the prospects for successful nation-building.[9]

When, too, the central concern, perhaps the only concern, of the bulk of the population in India is keeping body and soul together there is little disposition and less energy left over to respond to national efforts to induce greater participation in public affairs. The resultant listlessness, apathy, fatalism, acceptance of one's lot, are the very qualities that militate against forging common bonds and evolving common interests in national development. The failure of the bulk of the population to feel a stake and identify an interest in building the new state and its economy is among the greatest obstacles confronting India in its efforts to achieve national political and economic development. There is thus a direct link between economic development and successful nation-building. And the population problem, as we have seen, plays a crucial role in the prospects for economic development, and thus too, in the prospects for nation-building.

This same interrelationship of population, growth, and nation-building exists for all underdeveloped countries. The population burden weighs heaviest on Asian states. Communist China with a reputed 750 million people, India with over 450 million, Pakistan and Indonesia with an estimated 80 million each, and so on, have a burden that for the most part is not to be found in Africa or Latin America. Nigeria with a reputed 55 million has the largest African population, but the man/land ratio there as yet, with the possible exceptions of some pockets of heavy population in the Eastern Region, does not approach the population density found in so many Asian countries. Rwanda, Burundi, the Kingdom of Buganda in Uganda, and the Nile Valley in Egypt are among the other more heavily populated areas in Africa. There are, on the other hand, many large areas, such as the Congo (Kinshasa) and much of French-speaking Africa where the population density is very thin, averaging only ten to twelve persons per square mile. There are states too in Africa with populations under a half million, such as Gabon and the Gambia, and many with only two or three million or less, such as Liberia, Sierra Leone, and the Chad.

It is fair to conclude that on a continental basis the population burden of Asia is of a vastly different order of magnitude than that of Africa, and for that matter also of Latin America, whose continental population is similar to that of Africa's estimated 225 to 250 million people.

The population burden aside, the population mix—the composition of population—is also vastly different among the three areas, and particularly between Africa and Latin America. The latter continent is confronted with the historical legacy of three hundred years of Spanish and Portuguese rule, and as a result in many countries there are three quite distinct racial groups. First, in many countries there are the indigenous people, the unassimilated Indians, the Mayas, Aztecs, Chibchas, Incas, and others, who have remained apart from the main stream of modern Latin American life or only hover on its periphery. Second, the *mestizo*—"the new man"—resulting from the admixture of races, by concubinage and marriage, of Spaniards and Indians, has emerged, and plays an important role in many Latin-American countries of Spanish derivation. In Brazil too, a similar phenomenon has occurred, involving Portuguese, Indians, and Negroes brought from Africa, originally as slaves to work on plantations. Finally, there are the descendants of the Iberians—Spanish and Portuguese —who generally constitute a quite separate elite in all of the Latin-American countries.

In George Pendle's words:

> At the end of the colonial period, moreover, Spanish America contained a much greater variety of widely contrasting elements than English America. It was already an old and complex society, composed of locally-born *criollos*, who had inherited the pride of their Spanish ancestors but had acquired something of an American spirit; *mestizos*, who were partly Spanish, partly Indian, and really belonged to neither race; and Indians, who either laboured as serfs for the *criollos* and *mestizos* or lived in isolation among the highest mountains, where their forefathers had retreated from the foreign invaders. . . . When the wars of independence ended, no real social revolution had occurred. The structure of colonial society, inherited from Spain, remained essentially unaltered. . . . To the mass of the population the change of masters was of no great consequence.[10]

Although it would be wrong to imply that in the 150 years of independence changes in this inherited colonial social structure have not taken place, the basic structural divisions have persisted and have been very much a crucial factor in the efforts of most Latin-American countries to attain national cohesion. In Asian countries the population mix has generally not thrown up so distinctive a pattern as the Latin-American one just described. There, other cultural and social divisions, considered later in this chapter, based on religion and feudal systems, have played an important and somewhat comparable role in obstructing the achievement of national unity in newly independent Asian states or reawakened older ones.

In Africa there has been still another pattern. In the largest part of British, French, and Belgian Africa the Europeans came as traders, investors, and rulers. They did not come as settlers (except in North Africa, Kenya, the Rhodesias, and in South Africa, which we have excluded from the discussion as *sui generis*, and the Portuguese territories, which are outside our frame of reference of nation-building in the new states of Africa). They did not produce, except in limited degree, an intermixture of races and a large, recognizable, distinct class of "new men." And where the Europeans came as settlers, primarily in Algeria, Kenya, and the Rhodesias, they have with the notable exception of Southern Rhodesia either been ousted or relegated to a minority position, more or less commensurate with their numbers. The indigenous people—the Africans—under the "one man, one vote" doctrine have uniformly assumed control. The colonial powers left no rear guard of settlers who had captured control of the independence movements and thereafter, captured control of the newly independent states, as was often the case in Latin America. Simón Bolívar, "the Liberator," was born of *criollo* ancestors in Caracas. He and others like him made the Latin-American independence revolutions. In Africa the leaders of the African independence revolution were Africans, who then proceeded to assume power. So too, in Asia, Asians led the independence revolutions and now head the successor Governments.

In Africa, then, the Latin-American problem of building nation-states from multiracial populations does not exist, except in minor degree with respect to the Asian minorities in East Africa and the small European communities already discussed, and along the fringe of the Sahara in the states with Arabic and black African populations.

The African populations, however, are far from homogeneous in most instances. There usually are multiple tribal groupings within the boundaries of any one state. At one extreme, there is the near homogeneity of Somalia, and at the other, the multiplicity of the Congo (Kinshasa). The general pattern tends more toward the Congolese than the Somali with respect to large numbers of tribal groupings, which were assembled or thrown together by colonial powers, generally without regard to ethnic, cultural, religious, economic, or geographic considerations. The result has been a marked lack of cohesion and unity in most African states. For the most part they must now build a unifying national concept and make Nigerians, Sierra Leoneans, Ghanaians, Congolese, Tanzanians, Ugandans, etc., out of the tribal, subtribal, clan, and other groupings located within their respective geographic borders. In some instances this means evolving different nationalities for members of the same tribe. Thus, the Ewe, divided as they are between Togo and Ghana, are to become Togolese and Ghanaians. And the Bakongo, divided among the two Congos and Angola, are to become Congolese (Kinshasa), Congolese (Brazzaville) and eventually, one day, Angolans. And the Masai, divided between Kenya and Tanzania, are to become Kenyans and Tanzanians. And on and on.

Although the divided populations of Africa—of different tribes, ethnic origin (as the Watutsi and Bahutu in Rwanda and Burundi), religious (Christian, Islamic, animistic, etc.), and historical background—pose serious and major problems for nation-building, compared to the Latin American divisions, developed over centuries, and involving an intermixture of race, social structure, and economic status, they seem relatively manageable and over time susceptible of solution. The Latin American divisions have proved durable and today pose one of the gravest problems for the nation-building and development objectives of the "Alliance for Progress."

THE FACTOR OF FOOD

Implicit in the preceding discussion of the geopolitical and human factors is the question of food. The physical factor of land and the land/man ratio obviously relate directly to the availability of food. However, the question of food is so central that it warrants explicit treatment, to which we now turn briefly.

We have already alluded to the Indian population situation. High population density combined with extremely low agricultural productivity and limited additional cultivable land availability make agricultural development the critical section in India's development.

> India's struggle to achieve a radical economic transformation by peaceful means is apt to be won or lost in the countryside—not because rural problems have some sort of intrinsic priority in a development program over such other issues as heavy industrialization and foreign aid but because of the rural problems' combined quotient of importance *and* difficulty. Of all the essential achievements, success in the countryside may be the hardest to bring off.[11]

Professor Lewis, who is a friendly critic of India's development effort and hopeful about the possibilities and prospects for Indian agriculture, nevertheless found it necessary to conclude that:

> The policies that thus far have been mounted to seize India's opportunity for accelerated agricultural expansion, however, appear distressingly inadequate.[12]

The situation in Pakistan and Communist China, and elsewhere in Asia, with their "teeming millions" and traditional food shortages is not markedly different from that of India.   Speculation in foodstuffs which has resulted has long been endemic in Asia, and imposes a serious limitation not only on development, but, as we have already noted, also on nation-building.   In the words of a recognized Indian economist:

> The basic reason for speculative activity of this nature is the shortage of food and other consumer goods in relation to demand—and inflation is just another name for persistent speculation.[13]

And the subject of inflation offers a natural bridge to the consideration of the role of foodstuffs in the economic development of Latin America, where inflationary trends have been all too characteristic of the development efforts of many countries.[14]   In one cogent sentence about the "backwardness of agriculture in a large part of Latin America," Víctor Urquidi, the well-known Mexican economist stressed foodstuffs:

> The Achilles' heel of economic development is the inelasticity of food production.[15]

And again Urquidi comments:

> In particular, food supply usually lags behind demand, largely because increasing it requires changes in the system of land tenure, additional investments, improved farming methods, agricultural extension, and marketing—orientation services, more profitable prices, and social reforms—all of which can only be achieved slowly.   A developing country often has to import even basic foods.[16]

Although Latin America does not have anything like the population problem that afflicts India and many other Asian lands, it has according to Urquidi "the highest rate of population growth in the world." [17]   It also has "a lagging agriculture," which has only grown on a per capita basis of 1.1 percent per annum whereas populations has been growing at 2.5 percent per annum.   Cereal and livestock production have lagged most.[18]

As for Africa,[19] agriculture has long been the mainstay of the economy. Although generally of low productivity and largely of "subsistence-type" with respect to foodstuffs for internal consumption, in most African states agriculture makes the major contribution to gross domestic product and is the principal source of foreign exchange earnings.

Although African population has been growing at a rapid rate, probably at over 2 percent annually, its agriculture has kept pace expanding at 2-3 percent per annum, and there still remains in many localities the possibility of bringing new areas into production, to say nothing of the margin for increasing productivity. Generally in Africa there is not a shortage of food. Recently, fishing off the west coast of Africa has assumed a growing importance for supplying protein, a prime deficiency in African diet. The expansion of livestock production as well as the upgrading of the quality of beef output in such varied countries as Ethiopia and the Chad have also taken on new importance. Commercial poultry farming has also been introduced and is growing in importance in Nigeria, Malawi, and other African countries.

In sum, the improvement of the composition of the average diet, the improvement in storage facilities, and the development of the marketing system are the problems of African food consumption, rather than the more critical one of the absolute availability of an adequate supply of food for sheer survival as in many Asian countries. The African outlook on this score as well as for general agricultural expansion are relatively favorable, particularly when compared to Asian prospects.

The African attitude toward development of the agricultural sector has also been significantly different from that of many Asian and Latin-American countries. Most African development plans accord a leading priority to development of the agricultural sector, including the domestic food supply. There is, however, a discrepancy between proclaimed objectives and actual practices. Nevertheless, the African commitment to expanding agriculture seems much more serious than the general Asian and Latin-American commitment.[20]

Thus, in this tremendously important area of food production and agricultural development, Africa seems to have a definite lead over other areas of the underdeveloped world. This is a major asset in building sound economies and in nation-making. The possibilities seem much more promising in countries with an expanding agriculture and adequate food supplies for drawing more people into the market economy and more generally into the modern sector where the premium is on performance rather than status. Increasing participation in economic activity in response to incentives of growing segments of the population would seem to be a critical factor for successfully fusing disparate peoples into new national units and viable nation-states.

SOCIAL STRUCTURES

> The social aspects of economic development and the economic aspects of social development must blend together in a single drive towards progress.[21]

It is fitting that this conclusion should come from Dr. Urquidi, for in no part of the underdeveloped world is this more clearly demonstrable than in Latin America. Unfortunately, the failure to induce social development has imposed a most serious constraint on the economic development of most of Latin America. It is also fitting that this observation be made by an economist, who, in pursuit of his professional role of attempting to assist in the economic development of Latin America, came to know the formidable and seemingly intractable nature of the obstacles to development thrown up by the inherited social structures of the colonial era. The structures have been perpetuated and even strengthened, generally to the advantage of the governing class—more or less the class we have alluded to, which both made and inherited the independence revolutions in Latin America—and frequently to the disadvantage of the overall development, economic and social, of the countries-at-large and the bulk of their populations.[22] In the words of a former American Assistant Secretary of State for Latin-American Affairs and recognized specialist in this area of the world:

> Latin America is undergoing not one revolution but two. . . . There is a real and continuing indigenous effort, found everywhere in the region, which asserts greater rights of participation in government, in production, and in wealth for the Latin American masses. This is as endemic as it is justified.[23]

This is not the place for an extended narration and analysis of the Latin American social structures. For our purposes we shall, at the risk of over-simplifying, content ourselves by citing a brief generalized portrait which accords with most of the currently accepted analyses of the Latin American scene and is, more or less, tacitly accepted in the Act of Bogotá of 1960,[24] and the Declaration and Charter of Punta del Estes of 1961,[25] which underlie the Alliance for Progress. George Pendle has drawn the picture tautly:

> Until the second decade of the twentieth century there was little change in the social or political structure of any of the Latin American countries, the mass of the people continuing to regard government as not for them. . . . Wealth and power generally remained in the hands of the landowning oligarchy and their military allies, with the addition of a new class, the leaders of business, whose interests sometimes conflicted with those of the landowning families but whose views on labor were usually just as conservative. . . . In most of the republics, the carrying out of radical reforms could not be effected by parliamentary means, so that reformers had to resort to force . . . or they allowed an ambitious *caudillo* to assume the championship of their cause. . . .[26]

Coups d'état, revolutions, inflation, *caudillos*, social ferment and conflict, have been the continuing background for and limitation on economic development. They have also been the continuing background for and limitation on nation-building directly, and indirectly too, in their retarding effect on economic growth, which has become increasingly recognized as the motive power for achieving national unity and cohesion in Latin America (our point of departure in opening the discussion in this section).[27]

The Asian picture in many ways is still more difficult. Frequently the class structure is even more deeply rooted, stretching back centuries, with a religious sanction often attaching to the status of the privileged classes or, nearly the same thing, deriving from a quasi-mystical acceptance of one's position or status, and by inference, of that of the privileged classes as well. Frequently too, wealth, particularly in the form of vast landholdings, characterizes the monopoly of the privileged classes of political and economic power. In many instances the caste systems and lingering feudal traditions have been buttressed by the military, which, as in Latin America, has tended to be allied with and protective of the interests of the privileged classes.

When political change is under way, where social revolution has made a start, and where social ferment has appeared as a concomitant and cause of economic change, Asian as well as Latin-American social structures have tended to raise some of the most formidable barriers to successful economic growth, and to successful nation-building. As in Latin America, divesting vested interests in Asia has been the most intractable of tasks, resulting in the most formidable of all barriers to growth and development—in many ways in many countries, more important in imposing limitations on growth than the scarcity of resources.

The pivotal state of India, which, as Professor Lewis has rightly noted, has important implications for the rest of the underdeveloped world, offers a dramatic illustration of the problems posed by an entrenched social structure interacting with religious, tribal, and regional differences so characteristic of undeveloped countries. In Lewis' words (and he is a most sympathetic commentator):

> In the eyes of most thoughtful observers of Indian politics, however, the internal Communist danger in India would not be very great were it not being nurtured by a much more deeply indigenous threat to the maintenance of orderly national government. This is the age-old, now possibly resurgent, tendency of the Indian body politic to splinter into regional and communal fragments. An indication of this tendency is the fact that most of the non-Congress [ruling party] votes in recent central and state parliamentary elections have gone not to the Congress' national

party rivals but to religiously-, regionally-, and tribally-oriented groups. . . . It is evinced, further, by divisiveness . . . within the structure of the language-based states to which Mr. Nehru gave his profoundly reluctant acquiescence in 1955. Moreover, within many of the states, regional splintering is deeply cross-hatched by caste-group rivalries that not only are decisive within their own areas but do not even have the saving grace, it is said, of building much sense of interregional community within their own strata.[28]

Professor Lewis concludes:

Harrison [an American student of Indian Affairs] plainly is right to focus on the unity issue as the theme of India's coming political crisis. . . . The issue comes down to this: Can the nation hold together easily under the shocks of Mr. Nehru's retirement [he has since died] and/or a division in the Congress [Party]? Will it manage, under more routine leadership, to make an orderly transition to an effectively integrated two or few-party system of national government within the existing constitutional frame? Or will the nation so nearly come apart at the seams during the course of a succession crisis that constitutionalism will be swept aside? [29]

Whereas Harrison [30] is pessimistic, envisaging a probable military dictatorship or a possible communist totalitarian takeover, Lewis is hopeful that constitutionalism and democratic rule will survive and grow. He concludes that "the overwhelmingly important fact for our purposes is that India's political future will turn very largely on what happens to the Indian economy during the next few years." And again, "thus India's political future probably quite literally depends on the success of the Third Five Year Plan." [31]

Elsewhere in Asia, the Shah of Iran, the King of Afghanistan, the King of Nepal, and the King of Thailand preside over countries with social structures reflecting many of the aspects of the Indian one. The Hindu caste system of India also finds less rigid, perhaps, but nevertheless rough counterparts, in the Shinto military-religious system of Japan (said to have been considerably weakened in the aftermath of World War II) and, as a *de facto* matter if not as a matter of pure dogma and doctrine, in some of the fatalistic and contemplative religious practices of Buddhism, Islam, and other religions in various Asian countries.

Regional and tribal divisions thus tend to be reinforced by religious practices and caste structures, and the social immobility they imply, in Burma, the Indo-Chinese States, Indonesia, Korea, etc., as well as in India. And the largest state of all, mainland China, has traditionally had most and probably all of these concerns; and now has communism attempting through totalitarian techniques to expunge all these divisive factors. Will Communist China succeed or will it, in Djilas' terms only produce a "new class" of privileged party *cum* state bureaucrats? (China is, of course, the totalitarian route to unity—nation-building and development—compared to the pluralistic and democratic approach of India, a subject which we dealt with at some length in the African context, particularly in comparing Ghana and Nigeria.)

The African scene, by and large, differs considerably from those of Latin America and Asia—mostly by the absence of many of these constraining factors in their social structure. Thus, for the most part, Africa has not traditionally had a rigid, and in many instances even a recognizable class structure. In fact one of the deviations most widely accepted (if not always practised) of African Marxists is their rejection of the central Marxist doctrine of the class struggle. African Marxists, such as radical nationalist President Sékou Touré of Guinea, have insistently denied the existence of classes in African society, historically and currently. Former President Nkrumah of Ghana used to deny the existence of classes in African society too, but in his increasing turn to the left has not only dropped the word "African" from his proclaimed goal of "African socialism," but has also taken increasingly to talking about "crushing the working class's enemy" and "wiping out bourgeois opportunism," etc. The same transition has also occurred in Algeria where former President Ben Bella adopted an increasingly strident line against the "bourgeois class." But these are largely the exceptions; accepted African socialist doctrine still maintains the absence of the class structures in Africa.[32]

Although in the largest area of Africa there have not been clearly delineated class structures in the Marxist sense, there has been some class differentiation, and increasingly more, with economic development and postindependence political changes. Rwanda and Burundi in Central Africa and Ethiopia in East Africa, as we have already seen, have had types of feudal structures with classes based on an admixture of race, culture, and economic status. North Africa too, particularly Morocco and Egypt, at opposite ends of the Mediterranean, have had class structures. Elsewhere, although not absolutely absent, recognizable class structures in the Marxist sense tended to be exceptional. By and large, status societies in the Weberian sense rather than class structures in the Marxian sense, flourished in most of Africa. This has been in large part the consequence of the subsistence societies endemic and still prevalent in much of Africa.

In Weber's words:

> When the bases of the acquisition and distribution of goods are relatively stable, stratification by status [social position, prestige, family, tribe,

etc.] is favored. Every technological repercussion and economic transformation threatens stratification by status and pushes the [economic] class situation into the foreground. Epochs and countries in which the naked class situation is of predominant significance are regularly the periods of technical and economic transformations. And every slowing down of the shifting of economic stratification leads, in due course, to the growing of status structures and makes for resuscitation of the important role of social honour.[33]

Ascribed social status rather than achieved economic class has characterized African society; Africa has not generally experienced the vested interests problem of Latin America and Asia, where sharply differentiated classes have long been entrenched, based as much on wealth as on race, religion, and caste. Land ownership has gone hand in hand in these areas with race or religion or caste. So too has political power. Which came first, and which followed—wealth or status—no longer has importance in those areas where the concomitance exists. It is enough that they exist together and reinforce one another.

In Africa, on the other hand, for the most part, the lack of economic differentiation, of accumulated wealth, and of special land-holding groups, has left a residue of status differentiation based largely on region, tribe, and religion. In many instances, *intra*-regional, tribal, and religious differentiation have yielded to political change and economic development. For example, the suppression of the intertribal wars by the colonial powers caused the disappearance of the warrior group within tribal structures; the imposition of colonial authority diluted and frequently even destroyed the status of chiefs and other traditional ruling tribal authorities (with exceptions in certain British cases of "indirect rule"); the introduction of modern medicine diluted and impaired the position of the traditional medicine man and witch doctor; the introduction of western education has tended to break down traditional social classifications and replace them with new ones based on educational attainment or, often, on educational credentials which all too frequently have been confused with attainment; and the introduction of a market sector has had a tendency to produce new economic interest groups—cash-crop farmers, wage-earners, traders—to transmute traditional tribal gifts and tokens of respect into "dash" (common African usage for bribes), and to break down or transform extended family obligation into nepotism in the public services. A "new class" of politicians, who have frequently used their political position for personal economic advantages, has also emerged in many African states.

Inter-regional, tribal and religious differentiation, however, have persisted and thrown up major obstacles to African cohesion and growth.

Tribal and sectional antagonisms, reinforced in some areas like the Sudan, by religious differences, are perhaps the greatest problem for the new African states to resolve if they are to build modern nation-states.

There is tremendous social mobility in Africa within regional, tribal, and religious groupings. The conflicts and tensions arise not in vertical mobility within a group (tribe), but in horizontal mobility between groups (inter-tribal). Thus, for example, in Iboland—in the Eastern Region of Nigeria—modernization based on economic growth has broken down any number of status levels, but in Nigeria at large, the Ibo has had problems in being accepted in Yorubaland in Western Nigeria, and also tends to be rejected and, most recently, excluded, in Hausaland in Northern Nigeria.

Nonetheless, difficult as intertribal differences may be by themselves in interposing obstacles to national unity, they do not appear anywhere as intractable as the same or comparable tribal divisions are when reinforced by vested economic interests. On this important score, then, Africa for the most part has an important advantage. Its traditional freedom from class stratification (in the Marxist sense) generally, and in support of tribal division, means that there is not likely to be the type of bitter resistance to modernization encountered in Latin America and Asia.

THE RELIGIOUS FACTOR

Briefly, Africa has generally been free of many of the inhibitions imposed by religion on social change and economic growth in much of Asia and Latin America. As we have noted, historical and cultural continuity has been an important stabilizing and cohesive force in Asia in the period of the social, political, and economic transformation that followed World War II. As we have suggested, it has also had the opposite effect of solidifying customs and traditions so that they resist change. Thus, in India the Hindu religion, in Japan Shintoism, in much of the Middle East and Pakistan, Islam, in Southeast Asia and China Buddhism—all have provided either the basis for caste distinctions, or religious sanction for practices inimical to social and economic change, or institutions resistant to modernization, or clergy with motivations or attitudes frequently at cross purposes with development and change.

Although not absent in Africa, for the most part traditional African religions have not been anywhere as institutionalized and have not raised comparable barriers, or where they have tended to do so, the barriers have also tended to yield to the pressures of modern life. The influence of traditional African religions persists but does not seem to resist in the same way, as say Hinduism, the levelling effect of nation-building with respect to caste, or the taboo-destroying effect of economic deveolpment. The African "cattle complex," which has been described as a matter of social status and prestige, for example, will yield to economic incentives and needs, and has already done so where alternative social prestige symbols and alternative opportunities for asserting liquidity preferences have appeared, whereas the Indian belief in the sacred character of cattle has remained largely obdurate.

As for the external religions which have made headway in Africa—Islam and Christianity—they have not tended to throw up the obstacles encountered in Asian religions. Somehow Islam in Africa south of the Sahara seems less resistant to modernizing change than it does in, say, Morocco, Algeria, Tunisia, or in the Middle East generally. In Tunisia, President Bourguiba has made some headway, but slowly and at the cost of considerable controversy and opposition of the Islamic hierarchy, in his effort to rationalize the observance of the month of Ramadan, which, in its requirement of long periods of fasting and abstinence, has tended to interfere with the quality of workers' performance and with efficient public administration. In neighboring Algeria, confronted with even more serious problems of national development after seven years or more of guerrilla warfare, former President Ben Bella found it convenient to placate the Islamic hierarchy and refrain from undertaking a campaign for the reconciliation of religious practices with the needs of economic development, comparable to the program sponsored by President Bourguiba. Similarly, King Hassan in neighboring Morocco has found support for his political regime in the religious hierarchy he officially heads, and no effort of the Bourguiba type has been contemplated.

The difference in the quality of Islamic resistance in Africa south of the Sahara may be but a consequence of the overall social structure and cultural ambiance of the area,[34] or a result of the later appearance of Islam there, or due to still other causes not readily identifiable. For whatever reason, in most other areas of Africa, with the possible exception of the Sudan, Mauritania, and Northern Nigeria, Islam does not appear to have been a major factor in nation-building or economic development. Elsewhere in Africa, Christianity has facilitated national development with its introduction of mission schools and has provided one of the important pressures to which traditional animistic African religions have yielded. Christianity has also in various parts of Africa, with all other outlets denied it, provided a refuge or channel for early African nationalism or anticolonialism. Thus, in Kenya in the early 1950's the "Mau Mau religion" found support in the "preachers and leaders of the Independent Separatist Churches [who] were won over." [35] Elsewhere, too, in Africa syncretic breakaway separatist Christian Churches provided an outlet and sanctuary for protest movements. This was particularly true in the

Congo (Kinshasa). "In the countryside and in the big towns . . . hatred of the White is propagated mainly by the politico-religious sects called Kibanguism, Kitawala, and others, which can only operate secretly." [36] Preaching doctrine and sanctioning practices at odds with established or accepted ones, the syncretic and Messianic churches provided an emotional and psychological release, which, without too much manipulation, could be transformed into a wide political protest against the ruling colonial authorities. In his book, *Congo, My Country*, Patrice Lumumba recognized the importance of Kitawala.[37] And Kibanguism [38] had its supporters in the Abako Party in the Bas-Congo. The Abako was one of the earliest and best organized of the Congolese political parties seeking independence.

Whatever the reason, generally religion in Africa has not offered anywhere as much resistance to change as it has in Asia. And in Latin America too, the prevailing pattern has been different from that of Africa. From the early days of Spanish and Portuguese exploration and colonization the Catholic Church has been intimately involved in the colonial and postcolonial power structure and has played an important role in the pattern of national development of the Latin American countries.

This is not the place to attempt to record or analyze the role of the Catholic Church in nation-building and economic development in the Latin-American countries. We must content ourselves with noting its importance (not unlike many Asian religions) in influencing the pattern of such development, and with noting the difference between the Latin-American pattern and that of Africa generally. There has thus not been an African counterpart to the position of the Church at the time of the Mexican Revolution of the 1850's and 1860's with its "two chief aims":

> First, they aimed at subordinating the army and the Church to civil authority, hoping thereby to unite the country. . . . Second, they would curb the power of the landed aristocracy. . . .[39]

And again of the Mexican Revolution of 1926–29:

> The Church could not approve of the Revolution, which was undermining its authority, while from the point of view of the Revolution, the Church was still identified with the Spanish conquest and all the colonial system represented. In the event, however, both the Church and the Revolution proved to be realistic and flexible, and a war to the death was avoided.[40]

Although not necessarily typical, variations of the Mexican social structure involving the alliance or identification of the landed aristocracy, the military, and the Church have been quite common throughout the Latin American area.

Thus in Africa, once again, the absence of this type of highly structured vested interest resisting change has been a plus on the scale of prospects for nation-building and development.

LAND-HOLDING

Already touched on in the sections on social structure and religion, we shall deal briefly here with the land-holding factor. In both Latin America and Asia it has been widely recognized that the concentration of land ownership and rights deriving from its possession in the hands of a relatively small and compact group has been one of the major constraints on economic growth and on bringing into a common community the bulk of the populations in many Latin American and Asian countries. Time and again, the need for sweeping land reform has been identified throughout these two continents as *a* principal or *the* principal problem to be dealt with by developers and nation-builders.

The landed aristocracy has resisted in many parts of Asia and throughout Latin America. Sometimes, the religious hierarchy has been included; sometimes the military has also been included. Aside from the vested interest aspect of resistance to change, already dealt with, poorly exploited or totally unexploited land, which frequently is a factor in these situations, has interposed an additional obstacle to economic growth. Even where there is full and efficient exploitation, there are problems of adequate or equitable tax income to the state, wage payments to agricultural labor, use of savings, availability of foreign exchange earnings, price levels, etc., which are of serious importance to national development. All too often in the landed aristocracy cases, where status and class reinforce one another, these issues have been resolved against the general interest or in the interest of the limited class. The attendant consequences have not always contributed to a sense of national purpose and unity. On the contrary, they have frequently acted to divide the national populations in fundamental ways and to retard the growth which could serve to draw them together by expanding the market economy and the participation of and rewards to large masses of people now outside it or on the periphery.

In Africa, the general problem—Ethiopia and the North African states aside—has not been one of the landed aristocracy monopolizing the land and its product, and relating to its land ownership, political power, and social status. The problem rather has been—and remains—a problem of modernizing and adapting ancient and traditional systems of communal land holding. Land generally has been owned collectively by a tribe or subtribal group, and has been administered as a trust by a chief or chief-in-council in the interests of the collectivity. Clans or families have generally been assigned or acquired rights to use the land and its product, and within these groups, individuals have been assigned or acquired lesser rights or shares in the use of the land. There has been a tendency for these rights and shares to be passed on generation after generation—with the increasing introduction of stationary agriculture—and in some areas this has led to considerable fragmentation (as in large parts of East Africa).

The problem has become one of devising techniques of providing incentives to farmers in light of the insecurity of their rights in the land to improve its use and expand its productivity. One answer often put forward by Europeans has been the introduction of the concept of freehold ownership. Another has been the attempt to devise suitable cooperative concepts of land use. There has been, in this connection, considerable interest in the Israeli patterns of land ownership and use. Other techniques are being experimented with in various parts of Africa.

A related problem has been one of land consolidation and land registration in light of the division and redivision of the right to use land in various parts of Africa. In the Central Province of Kenya, where there is a relatively dense population, there has been serious land pressure among the Kikuyu and a large-scale program of consolidation and registration has been underway for some time. Elsewhere, there is the problem of how to bring together enough small parcels of land so that the benefits of plantation-scale agriculture could be attained. And so on with variants of the problem. The significant issue is one of how to alter and modernize traditional practices, rather than how to divest an entrenched and powerful class of the very basis of its wealth and status. The latter seems by far the more intractable problem. The general African position on this score appears more favorable to economic growth and building national cohesion.

THE MILITARY

We have had occasion to touch on the role of the military in the discussion of Latin American social structures. We now return to the military in Latin America briefly, as its basic roots and importance in the historical evolution of the independent Latin-American states are in sharp contrast to African experience. Starting with the Great Liberator, Bolívar, the seeds of *caudilloism* and militarism were sown, and they are still germinating. Thus:

Bolívar had liberated South America from the Spaniards, but his work was in ruins. The reasons for his failure provide the explanation of much of the later history of Spanish America. Bolívar destroyed Spanish authority. To replace it, he was eventually compelled to resort to despotism. Faced with the disorder in Colombia, he assumed dictatorial powers allowed by the Colombian Constitution in times of emergency. He was thus the forerunner of many Latin American *caudillos* who were to suspend Constitutions and depose elected authorities. Democratic aspirations—in the tradition of the early days of the revolution survived, but were not fulfilled, and it became customary to employ the army to impose order and to suppress liberalism, "the fountainhead of anarchy." [41]

In many Latin American countries the army *coup* to oust an unpopular leader, or a popular one who was too liberal or too reformist, or too independent of the military, has continued to the present day. In addition, we now find the military intervening and carrying out *coups d'état* where the civilian government has become too corrupt, or too indifferent to the welfare of the people, or too dictatorial. Thus, for example, we have the case of the largest of all South American countries, Brazil. "Presently, the political organization of the country is in full transition. . . . The army has been unjustly accused of fascism in opposing him [Vice-President João Goulart, who succeeded to the presidency after the abrupt resignation of President Quadro]; its real reason was desire to protect the democracy won when the army (with the backing of the country) compelled Getulio Vargas to end his dictatorship in 1945." [42]

And, in Argentina, Professor Berle has also written: "Democracy returned to Argentina, as to Brazil, via the army and the navy. The armed forces ended the Perón dictatorship in 1955. . . ." [43]

Thus it has been in other Latin American countries where the military has taken onto itself the function of protector of the public conscience or arbiter of social well-being of the population. The difficulty encountered in Brazil * and in Argentina, and elsewhere, is how does the military extricate itself? When does the new regime brought in under military auspices or with a military midwife stand on its own? And when it does, when does the military forego the assumed moral authority of judging the performance of the new government? When does it stop the practice intervening again and again, whenever the military determines that the new government's performance is not up to the expected standard?

* In the case of Brazil, its President, Arthur da Costa e Silva, assumed emergency one-man powers on December 13, 1968, after ordering Congress recessed. When he suffered a stroke in September 1969, a military junta took over. Shortly thereafter, young revolutionaries kidnapped U.S. Ambassador C. Burke Ellrick, who was ransomed by the release and transporting to Mexico of fifteen political prisoners. J.H.M.

And as if this were not enough, in Argentina and elsewhere, the question has arisen, at times with comic opera overtones, as to which part of the military is entitled to hold the keys to the public conscience. Interservice rivalries between the Army and Navy, and between the Air Force and the Army have arisen. Splits have occurred between age groups, younger officers and older senior commanders. Rivalries in the higher echelons have also not been unknown. As always, where there is no responsibility of the self-appointed ruler to a defined electorate, personal politics play an even greater role than otherwise, and deflect or divert the course of events in what might seem (and might in fact be) a highly capricious manner.

The burden of militarism on the public budget, with its diversion of resources to nonproductive investment in military establishments, to the purchase, maintenance, manufacturing, modernization, and replacement of armaments, and to maintaining large military forces has unquestionably imposed a serious restraint on Latin American development. This too has retarded the forging of national unity to the extent that these diverted resources were not available for productive investment to bring more Indians and others on the outer limits of the market economy into it with its leveling and integrating influence.

The Asian picture has been somewhat different, or at any rate more variegated. The Chinese war lords have been legendary, and now have been replaced by Communist Chinese militarism, leading to the ultimate incongruity of the twentieth century, of the People's Republic simultaneously pouring out its wealth to develop the atomic bomb and stoically accepting a bare subsistence level of sustenance for a large part of its large population. The other China, also bears a heavy burden of arms, partly in response to mainland China's militarism and partly in response to its own irredentist dream of reoccupying the mainland. In Japan, the role of Shintoism, in extolling the role of the warrior and encouraging Japanese aggression throughout the 1930's and up to the end of World War II, does not need retelling here. In Iran and Thailand the military have had a long tradition of power and alliance with the landed classes.

More recently, India and Pakistan, successor states of the dismantled British Empire, have borne a heavy burden of armed forces and modern arms. These two states, born in mutual distrust, suspicion, and at times seeming hatred of one another, have built up major and expensive military forces amidst stark poverty in both countries. And most recently as a result of Chinese Communist aggression, India has had an even heavier military burden to sustain. Burma too has with independence developed a significant military burden to maintain internal order in a state beset by serious tribal differences, armed political movements, and a constant Chinese Communist threat.

In addition to the arms burden and the major role the military have assumed in the histories of China and Japan and other Asian states, in the more recently independent states, particularly in Pakistan, Burma, and Indonesia, the military have undertaken a role through military takeovers comparable to the public conscience and reformist role already alluded to in the instances of Brazil and Argentina.

In Africa, the situation has been markedly different. There generally has been no military tradition or presence surviving European colonialism comparable to the Shinto tradition of Japan or the war-lordism of China or the landed aristocracy-military alliance of Iran. There has been no military *caudilloism* growing out of wars of independence as in Latin America (with the possible exception of Egypt and Algeria). On the contrary, there has been a very limited use of force in the independence revolution in Africa, involving the accession of three dozen African states to independence in the last decade, with the guerrilla war in Algeria against the French very much the exception.

As we have noted, the military age groups or warrior classes of traditional African society, where they existed, disappeared, partly because of the less rigid social structures to be found in Africa and partly because their functions became redundant with the imposition of the *Pax Europa* during the colonial era. In any event, with a few notable exceptions, there were not many military-run or dominated kingdoms in Africa at the time of the major European penetrations. Most African states have come to independence with modest armed forces, without a recent or continuous military tradition, with very few trained military personnel, and generally without institutions for training them, with limited arms and even more limited facilities for fabricating them.

Ethiopia has been something of an exception, with its feudal tradition and history of preserving its independence and repulsing European penetration. It has developed something of a military tradition, and by African standards a relatively large military establishment. The military too, as a result of the 1939 Italian conquest and subsequent liberation during World War II, and its participation in the Korean War and the UN Force in the Congo, has played an identifiable and important role in recent Ethiopian affairs. Morocco too, to a greater or lesser degree has been something of an exception, growing out of its feudal tradition, the history of the Moorish empire and its penetration of the Iberian peninsula, and the more recent guerrilla warfare involved in terminating the French protectorate in 1955. As in Ethiopia, the military has been renewed and modernized, and as we have noted, has provided major support for the reigning monarch.

Algeria too has been something of a special case. Its seven-year struggle for independence developed a fairly large and politically power-

ful military force. Since independence it has played a major role in
Algerian affairs, first as a major support for President Ahmed Ben Bella's
regime, and then in dispensing with it and assuming power itself. The
Congo (Kinshasa), which might also be thought of as something of a
special case, has been treated at length in Chapter 11.

By and large the rest of Africa, lacking a military tradition and as a
result of a peaceful road to independence, did not come to independence
with important military classes or forces or significant military burdens
to sustain. The support of small local defence forces, a natural attribute
of international sovereignty, appears to have been burden enough, and
in many states in the postindependence period the French Government
has continued to carry a large share of the expense of domestic African
forces, and of French forces maintained in Africa in lieu of or in supple-
ment to domestic forces.[44] And in various places in Africa for some
years after independence—as for example in Sierra Leone and Kenya—the
British have picked up a fair share of the bill for domestic military forces,
training missions, supplies, equipment, etc.

But sadly, in various African states, armed forces have been and are
being developed of questionable size and character, and with doubtful
missions. Inevitably, as a consequence, something of an arms race has
ensued. Pre-*coup* Ghana, with its military brand of Pan-Africanism and
build-up of its military forces, sparked off the bush-league African arms
race. Although still small in the world context, limited as it must be by
limited resources, the arms race is by no means insignificant on the
African scene. The author has dealt with this subject elsewhere at
length and now only cites it to round out the picture.[45] And as we have
noted in some detail earlier, there has been a rash of both successful and
abortive military *coups d'état* in many African countries. These have
occurred, in spite of the smallness of the armed forces and the lack of
military tradition, because of the weakness of the new state structures,
of the narrow base and lack of real support for the one-party authoritarian regimes (Dahomey, Congo-Brazzaville, Ghana, Upper Volta, Central African Republic, etc.), and the absence of any effective participation of other organized groups in society. In short, for all the reasons
analyzed in Part II of this book.

Thus, African states generally, if they do not throw it away, have a
marked advantage over both Latin American and Asian states on the score
of militarism. Once again it is the absence of a factor which affords the
advantage. The African states generally do not have the problem of
divesting the military of its special power and authority, breaking its
alliance with other vested interests, and taming its power and bringing it
under civilian authority. So too, generally, the crushing burden of arms
borne by states like the two Chinas, Korea, Viet Nam, India, Pakistan,

and in lesser but significant degrees, by any number of Latin-American countries, has been lacking in Africa.

To the extent Africa chooses to embark on an arms race then this dual advantage will diminish. It has already begun to in some states. To the extent national cohesion is not forged, and to the extent valid public participation in governmental and economic affairs is not fostered or is denied, then the procession of military coups of 1965–68 is likely to become an integral part of the African pattern. The growing role of the military in African country after African country has created the prospect of replaying in Africa the 150-year old Latin American drama of military *coups, caudilloism,* political instability, and inflation, with all of its disastrous implications for nation-building and development.

ECONOMIC DEVELOPMENT

Economic development, because of its close interrelationship with nation-building, is of central importance. It is also one of the hardest factors to assess. Latin American countries generally have a much higher per capita income than all of Africa (excepting the Republic of South Africa) and most all of Asia (excepting Japan). In Urquidi's words:

> Latin America's product per person of $366 was three and a half times that of central Africa and almost five times that of underdeveloped Asia. Nevertheless, Latin America has a low per capita product and a low standard of living . . . ; little comfort can be derived from comparison with central Africa or Southeast Asia.[46]

There can also be little question that many Latin-American countries have gone further in industrialization and in diversifying their economies than African countries and probably most Asian countries. The Latin-American countries also have larger quantities of trained manpower than African countries and many Asian countries. The resource base is as favorable as most and more favorable than many African and Asian countries. Latin America has also moved further in organizing a free trade area or areas than other regions of the underdeveloped world. All in all, it would seem that economic development prospects in Latin America are more favorable than those in most other underdeveloped areas of the world. This certainly is the view of Urquidi. Another prominent Mexican, this time the journalist Víctor Alba, although concurring, has raised an important question:

> It is well known that Latin America is now at a characteristic level of economic development which is higher than that of the Near or Far East, of the Maghreb or tropical Africa. It would be interesting, however, to

explore whether the Latin American development sequence and the type of disequilibrium it presents forms a pattern which might be followed by other underdeveloped countries, or whether it is the product of specific circumstances peculiar to Latin America. In other words, does there exist a Latin American style of developing? [47]

In the same way as the question was posed in the preceding discussion of the military—will the new African states reenact the Latin American drama of military coups and political instability—the comparable question must now be put with respect to the Latin-American development pattern. Will the new African states emulate the more-or-less standard Latin-American pattern of inflation, vastly uneven and disproportionate distribution of income and wealth, high-cost protected industrial development, lagging agriculture, large government participation in economic activity, and sporadic stop-and-go growth?

The Asian picture is far too diversified to project here beyond the point so vividly dramatized by the sharply contrasting routes to growth being followed by India and Communist China. As Professor Lewis makes clear in his book, India is engaged in a major program of planned economic growth by means compatible with democratic and constitutional principles and values. The Communist China program is the antithesis. Authoritarian and totalitarian in nature, the Communist Chinese are engaged in seeking development through state control, coercion and forced-march tactics. As Lewis has observed, the success or failure of the Indian attempt (particularly vis-à-vis the Chinese) will have important implications for Latin America and Africa.

It would not be possible to trace out in this section the comparative advantages and disadvantages of the three broad underdeveloped areas in their economic development efforts. Much of what we have discussed in the foregoing sections dealing with what are in effect the noneconomic factors that play a major role, and possibly a decisive one, in economic growth, suggests that the African states have some important structural and social advantages, or at any rate, opportunities for avoiding Latin-American pitfalls and the Asian handicaps. On the other hand, the Latin-American states clearly have a significant head start in economic development. Whether or not they have reached something of a plateau, and how much further they can go with their present inflation-ridden economies and highly protected industry enclosed in relatively narrow markets, remains to be seen. Suffice it to say that the African states, starting later and from a markedly lower level of development, have a long way to go to catch up in development terms with many Latin-American states. But by the same token, if they vary the pattern and learn from Latin-American experience, could they translate their impatience for development into practice and develop another route, different from the Latin-American and different from the Asian (with their special conditions, already discussed), which will, along with their other advantages with respect to noneconomic factors, afford them a less erratic and more steady rate of growth?

CONCLUDING WORD

The prospects for successful nation-building do not appear over bright for any of the three areas. Comparatively, African prospects do not appear worse than those of the other two areas, and in some respects African states—in theory at least—have important advantages. This of course does not mean individual states in other areas, such as Mexico, may not have better prospects for their nation-building than many African states, but it does mean that on a continental basis, the African states do have *opportunities* for successful nation-building that in some ways seem more promising than those of many other states in the other major areas. What the African states will do with their opportunities is the critical unknown in the equation. Based on the analysis in Part II and assessment in Part III, it is not at all clear that the theoretical advantages and opportunities of Africa will be realized in practice by more than a handful of African states.

APPENDIX I

TABLE OF MILITARY COUPS D'ETAT IN AFRICA RESULTING IN CHANGES OF GOVERNMENT SINCE 1960

(As of March 10, 1969)

Date	Country	Leaders	State Structure at time of Coup	Outcome
1. September 5, 1960	Congo (Kinshasa) (former Belgian Congo)	President Kasavubu dismissed Prime Minister Lumumba, who refused to resign and purported to "dismiss" the President; whereupon Colonel (now General) Mobutu, the army commander, declared army was assuming power.	Unitary, with quasi-federal aspects, multi-party structure.	The army with a "College of Commissioners" shared power with President Kasavubu. Subsequently Parliament was reorganized and a new government was installed with Cyrille Adouls as Prime Minister.
2. January 13, 1963	Togo * (former UN Trust Territory administered by France)	President Sylvanus Olympio was assassinated during army coup, involving unemployed ex-Togolese soldiers who had served in the French army. After a brief military interregnum M. Nicholas Grunitzky became President with military backing.	Unitary, *de facto* one-party structure.	President Grunitzky remained in power with military support. *De jure* one-party state structure established.
3. August 15, 1963	Congo (Brazzaville) † (former French colony)	The military deposed President Youlou, and sponsored the formation of a new government under President Massemba-Debat.	Unitary, *de facto* one-party structure.	M. Massemba-Debat became President in a *de jure* one-party state structure.
4. October 28, 1963	Dahomey (former French colony)	Colonel (now General) Soglo, Army Chief of Staff, deposed President Hubert Maga, and took power pending a new election in a *de jure* one-party structure.	Unitary, *de facto* one-party structure.	M. Apithy was elected President in the *de jure* one-party structure "election."
5. February 18, 1964	Gabon ‡ (former French colony)	M. Jean Aubame, Opposition Leader, headed a revolt supported by a group of young army officers. President Mba was arrested and Aubame assumed power. In a counter-coup the next day French troops restored the status quo ante.	Unitary, *de facto* one-party structure.	President Mba remained in power with French military support.
6. June 19, 1965	Algeria (former French territory, which France administered as a "province" of metropolitan France)	President Ben Bella overthrown and arrested by Colonel Houari Boumedienne, Chief of the Armed Forces, Minister of Defense and Vice President.	Unitary, *de jure* one-party structure.	Colonel Boumedienne became head of state and remained in power as head of military junta.
7. November 25, 1965	Congo (Kinshasa)	President Kasavubu deposed and former Prime Minister Tshombé "neutralized" by Lieut. General Mobutu and army.	Federal, multi-party structure.	General Mobutu announced a five-year military regime, and became President of country. Major-General Mulamba was appointed Prime Minister.

Date	Country	Leaders	State Structure at time of Coup	Outcome
8. November 29, 1965	Dahomey (former French colony)	General Soglo assumed power again and forced the ouster of President Apithy and Prime Minister Ahomadegbe.	Unitary, de jure one-party structure.	M. Congacou, President of the National Assembly, installed as President, as the next in line after the ousted President and Prime Minister.
9. December 22, 1965	Dahomey§ (former French colony)	General Soglo ousted civil government which was deadlocked over composition	Unitary, de jure one-party structure.	General Soglo became President and remained in power as head of military junta.
10. January 1, 1966	Central African Republic (former French colony)	Colonel Bokassa, chief of staff of the army, ousted President Dako, and seized power.	Unitary, de jure one-party structure.	Colonel Bokassa became President and remained in power as head of military junta.
11. January 4, 1966	Upper Volta (former French colony)	Colonel Lamizana, chief of staff of the army, deposed President Yaméogo and installed military government.	Unitary, de jure one-party structure.	Colonel Lamizana became President and remained in power as head of military junta.
12. January 15, 1966	Nigeria (former British colony)	A group of young army officers, primarily Ibos, assassinated Prime Minister and Premiers of Western and Northern Regions and numerous ranking officers, primarily Northerners. The remainder of cabinet passed power to Major-General Aguiyi Ironsi, the Army Commander, who negotiated settlement with rebellious military and installed military government.	Federal, multi-party structure.	Major-General Aguiyi Ironsi became head of state and of National Military Government. Issued decree on May 24, 1966, purporting to convert Nigeria from a federal to unitary state, and then after violent rioting in North reinterpreted decree and appeared to withdraw most of its effect.
13. February 24, 1966	Ghana‖ (former British colony)	Colonel (now General) Kotoka, commander of the Second Army Brigade, led a coup, which ousted President Nkrumah. Major-General Ankrah, former Army Commander, ousted by President Nkrumah, became chairman of the National Liberation Council.	Unitary, de jure one-party structure.	General Ankrah, as head of NLC, became de facto head of state and remained in power, and has associated selected civilians with various advisory and technical posts and functions of government.
14. July 8, 1966	Burundi*** (former UN Trust Territory administered by Belgium)	The King, Mwami Mwambutsa IV was ousted by his son, Crown Prince Charles Ndizeyé, with the support of the military.	Modernizing oligarchical state, de facto one-party structure.	Prince Charles assumed power as head of state, with the former Minister of Defense as Prime Minister.
15. July 29, 1966	Nigeria¶ (former British colony)	General Aguiyi Ironsi was kidnapped by rebellious northern troops. After several days of confused fighting, Lieut. Colonel Gowan, a Northerner, emerged as head of a successor military government.	Quasi-unitary, no-party structure.	Lieut. Colonel Gowon became head of the second National Military Government, with the stated intention of turning back rule to a civil government "at the earliest possible time."
16. November 19, 1968	Mali** (former French colony)			

Note: The abortive coup d'état of December 13, 1960, in Ethiopia and the suppressed military mutinies of January–February 1964 in Tanzania, Kenya and Uganda, all former British territories, are omitted. Also abortive coups involving military factions in Tunisia, Senegal, etc., are omitted. Similarly the rebellion in Zanzibar (a former British territory) of January 12, 1964, is omitted as the successful uprising involved only a makeshift armed gang, under a self-styled Field Marshall, John Okello of Uganda. The student uprising and general strike which toppled the Sudanese (a former Anglo-Egyptian condominium) military regime on October 30, 1964, is omitted. Finally, the "preventive coup" in the former British territory of Uganda, in April 1966, when Prime Minister Obote ousted the President, suspended the Constitution, divided up the Kingdom of Buganda, introduced a unitary state to replace a quasi-federal one, and himself became head of state is omitted, although he accomplished his acts with the support of the military.

* TOGO: Grunitzky was replaced without bloodshed in January, 1967, by Lt. Col. Etienne Eyadema who then became President on April 14, 1967.

† CONGO (BRAZZAVILLE): Army seized power on August 3, 1968, and forced President Massemba-Debat to form a new government. Massemba-Debat resigned on September 4, 1968, and was replaced by Captain Alfred Raoul who had been serving as Premier.

‡ GABON: Mba, reelected President in March 1967, died in November 1967. Vice President Albert Bongo became President and declared Gabon a one-party state as of March 1968. He dissolved and replaced the once powerful Gabonese Democratic Bloc by the new Gabonese Democratic Party.

§ DAHOMEY: Soglo, in power since 1965, was deposed in a bloodless army coup. Lt. Col. Alphonse Alley, heading a provisional military government, gave in to pressure resulting from massively boycotted May 1968 elections. He restored government by civilians headed by the former Minister of Foreign Affairs, Emile Zinsou.

‖ GHANA: In April 1967, young Gharaian military officers staged an unsuccessful attempt to overthrow the National Liberation Council.

¶ NIGERIA: The massacre of an estimated 30,000 Ibos in the Fall of 1966 and the expulsion of more than one million Ibos from the Northern Region of Nigeria were followed by the secession of the Eastern Region and the formation on May 30, 1967, of the Republic of Biafra by a young Ibo Colonel named Odumegwu Ojukwu. Biafran troops were still strongly resisting federal troops in March of 1969 despite heavy losses and despite mass starvation endangering millions of Ibos and others which resulted from the successful blockade maintained by federal troops.

** MALI: On November 19, 1968, President Modibo Keita of Mali was deposed in a bloodless coup led by Lt. Moussa Traore and other junior military leaders. Prior to his fall Keita had set up a unitary de facto one-party structure. His efforts to increase his power by dissolving the ruling Sudanese Union and replacing it with a seven-man Committee for the Defense of the Revolution (August, 1967), and by replacing the dissolved National Assembly by a twenty-eight member body (January, 1968) did not save Keita's regime. Traore and his colleagues felt threatened by Keita's people's militia, and they supposedly objected to Keita's constant implementation of Socialist economic policies. The thirty-two year old Traore formed a Military Committee of Liberation with political and administrative powers and sent out an appeal for help from private enterprise to promote Malian economic and social development. Shortly after the coup a new government composed largely of civilians and led by Captain Yoro Diakité was formed.

*** BURUNDI: Prince Charles became King (Mwami Natare V) on September 1, 1966, only to be overthrown on November 28, 1966, and replaced by Col. Michael Micombero, his Premier. Micombero declared Burundi a Republic and took over the presidency.

APPENDIX II

AFRICA, 1967
POPULATION AND GROSS NATIONAL PRODUCT PER CAPITA (U.S. DOLLARS)

No.	Country	Population	GNP Per Capita
1	Nigeria	57,500,000	80
2	United Arab Republic	29,600,000	150
3	Ethiopia	22,600,000	55
4	South Africa	18,441,000	520
5	Congo (Kinshasa)	15,627,000	65
6	Sudan	13,540,000	95
7	Morocco	13,323,000	180
8	Algeria	11,871,000	210
9	Tanzania	10,515,000	70
10	Kenya	9,365,000	85
11	Ghana	7,740,000	230
12	Uganda	7,551,000	100
13	Malagasy Republic	6,420,000	80
14	Cameroon	5,229,000	110
15	Upper Volta	4,858,000	50
16	Mali	4,576,000	60
17	Tunisia	4,414,000	200
18	Rhodesia	4,260,000	220
19	Malawi	3,940,000	40
20	Ivory Coast	3,835,000	210
21	Zambia	3,710,000	200
22	Guinea	3,500,000	75
23	Senegal	3,490,000	170
24	Niger	3,328,000	70
25	Chad	3,307,000	65
26	Burundi	3,210,000	45
27	Rwanda	3,110,000	50
28	Somalia Republic	2,500,000	55
29	Sierra Leone	2,367,000	140
30	Dahomey	2,365,000	60
31	Togo	1,638,000	90
32	Libya	1,617,000	490
33	Central African Rep.	1,352,000	75
34	Liberia	1,070,000	180

35	Mauritania	1,050,000	150
36	Congo (Brazzaville)	840,000	120
37	Lesotho	838,000	55
38	Botswana	559,000	55
39	Gabon	463,000	250
40	Swaziland	375,000	240
41	Gambia	330,000	75

Source: World Bank Atlas of Per Capita Product and Population (Washington, D.C., September, 1967).

NOTES

Introduction

1. Michael Crowder, *Senegal: A Study in French Assimilation Policy* (London: Oxford University Press, 1962), pp. 1–6.

2. In North Africa, Algeria, Morocco and Tunisia; in West Africa, Dahomey, Guinea, Ivory Coast, Mali, Mauritania, Niger, Senegal, Togo and Upper Volta; in Central Africa, Cameroun, Central African Republic, Chad, Congo (Brazzaville) and Gabon; and in the Indian Ocean, Madagascar (or Malagasy Republic).

3. Sir Andrew Cohen, *British Policy in Changing Africa* (London: Routledge and Kegan Paul, 1959), pp. 22–30; and Margery Perham, *The Colonial Reckoning* (London: Collins, 1961), pp. 56–61.

4. In West Africa, Gambia, Ghana, Nigeria and Sierra Leone; in East Africa, Kenya, Uganda, Tanganyika and Zanzibar (the latter two have formed the United Republic of Tanzania); in Central Africa, Malawi and Zambia; and in Southern Africa, Botswana and Lesotho.

5. Angola, Guinea (Bissau), and Mozambique. There are also the small islands of Principe and San Tomé in the Gulf of Guinea and the curious Portuguese enclave—Cabinda—lodged between the two Congos.

6. Ceuta, Ifini, Melilla, and Spanish Sahara. There are also the Canary Islands in the Atlantic Ocean and the island of Fernando Po in the Gulf of Guinea.

7. Charles D. Cremeans, *The Arabs and the World: Nasser's Arab Nationalist Policy* (New York: Praeger, 1963), pp. 92–95.

8. Gamal Abdul Nasser, *Egypt's Liberation: The Philosophy of the Revolution* (Washington Public Affairs Press, 1955), pp. 109–110.

Chapter 1

1. Judd Teller, *The Jews: Biography of a People* (New York: Bantam Books, 1966), pp. 14–16.

2. *Ibid.*

3. *Ibid.*, p. 16.

4. *Ibid.*, p. 20.

5. See, for example, Max F. Millikan and Donald L. M. Blackmer (eds.), *The Emerging Nations: Their Growth and United States Policy* (Boston: Little, Brown, 1961) and W. W. Rostow: *The Stages of Economic Growth* (London: Cambridge University Press, 1960), two important studies relating to nation-building in which the authors' views of traditional societies and underdeveloped countries are clearly predicated on Asia and Latin American models, although the studies purport to be applicable to Africa as well.

6. Arnold Rivkin, *The African Presence in World Affairs: National Development and Its Role in Foreign Policy* (New York: Free Press of Glencoe; and London: Collier-Macmillan Ltd.), 1963, pp. 304.

CHAPTER 2

1. See Arnold Rivkin, *ibid.*, and "The Organization of African Unity" in *Current History*, Vol. 48, No. 284 (April, 1965), pp. 193–200, 240–242.

2. The Union of African and Malagasy States was originally the Brazzaville bloc, an *ad hoc* association of most of the former French-African territories. As the UAM (after its French initials), the Brazzaville bloc took on formal shape. With the advent of the Organization of African Unity the UAM was under considerable pressure to dissolve itself. Instead, it transformed itself into the Union of African and Malagasy States for Economic Corporation, ostensibly shedding its political functions. In February 1965, the UAMCE reverted to its earlier form—a political as well as economic association of most of the French-speaking African states (thirteen in number)—under the style of the Common Organization of African and Malagasy States (or OCAM after its French initials). Mauritania has since withdrawn from OCAM. Rwanda and Congo (Kinshasa) are also members.

3. As quoted in *Cahiers de l'Afrique Occidentale et de l'Afrique Equatoriale* (Paris, June 15, 1963), pp. 33–34; translation from French by the present author.

4. As quoted in *Federal Nigeria*, Vol. VI, No. 5 (June–July, 1963), p. 6.

5. Article III, Charter of the Organization of African Unity.

6. *Federal Nigeria, op. cit.*, p. 6.

7. See Kwame Nkrumah, *Africa Must Unite* (New York: Praeger, 1963), published to coincide with the Addis Ababa Conference, and ever since, the standard reference for Dr. Nkrumah and his followers in all discussions on African unity; see also Editors of *The Spark, Some Essential Features of Nkrumaism* (New York: International Publishers, 1965), C. 4, for an authorized version of Nkrumah's views on African unity by the editors of the former Ghanaian doctrinaire journal, *The Spark.*

8. See Arnold Rivkin, *Africa and the European Common Market: A Prospective* (World Monograph Series, University of Denver), revised second edition, 1966, for a discussion of the relation of the African Associated Members and the nonassociated African states with the EEC and with each other; see also the author's article, *Africa and the European Common Market*, in *Finance and Development*, Vol. III, No. 2 (June, 1966).

9. See *ibid.* for discussion of the implications of the Addis Ababa Conference and the founding of the Organization of African Unity for Eurafricanism and the association of African states with the European Economic Community.

10. *New York Times*, July 21, 1964, p. 5.

11. *Washington Post and Times Herald*, July 21, 1964, p. 1.

12. Colin Legum in *The Observer* (London), reprinted in the *Washington Post and Times Herald*, July 21, 1964, p. 1.

13. *New York Times, op. cit.*

14. As quoted in *East Africa and Rhodesia* (London, July 9, 1964), p. 850.

15. As quoted in *Reporter* (Nairobi), IV, No. 140 (August 27, 1965), p. 10.

16. *Ibid.*, p. 11.

17. Donald H. Louchheim, "Accra Conference Wove Realism into Fragile OAU Fabric," in the *Washington Post and Times Herald*, October 27, 1965, p. 16.

18. *Ibid.*

19. *New York Times,* October 27, 1965, p. 9.

20. As quoted, *ibid.*

21. As quoted in the *New York Times,* October 25, 1965, p. 22.

22. *Washington Post and Times Herald,* October 21, 1965, p. 31.

CHAPTER 3

1. "Mali: Timbuktu Is Still Far Away," *The Economist* (London, March 21, 1964), p. 1094.

2. *Cahiers de l'Afrique Occidentale et de l'Afrique Equatoriale* (Paris), No. 262 (September 5, 1964), p. 31; translation from the French by the author.

3. *The Economist, op. cit.;* see also Bakari Kamian, *Connaissance de la République du Mali* (Bamako: *Le Secrétariat d'Etat à l'Information et au Tourisme,* undated), p. 119, from which some of the geographical, ethnographic, and anthropological material in this discussion of Mali has been drawn.

4. *Ibid.;* see also *Public International Development Financing in Senegal: Report No.* 7 of the Research Project of Columbia University Law School (New York, Columbia University, 1963), especially page 23, for the cost to Senegal of the disrupted Federation of Mali, and the discussion below on problems of achieving internal cohesion based in part on this Report.

5. "Sudan Tragedy," *The Observer* (London, September 5, 1965), p. 10.

6. C. D. Makuei, "Southern Sudan: A Test Case in Afro-Arab Cooperation," *New Africa* (London), Vol. 6, No. 4 (April, 1964), pp. 11–12.

7. Mohammed O. Beshir, "The Sudan: A Military Surrender," *Africa Report,* Vol. 9, No. 11 (December, 1964), pp. 3–6.

8. *The Economist* (London, August 4, 1965), p. 597.

9. *New Africa, op. cit.,* p. 11.

10. *Ibid.*

11. *Ibid.,* p. 12.

12. Letter of Mr. M. A. Bereir, Press Attaché, Embassy of Sudan, London, in *New Africa,* Vol. 6, No. 5 (May, 1964).

13. *Afrique Nouvelle* (Dakar), No. 939 (August 5–11, 1965), p. 12; *Afrique Nouvelle,* No. 941 (August 19–25, 1967), p. 7; *Reporter* (Nairobi, July 30, 1965), pp. 15–16; *Reporter* (August 15, 1965), p. 15; *East Africa and Rhodesia* (London), Vol. 41, No. 2131 (August 12, 1965); *East Africa and Rhodesia,* Vol. 42, No. 2133 (August 26, 1965), p. 11; *The Economist, op. cit.*

14. A typical straw in the wind was the announcement of the then Sudanese Minister of the Interior:

"Surveillance of the frontier between the Sudan and Chad is going to be considerably reinforced, Major General Ahmed Irwa, Minister of the Interior of the Sudan announced.

The Minister indicated that the government had judged it necessary to establish 13 police posts on the frontier with Chad as the consequence of a certain number of incidents which have taken place in this region. He added that the Sudanese government had the intention of entering conversations with the Republic of Chad for the establishment of a system of permits for travelling from one country to another . . ." *Cahiers de l'Afrique Occidentale et de l'Afrique Equatoriale* (Paris), No. 251 (April 4, 1964), p. 35.

15. As quoted in *Africa Diary* (New Delhi), Vol. V, No. 29, July 10–26, 1965, p. 2410, and also reported in the *Washington Post and Time Herald*, August 25, 1966.

16. *The Economist* (London, October 9, 1965), p. 152.

17. Sir Thomas Southorn, *Journal of the Royal African Society*, 1944, as quoted in *New Africa* (London), Vol. 6, No. 5 (May, 1964), pp. 9–10.

18. *The Times* (London), April 15, 1964, p. 11.

19. *Ibid.*

20. *Ibid.*

21. *New Africa, op. cit.,* pp. 10–11.

22. However, for a brief period, 1763–83, the British used the term, Senegambia, to describe the new crown colony of Gambia and the captured French posts in "Upper Guinea," which the French recaptured during the American Revolutionary War. A British presence was not impressed on the French posts and for our purposes the interlude can be regarded as an historical curiosity.

23. See David E. Gardinier, *Cameroun: United Nations Challenges to French Policy* (London: Oxford University Press for the Institute of Race Relations, 1963), especially Chapter IX.

24. See, for example, two articles in *Current History* by the author, which in passing allude to the geographical problems of Nigeria in connection with discussions of the country's economic and political development: *"Nigeria's National Development Plan,"* Vol. 43, No. 256 (December, 1962), pp. 321–328, 368, and *"Nigeria: A Unique Nation,"* Vol. 45, No. 268 (December, 1963), pp. 329–334.

25. C. L. Sulzberger, "Emotion Alone Is Not Enough," *New York Times,* April 22, 1964, p. 46.

26. This use of contradictions was carried to a delightful *reductio ad absurdum* in what has become a classic among motion pictures, *Never on Sunday,* where two obvious Soviet sailors "on liberty" in Athens are frustrated by a sign on a well-known brothel, "Closed. Never on Sunday." One sailor is heard mumbling to the other as they descend the stairway "a contradiction of capitalism."

27. A. J. Hughes, *East Africa: The Search for Unity* (Baltimore: Penguin Books, 1963), p. 13.

28. Appendix, *ibid.,* p. 267.

29. "Reconstructing Mali," *West Africa* (London), No. 2447 (April 25, 1964), p. 451.

CHAPTER 4

1. The author analyzes this phenomenon at length in his book, *The African Presence in World Affairs: National Development and Its Role in Foreign Policy* (New York: Free Press of Glencoe-Macmillan, 1963), especially in Part III. See also, Rupert Emerson, *Political Modernization: The Single-Party System* (University of Denver Monograph Series in World Affairs, No. 1, 1963–1964), p. 30.

2. Emerson *ibid.*, p. 29.

3. As quoted in Charles Debbasch, *"Ahidjo laisse la porte ouverte: Elections Camerounaises" Jeune Afrique* (Tunis), No. 180 (April 20, 1964), p. 10; translation from the French by the present author.

4. *Ibid.*, p. 11.

5. Gwendolen M. Carter, Introduction, in Carter (ed.), *Politics in Africa: 7 Cases* (New York: Harcourt, Brace & World, 1966), p. 8.

6. Alhaji Sir Abubakar Tafawa Balewa, *Federal Nigeria*, Vol. VI, No. 15 (June–July 1963), p. 6 (emphasis supplied).

7. There is also opinion in Africa (as well as beyond) to the effect that the unitary one-party structure is not necessary, and is not the most desirable structure within which to build unity and achieve growth. The Federal Republic of Nigeria and Sierra Leone, for example, have been committed among the African states to trying a multi-party decentralized structure, and we shall examine this further in the next chapter. Sir Albert Magai, Prime Minister of Sierra Leone, however, has equivocated and flirted with the possibility of transforming Sierra Leone into a one-party state. He has run into forceful and articulate opposition internally, and has apparently also been frightened by the fate of President Nkrumah and the Convention People's Party in Ghana, which were jettisoned unceremoniously in a *coup d'état* in February 1966. Ghana had been Sir Albert's model of a successful one-party state structure.

8. Sir John Fletcher-Cooke, "The Failure of the Westminster Model in Africa," an address to the Royal Africa and Commonwealth Societies, as reported in *East Africa and Rhodesia* (London), Vol. 40, No. 2061 (April 9, 1964), p. 624.

9. Erskine B. Childers, "Where Democracy Doesn't Work . . . Yet," *Harper's Magazine* (April, 1960), p. 83.

10. Carter, *op. cit.*

11. For example, see the *New York Times*, May 2, 1964, p. 4, for a report on the evolving pressures making the Congo (Brazzaville) "lean to the left."

12. St. Clair Drake and L. A. Lacy, "Government Versus the Unions," in Carter, *op. cit.*, p. 116.

13. *New York Times*, May 6, 1964, p. 6.

14. Geoffrey Godsell, "Destourian Socialism in Tunisia," *Christian Science Monitor*, February 14, 1964, p. 16 (ed.).

15. Béchir Ben Yamed, *"Pour ou Contre le Parti Unique," Jeune Afrique*, No. 166 (January 11, 1964), p. 5; translation from the French by the present author.

CHAPTER 5

1. Winston S. Churchill, *The River War: The Reconquest of the Sudan* (London: Eyre & Spottiswoode Ltd., 1899; reissued, Landsborough Publications, 1960), p. 69.

2. James S. Coleman and Belmont Brise, Jr., "The Role of the Military in Sub-Saharan Africa," in Rand Corporation (ed.), *The Role of the Military in Underdeveloped Countries* (Princeton: Princeton University Press, 1962), p. 402.

3. *Ibid.*, p. 366.

4. *Ibid.*, p. 368.

5. Robert West, as quoted in the *African Studies Bulletin*, Vol. V, No. 4 (December, 1962), p. 33.

6. Coleman and Belmont, *op. cit.*, p. 359.

7. See, for example, Max F. Millikan and Donald L. M. Blackmer, *op. cit.*, which, although it notes that "with the exception of most parts of Africa, substantial military groups having considerable political and social influence have played a significant role in the modernization process" (p. 31), concludes "what we would particularly emphasize is that in addition to assisting in the relatively conventional military task of defense, American military assistance properly administered, can have a strong constructive influence on the evolution of the transitional societies" (pp. 111–112). Millikan and Blackmer continue: "There are two broad areas in which local military forces can make valuable contributions to the case of modernization. First, they can contribute to major tasks of economic development. . . . Second, they can assist in training large numbers of people in the skills and attitudes demanded by a society undergoing social and economic transformations. . . ." (p. 112).

8. William Gutteridge, *Armed Forces in New States* (London: Oxford University Press, 1962), p. 66.

9. *New York Times*, July 30, 1966, pp. 1, 7; July 31, 1966, p. 9; August 1, 1966, p. 8; August 2, 1966, p. 1; August 3, 1966, pp. 6, 36; August 4, 1966, p. 10; August 5, 1966, p. 2.

10. Radio Lagos, August 1, 1966, 1130 Local Time, and Radio and T.V. Enugu, August 1, 1966, 1945 Local Time.

11. Germain Mba, *"L'Ombre des Politiciens"* in *Jeune Afrique*, No. 296 (September 11, 1966), p. 9; translation by the present author.

12. *Quarterly Economic Review: Algeria, Morocco and Tunisia* (London: The Economist Intelligence Unit), No. 23 (September, 1965), p. 3.

13. *Ibid.*, p. 4.

14. *New York Times*, August 5, 1966, p. 2.

15. Donald H. Louchheim, *Washington Post and Times Herald*, August 6, 1966.

16. As quoted in the *New York Times*, August 5, 1966, p. 2.

17. *Washington Post, op. cit.*

18. Germain Mba, *op. cit.*

19. Germain Mba, *op. cit.*

20. S. E. Finer, *The Man on Horseback* (London: Pall Mall Press, 1962), pp. 240–243 (emphasis supplied).

CHAPTER 6

1. Douglas E. Ashford, "Local Reform and Social Change in Morocco and Tunisia" in William H. Lewis (ed.), *Emerging Africa* (Washington, D.C.: Public Affairs Press, 1963), p. 126.

2. *New York Times*, April 29, 1964, p. 40.

3. Quoted in Czeslaw Jesman, *The Ethiopian Paradox* (London: Oxford University Press, 1963), p. 73. This theme repeats itself in Ethiopian state papers. See, for example, Ethiopia's *Second Five Year Plan*, 1955–1959 (G.C.) (Addis Ababa), Chapter I, p. 1: "Inspired by the far-sightedness of H.I.M. Haile Selassie I, The Five Year Development Plan, 1959–1961 (G.C.), was introduced as the first document of overall economic and social policy of Ethiopia. By this, Ethiopia became the first African country to commence comprehensive planning of her economic and social development."

4. See Jean and Simone Lacouture, *Le Maroc à l'Epreuve* (Paris, Editions du Seuil, 1958), for an interesting account by two knowledgeable French writers on North African affairs, of the evolution of the French protectorate in Morocco, from its inception, through the long independence movement period, to the termination of the protectorate and the achievement of independence.

5. King Hassan is fond of comparing his powers with those of other African heads of state, and thus in the campaign for popular ratification of the new Constitution, his then ardent supporters, the political party *l'Istiqual* ran a series of comparisons in its newspaper. A particularly interesting comparison is the one drawn between the powers of the Presidents of Tunisia and Guinea and the King of Morocco. The constitutional provisions relating to the chief executive in the three states were printed side by side, without editorial comment, in the newspaper *Al Istiqual* (Rabat), No. 297, November 28, 1962. Which chief executive has more formal constitutional power is a toss-up. The comparison and even more important the fact that it appeared in *Al Istiqual* is particularly important as *l'Istiqual* or the Independence Party was one of the leading and one of the earliest nationalist groups to oppose the continuation of the French protectorate over Morocco. Of equal interest is the opposition of the *Union Marocaine du Travail* to "La Constitution Monarchique." The UMT campaigned against ratification with the slogan "the remedy is worse than the ailment." See, for example, the UMT newspaper, *l'Avant Garde* (Casablanca), No. 192, December 1, 1962. The UMT objected particularly to the concentration of power in the hands of the monarchy and its supporting institutions. It was extremely skeptical about the limited role of the Parliament.

6. See Jean Lacouture, *Cinq Hommes et La France* (Paris: Editions du Seuil, 1961), for a sympathetic biography of King Mohammed V, and his role in the achievement of Moroccan independence.

7. Douglas E. Ashford, *op. cit.*, pp. 113–127.

8. *The Economist* (London, December 18, 1965), p. 1306.

9. *Ibid.*

10. "Burundi, Quand Le Roi Fait Le Coup de Feu," in *Jeune Afrique*, No. 254 (November 7, 1965), p. 12 and the *Washington Post*, January 18, 1966, pp. 1, 8.

11. In the words of *The Economist*: "Haile Selassie's record of successful centralisation, of struggle against chiefly and tribal separatisms, of obtaining development aid from many foreign sources without loss of dignity, and now

of leadership in the creation of Africa's own organizations, add up to quite a lot, even in the eyes of the younger and more ardent of African politicians." *The Economist* (London, April 25, 1964), p. 372.

CHAPTER 7

1. The balkanization doctrine has become part of the glossary and one of the axioms of African politics. The superstructure of doctrine and decision built on this belief obscures the limitations of this view of history. Without ignoring the greed, competition, and indifference or ignorance of European colonialists with respect to ethnic, tribal, geographic, economic or other African realities, the fact is that in large areas of Africa the process of colonization was a consolidating and integrating force rather than a fragmenting one, combining relatively limited or small tribal groupings into larger geographic and political units. To acknowledge this in no way denies any of the vices of colonialism, or fails to recognize that at various times in African history kingdoms and empires made up of several kingdoms have existed, or that at various points in Africa European colonial powers encountered resistance to their penetration from African kingdoms or tribal groupings. What it does do, is to recognize that at the time of the main thrust of European territorial colonialism—the scramble for Africa in the 1890's and 1900's—in the largest part of Africa, the tribal unit was the most common unit, and there was little, if any, balkanization of larger units, states, kingdoms, or empires, as is frequently implied, into smaller units. Where larger units had existed, for the most part they had long since disintegrated or were well along in the process of doing so.

2. See the *Report of the Uganda Relationships Commission, 1961* (Entebbe Uganda: Government Printer, 1961), which was largely accepted by the British Colonial Office in drafting the constitution under which Uganda has come to independence. The terms "federal relationship" and "semi-federal relationship" are from the *Commission Report*. "The picture which emerges, therefore is of a composite state containing a single federal kingdom (Buganda) in association with the rest of the country, which would be governed unitarily." (*Ibid.*, p. 55.)

3. See Guy Clutton-Brock, *Dawn in Nyasaland* (London: Hodder and Stoughton, 1959), for a particularly outspoken analysis of the African opposition in Nyasaland to the imposed federation from the outset. Also, see the *Report of the Nyasaland Commission of Inquiry* (the report of the Devlin Commission) (London: HMSO, 1959), Cmnd. 814, particularly Section 3, paragraphs 19–30.

4. See Kenneth Kaunda, *Zambia Shall Be Free* (London: Heinemann, 1962), for a brief but interesting account of "Zambia's struggle for freedom" by the country's first president, including Northern Rhodesia's view of the imposed federation.

5. As quoted from an address by M. Moïse Tshombé to the Royal Institute of International Affairs in London in *East Africa and Rhodesia* (London), Vol. 40, No. 2062 (April 16, 1964), p. 646.

6. In a way the Congo experience illustrates one of the risks of attempting to install a centralized, unitary structure in a situation not ready for it. In-

stead of a federal structure with six provinces or "states" or even eight or ten the Congo has reacted, the pendulum has swung to the other extreme, and the pluralistic drives have been given their full expression in the large number of provinces created. In some instances, such as the old province of Katanga, whatever "unity" had been achieved during the colonial period was fragmented, and three smaller units have resulted, the provinces of Nord-Katanga, Sud-Katanga and Lualaba.

7. Margery Perham, *The Colonial Reckoning* (London: Collins, 1961), p. 70.

8. Alexis de Tocqueville, *Democracy in America*, I (New York: Vintage Books, 1945 edition), 61–62.

9. *Ibid.*, p. 63.

10. Robert Delavignette, *Freedom and Authority in French West Africa* (London: Oxford University Press, 1950), pp. 11–12.

11. See Georges Brausch, *Belgian Administration in the Congo* (London: Oxford University Press, 1961), Chapter III, for an interesting account of Belgian Policy with respect to local administration and the contention of the author that Belgian Minister Louis Franck was "Belgium's Lord Lugard" (p. 43).

12. Sir Andrew Cohen, *British Policy in Changing Africa* (London: Routledge & Kegan Paul, 1959), p. 2.

13. *Ibid.*, p. 24.

14. Charles Debbasch, *op. cit.*

15. Certainly one of the things that have come to light in the break-up of the Federation of Rhodesia and Nyasaland is the significant degree to which Northern Rhodesia had been subsidizing the industrial development of Southern Rhodesia with the transfer of public revenues received from the exploitation of the Northern Rhodesian copper mines, and also through paying higher prices in the "protected market" it provided for Southern Rhodesia manufactures. What cannot be measured precisely is the amount of industrial development Northern Rhodesia has also had to forego for the benefit of its neighbor to the south. It seems clear though, from the new postfederation boom in Northern Rhodesia, that it has had to sacrifice a good deal of such development. See William J. Barber, "Federation and the Distribution of Economic Benefits" in Colin Leys and Crawford Pratt, *A New Deal in Central Africa* (London, Heinemann, 1960), pp. 81–97.

16. The weaker unit may gain, but this is certainly not to be taken for granted, nor is it the automatic result. Thus, it has been argued with considerable evidence by Hazlewood and Henderson that Nyasaland, the weaker economic unit in the Federation of Rhodesia and Nyasaland, benefited at the expense of Northern Rhodesia, but not particularly at the expense of Southern Rhodesia. In fact they contend that Nyasaland would have benefited more from a simple federation with Northern Rhodesia than it did from membership in a federation with the two Rhodesias. A. Hazlewood and P. O. Henderson, *Nyasaland: The Economics of Federation* (Oxford: Basil Blackwell, 1960). See also footnote 15.

17. Although not a political union, just as a common market, it has become clear in East Africa that Kenya, the most developed of the three territories as

an industrial base, benefited most from the East African Common Market, and Tanganyika (now Tanzania), the least developed, benefited least. See *East Africa: Report of the Economic and Fiscal Commission* (London: HMSO, 1961), Cmnd. 1279, particularly Part III. In fact, in the protracted and difficult negotiations over transforming the East African Common Services Organization (EACSO) and the associated common market into a political and economic union, President Julius K. Nyerere of Tanganyika repeatedly brought up this point. He has demanded a better deal for Tanganyika in the sharing of custom duties to compensate Tanganyika for "loss" of income on foreign imports and the higher prices it has had to pay for Kenya manufactures, a degree of protection for "local" industry through imposition of quotas on Kenya's "exports" to Tanganyika, and an agreement on the location of new industrial investment in order to ensure that Tanganyika would receive a "fair share" of industrial investment.

President Nyerere received a promise of some reform in each of these fields as his price for staying in the East African common market. However, these problems have continued to trouble the association of the three East African states, and have contributed to the breakup of the common East African currency pool, to the development of separate Central Banks, to the loosening of ties in the EACSO, and to the growth of constraints on the functioning of the Common Market itself. The Tanganyika experience is consistent with the general pattern of industrial investment elsewhere: investment tends to flow to the most developed areas, affording facilities, services, complementary industrial establishments, skilled labor, marketing arrangements, financing institutions, etc., rather than to pioneer in new areas within the same marketing zone. For a generally interesting exposition on the East African common market, see K. G. V. Krishna, "Some Economic Aspects of an East African Federation," in *The East African Economic Review* (Nairobi, Kenya), Vol. 8, No. 2 (December, 1961), pp. 99–110. The concentration of investment in Southern Rhodesia, particularly around Salisbury, in preference to investment in either Northern Rhodesia or Nyasaland is another example of this principle in action. See footnotes 15 and 16, *supra*.

18. See the author's monograph, *Africa and the European Common Market: A Perspective* (Denver: University of Denver Press), Revised Second Edition, 1966, for an analysis of the transitional stages established under the Treaty of Rome, 1957, with particular attention to the relation of these stages to the benefits accorded the eighteen African Associated Members, first under the Implementing Agreement, 1957, and then under the Yaoundé Convention of Association, 1964.

19. See the author's article "Nigeria: A Unique Nation," *Current History*, Vol. 45, No. 268 (December, 1963), pp. 329–334.

20. Lagos Nigeria Domestic Radio Service (in English), 1400 GMT, April 13, 1964.

21. The federation of the former Italian colony Eritrea with the Empire of Ethiopia under UN auspices in 1952, was terminated in late 1962, when Eritrea was fully integrated into the unitary structure of Ethiopia. The Kingdom of

Libya was also constituted as a federation out of the former Italian North African colonies of Cyrenaica, Tripolitania, and the Fezzan, under UN auspices in 1951; it transformed itself on April 27, 1963, into a unitary state.

22. The Federation of Rhodesia and Nyasaland, established by the United Kingdom in 1953 by putting together two protectorates, Northern Rhodesia and Nyasaland (the African populations of which generally opposed federation), with the "self-governing colony" of Southern Rhodesia, ten years later, with the approaching independence of Nyasaland and Northern Rhodesia, has been dissolved.

23. The Federal Republic of Cameroon only came into being a year after Nigerian independence as the result of a fusion of the former British Southern Cameroons with the already independent Cameroon Republic. The ill-fated Federation of Mali, a union of Senegal and the former French Soudan (which has retained the name Mali), constituted while the two units were "autonomous republics" within the Franco-African Community, only months before independence, broke apart in August 1960, within two months of achieving full independence.

24. Obafemi Awolowo, *Awo* (Cambridge: Cambridge University Press, 1960), pp. 160–212.

25. *Ibid.*, p. 160.

26. *Ibid.*, p. 181.

27. Nnandi Azikiwe, *Zik: Selected Speeches* (Cambridge: Cambridge University Press, 1961), pp. 120–121. Cf. Awolowo, *op. cit.*, pp. 164–165.

28. *Ibid.*, p. 121.

29. *Ibid.*, p. 120.

30. Ahmadu Bello, *My Life* (Cambridge: Cambridge University Press, 1962), p. 151.

31. *Ibid.*, p. 228.

32. Awolowo, *op. cit.*, pp. 164–165.

33. Official figures of the 1963 census, published in 1964, give a total population figure of 55,653,821, with over ½ in the Northern Region. *Federal Nigeria*, Vol. VII, No. 2 (March–April, 1964), p. 12.

34. See the author's article "Nigeria's National Development Plan," in *Current History*, Vol. 43, No. 256 (December, 1962), pp. 321–328, 368, for a full discussion of the Plan, with emphasis on the role of the Regions.

35. The parallel of the Nigerian experience with that of the United States is striking. The recent U.S. national issue of federal aid to education, and during the Roosevelt era of federal aid to and regulation of agriculture, foreshadowed analogous developments in Nigeria.

36. Paul O. Proehl, *Foreign Enterprise in Nigeria: Law and Policies* (Chapel Hill: University of North Carolina Press, 1965), p. viii.

37. The highest estimate was reported by Lloyd Garrison, African correspondent for the *New York Times*: "After a week of rioting and looting 200,000 Ibos were reported to have been killed [in May in the North]," the *New York Times*, August 9, 1966, p. 7. Other estimates referred to "several hundred" and "several thousands."

38. Donald S. Louchheim, African correspondent for the *Washington Post*, reported: "In June after Northern rioting against Easterners, an estimated 60,000 Ibos fled the region." *Washington Post*, August 9, 1966, p. 10.

39. See Richard L. Sklar, "Nigerian Politics: The Ordeal of Chief Awolowo, 1960–65," in G. M. Carter (ed.), *Politics in Africa: 7 Cases* (New York: Harcourt, Brace & World, 1966), pp. 128–129, for a discussion of Chief Awolowo's "swing" to "radical antiregionalism" after the federal elections of 1959.

40. *New York Times*, August 12, 1966.

41. As quoted in the *New York Times*, August 11, 1966, p. 9.

42. Donald H. Louchheim, the *Washington Post*, August 11, 1966, p. 16 (Sec. D).

CHAPTER 8

1. Immanuel Wallerstein, *Africa: The Politics of Independence* (New York: Vintage Books, 1961), p. 163.

2. *African Conference on the Rule of Law*, Lagos, Nigeria, January, 1961 (Geneva: International Commission of Jurists, 1961), p. 86. See also Folarin Coker, *Sir Adetokunbo Ademola* (Lagos: Times Press, 1962), for a brief but interesting biography of the Chief Justice. The book also contains a brief foreword by the Hon. Chief F. R. A. Williams, Q.C., the then President of the Nigerian Bar Association, wherein he states that Sir Adetokunbo "will not have to stage the type of battle that Chief Justice Marshall of the United States Supreme Court had to stage in order to establish the right and duty to pronounce upon the validity of laws passed by the various legislatures. It is already provided in the Constitution that in Nigeria this right and duty squarely rests upon the shoulders of the Judiciary" (p. ii).

3. *Ibid.*, pp. 87–88.

4. *Ibid.*, p. 89.

5. Wallerstein, *op. cit.*, p. 159 (emphasis provided).

6. *African Conference on the Rule of Law*, pp. 45, 55.

7. For an interesting account of the trial, which is sympathetic to the defendant, see Richard Sklar, "Nigerian Politics: The Ordeal of Chief Awolowo," in G. M. Carter (ed.), *Politics in Africa: 7 Cases* (New York: Harcourt, Brace & World, 1966), pp. 119–165.

8. *New York Times*, July 28, 1963, p. 22.

9. Lagos, Nigeria Domestic Radio Service (in English), 1800 GMT, May 15, 1964.

10. Wallerstein, *op. cit.*, p. 165.

11. *African Conference on the Rule of Law*, pp. 48–49.

12. International Commission of Jurists, *Bulletin* (Geneva), No. 18 (March, 1964), pp. 12–13. See also *African Conference on the Rule of Law, op. cit.*, and International Commission of Jurists, *Newsletter* (Geneva), No. 11 (February, 1961).

13. Quoted in full in *Newsletter* of International Commission of Jurists (Geneva), No. 15 (February, 1964), p. 5.

14. *Ibid.*, p. 6.

15. *Bulletin*, pp. 9–13.

16. Thomas Hodgkin, "Counter-Revolution in Ghana," *Labour Monthly* (London, April, 1966), pp. 162–167.

17. Dar-es-Salaam, Tanganyika Domestic Radio Service (in English), 1600 GMT, May 13, 1964.

18. As quoted in *Africa Digest* (London), Vol. XI, No. 5 (April, 1964), p. 150.

19. *Ibid.*, p. 141.

20. Ruth Schachter Morgenthau, "African Elections: Tanzania's Contribution," in *Africa Report*, Vol. 10, No. 11 (December, 1965), pp. 12–16.

21. *Ibid.*, p. 14.

22. Chief Arthur Prest, *op. cit.*

23. *The Reporter* (Nairobi, July 29, 1966), p. 1.

CHAPTER 9

1. See Immanuel Wallerstein, *op. cit.*, and Thomas Hodgkin, "Counter-Revolution in Ghana," in *Labour Monthly* (London, Africa, 1966), pp. 162–167.

2. *Africa Digest* (London), Vol. XI, No. 5 (April, 1964), pp. 156–157.

3. Ministry of Information, *Ghana Press Release No. 142/64* (Accra, March 15, 1964).

4. As reported in *Africa Digest, op. cit.*, p. 155.

5. As reported, *ibid.*

6. *Ghana Radio Service*, Accra, 0600 GMT, May 17, 1964.

7. The sanctuary afforded African political exiles has been one of the unanticipated and uncounted blessings of the United Nations organization and its affiliates.

8. *West Africa* (London), No. 2450 (May 16, 1964), p. 552.

9. *Ibid.*

10. As reported, *Africa Digest, op. cit.*, p. 155.

11. The Kwame Nkrumah Ideological Institute at Winneba, Ghana, was the official center for the propagation of Nkrumahism. It laid down and articulated party doctrine.

12. Morgenthau, *op. cit.*, p. 14.

13. Dar-es-Salaam, Tanganyika Domestic Service (in English) 1430 GMT, June 29, 1964. See also, "Tanganyika and Zanzibar Unite" in *Africa World* (London), June 1964, p. 21, for report on the "Union of Tanganyika and Zanzibar," including a note on the new "Russian-trained Zanzibar army."

14. "Suicide of M. Boka," *Africa Digest* (London) XI, No. 6 (June, 1964), 190.

15. *Central African Examiner* (Salisbury, So. Rhodesia), Vol. 7, No. 10 (April, 1964), pp. 3–4.

16. *Ibid.*

17. *Malawi News* (Blantyre, Nyasaland), April 10, 1964. "No votes were cast, and on April 6, nomination day, three weeks before the official polling date of April 28, the M.C.P. victory was announced." *Africa Digest, op. cit.*, p. 162.

18. As quoted in *East Africa and Rhodesia* (London), Vol. 40, No. 2070 (June 11, 1964), p. 785.

19. See *West Africa* (London), No. 2449 (May 9, 1964), p. 511.

20. Nairobi, *Kenya Domestic Radio Service,* 1600 GMT, May 19, 1964.

21. See "Kenya Trade Union Split," in *East Africa and Rhodesia* (London), Vol. 40, No. 2064, April 30, 1964, p. 683, for an interesting account of the complicated trade union split in Kenya.

22. The All-African Trade Union Federation, or *l'Union Syndicate Pan-africaine* (USPA in French), convened in Bamako, Mali, June 10–14, 1964, and laid down its line on affiliation with the ICFTU. In a thinly disguised resolution directed at affiliation with the ICFTU, it condemned "hypocritical action by international organizations designed to divide the African workers" and "the organizations and infiltrating agents of imperialism in Africa." The charter of the organization adopted at Bamako affirms that the organization is independent "of all international trade union federations and adds that the unity of African workers is incompatible with the organization of several national unions." *Cahiers de l'Afrique Occidentale et de l'Afrique Equatoriale* (Paris), No. 257 (June 27, 1964), pp. 24–26; translation by the author.

23. "I.C.F.T.U. Criticizes Governments," *East Africa and Rhodesia,* Vol. 40, No. 2066 (May 14, 1964), p. 721.

24. *Ibid.*

25. *New Africa* (London), Vol. 6, No. 7 (July, 1964), p. 5.

26. *New York Times,* July 28, 1963, p. 22.

27. *Report of the Commission on the Review of Wages, Salary and Conditions of Service of the Junior Employees of the Governments of the Federation and in Private Establishment,* 1963–64 (Lagos: Federal Ministry of Information, Printing Division, 1964).

28. See "Nigeria's £10 Minimum," *West Africa* (London), No. 2457 (July 4, 1964), p. 735, for a discussion of the final settlement reached in the government's negotiations with the trade unions.

29. As quoted in *West Africa,* No. 2456 (June 27, 1964), p. 706 (emphasis provided).

30. *West Africa,* No. 2455 (June 20, 1964), p. 678.

31. In Sierra Leone one finds on a smaller scale traditions and practices in the civil service comparable to those in Nigeria. The same could also be said about the Gambia.

Chapter 10

1. See *The African Presence in World Affairs: National Development and Its Role in Foreign Policy* (New York: Free Press of Glencoe, 1963), particularly Chapter 2.

2. *Programme of the Convention People's Party* (Accra: Ministry of Information and Broadcasting, 1962), p. 7.

3. *Ibid.,* p. 15.

4. "Ghana after Nkrumah," *The Economist* (London, August 6, 1966), pp. 549–564.

5. *Ibid.,* p. 552.

6. Only South Africa and Gabon had a higher per capita income. The former is *sui generis* and outside our frame of reference, and the latter is a special case of a small country with a population of under 500,000 and rich mineral and timber resources.

7. G. Warburg, "Guinea: In the Grip of U.S. Aid?", *New Africa* (London), Vol. 6, No. 7 (July, 1964), p. 11.

8. See the author's monograph, *Africa and the European Common Market* (University of Denver, World Affairs Monograph Series, Second Revised Edition, 1966) for a discussion of Guinea and the E.E.C.

9. D. K. Chisiza, *Africa—What Lies Ahead?* (New York: The African-American Institute, 1962), pp. 11–12.

10. *Ibid.*, pp. 29, 31.

11. The author, in writing this and the succeeding sections on intersectoral *and intrasectoral priorities*, has drawn on his paper, *The Role and Scope of Industrialization in Development*, which he delivered to the Cambridge Conference on Industrialization in Developing Countries, at King's College, Cambridge, England, in September 1964, and has since been published in Ronald Robinson (ed.) *Industrialization in Developing Countries* (Cambridge University Overseas Studies Committee, 1965), pp. 54–66.

12. P. T. Bauer and B. S. Yamey, *The Economics of Under Developed Countries* (Cambridge: Cambridge University Press, 1957), p. 235.

13. *Ibid.*, p. 76.

14. Dudley Seers, "The Role of Industry in Development: Some Fallacies": *The Journal of Modern African Studies*, Vol. 1, No. 4 (December, 1963), p. 464.

15. W. Arthur Lewis, *The Theory of Economic Growth* (London: Allen and Unwin, 1955), p. 141.

16. The foregoing discussion has emphasized the aggregate allocation of resources to education and the composition of the expenditure on education. It treats with the *content* of education by implication only, not because it is an unimportant or irrelevant consideration, but because it would tend to divert the discussion from its principal focus on political decisions and economic choices and the implications for nation-building, to the technical question of what are appropriate curricula for educational institutions in the new African states.

17. Lewis, *op. cit.*

18. P. N. Rosenstein-Rodan, "Problems of Industrialization of Eastern and South-Eastern Europe," *The Economic Journal* (June–September, 1943), reprinted in Agarwala and Singh, *The Economics of Underdevelopment* (London: Oxford University Press, 1958), p. 245 (footnote 1).

19. Bauer and Yamey, *op. cit.*, p. 236.

20. See *The African Presence in World Affairs: National Development and Its Role in Foreign Policy*, *op. cit.*, Chapter IV, "Modernization of Agriculture," for a comprehensive treatment of the role of agriculture in African development, and the principal problems for its growth.

21. W. W. Rostow, *The Stages of Economic Growth* (Cambridge: Cambridge University Press, 1960), pp. 21–24.

22. See Bauer and Yamey, *op. cit.*, pp. 237–242.

23. *Ibid.*, p. 239.

24. *Federation of Nigeria National Development Plan, 1962–68* (Lagos: Ministry of Economic Development, 1962), p. 23.

25. *Programme of the Convention People's Party* (Accra: Ministry of Information and Broadcasting, 1962), p. 15.

26. Joseph Bognar to H. E. Dr. Kwame Nkrumah, a paper with recommendations for Ghana's Seven-Year Plan (Accra, February, 1962), pp. 116, 10 appendices (mimeographed).

27. *Ibid.*, pp. 2, 3 and 4.

28. *Ibid.*, p. 15.

29. *Plan Quinquennal de Développement Economique et Social de la République du Congo: Principaux Généraux* (Léopoldville: Ministry of Plan and Industrial Development, 1963), p. 23; translation by the author.

30. *Ibid.*, p. 9.

31. James S. Coleman, "Introduction to Patterns of Policy-Directed Educational Development," in J. S. Coleman (ed.), *Education and Political Development* (Princeton: Princeton University Press, 1965), pp. 231–232.

Chapter 11

1. *West Africa* (London), No. 2447 (April 25, 1964), p. 450.

2. *Washington Post and Times Herald*, August 25, 1966, and *West Africa*, No. 2569, August 27, 1966, p. 985. Also *Cahiers de l'Afrique Orientale et de l'Afrique Equatoriale* (Paris), No. 313 (August 20, 1966), p. 37: "President Tombalbaye issued a veritable ultimatum to the Sudan, which he accused of failing to respect the Sudanese-Chadian agreement concerning the operations of the 'network of bandits' in the frontier province of Ouaddi from bases in the Sudan."

3. Former Prime Minister Kimba, a relatively obscure member of the former secessionist government of Katanga was arrested, tried summarily by a military government, sentenced to death and executed early in 1966 by the Mobutu government, for allegedly plotting to overthrow the government and assassinate President Mobutu. Three former cabinet members were hanged along with Kimba.

4. Material in this and the following sections has been drawn from two papers delivered by the author on "The Role of Government in African Development" in May and July, 1964, respectively, to an intercollegiate faculty seminar at the Wharton School of Finance at the University of Pennsylvania and to a special seminar at the School of Foreign Service at Georgetown University, as well as from successive monthly issues of the publication, *Etudes Congolaises*, published by the *Institut National d'Etudes Politiques* in Kinshasa in conjunction with the *Centre de Recherche et d'Information Socio-Politique* in Brussels, the C.R.I.S.P. study by J. Gérard-Libois, *Secession au Katanga* (Brussels, 1963), and from numerous other C.R.I.S.P. publications on Congolese affairs.

5. *"A la Commission Constitutionnelle de Luluabourg,"* *Congo Magazine* (Kinshasa, April, 1964), pp. 16–17, 27.

6. From the text of the report as quoted in the *New York Times*, July 1, 1964, p. 34.

7. *Washington Post and Times Herald*, August 1, 1964, p. 6.

8. President Nicholas Grunitzky's intervention was particularly pertinent as he had been excluded from the first Heads of State Conference a year earlier at Addis Ababa at which the OAU was founded. However, in his case, there was an important difference. Grunitzky came to power after a *coup d'état* in which President Sylvanus Olympio was assassinated, and at the time of the first OAU meeting quite a few African countries had not yet recognized the Grunitzky government.

9. As quoted in *Jeune Afrique* (Tunis), No. 194 (July 27, 1964), p. 15; translation by the author.

10. "OAU on the Nile" in *West Africa* (London), No. 2460 (July 25, 1964), p. 819.

11. *West Africa*, No. 2459 (July 18, 1964), p. 1790.

12. *The Economist* (London, July 25, 1964), pp. 347–348.

CHAPTER 12

1. *Ruanda-Urundi: Geography and History* (Brussels: Belgian Congo and Ruanda-Urundi Information and Public Relations Office, 1960), p. 23.

2. See Richard Cox, *Pan-Africanism in Practice* (London: Oxford University Press, 1964), p. 30, *e.g.,* "The Bahutu party (Parmehutu) was (alleged to be) a Belgian creation, which indeed it very largely was." *Cf.* the Soviet view: "Parmehutu while fighting against feudalism really played into the hands of the Belgian administration." V. Karpushina, *Sovetskaya Etnografiya*, No. 1, 1963, pp. 106–111, quoted in David Morison, *The U.S.S.R. and Africa* (London: Oxford University Press, 1964), pp. 108–109.

3. *Pan Africanism in Practice, op. cit.*

4. Benoît Verhagen in the Preface to *Rwanda Politique, 1958–1960* (Brussels: Centre de Recherche et d'Information Socio-Politique, Les Dossiers du C.R.I.S.P., 1963(?), p. 7.

5. In an important book on the 1956 "consultations" in Ruanda-Urundi, which provided for a universal secret ballot for males to elect an electoral college to elect in turn *le conseil du sous-chefferie*, the likely outcome of a direct election for a national parliament, if the Hutu inhibitions about their Tutsi ruling class were removed, was forcefully demonstrated. The book, at the time it appeared in 1959, was critically received by the Tutsi rulers as a "Belgian incitement to the Bahutu." See J. J. Maquet and M. d'Hertefelt, *Elections en Société Féodale* (Brussels: Royal Academy of Colonial Sciences, 1959), p. 231.

6. The comparable population densities in the neighboring Congo (Kinshasa) are 14, in Tanganyika, 24, and in Uganda, 61.

7. Maquet and d'Hertefelt, *op. cit.*, p. 4.

8. *Afrique Nouvelle* (Dakar), No. 966 (February 10–16, 1966), pp. 8–9.

9. *Washington Post and Times Herald,* January 18, 1966, pp. 1, 8.

10. *West Africa* (London), No. 2569 (August 27, 1966), p. 985.

11. "Chinese in Africa: The Aims Behind the Acrobats," *The Economist* (London, September 26, 1964), pp. 1226–1228.

12. *Ibid.*

13. Bujumbura, Burundi Radio Domestic Service (in French) 10:45 GMT, September 28, 1964.

14. See *General Assembly Resolution No. 21* (1949), and the related debates.

15. *Instituto Centrale di Statistica, VII Censimento Generale della Popolazione,* V (Rome, 1935), quoted in Mark Karp, *The Economics of Trusteeship in Somalia* (Boston: Boston University Press, 1960), p. 23.

16. *Ibid.*

17. *Ibid.,* p. 34.

18. See *Agreements and Exchanges of Letters Between the United Kingdom and the Government of Somaliland (British) in Connexion with the Attainment of Independence by Somaliland, Hargeisa, June 26, 1960* (London: HMSO, Treaty Series No. 44 (1960), Cmnd. 1101 (July, 1960), p. 15.

19. Abdirashid Ali Sharmarke, in the Preface to *The Somali Peninsula: A New Light on Imperial Motives* (Mogadiscio: Information Service of the Somali Government, 1962), p. vi.

20. *Ibid.,* p. 76.

21. E. Sylvia Pankhurst, *Ex-Italian Somaliland ("The Benadir")* (London: Watts and Co., 1951), p. 457.

22. *Ibid.,* pp. 457–458.

23. President de Gaulle was greeted by demonstrations in Djibouti, the capital of French Somaliland, demanding independence and union with Somali on a trip to French Somaliland (and thereafter to Ethiopia) in late August 1966. Several demonstrators were killed and President de Gaulle's plans for a public address in Djibouti had to be altered. Subsequently, the French government announced a referendum would be held in mid-1967 to determine the territory's future status.

24. "Somali Republic," in *Africa Report* (November, 1963), p. 40.

25. Anthony Sampson in *The Observer* (London), February 9, 1964.

26. *Africa Report, op. cit.*

27. *Dalka* (Mogadishu), Vol. 1, No. 10 (April 1, 1966), p. 8.

28. *Ibid.,* p. 1.

29. Apparently "balkanization" is a matter of vantage point. Lord Rennell and Sylvia Pankhurst in the same context—Greater Somalia—draw diametrically opposite conclusions about who was "balkanizing" whom. The Rwandese and Burundese situation discussed earlier in this chapter throws up still another example or version of "balkanization." How would Dr. Nkrumah with his opposition to regional groupings as a type of "balkanization" decide these "special cases"?

30. See Evelyn Waugh, *Scoop,* and *Black Mischief* in the Penguin Paperback Series (London: Penguin, 1963).

31. *Preamble—Declarations of Rights, Constitution of Liberia,* promulgated in 1847.

32. Ernest Jerome Yancy, *The Republic of Liberia* (London: Allan and Unwin, 1959), pp. 11–13. Also see, by the same author, *Historical Highlights of Liberia's Yesterday and Today* (New York: Herman Jaffe, 1954), and Esther Warner, *Trial by Sasswood* (London: Gollancz, 1955).

33. See Arthur T. Porter, *Creoledom* (London: Oxford University Press, 1963), for an account of the evolution of "Creoledom" in Sierra Leone, down the coast from Liberia, where a somewhat comparable problem has obtained as a result of the resettling of freed slaves by English abolitionists and philanthropic groups. The Sierra Leoneans, however, have gone further in building national unity, and the "protectorate peoples" as those from the interior are called, in contrast to the "colonial peoples" who populate the coast, the Creoles, have gone far to capture political power. The first two Prime Ministers, for example, have been "Mende men" from the interior, the late Sir Milton Margai, and his successor, his brother, Sir Albert M. Margai, former Minister of Finance.

34. For an interesting account of the development of the first rubber industry in Liberia, see Wayne C. Taylor, *The Case Study of the Firestone Operation in Liberia* (Washington, D.C., National Planning Association, 1956), p. 113.

35. See Jack Bennet, *Small Business in Liberia: Development of Private Enterprise in an Underdeveloped Country* (Washington, D.C.: The Continental Allied Co., 1956), p. 20 (mimeographed).

36. Liberia did get into serious economic and financial difficulties in 1964, and it became necessary for the International Monetary Fund to negotiate a debt rescheduling with Liberia's major creditors.

CHAPTER 13

1. *East Africa and Rhodesia* (London), Vol. 40, No. 2070 (June 25, 1964), p. 823.

2. *Washington Post and Times Herald*, July 27, 1964.

3. Zanzibar Domestic Radio Service (in Swahili), 10:35 GMT, July 15, 1964.

4. Carl G. Rosberg, Jr., "Democracy and the New African States," in Kenneth Kirkwood (ed.), *African Affairs: Number Two* (London: Chatto & Windus, 1963), p. 44.

5. *The Times* (London), June 8, 1964, p. 9.

6. *Washington Post and Times Herald*, July 21, 1964, p. 17.

7. *The Times* (London), April 7, 1964, p. 90.

8. *The Economist* (London, July 11, 1964), p. 142.

9. *New York Times*, July 31, 1964, p. 5.

10. *Ibid.*

11. *Ibid.*

12. *Jeune Afrique* (Tunis), No. 193 (July 20, 1964), p. 12; translation from French by the present author.

13. In former French West Africa, Mauritania, Niger, Upper Volta, Dahomey and Togo in former French Equatorial Africa, Chad, Central African Republic (Centrafrica), the Congo (Brazzaville), Gabon and the Federal Republic of Cameroon, in North Africa, Algeria, and in the Indian Ocean, the Malagasy Republic.

14. Martin Kilson, "African One-Party States" in *AMSAC Newsletter* (American Society of African Culture), Vol. 6, No. 9 (May, 1964), p. 3.

15. For example: "Following a month-long, calm campaign, final results of Mali's first election since independence have been released this week. They show 100 percent of the voters in favor of Union Soudanaise RDA, the ruling party. Thus, Mali has surpassed the results achieved by Chad, Dahomey, Niger and Centrafrica, whose percentages in their recent elections were in the region of 95 percent." *West Africa* (London), No. 248 (May 2, 1964), p. 451. In fact, the official vote claimed for the Union Soudanaise was 99.89 percent, which like the claim of the makers of Ivory Soap that it is $99\,4\,\frac{4}{100}$ percent pure, allows a margin for human fallibility, but not much.

16. Christopher Fyfe, *A History of Sierra Leone* (London: Oxford University Press, 1962), p. 619.

Chapter 14

1. Albert O. Hirschman, "Ideologies of Economic Development in Latin America," in A. O. Hirschman (ed.), *Latin American Issue* (New York: The Twentieth Century Press, 1961), p. 11.

2. John Beattle, *Bunyoro: An African Kingdom* (New York: Holt, Rhinehart & Winston, 1962), p. 24; cf. Jucker-Fleetwood, *op. cit.*

3. Ardath W. Burks, *The Government of Japan* (New York: Crowell, 1961), p. 2.

4. *Ibid.*

5. *Ibid.*, p. 266.

6. And lest we forget that nation-building existed at other times and places: "What was the political counterpart of this cultural unity? In Egypt after Menes the cultural unity subsisting from the Delta to the First Cataract [Third Millennium B.C.] corresponded not only to a uniformity of environment, traditions, language and racial stocks, but also to political unification under a single sovereign." Gordon Childe, *New Light on the Most Ancient East* (New York: Grove Press, 1957), pp. 173–174.

7. George Pendle, *A History of Latin America* (Baltimore, Md.: Penguin Books, 1963), p. 15.

8. See John P. Lewis, *Quiet Crisis in India* (Washington, D.C.: Brookings Institution, 1962), pp. 24–26, for the discussion underlying these brief observations.

9. The argument advanced on this score by Thomas R. Malthus in his classic work, *An Essay on the Principle of Population* (8th ed., London: Reeves and Turner, 1878), still remains fundamental in any consideration of the development and nation-building prospects of underdeveloped countries.

10. Pendle, *op. cit.*, pp. 85–86.

11. Lewis, *op. cit.*, p. 148.

12. *Ibid.*, p. 178.

13. Bhabatosh Datta, "Growing Pains," *The Economic Weekly* (Bombay, July 6, 1957), reprinted as "Growing Pains in the Second Five Year Plan," in Samuelson, Bishop and Coleman, *Readings in Economics* (3rd ed., N.Y.: McGraw-Hill, 1958), p. 372.

14. "The background of this controversy [between monetarists and structuralists in Latin America] is the chronic inflation that has plagued Latin America since the late 1930's." See David Felix, "An Alternative View of the 'Monetarist-Structuralist' Controversy," in A. O. Hirschman, *op. cit.*, p. 81. "But in many of the principal Latin American countries, the rise in prices has not been moderate; on the contrary, there have been several cases of runaway inflation, some others of considerable inflation, and many instances of external monetary disturbances. Moreover, the countries experiencing the severest inflation have not always been those with the highest rate of development." See V. L. Urquidi, *The Challenge of Development in Latin America* (New York: Praeger, 1964), p. 37.

15. Víctor L. Urquidi, *The Challenge of Latin America* (Baltimore, Md.: Penguin Books, 1963), p. 16.

16. *Ibid.*, p. 35.

17. *Ibid.*, p. 1.

18. *Ibid.*, pp. 8–9.

19. See Arnold Rivkin, *The Role of Industrialization in Development of Underdeveloped Countries*, a paper delivered to the Cambridge Conference on Industrialization in Developing Countries, Kings' College, Cambridge, September 1964, and published in R. Robinson (ed.), *Industrialization in Developing Countries* (Cambridge: Cambridge University Overseas Committee, 1965), pp. 54–66.

20. "Strategy for Development," *The Economist*, September, 1964, p. 1010.

21. Víctor L. Urquidi, *The Challenge of Development in Latin America* (New York: Praeger, 1964), p. 86.

22. *Ibid.*, particularly chapter 6; also Víctor Alba, "The Latin American Style and the New Social Forces," and Thomas F. Carroll, "The Land Reform Issue in Latin America," in Hirschman, *op. cit.*, pp. 43–51 and 161–201, respectively; A. A. Berle, *Latin America: Diplomacy and Reality* (New York: Harper & Row, 1962), pp. 12–13, 22–23, and chapter VIII generally, and Pendle, *op. cit.*, pp. 186–216.

23. Berle, *op. cit.*, p. 12.

24. *Preamble to the Act of Bogotá, September 12, 1960.*

25. See "Organization of American States," *Alliance for Progress: Official Documents Emanating from the Special Meeting of the Inter-American Economic Council*, Punta del Estes, August 5–17, 1961.

26. Pendle, *op. cit.*, pp. 186–187; cf. Berle, *op. cit.*, pp. 12–13.

27. Urquidi, *op. cit.*, Berle, *op cit.*, and Hirschman, *op. cit.*

28. Lewis, *op. cit.*, p. 16.

29. *Ibid.*, pp. 17–18.

30. S. Harrison, *India: The Most Dangerous Decades* (Princeton: Princeton University Press, 1960).

31. Lewis, *op. cit.*, p. 19.

32. See Arnold Rivkin, *The African Presence in World Affairs* (New York: Free Press of Glencoe-Macmillan, 1963) for a discussion of African socialist doctrine.

33. Max Weber, *from Max Weber: Essays in Sociology* (translated by H. H. Gerth and C. W. Mills) (New York: Oxford University Press, 1946), p. 47.

34. See M. S. Herskovits, *The Human Factor in Changing Africa* (New York: Knopf, 1962), pp. 417–429, for a discussion of the "resilience" and "flexibility" of traditional African religions and their capacity for adapting themselves to the new external religion; and *vice versa*.

35. L. S. B. Leakey, *Defeating Mau Mau* (London: Methuen, 1954), p. 47.

36. Father R. P. Van Wing, prominent Belgian missionary in the Congo and Member of the Colonial Council, as quoted in footnote in Patrice Lumumba, *Congo, My Country* (London: Pall Mall Press, 1962), p. 8.

37. *Ibid.*, pp. 8–9.

38. See Jules Chomé, *La Passion de Simon Kimbangu* (Brussels: *Les Amis de Présence Africaine*, 1959) for an interesting and sympathetic account.

39. Pendle, *op. cit.*, p. 131.

40. *Ibid.*, p. 195.

41. *Ibid.*, pp. 109, 125–128.

42. Berle, *op. cit.*, p. 17.

43. *Ibid.*, p. 20.

44. France decided in 1964 to cut its military expenditures in Africa by seriously reducing its own forces maintained on the continent. By mid-1965 the forces were reduced by more than three-quarters, *i.e.*, from 27,800 in October 1964 to 6,600 in July 1965. See "French Armies Out of Africa" in *West Africa* (London), No. 2471 (October 10, 1964), p. 1137.

45. See Arnold Rivkin, "Arms for Africa:" in *Foreign Affairs,* Vol. 38, No. 1, October 1959, pp. 84–94, and Arnold Rivkin, "Lost Goals in Africa," *Foreign Affairs* (October, 1965), pp. 111–126.

46. Urquidi, *op. cit.*, pp. 5–6.

47. Víctor Alba, "The Latin American Style and the New Social Forces," in Hirschman, *op. cit.*, p. 43.

BIBLIOGRAPHY

Books

Alba, Víctor. "The Latin American Style and the Social Forces," A. Hirschman (ed.), *Latin American Issue*, New York: The Twentieth Century Press, 1961.

Ashford, Douglas E. "Local Reform and Social Change in Morocco and Tunisia," in William H. Lewis, *Emerging Africa*, Washington, D.C.: Public Affairs Press, 1963.

Awolowo, Obafemi. *Awo.* Cambridge: Cambridge University Press, 1960.

Azikiwe, Nnandi. *Zik: Selected Speeches.* Cambridge: Cambridge University Press, 1961.

Barber, William J. "Federation and the Distribution of Economic Benefits" in Colin Leys and Crawford Pratt, *A New Deal in Central Africa.* London: Heineman, 1960.

Beattle, John. *Bunyoro: An African Kingdom.* New York: Holt, Rinehart and Winston, 1962.

Bello, Ahmadu. *My Life.* Cambridge: Cambridge University Press, 1962.

Bennet, Jack. *Small Business in Liberia: Development of Private Enterprise in an Underdeveloped Country.* Washington, D.C.: The Continental Allied Co., 1956.

Berle, A. A. *Latin America: Diplomacy and Reality.* New York: Harper & Row, 1962.

Brausch, Georges. *Belgian Administration in the Congo.* London: Oxford University Press, 1961.

Burks, Ardath W. *The Government of Japan.* New York: Crowell, 1961.

Carroll, Thomas F. "The Land Reform Issue in Latin America," A. Hirschman (ed.), *Latin American Issue*, New York: The Twentieth Century Press, 1961.

Carter, Gwendolen M. (ed.). "Introduction," *Politics in Africa. 7 Cases.* New York: Harcourt, Brace and World, 1966.

———. *Politics in Africa: 7 Cases.* New York: Harcourt, Brace and World, 1966.

Childe, Gordon. *New Light on the Most Ancient East.* New York: Grove Press, 1957.

Chisiza, D. K. *Africa—What Lies Ahead?* New York: The African-American Institute, 1962.

———. Paper delivered to Nyasaland Economic Symposium in 1962, published in shortened version in *Africa's Freedom* (London: Unwin Books, 1964).

Chome, Jules. *La Passion de Simon Kimbangu.* Brussels: Les Amis de Présence Africaine, 1959.

Churchill, Winston S. *The River War: The Reconquest of the Sudan.* London: Eyre and Spottiswood Ltd., 1899 (reissued, Landsborough Publications, 1960).

287

Clutton-Brock, Guy. *Dawn in Nyasaland.* London: Hodder and Stoughton, 1959.

Cohen, Sir Andrew. *British Policy in Changing Africa.* London: Routledge and Kegan Paul, 1959.

Coker, Folarin. *Sir Adetokunbo Ademola.* Lagos: Times Press, 1962.

Coleman, James S. (ed.). "Introduction to Patterns of Policy-Directed Educational Development" in *Education and Political Development.* Princeton: Princeton University Press, 1965.

Coleman, James S. and Buse, Belmont, Jr. "The Role of the Military in Sub-Saharan Africa" in Rand Corporation (ed.), *The Role of the Military in Underdeveloped Countries.* Princeton: Princeton University Press, 1962.

Cox, Richard. *Pan-Africanism in Practice.* London: Oxford University Press, 1964.

Cremeans, Charles D. *The Arabs and the World: Nasser's Arab Nationalist Policy.* New York: Praeger, 1963.

Crowder, Michael. *Senegal: A Study in French Assimilation Policy.* London: Oxford University Press, 1962.

Dalta, Bhabatosh. "Growing Pains," *The Economic Weekly* (Bombay, July 6, 1957 reprinted as "Growing Pains in the Second Five-Year Plan" in Samuelson, Bishop and Coleman, *Readings in Economics,* New York: McGraw-Hill, 1958).

Debenham, Frank. *Nyasaland: The Land of Lake.* London: HMSO, Carone Library, 1955.

Delavignette, Robert. *Freedom and Authority in French West Africa.* London: Oxford University Press, 1950.

De Tocqueville, Alexis. *Democracy in America,* Vol. I. New York: Vintage Books, 1945.

Dia, Mamadou. *The African Nations and World Solidarity.* New York: Praeger, 1961.

Drake, St. Clair and Lacy, L. A. "Government Versus the Unions," G. Carter (ed.), *Politics in Africa,* New York: Harcourt, Brace and World, 1966.

Etudes Congolaises. *Institut National d'Etudes Politique au Kinshasa* in conjunction with the *Centre de Recherche et d'Information Socio-Politique* in Brussels, the C.R.I.S.P. study by J. Gérard-Libois, *Secession au Katanga* (Brussels, 1963).

Felix, David. "An Alternative View of the 'Monetarist-Structuralist' Controversy" in A. O. Hirschman (ed.), *Latin American Issue.* New York: The Twentieth Century Press, 1961.

Finer, S. K. *The Man on Horseback.* London: Pall Mall Press, 1962.

Fyfe, Christopher. *A History of Sierra Leone.* London: Oxford University Press, 1962.

Gardinier, David E. *Cameroun: United Nations Challenge to French Policy.* London: Oxford University Press, for the Institute of Race Relations, 1963.

Gutteridge, William. *Armed Forces in New States.* London: Oxford University Press, 1962.

Harrison, S. *India: The Most Dangerous Decades.* Princeton: Princeton University Press, 1960.

Hazelwood, A. and Henderson, P. O. *Nyasaland: The Economics of Federation.* Oxford: Basil Blackwell, 1960.

Herskovits, M. S. *The Human Factor in Changing Africa.* New York: Knopf, 1962.

Hirschman, Albert O. "Ideologies of Economic Development in Latin America" in A. O. Hirschman (ed.), *Latin American Issue.* New York: The Twentieth Century Press, 1961.

Hughes, A. J. *East Africa: The Search for Unity.* Baltimore: Penguin Books, 1963.

Jesman, Czeslaw. *The Ethiopian Paradox.* London: Oxford University Press, 1963.

Jucker-Fleetwood, Erin E. *Money and Finance in Africa.* London: Allen and Unwin, 1964.

Kaunda, Kenneth. *Zambia Shall Be Free.* London: Heineman, 1962.

Lacouture, Jean. *Cinq Hommer et la France.* Paris: Editions du Seuil, 1961.

Lacouture, Jean and Simon. *Le Maroc à l'Epreuve.* Paris: Editions du Scuil, 1958.

Leakey, L. S. B. *Defeating Mau Mau.* London: Methuen, 1954.

Lewis, John P. *Quiet Crisis in India.* Washington, D.C.: Brookings Institution, 1962.

Lewis, W. Arthur. *Development Planning.* London: Allen and Unwin, 1966.
———. *The Theory of Economic Growth.* London: Allen and Unwin, 1955.

Lumumba, Patrice. *Congo My Country.* London: Pall Mall Press, 1962.

Malthus, Thomas R. *An Essay on the Principle of Population.* London: Reeves and Turner, 1878.

Millikan, Max F. and Blackmer, Donald L. M. (eds.). *The Emerging Nations: Their Growth and United States Policy.* Boston: Little, Brown, 1961.

Morrison, David. *The U.S.S.R. and Africa.* London: Oxford University Press, 1964.

Nasser, Famal Abdul. *Egypt's Liberation: The Philosophy of the Revolution.* Washington: Public Affairs Press, 1955.

Nkrumah, Kwame. *Africa Must Unite.* New York: Praeger, 1963.

Pankhurst, E. Sylvia. *Ex-Italian Somaliland ("The Benadir").* London: Watts & Co., 1951.

Pendle, George. *A History of Latin America.* Baltimore, Maryland: Penguin Books, 1963.

Pernham, Margery. *The Colonial Reckoning.* London: Collins, 1961.

Porter, Arthur T. *Creoledom.* London: Oxford University Press, 1963.

Proehl, Paul O. *Foreign Enterprise in Nigeria: Law and Policies.* Chapel Hill: University of North Carolina Press, 1965.

Richardson, Sam S. *The Evolving Public Service in Africa.* Madison, Wisconsin: Institute of Governmental Affairs, University of Wisconsin, 1964.

Rivkin, Arnold. *Africa and the West: Elements of Free World Policy.* New York: Praeger, 1962.

Rivkin, Arnold. *The African Presence in World Affairs: National Develop-ment and Its Role in Foreign Policy.* New York: Free Press of Glencoe; and London: Collier-Macmillan Ltd., 1963.

————. "The Role and Scope of Industrialization in Development," Ronald Robinson (ed.), *Industrialization in Developing Countries.* Cambridge University Overseas Studies Committee, 1965.

Rosberg, Carl S., Jr. "Democracy and the New African States" in Kenneth Kirkwood (ed.), *African Affairs: Number Two.* London: Chatto & Windus, 1963.

Rostow, W. W. *The Stages of Economic Growth.* Cambridge: Cambridge University Press, 1960.

Ruanda-Urundi: Geography and History. Brussels: Belgian Congo and Ruanda-Urundi Information and Public Relations Office, 1960.

Sharmarke, Abdirashid Ali, in the Preface to *The Somali Peninsula: A New Light on Imperial Motives.* Mogadiscio: Information Service of the Somali Government, 1962.

Sklar, Richard L. "Nigerian Politics: The Ordeal of Chief Awolowo, 1960–65," in G. C. Carter (ed.), *Politics in Africa: 7 Cases.* New York: Harcourt, Brace and World, 1966.

Taylor, Wayne C. *The Case Study of the Firestone Operation in Liberia.* Washington, D.C.: Washington National Planning Association.

Teller, Judd. *The Jews: Biography of a People.* New York: Bantam Books, 1966.

Urquidi, Víctor L. *The Challenge of Development in Latin America.* New York: Praeger, 1964.

Wallerstein, Immanuel. *Africa: The Politics of Independence.* New York: Vintage Books, 1961.

Warner, Esther. *Trial by Sasswood.* London: Gollancy, 1955.

Waugh, Evelyn. *Scoop.* London: Penguin, 1963.

————. *Black Mischief.* London: Penguin, 1967.

Weber, Max. *Essays in Sociology* (translated by H. H. Gerth and C. W. Mills). New York: Oxford University Press, 1946.

Yancy, Ernest Jerome. *The Republic of Liberia.* London: Allen and Unwin.

————. *Historical Highlights of Liberia's Yesterday and Today.* New York: Herman Jaffe, 1954.

JOURNALS AND PERIODICALS

Africa Diary (New Delhi), Vol. V, No. 29 (July 10–26, 1956), p. 2410.

Africa Digest (London), Vol. XI, No. 5 (April 1964), p. 150.

Afrique Nouvelle (Dakar), No. 939 (August 5–11, 1965), p. 12; No. 966 (February 10–16, 1966), pp. 8–9; No. 941 (August 19–25, 1967).

Al Istiqual (Rabat), No. 297 (November 28, 1962).

"A la Commission Constitutionnelle de Luluabourg," *Congo Magazine* (Kinshasa, April 1964), pp. 16–17, 27.

Balewa, Sir Abubakar Tafawa. "Report on Addis Ababa Conference," *Federal Nigeria*, Vol. VI, No. 15 (June–July 1963), p. 6.

Banda, Dr. H. Kamuzu. Quoted in *East Africa and Rhodesia* (London, July 9, 1964), p. 850.

Beshir, Mohammed O. "The Sudan: A Military Surrender," *Africa Report*, Vol. 9, No. 11 (December 1964), pp. 3–6.

"Burundi, Quand le Roi Fait le Coup de feu," *Jeune Afrique*, No. 254 (November 7, 1965), p. 12.

Cahiers de l'Afrique Occidentale et de l'Afrique Equatoriale (Paris), No. 257 (June 27, 1964), pp. 24–26; No. 313 (August 20, 1966), p. 37.

The Central African Examiner (Salisbury, South Rhodesia), Vol. 7, No. 10 (April 1964), pp. 3–4.

Childers, Erskine B. "Where Democracy Doesn't Work . . . Yet," *Harper's Magazine* (April 1960), p. 83.

"Chinese in Africa: The Aims Behind the Acrobats," *The Economist* (London, September 26, 1964), pp. 1226–1228.

"Congo Strong Man?", *West Africa* (London), No. 2447 (April 25, 1964).

Dalka (Mogadishu), Vol. 1, No. 10 (April 1, 1966), pp. 5, 8.

Debbasch, Charles. "Ahidjo laisse la porte ouverte: Elections Camerounaises," *Jeune Afrique* (Tunis), No. 180 (April 20, 1964).

East Africa: Report of the Economic and Fiscal Commission (London: H.M.S.O., 1961), Cmnd. 1279.

East Africa and Rhodesia (London), Vol. 40, No. 2070 (June 11, 1964), p. 785; Vol. 41, No. 2131 (August 12, 1965); Vol. 42, No. 2133 (August 26, 1965), p. 11.

The Economist (London, April 25, 1964), p. 372; (July 25, 1964), pp. 347–348; (August 4, 1965), p. 597; (October 9, 1965), p. 152; (December 18, 1965), p. 1306.

Fletcher-Cooke, Sir John. "The Failure of the Westminister Model in Africa," *East Africa and Rhodesia*, Vol. 40, No. 2061 (April 9, 1964), p. 624.

"French Armies Out of Africa," *West Africa* (London), No. 2471 (October 10, 1964), p. 1137.

"Ghana After Nkrumah," *The Economist* (London, August 6, 1966), pp. 549–564.

Hodgkin, Thomas. "Counter-Revolution in Ghana," *Labour Monthly* (London, April 1966), pp. 162–167.

"I.C.F.T.U. Criticizes Governments," *East Africa and Rhodesia*, Vol. 40, No. 2066 (May 14, 1964), p. 721.

Jeune Afrique (Tunis), No. 180 (April 20, 1964), pp. 10–11; No. 193 (July 20, 1964), p. 12; No. 194 (July 27, 1964), p. 15.

Karpushina, V. *Sovetskaya Etnografiya*, No. 1, 1963, pp. 106–111.

Keita, Modibo. *Cahiers de l'Afrique Occidentale et de l'Afrique Equatoriale* (Paris), No. 251 (April 4, 1964), p. 35; No. 262 (September 5, 1964), p. 31.

"Kenya Trade Union Split," *East Africa and Rhodesia* (London), Vol. 40, No. 2064 (April 30, 1964), p. 683.

Kilson, Martin. "African One-Party States" in AMSAC *Newsletter*, Vol. 6, No. 9 (May, 1964), p. 3.

Krishna, K. G. V. "Some Economic Aspects of an East African Federation," *The East African Economic Review* (Nairobi, Kenya), Vol. 8, No. 2 (December, 1961), pp. 99–110.

Letter of Mr. M. A. Bereir, Press Attaché, Embassy of Sudan, London, in *New Africa*, Vol. 6, No. 5 (May 1964).

"Mali: Timbuktu Is Still Far Away," *The Economist* (London, March 21, 1964), p. 1094.

Makuei, C. D. "Southern Sudan: A Test Case in Afro-Arab Cooperation," *New Africa* (London), Vol. 6, No. 4 (April 1964), pp. 10–12.

Mba, Germain. "L'Ombre des Politiciens," *Jeune Afrique*, No. 296 (September 11, 1966), p. 9.

Morgenthau, Ruth Schachter. "African Elections: Tanzania's Contribution," *Africa Report*, Vol. 10, No. 11 (December 1965), pp. 12–16.

New Africa (London), Vol. 6, No. 7 (July 1964), p. 5.

"Nigeria's 10£ Minimum," *West Africa* (London), No. 2457 (July 4, 1964), p. 735.

Nyerere, Julius K. "A Parable on African Unity and Development," *The Economist* (London, July 25, 1964); also reported in slightly different form in *New Africa* (London), Vol. 6, No. 9 (September 1964).

———. Quoted in *Reporter* (Nairobi), Vol. IV, No. 140 (August 27, 1965), pp. 10, 11.

"O.A.U. on the Nile," *West Africa* (London), No. 2460 (July 25, 1964), p. 819.

"Pan Africa: The Hole in the Doughnut" (Special Correspondent) *The Economist* (Cairo, July 25, 1964, pp. 347–348.

Quarterly Economic Review: Algeria, Morocco and Tunisia (London: The Economist Intelligence Unit, No. 23 (September 1965), p. 3.

"Reconstructing Mali," *West Africa* (London), No. 2447 (April 25, 1964), p. 451.

Reporter (Nairobi, July 30, 1965), pp. 15–16; (August 15, 1965), p. 15; (July 29, 1966), p. 1.

Rivkin, Arnold. "Arms in Africa," *Foreign Affairs*, Vol. 38, No. 1 (October, 1959), pp. 84–94.

———. "Lost Goals in Africa," *Foreign Affairs* (October, 1965), pp. 111–126.

———. "Nigeria's National Development Plan," *Current History*, Vol. 43, No. 256 (December, 1962, pp. 321–328.

———. "Nigeria: A Unique Nation," *Current History*, Vol. 45, No. 268 (December, 1963), pp. 329–334.

———. "The Organization of African Unity," *Current History*, Vol. 48, No. 284 (April, 1965), pp. 193–200, 240–242.

———. "Africa and the European Common Market," *Finance and Development*, Vol. III, No. 2 (June, 1966).

Rosenstein-Rodan, P. N. "Problems of Industrialization of Eastern and South-Eastern Europe," *The Economic Journal*, June–September, 1943, reprinted in Agarwala and Singh; *The Economics of Underdevelopment* (London: Oxford University Press, 1958), p. 245 (footnote 1).

Scotton, C. M. M. "Some Swahili Political Words," *Journal of Modern African Studies*, Vol. 3, No. 4 (December, 1965), pp. 527–541, 532.

Seers, Dudley. "The Role of Industry in Development: Some Fallacies," *The Journal of Modern African Studies* (December, 1963), Vol. I, No. 4, p. 464.

Senghor, Léopold Sédur. "Addis Ababa Conference," *Cahiers de l'Afrique Occidentale et de l'Afrique Equatoriale*. Paris: June 15, 1963.

"Somali Republic," *Africa Report* (November, 1963), p. 40.

"Some Essential Features of Nkrumahism," *The Sparks* (New York: International Publishers, 1965), C. 4 by the Editors of *The Sparks*, former Ghanaian doctrinaire journal.

Southorn, Sir Thomas. *Journal of the Royal African Society*, 1944, as quoted in *New Africa* (London), Vol. 6, No. 5 (May, 1964), pp. 9–10.

"Strategy for Development," *The Economist* (September 12, 1964), p. 1010.

"Suicide of M. Bolka," *Africa Digest* (London), Vol. XI, No. 6 (June, 1964), p. 190.

"Tanganyika and Zanzibar Unite," *Africa World* (London, June, 1964), p. 21.

Tshombé, Moïse. (Address to Royal Institute of International Affairs) *East Africa and Rhodesia* (London), Vol. 40, No. 2062 (April 16, 1964), p. 646.

Verhagen, Benoît. *Rivanda Politique, 1958–1960* (Brussels: Centre de Recherche et d'Information Socio-Politique, Les Dossiers du C.R.I.S.P., 1963), p. 7.

Warburg, G. "Guinea: In the Gift of U.S. Aid?" *New Africa* (London), Vol. 6, No. 7 (July, 1964), p. 11.

West Africa (London), No. 2447 (April 25, 1964), p. 450; No. 2449 (May 9, 1964), p. 511; No. 2450 (May 16, 1964), p. 552; No. 2455 (June 20, 1964), p. 678; No. 2456 (June 27, 1964), p. 706; No. 2459 (July 18, 1964), p. 1790; No. 2569 (August 27, 1966), p. 985.

West, Robert. *African Studies Bulletin*, Vol. V, No. 4 (December, 1962), p. 33.

Yamed, Béchir Ben. "The Limits of the One-Party Structure," *Croissance des Jeunes Nations* (Paris), No. 32 (April, 1964), p. 23.

———. "Pour ou Contre le Parti Unique," *Jeune Afrique*, No. 166 (January 11, 1964), p. 5.

DOCUMENTS AND PAPERS

Ademola, Sir Adetokunbo A. *African Conference on the Rule of Law* (Lagos, Nigeria), January 3–7, 1961, Report of the Proceedings of the Conference (Geneva: International Commission of Jurists), 1961.

Agreements and Exchanges of letters between the United Kingdom and the Government of Somaliland (British) in Connection with the Attainment of Independence by Somaliland, Hargeisa, June 26, 1960 (London: HMSO, Treaty Series No. 44, 1960), Cmnd. 1101, July 1960, p. 15.

Bognar, Joseph, to H. E. Dr. Kwame Nkrumah. A paper with recommendations for Ghana's Seven-Year Plan (Accra, February, 1962), pp. 116, 10 appendices (mimeographed).

Charter of the Organization of African Unity (Article III).

"The Constitutional Institutions of the Algerian Republic," *Bulletin of the International Commission of Jurists* (Geneva, No. 19, May, 1964).

Ethiopia's Second Five-Year Plan, 1955–1959 (Addis Ababa), Chapter I, p. 1.

Federal Nigeria, Vol. VI, No. 5 (June–July, 1963), p. 6.

Federal Nigeria, Vol. VII, No. 2, March–April, 1964, p. 12.

Federation of Nigeria National Development Plan, 1962–1968 (Lagos: Ministry of Economic Development, 1962), p. 23.

General Assembly Resolution (No. 21, 1949).

Instituto Centrale di Statistica, VII Censimento Generale della Popolazione, V (Rome 1935), quoted in Mark Karp, *The Economics of Trusteeship in Somalia* (Boston: Boston University Press, 1960), p. 23.

International Commission of Jurists, *Bulletin* (Geneva), No. 18 (March, 1964), pp. 12–13.

International Commission of Jurists, *Newsletter* (Geneva), No. 11 (February, 1961); No. 15 (February, 1964), p. 5.

Kamian, Bakari. *Connaissance de la République du Mali* (Bamako: Le Secrétariat d'Etat à l'Information et au Tourisme, undated), p. 119.

"The Mobilisation Budget 1962," *The Six Budget Speeches 1958–1963* (Lagos: Federal Ministry of Finance).

Organization of American States, *Alliance for Progress: Official Documents from the Special Meeting of the Inter-American Economics Council,* Punta del Estes, August 5–17, 1961.

Plan Quinquennal de Développement Economique et Social de la République du Congo: Principaux Généraux (Léopoldville: Ministry of Plan and Industrial Development, 1963), p. 23.

Preamble to the Act of Bogota, September 12, 1960.

Programme of the Convention People's Party (Accra: Ministry of Information and Broadcasting, 1962).

Public International Development Financing in Senegal: Report No. 7 of the Research Project of Columbia University Law School (New York: Columbia University), 1963.

Report of the Commission on the Review of Wages, Salary and Conditions of Service of the Junior Employees of the Governments of the Federation and in Private Establishment, 1964–1965 (Lagos: Federal Ministry of Information, Printers Division, 1964).

Report of the Nyasaland Commission of Inquiry (the report of the Devlin Commission; London: HMSO, 1959), Cmnd. 814, particularly Section 3, paragraphs 19–30.

Report of the Uganda Relationships Commission, 1961 (Entebbe, Uganda: Government Printer, 1961).

Rivkin, A. "The Role of Government in African Development," two papers delivered in May and July, 1964, to an inter-collegiate faculty seminar at the Wharton School of Finance at the University of Pennsylvania and to a special seminar at the School of Foreign Service at Georgetown University.

World Bank Atlas of Per Capita Product and Population (Washington, D.C., 1967).

NEWSPAPERS

Colin, Legum. *The Observer* (London), reprinted in *Washington Post and Times Herald*, July 21, 1964.

Godsell, Geoffrey (ed.). "Destourian Socialism in Tunisia," *The Christian Science Monitor*, February 14, 1964, p. 16.

Louchheim, Donald H. "Accra Conference Wove Realism into Fragile OAU Fabric," *Washington Post and Times Herald*, October 27, 1965.

————. *Washington Post*, August 6, 1966, p. 15 (Sec. A).

————. *Washington Post*, August 9, 1966, p. 10 (Sec. A); August 11, 1966, p. 16 (Sec. O).

Malawi News (Blantyre, Nyasaland).

New York Times, July 28, 1963, p. 22; April 29, 1964, p. 40; May 2, 1964, p. 4; May 6, 1964, p. 16; July 21, 1964, p. 5; July 31, 1964, p. 5; October 27, 1964, p. 9; October 25, 1965, p. 22; July 1, 1966, p. 34; July 30, 1966, pp. 1 and 7; July 31, 1966, p. 9; August 1, 1966, p. 8; August 2, 1966, p. 1; August 3, 1966, p. 6 and (ed.) p. 36; August 4, 1966, p. 10; August 5, 1966, p. 7; August 9, 1966, p. 7; August 12, 1966, p. 11.

Sampson, Anthony. *The Observer* (London), February 9, 1964.

"Sudan Tragedy," *The Observer* (London), September 5, 1965, p. 10.

Sulzberger, C. L. "Emotion Alone Is Not Enough," *New York Times*, April 22, 1964, p. 46.

The Times (London), April 7, 1964, p. 9; April 15, 1964, p. 11; June 8, 1964, p. 9.

UMT newspaper, *L'Avant Garde* (Casablanca), No. 192, December 1, 1962.

Washington Post and Times Herald, July 19, 1964, p. 17 (Sec. A); July 27, 1964, p. 10 (Sec. A); August 1, 1964, p. 6 (Sec. A); October 21, 1964, p. 31 (Sec. A); January 18, 1966, pp. 1, 8 (Sec. A); August 25, 1966.

MONOGRAPHS

Emerson, Rupert. *Political Modernization in the Single-Party System* (University of Denver Monograph Series in World Affairs), No. 1, 1963–1964, pp. 1–30.

Gérard-Libois, J. *Secession au Katanga* (Brussels: *Centre de Recherche et d'Information Socio-Politique*, 1963).

Rivkin. "Africa and the European Common Market: A Prospective" (World Monograph Series, University of Denver), revised edition, 1966.

OTHER SOURCES

Adoula, Cyrille. Radio Léopoldville (now Kinshasa) Domestic Service (in French), 1830 GMT, January 2, 1964.

Bujumbura, Burundi Radio Domestic Service (in French), 1045 GMT, September 28, 1964.

Dar-es-Salaam, Tanganyika, Domestic Radio Service (in English), 1600 GMT, May 13, 1964.

Dar-es-Salaam, Tanganyika, Domestic Service (in English), 1430 GMT, June 29, 1964.

Ghana Radio Service, Accra, 0600 GMT, May 17, 1964.

Lagos Nigeria Domestic Radio Service (in English), 1400 GMT, April 13, 1964.

Lagos Nigeria Domestic Radio Service (in English), 1800 GMT, May 15, 1964.

Ministry of Information, *Ghana Press Release*, No. 142/64 (Accra), March 15, 1964.

Nairobi, *Kenya Domestic Radio Service*, 1600 GMT, May 19, 1964.

Radio Lagos, August 1, 1966, 1130 Local Time.

Radio and T.V. Enugu, August 1, 1966, 1945 Local Time.

INDEX

Abako Party (Congo), 248
Abboud, Ibrahim, deposition, 35–36, 37, 38, 39, 63, 66, 69, 212
Abidjan, Ivory Coast, 32
Accra, Ghana, 58, 70, 145, 158; OAU Conference (1965), 18, 22–24
Act of Bogotá (1960), 241
Action Group Party (Nigeria), 101, 109, 117, 118, 119, 153
Adamafio, Tawaia, Ghana Minister of Information, 122
Addis Ababa, Ethiopia, 81, 199; Heads of State Conference, 281n8; OAU Conference (1963), 1, 14–19, 20, 24, 46, 50, 88, 104, 178, 188, 266nn7–9
Addison, Koduro, quoted, 136
Adebola, Alhaji H. P., quoted, 146
Ademola, Adetokunbo A., 118, 132, 276n2; quoted, 112, 113–14
Adoula, Cyrille, 72, 133, 181, 182, 192, 259(tab.); quoted, 1, 13
Afghanistan, 231, 243
Africa: geopolitical problems, 27–46, 233–34; nationalism and, 1–24, 25, 229–33; population, 234–36, 262–63 (tab.); regional federations and, 87
Africa Digest (periodical), 133
Africa Must Unite (Nkrumah), 266n7
Africa: The Politics of Independence (Wallerstein), 113
African Associate States, 223–24
African Conference on the Rule of Law (Lagos, 1961), 112–17, 121–22, 124, 276n2
Africanization policies, 137, 139–40; Ivory Coast, 218; Malawi, 143; Nigeria, 152–53
African Studies Association of the United States, 64
Afrifa, Akwai A., 207n
Afro-Shirazi Party (ASP), Zanzibar, 153, 209–10, 211
Agricultural equipment industry, 168
Agriculture, 163–64, 167–69, 173, 217, 245, 256, 279n20; cooperatives, 84, 120, 165; Ghana, 70, 138, 223; Ivory Coast, 219; land ownership and, 249, 250; Malawi, 143; Mali, 33, 43; Morocco, 80; Nigeria, 103, 105, 106, 165, 166, 223, 240, 275n35; population density and, 238–40; trade, 168, 223–24
Ahidjo, Ahmadou, 97, 105; quoted, 48–49

Ahmadu Bello, University of, 151
Ahomadegbe, Justin, vice-pres. of Dahomey, 66, 260(tab.)
Airlines, 9, 111, 158
Alba, Víctor, quoted, 255–56
Algeria, 30, 70–71, 84, 218, 237, 244, 253–54; Addis Ababa Conference (1963) and, 16, 17, 18; GNP, 262 (tab.); Islam in, 216, 247; one-party system in, 51, 52–53, 58, 61, 69, 73, 153, 215–17, 259(tab.); trade unions and, 53, 144; Tshombé in, 181n
Algeria. Ministry of Defense, 217, 259 (tab.)
Algeria. Ministry of Justice, 217
Algerian National Liberation Front (FLN), 53, 153, 216
Algerian War, 53, 217, 253–54
All-African Trade Union Federation (AATUF), 144, 145, 146–47, 278n22
Alley, Alphonse, 69n, 261
All People's Congress Party (Sierra Leone), 96
American Civil War, 201
Amharic tribe, 199
Angola, 238, 265n5
Ankole, Kingdom of, 89
Ankrah, Joseph A., 207n, 260(tab.)
Anti-colonialism, 19, 20–21, 45; Burundi, 192–93; federalism and, 87, 88–91, 94, 97, 272n1; in Gambia, 41, 42–43; in Ghana, 133–34, 170–71; in Mali, 30; the military and, 250–51, 253–54; religion and, 247–48; in the Sudan, 36
Apapa, Nigeria, 103
Apartheid, doctrine of, 6
Apithy, Sourou-Mignan, 72, 187, 259 (tab.), 260(tab.)
Arabian Peninsula, 199
Arabs, 219, 237; in Algeria, 216; in Mali, 33, 34, 35, 43; in Morocco, 44; in Somalia, 195; in Sudan, 35–36, 38, 39, 43, 61, 65, 152, 212; in Zanzibar, 68
Arab states, 5, 73, 230. See also specific countries
Argentina, 251, 252, 253
Armaments, 22, 252–53, 254–55; shipping, 38, 39; Somalia and, 17, 195, 197
Armed Forces in New States (Gutteridge), 64
Armed hostilities, 17, 57, 70–71; Congo, 39, 179, 180–81, 187; Rwanda, 191;

297